The New York Times

what's doing
around the world

The New York Times

what's doing around the world

A TRAVELER'S
PREVIEW TO 65 OF
THE WORLD'S TOP
DESTINATIONS

EDITED BY **Joseph Siano**

FROM THE PAGES OF *THE NEW YORK TIMES* TRAVEL SECTION

LEBHAR-FRIEDMAN BOOKS

NEW YORK • CHICAGO • LOS ANGELES • PARIS • TOKYO

Lebhar-Friedman Books
425 Park Avenue
New York, NY 10022

Published by Lebhar-Friedman Books
Lebhar-Friedman Books is a company of Lebhar-Friedman, Inc.

Printed in the United States of America

Library of Congress Cataloging-in-Publication Data

The New York Times what's doing around the world : a traveler's
    preview to 65 of the world's top destinations.
        p. cm.
    ISBN 0-86730-833-8
    1. Travel. I. Title: What's doing around the world. II. New York
    Times Company.

G153.4 .N49 2001
910.4—dc21   00-052170

Text design by Erin L. Matherne and Tina Thompson
Line drawings by Roxie Munro

Call (212) 756-5248 for information on volume discounts

Visit our Web site at lfbooks.com

Contents

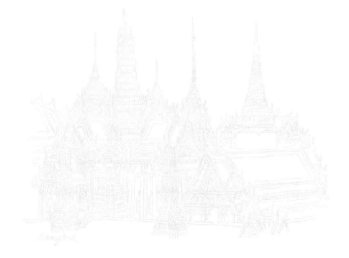

Acknowledgments

Runzheimer International has provided much of the data contained in the Vital Statistics charts, which were ably assembled by Timothy S. Bralczyk, a member of *The Times*'s Travel section staff. Thanks to Mike Levitas, Editorial Director, Book Development, who made this book possible, and to Nancy Newhouse, the editor of *The Times* Travel section.

A large measure of thanks also goes to researchers in the tourism offices of the cities and countries represented in these articles, who double-checked prices, telephone numbers, menus and admission fees. And all the articles in this book were originally checked and edited by some of the sharpest eyes in the business: the copy editors in *The New York Times* Travel section.

Introduction

No matter how many guidebooks you carry along on a trip to an unfamiliar city, nothing beats knowing someone who lives there—someone who is ready to show you the town as only a resident can.

And that is the purpose of this book. Each author of these "What's Doing in . . ." articles, which originally appeared in *The New York Times* Travel section, can report about his or her city as an insider. Many writers are *Times* correspondents who have spent years on assignment in national and foreign bureaus. And the others are free-lance writers who live in or near that city and who meet the Travel section's standards for accuracy and objectivity (no industry- or government-sponsored trips allowed—ever). In every case, think of the writers as insiders who are leading you on a weekend escape, guiding you to the sights, experiences and tastes that capture the essence of the city as they know it personally.

Naturally, the authors' individual tastes are a factor in selecting sights, hotels and restaurants—but that's meant to work in your favor, often giving you offbeat glimpses of a city not found in a mainstream guidebook. And if you find yourself in, say, Brussels, and are wondering what awaits on a spur-of-the-moment day trip to Amsterdam, think of this book as a serendipitous source of counsel.

The weekly "What's Doing in . . ." feature made its debut in the Travel section on July 22, 1973. The first subject was Rome, written by Paul Hofmann, then chief of *The Times*'s bureau in that city. (Although Paul has since retired, he remains a frequent and enthusiastic "What's Doing" author, as his two chapters in this volume demonstrate.) The purpose in launching the feature was to find a channel for *The Times*'s foreign correspondents to share with readers their knowledge of the cities they covered. For the first few years, it was printed surrounded by a dotted line—as if *Times* readers needed instruction on how to tear out an article that they might find useful on an upcoming trip. Indeed, it may have had the opposite effect, since it made "What's Doing" look like appendages to the adjacent advertisements. Thankfully, this distinctly un-Timesian touch is long gone.

So, without the dotted lines, here are a few tips on making the most of the information you will find in these pages. Regular "What's Doing" readers will immediately notice that the "Events" section found in each original article is gone, replaced instead by a

"Best of Times" feature. Here, you'll find advice on what kind of weather to expect when you visit, as well as a quick sampling of major annual events in that city.

All prices for foreign cities are in U.S. dollars, using conversion rates valid in early autumn of 2000; although we have attempted to make sure prices are reliable, please allow for variations due to fluctuating currency values and rate changes since this book went to press. For more information on any destination, a local telephone number for a city tourism office and a Web address for the same are provided under the heading "Vital Statistics."

Amsterdam

Built for walking,
and for pleasures of all kinds

ERIC WEINBERGER

Eric Weinberger, who grew up in the Netherlands,
teaches expository writing at Harvard.

"I stroll about every day among the noise and bustle of a great nation," Rene Descartes wrote while staying in Amsterdam in 1631. But the philosopher did not fret. "The commotion," he went on, "does not disturb my train of thought any more than would the babbling of some stream for I see that all efforts serve to embellish my place of residence, and to ensure that I lack for nothing."

The Netherlands of the new millennium is one of earth's most crowded countries; unsurprisingly, its capital Amsterdam can feel like one of its more crowded cities. But Amsterdammers, packed in as they are, know how to enjoy themselves, and Amsterdam is built for pleasures of all kinds. The simplest, as Descartes understood, involve walking. Most visitors soon discover for themselves the pleasures of aimless strolling in the Jordaan, usually as an offshoot of a visit to the Anne Frank House, on the Prinsengracht. The Jordaan begins on the other side of this canal: a former working-class neighborhood that still retains its run-down, neighborhood feel, with odd little shops, cafes, artists' studios and hofjes (former almshouses collected around an inner courtyard) in unexpected places.

Amsterdam has largely resisted gentrification. This is a city whose rough edges remain, although in Amsterdam at least they are never dangerous, or even threatening; still, do watch out for the endless stream of cyclists, and the trams.

best of times

Like any great city, Amsterdam is a place for all seasons, although all of them can be wet, cloudy or cool. June is perhaps Amsterdam's best month; the weather is usually sunny and dry. It is warm (or at least mild), and for those who haven't had their fill of culture after trips to the Concertgebouw or the "Big Three" museums (the Rijksmuseum—with its collection of Dutch paintings and drawings by Rembrandt, Vermeer, Ruisdael and the Dutch primitives—the Van Gogh, and the Stedelijk Museum of Modern Art), there is the bonus of the annual Holland Festival, and its program of often avant-garde music, theater and dance.

An advantage of the season is that you needn't be suffocated in the stained, murky depths of a smoky Amsterdam brown cafe. In spring and summer tables are set up outdoors in impromptu fashion, and the choice spots are always along (or in some cases, above) the water of the canals, where some of the best entertainment is watching the passing boats.

what to see

Holland's wealth in the Golden Age was founded on its far-reaching sea trade, an era depicted in the Maritime Museum, 1 Kattenburgerplein, (31-20) 523-2222, with particular attention to the exploits of the Dutch East India company. There are also exhibits on naval warfare, domestic and foreign trade, and the history of navigation and cartography. Admission includes entrance to the replica merchant ship Amsterdam, where a costumed crew can be seen going about their duties on board. Listen for a cannon shot at noon and 3 p.m. Monday to Saturday. Admission: $5.80 for adults, ages 6 to 17 $3.20.

The most notable expression of the Amsterdam School of architecture is the 1921 public housing known as Het Schip (The Ship), on the Oostzaanstraat, by Michel de Klerk. This triangular block of apartments is unusual in nearly every way, from its oddly placed little windows and spiky steeple at the stern, to the still-functioning post office at the bow. Beyond the taste for expressionistic ornament and red tile and brick, the architects were concerned with social issues; two of de Klerk's earlier buildings, also designed as working-class housing, can be seen on the adjacent Spaarndammerplantsoen.

Amsterdam's club team, Ajax (pronounced EYE-yahks), is one of the legends of European soccer, and it plays in the space-age stadium on the city outskirts, the Amsterdam Arena. The Ajax Museum, presenting a history of Dutch soccer in video, photographs and other memorabilia, will interest sports fans and children alike. It's at 3 Arena Boulevard, (31-20) 311-1333. Open daily, except game days. Admission is $6 for adults, $5 for children.

The Anne Frank House, 263 Prinsengracht, (31-20) 556-7100, is where Otto Frank, Edith Frank-Hollander and their daughters Margot and Anne went into hiding in July 1942 to escape the Nazis. The building consists of two parts: a front house and a back annex, whose uppermost floors became the hiding place. After more than two years the group was betrayed and deported. Anne and Margot died of typhus in Bergen-Belsen in March 1945, only a few weeks before it was liberated. Otto Frank, the only family member to survive, returned after the war. Open daily 9 a.m. to 7 p.m., until 9 p.m. in summer. Admission: $4 for adults, $2 ages 10 to 17.

A new Jordaan attraction is the Houseboat Museum, 296 Prinsengracht, (31-20) 427-0750, with a very short self-guided tour of life on board this most characteristic Amsterdam housing. Open 10 a.m. to 5 p.m. Tuesday to Sunday; admission is $1.50 for adults, $1 children.

The Van Gogh Museum, 7 Paulus Potterstraat, (31-20) 570-5200, reopened in 1999 after extensive renovations. A new wing has been added for temporary exhibitions. Open 10 a.m. to 6 p.m. daily; admission is $6.20 for adults, $2 ages 12 to 17.

where to stay

BUDGET: For those who would like a chance to sleep on water, the Amstel Botel, (31-20) 626-4247, fax (31-20) 639-1952, is moored at 2-4 Oosterdoks kade, near Central Station. The 176 rooms (all with private bath and TV) are basic, but there are nice views on the canal side. Doubles are $63.60, $4 cheaper on the land side.

A modern canal house on the Bloemgracht very close to the Anne Frank House, Hotel van Onna, 102-108 Bloemgracht, (31-20) 626-5801, offers good, clean double rooms, with separate bathrooms, for only $64 (no credit cards), including breakfast. Furnishings are rather spartan but comfortable.

MODERATE: The 62-room Jan Luyken Hotel, 58 Jan Luykenstraat, (31-20) 573-0730, fax (31-20) 676-3841, is well situated for visitors to the Concertgebouw and the Big Three museums; the fancy shops of the P. C. Hooftstraat are right around the corner. Rooms are quiet and well appointed. Doubles are $148 to $216, with breakfast.

The 38-room Amsterdam Wiechmann Hotel, 328-332 Prinsengracht, (31-20) 626-3321, fax (31-20) 626-8962, is a true Jordaan find, a corner grouping of three old canal houses converted into an idiosyncratic small hotel and outfitted tastefully in traditional Dutch style. About one-third have canal views; there is a large, sunny breakfast room on the corner of two canals. But watch for those steep Dutch staircases (no elevator). Doubles range from $90 to $120.

LUXURY: The grande dame of Amsterdam hotels, the 79-room Amstel Inter-Continental, (31-20) 622-6060, sits astride the banks of the river Amstel, some distance from the city's chief attractions. Its palatial splendor perfectly suits its role as an occasional perch for royalty and other notables. The terrace along the river is particularly inviting. Doubles begin at $358 overlooking the square, $398 overlooking the river, without breakfast.

The American Hotel, 97 Leidsekade, (31-20) 556-3000, fax (31-20) 556-3001, completed in 1902, is a landmark Art Nouveau building dominating Amsterdam's liveliest square, and was an inspiration for the architects of the Amsterdam School. There's an equally stylish cafe fronting the Leidseplein, and the 188 rooms are designed with broad touches of Art Deco. A standard double is $190, with breakfast at the cafe $15.80 apiece.

where to eat

Excelsior, the restaurant of the grand luxe Hotel de l'Europe, 2-8 Nieuwe Doelenstraat, (31-20) 531-1777, provides traditional haute cuisine in a plush dining room overlooking the Rokin Canal as it joins the river Amstel. Fresh lobster salad is prepared at your table ($35.40). A four-course dinner for two with a glass of wine with each course is $148.

Christophe, 46 Leliegracht, (31-20) 625-0807, offers fine dining in an airy, pleasant room on a side canal just around the corner from the Anne Frank House. There are two four-course menus (at $38 and $50); also lobster served at the daily market price, and milk-fed Pyrenees lamb with ravioli of ratatouille for $26. Dinner for two, with wine, is $160.

Near the Concertgebouw and the big museums, De Knijp, 134 Van Baerlestraat, (31-20) 671-4248, is an informal brasserie with a Dutch twist to its cooking and décor, notably the dark wooden hue of the furniture and balcony floor. Main courses begin at $15. A two-course dinner with dessert and wine for two, about $75.

A Dutch specialty, left over from Holland's time as a colonial power in Indonesia, is the rijsttafel, or rice table. Kantijl en de Tijger, 291 Spuistraat, (31-20) 620-0994, offers three variants (at $31, $35 and $39) in a spacious dining room more like an upscale bar than a restaurant, on a street full of notable places to eat. The most expensive rijsttafel, the Matjan, comes with everything: chicken, fish, beef, vegetable, beans, potato and corn.

There are few rooftop views of Amsterdam, but the sixth-floor restaurant of the fashionable Metz & Company department store, 34-36 Leidsestraat, (31-20) 520-7020, offers breakfast, light meals and salads with sweeping views of the city and canals. Club sandwiches are $9.80, and English high tea $13.80. Open until 6 p.m. except Thursday (9 p.m.) and Sunday (5 p.m.).

Keuken van 1870, 4 Spuistraat, (31-20) 624-8965, offers the plainest Dutch cooking at the cheapest prices, including a daily two-course menu for $5 weekdays and $8.20 weekends. A dinner of tomato soup with sausage, mashed potato and cauliflower was $7; bottled beer and wine are served. The surroundings are as basic as the food, and you may have to share a table with strangers, but it's a good place to mingle with Amsterdammers.

vital statistics

POPULATION (1998): City 724,908; Metro area 1,268,908

HOTEL: Room for one with tax $251.50

DINNER FOR ONE: With tax and tip but not drinks $25.70

TAXI: Upon entry $2.30; Each additional kilometer $1.15; From the airport $21.80

CAR RENTAL FOR A DAY: Midsize car with unlimited free mileage $133.00

FOR MORE INFORMATION: Telephone: (31-20) 900-400-4040; Web: www.visitamsterdam.nl

Sources: Runzheimer International, Amsterdam Tourist Board, Netherlands Board of Tourism, local businesses

Athens

The rebuilding never stops;
even the Parthenon is getting a face-lift

The Parthenon, Athens

SHERRY MARKER

Sherry Marker is a journalist who travels to Greece frequently.

Ask an Athenian where he's from and he'll usually reply not with the name of the neighborhood where he lives, but with the name of the village where he—or his parents—were born. At Christmas and Easter, and for much of August, virtually every Athenian who can leaves the capital and heads into the country-side, where village life changes slowly. Then, laden with olive oil, and fresh fruits and vegetables, families return to Athens, the city that seems to reinvent itself constantly. One example: a few years ago, many abandoned warehouses and shops in the down-at-the-heels district of Psirri between Hermou and Athinas Streets began to be transformed into cafes, galleries, and restaurants. Now the districts of Gazi, once known only for the gasworks just west of Psirri, and Rouf, home of the fruit and vegetable market, are sprouting trendy eateries and galleries.

Despite the competition, the chic Kolonaki district, on the slopes of Mount Lycabettus, still draws cafe-loungers and shop-pers. When Athens's long-awaited subway is finally completely up and running (perhaps by 2002), the city's endemic gridlock should diminish. The initial Metro extension that opened in January 2000 immediately diminished both pollution and congestion—and drew sightseers to the Syntagma Square station, which has displays of ancient artifacts found during excavations for the Metro tunnels.

Even the Parthenon is getting a face-lift: eight columns along the north side are being totally dismantled and reconstructed. It will be some time before visitors see the Acropolis without scaffolding on one or another monument. And it's likely to be several years before the second floor of the National Archaeological Museum—damaged by the 1999 earthquake—reopens.

best of times

Athens is now a year-round tourist destination, although relatively quiet from December through March, when blustery rainy spells alternate with glorious halcyon days and the first flowers and flowering trees are in bloom on city streets and in the ancient Agora. From April through June, and again from September through November, Athens is usually at its most delightful: sunny and not too hot. If at all possible, try to avoid the parching heat (and not infrequent electrical brown- and blackouts) of July and August, when Athens's notorious nefos (smog) is usually at its worst.

The Athens Festival runs from June into September and has concerts and performances of ancient and contemporary plays in the Herodes Atticus theater on the slopes of the Acropolis. In June, the Lycabettus Festival features jazz and pop music in the outdoor theater on Lycabettus Hill. Information for all performances should be available at the Athens Festival Office, 23 Hatzihristou Street; (30-1) 928-2900 or 928-2923.

This is also the place to find out about what's going on at the Epidaurus Festival, which stages classical drama in July and August in the handsome fourth-century B.C. theater at Epidaurus and in September at the Melina Mercouri Theater (also known as the Theatro Vrahon) in the suburb of Vyronas. The festival box office also has information on transportation to Epidaurus, some two hours outside Athens in the Peloponnese.

There's usually nothing going on at the handsome Megaron Mousikis Concert Hall, at Vasilissis Sofias and Kokkali, (30-1) 728-2333, during the Athens Festival, but for the rest of the year you can catch operatic performances here. This is a wonderful place to slip away from tourist Athens and see elegantly dressed Athenians enjoying everything from opera to solo performances.

Information on many cultural events is released less than a month in advance. The Weekend section in *The Athens News* on Friday is a good way to stay up to date; *Now in Athens,* published every other month and available free in many hotels and museums, is a comprehensive guide for events in and outside Athens.

what to see

Athenians take refuge from the midday sun and enjoy the cool of the evening while strolling the leafy paths of the National and Zappeion Gardens, between Syntagma Square and Hadrian's Arch. A bust of the actress and politician Melina Mercouri stands across from the arch on Vasilissis Amalias. The gardens, open from sunrise to sunset, with a wide variety of plants and subtropical trees, have a small zoo, duck ponds and several cafes.

Summer in Athens was once synonymous with open-air cinemas. A few remain, including the Athinea, 50 Haritos, Kolonaki, (30-1) 721-5717; Dexameni, Dexameni Square, Kolonaki, (30-1) 360-2363; and Cine Paris, Kidathenion Square, Plaka, (30-1) 322-2071. Tickets: about $6.75. Feature films are often American imports with Greek subtitles, and there's usually an intermission, when ice cream and snacks are sold. The mood is casual, with many family groups, and there are generally wooden chairs for the audience.

The city's museums have caught the special-exhibition bug. It is well worth checking with the Greek National Tourist Office at 2 Amerikis, (30-1) 331-0561, to see what is going on at the National Archaeological Museum, 44 Patission, (30-1) 821-7717, and the National Gallery, 50 Vasileos Konstantinou, (30-1) 721-1010. The N.P. Goulandris Foundation Museum of Cycladic Art, 4 Neophytou Douka (Kolonaki), (30-1) 722-8321, uses the handsome 19th-century Stathatos Mansion, linked by a walkway to the original museum, for its special exhibitions.

where to stay

BUDGET: Pedestrian-only Angelikes Hatzimihali Street runs alongside the 16-room Nefeli Hotel, 16 Iperidou, making this as quiet a location as you're likely to find in the Plaka. Simply decorated small bedrooms are bright and pleasant (no TV), and the staff is very helpful. Rates: $68 with air-conditioning and breakfast; (30-1) 322-8044, fax (30-1) 322-5800.

The 22-room Art Gallery Hotel, 5 Erechthiou, south of the Acropolis in the residential neighborhood of Koukaki, has solid Victorian furniture in its breakfast room, and bedrooms with ceiling fans and polished hardwood floors. Rates: $51; (30-1) 923-8376, fax (30-1) 923-3025.

MODERATE: The 453 rooms at the Athens Hilton, 46 Vasilissis Sophias, a 10-minute walk from Syntagma Square, face either the Acropolis or the city and its surrounding hills. The hotel's Byzantine and Ta Nissia restaurants are popular with Athenians. Rooms are comfortable, done in pastels, with large bathrooms; some have balconies. Rates are lowest August through October, from $245 weekdays, $186 weekends, with breakfast but not tax; (30-1) 728-1000, fax (30-1) 728-1111.

The 28-room Athenian Inn, 22 Haritos (Kolonaki), draws many repeat visitors, including archaeologists and academics, with its simply furnished rooms (the nicest have balconies), quiet atmosphere and congenial staff. No TV in rooms, although one has infiltrated the lobby. Rates: $99 including breakfast; (30-1) 723-8097, fax (30-1) 724-2268.

LUXURY: In a quiet residential neighborhood, the Andromeda, 22 Timoleontos Vassou, has 12 one- and two-bedroom suites with kitchenettes and balconies across the street from the original 30-room boutique hotel. The suites are sleek and elegant, while the rooms across the street are country-house posh. Service here is flawless, and the in-house restaurant is excellent. Rates: $285 to $440 (special rates sometimes available); (30-1) 643-7302, fax (30-1) 646-6361.

Ten miles outside Athens, the three Astir Palace Vouliagmeni Hotels, all renovated in 1997, sprawl beside the sea along a private peninsula. This is a good place to balance sightseeing (there is a twice-daily shuttle into central Athens) with swimming, tennis, sailing and golf. Rooms: from $260 (Aphrodite), $275 (Arion) and $310 (Nafsika); (30-1) 896-0211, fax (30-1) 896-3194.

where to eat

Vardis, in the neo-Classical Hotel Pentelikon, 66 Deligianni, in the tony suburb of Kifissia, has earned a Michelin star. The décor is elegant, the food—linguini with crayfish, red mullet with coriander, oyster confit with tomatoes—is French-Mediterranean, and the wine list is outstanding. Dinner for two with a simple wine: from $150; (30-1) 623-0650.

Varoulko occupies a former warehouse at 14 Deligeorgi in Piraeus, and is done in minimalist style. The seafood is magnificent. This is the place to try monkfish livers with soy sauce, honey and balsamic vinegar; sea bass carpaccio; mussels with oregano sauce, and virtually every other fish. Reserve several days ahead. Closed Sundays. Dinner for two with wine: from $100; (30-1) 411-422-1283.

There are Pompeiian frescoes on the walls and fragments of an ancient Greek building in the garden of Daphne's, 4 Lysikratous (Plaka), a lovingly restored neo-Classical town house. Traditional dishes—rabbit in mavrodaphne sauce, veal with quinces—are prepared with a light nouvelle-Greek touch. The food, service and beautiful surroundings make Daphne's very popular; reservations essential. Dinner for two with wine: $75; (30-1) 322-7971. Open daily.

In an unlikely corner near the fruit and vegetable market, Aristera Dexia, 3 Andronikou (Rouf), features a see-through catwalk over the wine cellar and an in-house art gallery. Diners can sit at a stainless-steel counter flanking the open kitchen and watch the chefs prepare dishes like crab risotto with tarragon and dry vermouth or crayfish in lavender, sweet moschato wine and soy sauce. Dinner for two with wine: from $85; (30-1) 342-2380. Usually closed from July to early September.

Market workers, businesspeople and all-night revelers head to two hole-in-the-wall restaurants in the city's Central Market on Athinas Street. Papandreou, in the meat market, specializes in tripe dishes; (30-1) 321-4970. Diporto, in the basement under the olive shop at the corner of Theatrou and Sofokleos, has terrific revithada (chickpea soup). Both are open from about 6 a.m. to 6 p.m., except Sunday. No telephone. Lunch for two: from $25.

vital statistics

POPULATION (2000 estimate): Greater Athens 4 million

HOTEL: Room for one with tax $221.00

DINNER FOR ONE: With tax and tip but not drinks $19.60

TAXI: Upon entry 52 cents; Minimum charge $1.30; Each additional kilometer 18 cents; From the airport $6.45

CAR RENTAL FOR A DAY: Midsize car with unlimited or 100 free kilometers $86.66

FOR MORE INFORMATION: Telephone: (30-1) 331-0561; Web: www.gnto.gr

Sources: Runzheimer International, Greek National Tourist Office, local businesses

Atlanta

Beyond a giant airport and convention center,
a friendly bunch of pretty neighborhoods

KEVIN SACK

Kevin Sack is chief of the Atlanta bureau of *The Times*.

Atlanta now has the world's busiest airport, but all too often the passengers are just passing through. And those who do stay, usually recognizable by the conventioneers' badges dangling from their necks, seem to spend most of their time wandering the downtown corridors that link the hotels to the Georgia World Congress Center. One week it's the ophthalmologists, the next it's the sports-collectibles crowd.

That is a shame, because Atlanta is a worthy tourist destination in its own right. With the exception of Stone Mountain, the mammoth granite monolith that has outgrown its reputation as the Rushmore of the Confederacy, there are few natural wonders. But wander the city's in-town neighborhoods or stroll Peachtree Street through the arts-center district or take in a Braves game at Turner Field and you will quickly see what attracts thousands of migrants to Atlanta each year. They may note, accurately, that Atlanta does not have the character, culture or vibrancy of New York, Washington, Chicago or San Francisco, but those who look in the right places can find all of those qualities, along with a lushness and friendliness that few cities can match.

The city's strengths are its neighborhoods and its history. Charming Virginia-Highlands and Victorian Inman Park, bustling Buckhead and funky Little Five Points, even up-from-nowhere East Atlanta, are all worth exploring on a sunny afternoon or festive Friday night. Visitors often remark on the things that natives take for granted, like how heavily forested the neighborhoods are.

As for history, the Martin Luther King Historic District will touch most anyone with an interest in the civil rights movement, or a memory that stretches back to that day in 1968 when two mules pulled King's casket slowly down Auburn Avenue. And, while no one was looking, Atlanta has become a pretty fair museum town. The High Museum of Art, the Fernbank Museum of Natural History and Scitrek, a hands-on science and technology museum, are all legitimate attractions these days.

best of times

Atlanta can be blistering in the summer and chilly in the winter, but springtime is paradise. When the azaleas and dogwoods color the streetscapes in riotous shades of pink and white, it is as if someone has spiked the water supply with Prozac. It simply becomes difficult to stay in a bad mood for long (unless, of course, you are stuck in Atlanta traffic).

The city exploits the season with a pair of outdoor festivals that bring locals and visitors into the sunshine to celebrate the rites of spring. The Atlanta Dogwood Festival, typically held in early April when the flowers are in full bloom, will observe its 65th anniversary in 2001. The three-day event brings 250,000 people to Piedmont Park, the city's most elegant green space, for music from three stages, a regional artists' market, children's games and a canine Frisbee competition.

A month later, usually in early May, the Music Midtown Festival takes over a large quadrant of asphalt and parkland. In 2000, the festival's seventh year, Music Midtown featured eight stages with acts as diverse as the Allman Brothers, Jimmy Cliff, Joe Walsh, Koko Taylor and BR5-49. Some concertgoers complained about the drift of sound from one stage to the next, but many came back for all three days of music, food and laid-back camaraderie.

what to see

There are only a handful of giant pandas in the United States, and two of them are at Zoo Atlanta, 800 Cherokee Avenue SE, (404)

624-5600. Lun Lun and Yang Yang arrived from China in November 1999 as 2-year-old cubs and have been winning hearts in their new home. The zoo's gates are open 9:30 a.m. to 4:30 p.m. daily, and the park remains open until 5:30. Admission is $12 for adults, $10 for ages 55 and up, and $8 ages 3 to 11. Upon admission, visitors get timed tickets to the panda exhibit. On busy days, waits typically have been 20 to 30 minutes.

The latest addition to the Martin Luther King Jr. National Historic Site, 450 Auburn Avenue NE, is Ebenezer Baptist Church, the pulpit where King, his father and his grandfather all preached. After the congregation moved to a new church across the street, the original building, at 407 Auburn Avenue NE, became available for National Park Service interpretive displays. Visitors can listen to King's speeches and sermons. The church and other historic sites are open 9 a.m. to 5 p.m.; free; (404) 331-6922.

The Atlanta Botanical Garden, 1345 Piedmont Avenue NE, (404) 876-5859, provides a lovely oasis on a sunny day. The Dorothy Chapman Fuqua Conservatory is lush with orchids and other tropical plants; the children's garden is fun and educational. Open Tuesday to Sunday 9 a.m. to 6 p.m.; $7 for adults, $5 for ages 65 and up, $4 for students. No charge after 3 p.m. Thursday.

The High Museum of Art, 1280 Peachtree Street NE, (404) 733-4444, is open 10 a.m. to 5 p.m. Saturday through Wednesday, and 10 a.m. to 9 p.m. Thursday and Friday. Tickets for special exhibitions may be purchased through Ticketmaster, (404) 817-8700, or www.ticketmaster.com, or the Woodruff Arts Center box office, (404) 733-5000 or www.high.org.

The Fernbank Museum of Natural History, 767 Clifton Road, (404) 378-0127, includes an IMAX theater. Open 10 a.m. to 4 p.m. Monday through Saturday and noon to 4 p.m. Sunday.

where to stay

BUDGET: The Embassy Suites Hotel, Centennial Olympic Park, 267 Marietta Street, (404) 223-2300, fax (404) 223-0925, is wonderfully convenient, and includes a Ruth's Chris Steak House overlooking the park. The 321 suites, which have refrigerators, microwaves and coffeemakers, cost $105 to $265, with breakfast and afternoon cocktails.

MODERATE: Vivien Leigh and Clark Gable stayed at the Georgian Terrace, 659 Peachtree Street, (800) 651-2316, fax (404) 724-0642, for the premiere of *Gone With the Wind* in 1939. Opened in 1911 and substantially renovated in 1992, the "Grand Old Lady of Peachtree" is a national landmark that sometimes shows its age. But rooms are large and comfortable, particularly the many family-friendly suites, and the 360-degree view from the rooftop is breathtaking. Rates start at $149 and run to $499 for a three-bedroom suite.

The newly renovated Omni Hotel at CNN Center, 100 CNN Center, (404) 659-0000, fax (404) 525-5050, will place you closest to the Georgia Dome and Centennial Olympic Park. Prices for the 470 rooms can run as low as $149 on slow weekends and as high as $350 at busier times.

LUXURY: The Ritz-Carlton, Buckhead, 3434 Peachtree Road NE, (404) 237-2700, fax (404) 240-7191, across from Atlanta's premier malls, Lenox Square and Phipps Plaza, exudes elegance, from its wood-paneled lobby to its rooftop indoor heated pool. The Dining Room, one of two restaurants, is considered one of the best in town. Rates for the 553 rooms begin at $275.

The Ritz's primary competition (besides its sister hotel downtown) is the Four Seasons Hotel Atlanta, 75 14th Street, (404) 881-9898, fax (404) 253-3915, an easy walk to the Woodruff Arts Center. It offers beautiful views from its 244 tastefully decorated rooms; an indoor heated pool is infused with sunlight. The restaurant here, Park 75, is also highly regarded. Doubles cost $275 to $360.

where to eat

Try to get to Canoe, 4199 Paces Ferry Road NW, (770) 432-2663, before sundown, because it may enjoy the prettiest setting of any of Atlanta's fine restaurants. Fast by the Chattahoochee River, Canoe features a terrace that is delightful during warmer seasons, and a cozy interior. The seasonal menu highlights fish, like seared trout with horseradish mashed potatoes, and pasta dishes, like saffron fettuccini with seared shrimp, mussels, leeks, fennel and pesto. Dinner for two with wine approaches $100.

South City Kitchen, 1144 Crescent Avenue, (404) 873-7358, remains one of the best of Atlanta's many bastions of new Southern cooking. It's hard to go wrong with dishes like crayfish and tasso tossed with penne, she-crab soup, and fried green tomatoes with goat cheese and sweet red pepper coulis. Again, dinner for two with a bottle of wine should not exceed $100.

For seafood that is a tad less expensive, try Atlanta Fish Market, 265 Pharr Road, (404) 262-3165, a cavernous Buckhead mainstay where the food is far classier than the 65-foot-tall bronze fish outside. There is a vast menu, but the specialty is a trout fillet with mushroom mashed potatoes, green beans and brown sage butter. Count on spending $75 for dinner for two with wine.

Atlanta has become a mecca for Latin food, and one of the best purveyors is La Fonda Latina, a hard-to-categorize chain where the colorful décor is Caribbean, the music leans toward salsa and the cooking borrows from Spanish, Mexican and Cuban influences. Of all the branches, the funkiest is at 1150 Euclid Avenue, (404) 577-8317, where it fits in with the piercing parlors and natural-foods groceries of bohemian Little Five Points. The paella, arroz con pollo and quesadilla con maiz y jalapeños are all wonderful, and served steaming hot. You'll have trouble spending more than $35 for dinner for two with beer or sangria.

For a flavor of old Atlanta, try lunch at Mary Mac's Tea Room, 224 Ponce de Leon Avenue, (404) 876-1800, a landmark where you may find yourself seated next to the governor. The fried chicken is worthy, but the real attractions are side dishes like squash soufflé, black-eyed peas and Brunswick stew. Hardly anywhere else still serves potliquor (the juice of turnip greens, sopped with cornbread). Meat and three sides runs $9.75.

vital statistics

POPULATION (1998 estimate): City 403,819; Metro area 3,746,059

HOTEL: Room for one with tax $187.00

DINNER FOR ONE: With tax and tip; but not drinks $24.20

TAXI: Upon entry $1.50; Each additional mile $1.40; From the airport $18.00

CAR RENTAL FOR A DAY: Midsize car with unlimited free mileage $76.00

FOR MORE INFORMATION: Telephone: (404) 521-660; Web: www.atlanta.com

Sources: Runzheimer International, U.S. Census Bureau, local businesses

Baltimore

Parts of it haven't changed in 50 years,
thank goodness

LAURA MANSNERUS

Laura Mansnerus is a reporter for The Metro Section of *The Times*.

If time has passed Baltimore by, that is to Baltimore's advantage. Its successes—the Inner Harbor's glassy hotels and franchise restaurants, Camden Yards, the rehabbed row houses of Federal Hill—have become advertisements for urban revitalization. Yet just beyond, in neighborhoods happy to look pretty much the way they did in 1949, the city cultivates the oddball appeal that set John Waters and Barry Levinson to work.

What the visitor finds there is not marketed amusement but live blues and corner taprooms, vegan cafes and unreconstructed diners, rehabbers in ponytails and women in housedresses surveying them from webbed plastic lawn chairs—in short, an affection for urban life.

Mount Vernon and Bolton Hill, for example, were always stately neighborhoods, though they had frayed at the edges. Both are still stately neighborhoods—and still a bit frayed. The difference is that homegrown enterprises have burrowed in here and there, so that visitors to Mount Vernon's cultural institutions can stop for latte or Indian food in one of the gracious stone apartment buildings, joining the multiple-pierced music and art students who keep Charles Street alive at night.

Fell's Point and Canton, by contrast, were raw waterfront districts 20 years ago, the streets kept alive at night largely by prostitution. Fell's Point remade itself first. Its saloon-studded waterfront has become a Saturday-night teen paradise, with the smaller streets dotted with little pubs, shops and antique stores. Now Canton is following.

At the same time, the Inner Harbor's glassy jumble of malls and hotels offers more than shopping. For example, the new Port Discovery Museum for children is a three-story funhouse with interactive exhibits. The National Aquarium provides a day's worth of exploration.

And the cultural district as always offers music—in the modern Meyerhoff Symphony Hall and the 140-year-old Peabody Institute—and art museums, all near downtown.

best of times

This much-filmed city shows films, too—more than 100 in a four-day binge in April called the Maryland Film Festival. Most are shown at two reclaimed movie palaces, the Charles and the Senator. Call (410) 752-8083; www.mdfilmfest.org.

The Preakness Stakes, the second race for the thoroughbred Triple Crown, is over in a flash on the third Saturday in May at Pimlico Race Course. The Preakness celebration starts more than a week earlier, with concerts, block parties, a parade, and parties at restaurants and hotels. Festival information: (410) 837-3030 or see www.preaknesscelebration.com; Preakness ticket information: (410) 542-9400.

Artscape, a three-day weekend festival in July, explores every art form: performing, visual and literary. At the festival site, on Mount Royal Avenue, near Penn Station and the Meyerhoff Symphony Hall, outdoor stages offer concerts and theater, while writers' workshops and art shows are under way at the many nearby cultural institutions. Everything is free. Information: (410) 396-4575; www.artscape.org.

In August, the state fair comes to town—or to Timonium, just north of the city limits—for 11 days, through Labor Day. The fair has livestock and horse shows, 4-H exhibitors, concerts and rides. There are competitions in "home arts," like quilting and baking, and in farm products, including wine. You can buy crab cakes, too. Information: (410) 252-0200, extension 227; www.marylandstatefair.com.

The Baltimore Book Festival brings booksellers, writers and publishers to Mount Vernon Place, a wide green on North Charles Street, on the last weekend in September. There are also puppet shows and crafts, a literary walking tour, cookbook demonstrations and tastings, street theater and plenty of street food. All events are free. Information: (410) 752-8632; www.bop.org.

what to see

One way to see a swath of Baltimore is from the Water Taxi, which travels the long arm of Northwest Harbor. The Inner Harbor, which would be the fist burrowing into downtown, is the main stop on a route that includes other major attractions. The boats (open in good weather, enclosed and warm in bad) pass marinas, dockyards, working wharves, rotting piers and, at the harbor's opening, the wide lawns of Fort McHenry. The $5 ticket is good for trips all day.

Fell's Point and Canton easily provide a day of walking, shopping and eating. Don't miss the quieter back streets. O'Donnell Square, with the stone Messiah Lutheran Church anchoring one end, has the air of a European town.

Camden Yards is a sight, even when the home teams are away. Much of Orioles Park (the other half of Camden Yards is Ravens Stadium, home of the National Football League team) can be seen from the outside, and from the restaurants and bars in the B & O warehouse along the park's shoulder. Orioles tickets might be available; call (410) 685-9800.

The city's museums include the Baltimore Museum of Art, off North Charles Street at 10 Art Museum Drive, and the elegant Walters Art Gallery, 600 North Charles Street in Mount Vernon, (410) 547-9000, known for its collection of ancient, medieval and Renaissance art. The Museum of Art, (410) 396-7100, has a collection of modern works by Matisse, Picasso and Warhol, among others, and two sculpture gardens. Admission is $6 for adults, $4 for seniors, free on Thursday and for ages 18 and under. Closed Monday and Tuesday. At the Walters, it's $5 for adults, $3 for seniors and young adults (18 to 25), $1 ages 6 to 17. Free admission Saturday 11 a.m. to 1 p.m. Closed Monday.

Baltimore is a logical place to buy something old. Antique Row, on Howard Street in Mount Vernon, offers more than 30 shops, and there are two dozen more in Fell's Point. On the second Sunday of each month from late spring to early fall, a flea market sets up on Broadway Market Square, starting at 8 a.m.

Fell's Point and Canton also offer rich book shopping, all the richer if you're hungry. At Adrian's Book Cafe, 714 South Broadway, break for cake or biscotti upstairs and check out the used books. And then there's the intensely unpretentious Funk's, 1818 Eastern Avenue, which, in addition to desserts and vegetarian-oriented bistro dishes, sells used books. It's open until midnight Friday and Saturday, until 11 p.m. otherwise.

where to stay

Most hotels are clustered around the Inner Harbor. Expect decent views and the standard Federal reproductions and chintz bedspreads; also expect streams of sightseers. Here are a few other choices.

BUDGET: The Mount Vernon Hotel and Washington Cafe, 24 West Franklin Street, (410) 727-2000, fax (410) 576-9300, a solid, well-kept old building, is near the Walters. The 191-room hotel helps train hotel management students, and culinary students train in the cafe, better described as a dining room, with fireplace and white tablecloths. Rooms are $69 to $109.

MODERATE: The Hilton Baltimore and Towers, 20 West Baltimore Street, (410) 539-8400, fax (410) 625-1060, is between the Inner Harbor's glass and steel and the city's old downtown. Built in 1928, the 439-room hotel has the potted palms and dark, paneled lobby bar that could be the set of a Bogart movie. The rooms are smallish but nicely appointed in traditional style. Rates range from $125 to $239.

The Admiral Fell Inn, 888 South Broadway, (800) 292-4667, fax (410) 522-0707, places you smack in the center of Fell's Point's waterfront. With canopied four-poster beds in the 80 rooms and a fireplace in the lobby, it matches the neighborhood's vintage. The standard rate is $199.

For a bed-and-breakfast in a quiet precinct, many Baltimoreans tell visitors about Mr. Mole, 1601 Bolton Street, (410) 728-1179, fax (410) 728-3379, a town house in Bolton Hill, not far from Mount Vernon. It has five meticulously and distinctly decorated suites, all with private baths and telephones. Rates are $115 to $175.

LUXURY: The Harbor Court Hotel, 550 Light Street, (410) 234-0550, fax (410) 659-5925, is downright opulent, with Asian antiques gracing the corridors and leather-bound books in the first-floor library. Many of its 203 rooms, each big enough for a cocktail party, command harbor views. Doubles are $310 to $340; suites are $500 to $3,000.

where to eat

A magnet on the Canton waterfront is Atlantic, 2400 Boston Street, (410) 675-4565, all chrome and black steel. The menu is almost all seafood—thick and rare tuna steak, wafers of grilled squid, flaky crab cakes. Dinner for two, with drinks, about $75.

In Fell's Point, Peter's Inn, 504 South Ann Street, (410) 675-7313, is a bar without bar food; instead, it offers serious entrees like filet mignon, chicken, seafood and always a vegan dish. The ambience is loose, a point made by the herb garden in the clawfoot bathtub on the sidewalk. The menu changes weekly. Dinner for two, with wine, about $55.

Gunnings Crab House, 3901 South Hanover Street, (410) 354-0085, is in the untouristed neighborhood of Brooklyn, south of downtown. Gunnings looks like a neighborhood bar (it is) that grew in an ungainly way to fit crab-eaters into two dining rooms and a covered patio. With the hard shells, try the gigantic pepper rings—green-pepper rings dipped in ultrathick batter, deep-fried till they look like doughnuts and sprinkled with confectioner's sugar. Dinner for two, with beer, about $50.

Breakfast is the main item at the Blue Moon Cafe, 1621 Aliceanna Street, (410) 522-3940, in a skinny row house in Fell's Point. French toast is the specialty, and there are five varieties of eggs Benedict (including Maryland crab). But you could come back for the lunch dishes, too, like quesadillas. It closes at 3 p.m. most days, but stays open all night Friday and Saturday. Breakfast for two is $15 to $20.

The Sip & Bite, 2200 Boston Street, (410) 675-7077, is open 24 hours. This waterfront diner in Canton is a 1950's kind of place: pink and gray Formica and a long counter, and mainstays like pork chops and liver and onions. Breakfast is served with crispy home fries. With a glass or two of beer or wine, if you worked at it, dinner could cost $10 or $12.

vital statistics

POPULATION (1998 estimate): City 645,593; Metro area 2,483,952

HOTEL: Room for one with tax $151.50

DINNER FOR ONE: With tax and tip but not drinks $26.00

TAXI: Upon entry $1.50; Each additional mile $1.20; From the airport $19.00

CAR RENTAL FOR A DAY: Midsize car with unlimited free mileage $65.50

FOR MORE INFORMATION: Telephone: (800) 343-3468; Web: www.baltimore.org

Sources: Runzheimer International, U.S. Census Bureau, local businesses

Bangkok

Once the seat of Chakri kings, now home to princes of finance

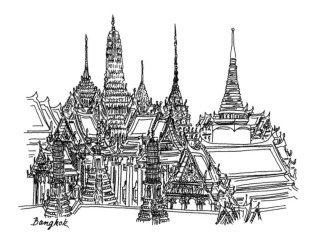

Bangkok

SETH MYDANS

Seth Mydans is chief of the Bangkok bureau of *The Times*.

Bangkok is dead; long live Bangkok.

Just as the first of the Chakri kings transformed a swampy village two centuries ago into a wonderland of canals and temples, the bankers and businessmen who run Thailand today have remade Bangkok once again into an overpowering jumble of big buildings, big traffic and unending bustle.

Thailand is plunging pell-mell into the 21st century, and its capital city is bursting with a population of 10 million—nearly one-sixth of the country's people—many trying to get rich as quickly as they can.

There are still canals and temples, teak houses and saffron-robed Buddhist monks, but they are all but buried by the roar of the modern world. At the Erawan shrine, one of the city's most vener-ated spots on a corner outside the Grand Hyatt Hotel, traditional dancers still perform to delicate melodies, surrounded by clouds of incense. But the music and the incense are lost in the clamor of a major intersection.

Thais ask themselves today: What has become of our culture? Who are we? What does it mean to be Thai? Yet with all the rapid change, Bangkok remains one of the world's distinctive cities— chaotic, heedless, maddening, energetic and unmistakably Thai.

For visitors as much as for themselves, the Thais have preserved their monuments and traditions, and the city still offers quiet temples, ancient dance, fine restaurants and marvelous street food, traditional massage, clamorous markets and hidden canals. And beyond the tourist sites, in the shopping malls and on the back streets, you'll find an energy, a warmth and a delicacy that have outlasted the changes.

When people complain about Bangkok, their grievances usually come down to one thing: the traffic, which seems each year to reach a new level of impossibility.

best of times

Climatically, the best time to visit Thailand is during the winter months, from December to February, when temperatures "cool" into merely balmy. Rainy season runs more or less from June to November, and the hot, hot season is from March to June.

There are festivals and events pretty much throughout the year, including the very wet water festival of Songran in mid-April and the Loy Kratong festival in November when small offerings are floated in ponds and canals. There is the popular elephant roundup in Surin in November and the rocket festival in the northeastern provinces in May, as well as the let-it-all-hang-out vegetarian festival in Phuket in September. In towns to the north of Bangkok, the Dragon and Lion Parade, a Chinese tradition, is held near the time of the lunar new year in January and February in Nakhon Sawan. The Straw Bird fair runs at about the same time in Chai Nat, and in early February Buddhist devotees make a pilgrimage to the Holy Footprint at a hillside shrine in Saraburi.

Excursions to any of these events, and others in this tourist-friendly country, are easy to arrange through hotels and travel agencies. In addition, the Siam Society, (66-2) 661-6470, fax (66-2) 258-3491, conducts imaginative tours and lectures.

what to see

No visitor to Bangkok should miss the Grand Palace, whose insouciant gaudiness rivals that of St. Basil's Cathedral in Moscow. It is on Na Phralan Road, on the banks of the Chao Phraya River, and is open daily. Admission: $5.

Thailand has an overpowering tourism industry, and you can put yourself in the hands of highly professional guides who will assure that you will be comfortable and will spend plenty of money. Or you can search the alleys and canals behind the modern office buildings for a grittier Bangkok. Long-tail boats—sleek, narrow rivercraft driven by propellers at the end of a long metal shaft—can be rented for about $12 an hour at the Oriental Hotel or directly from piers behind the hotel. They will take you careering up the broad Chao Phraya among the rice barges and river taxis, or winding through the fetid canals of Thonburi, where dilapidated homes are a reminder of the city's past. If you allow a guide to persuade you to visit the famous floating market—no longer relevant to the city's commerce—go for the experience of the ur-tourist trap.

It is also possible to take a cheap seat on a river taxi and join Thai commuters through the winding canals. A riverboat is a good way to visit the Grand Palace—as well as Pak Klong Talaad, one of the city's main fruit and vegetable markets. Adjacent to that market is the city's flower market on Maharaj Road, where from dusk until dawn the sidewalks spring to life with colors and scents.

Traditional dance and music are dying forms. They have been preserved for tourists, and luxury hotels are the easiest places to see truncated performances. But traditional dance is still required for university art students, and outsiders can see more authentic, sparsely attended performances of the Khon masked plays and the Lakon dance-dramas at the National Theater on Saturday and Sunday at 10 a.m. and 2 p.m. Tickets range from $2.37 to $23.70. Check on performances with the box office at (66-2) 224-1342.

Thai boxing belies this country's reputation for gentleness, employing bare feet, knees, shins and fists with frightening aggressiveness. Audiences go wild, screaming their bets and waving their arms. But it is also possible to go not for the sport but for the music—a mesmerizing performance of the squealing pi-chawa horn, drums and finger cymbals that follows the ebb and flow of the bout, rising to hysterical intensity as the kicks and jabs draw blood. Matches are Tuesday and Friday at 6 p.m. and Saturday at 5 p.m. at Lubpini Stadium, Rama IV Road, telephone (66-2) 251-4303 or 260-4550; and Monday and Wednesday at 6 p.m. and Sunday at 5 p.m. at Rajdamneun Stadium, 1 Rajdamneun Road, (66-2) 281-0879. Ringside is expensive at $23.70, but it's the only way to really hear the music, and the seats are far enough away to avoid getting splattered with blood.

Traditional Thai massage is also not so gentle—from the $160 half-day luxury treatment at the Oriental Hotel's spa to the $12 two-hour workover at no-frills streetside parlors. A good masseusse can draw cries of protest as she probes pressure points and twists the back and neck. The best practitioners have studied at Wat Po in central Bangkok, a school of ancient medicine where a visitor can buy an hour's sweaty treatment that costs $4 for Thais and $7.20 for foreigners. (A school official said that Thai customers would be offended if they were charged as much as rich foreigners.)

where to stay

BUDGET: Swiss Lodge, 3 Convent Road, (66-2) 233-5345, fax (66-2) 236-9425, is a clean, friendly hotel with 57 rooms, close to nightspots. Doubles: $92.

The 210-room Manhattan Hotel, 13 Soi 15, Sukhumvit Road, (66-2) 255-0166, fax (66-2) 255-3481, is convenient for shopping and business.

MODERATE: Ambassador Hotel, 171 Soi 11-13, Sukhumvit Road, (66-2) 254-0444, fax (66-2) 253-4123, is centrally located and close to the airport toll road. Its 750 rooms are decorated in mainstream hotel décor. Doubles start at $92.

LUXURY: The Oriental Hotel, 48 Oriental Avenue, (66-2) 236-0400, fax (66-2) 236-1937, sets the standard for elegance and service. Almost all the 396 rooms have river views. Double rooms are $268 to $336.

The lobby of the 356-room Regent Hotel, 155 Rajdamri Road, (66-2) 251-6127, fax (66-2) 251-5390, is dominated by a classical Thai mural. Doubles: $244.

where to eat

Thai cooks are geniuses, whether frying pork and squid at roadside braziers or preparing a French soufflé. Street vendors offer everything from deep-fried grasshoppers to tart papaya salad to neon-bright jellied desserts to sticky rice sweetened with coconut milk and roasted inside shafts of bamboo.

To feast on finger food, visit a produce market known by its initials as Aw-Taw-Gaw, off Paholyothin Road on the way to the airport, just beside the seemingly endless Sunday Market. Among other discoveries at Aw-Taw-Gaw is the mieng kam, a bite-size snack made up of tiny bits of lime, onion, garlic, chili, peanut, coconut, dried shrimp and sugar paste, all wrapped in an aromatic leaf and exploding with flavors when you bite into it. Vendors specialize in foods from around the country, none of which costs more than a dollar or two. The beverage of choice is usually a soft drink.

For ambience, there is nothing quite like a dinner cruise along the Chao Phraya River. One of the best is on board the Manohra, a converted teak rice barge that leaves daily at 7:30 p.m. from the Marriott Royal Garden Riverside Hotel for a three-hour cruise that costs $28.50 a person. Reserve at (66-2) 476-0022. Another is the Pearl of Siam, a three-deck motor yacht that departs at 7:15 p.m. from the River City Pier at the Royal Orchid Sheraton for a two-hour cruise that costs $26, including buffet and drinks. Reservations at (66-2) 236-777, extension 1204. Both serve mainstream Thai dishes, such as sweet-and-sour fish and tom yam gung, the popular spicy shrimp soup.

Harmonique, 22 Charoenkrung Soi 34, (66-2) 237-8175, serves some of the city's best Thai and southern Chinese food in a jungle-green terrarium within a gift shop of antique furniture, Burmese-Thai lacquerware and jewelry. Especially good are the mango chicken salad (yam saab gai) and baked rice with olives (khao op ngam liab). Dinner for two is $32 ($40 with beer). Closed Sunday; reservations recommended.

Crepe and Company Cafe, 18 Sukhumvit Soi 12, (66-2) 251-2895, is a friendly restaurant serving dozens of crepes ranging from standard cheese or meat or seafood dishes, to crepes featuring Thai curry fillings. Dinner for two with wine is $40.

vital statistics

POPULATION (1998 estimate): City 9 million

HOTEL: Room for one with tax $179.00

DINNER FOR ONE: With tax and tip but not drinks $25.55

TAXI: Upon entry 85 cents; Each additional kilometer 12 cents; From the airport $10.00

CAR RENTAL FOR A DAY: Midsize car with unlimited free mileage $46.00

FOR MORE INFORMATION: Telephone: (66-2) 694-1222; Web: www.tat.or.th

Sources: Runzheimer International, Tourism Authority of Thailand, local businesses

Barcelona

Thanks to the Olympics and new cultural
freedom, as vibrant and self-assured as ever

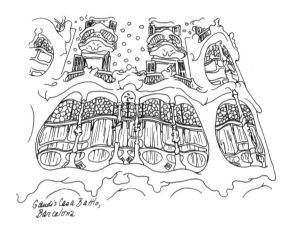

Gaudi's Casa Batllo,
Barcelona

STEVEN GREENHOUSE

Steven Greenhouse is a reporter for *The Times.*

Barcelona is a walker's paradise. It has old and new, sea and
mountain, postmodern and primitive. To saunter through its
Gothic Quarter, along the dark, narrow streets and past the ancient
artisans' shops, is to be transported back to the Middle Ages.

Walk up Passeig de Gràcia, past the chic boutiques and the dar-
ing, whimsical buildings by Antonio Gaudí, Barcelona's favorite
architectural son, and it is easy to appreciate why this city is known
as Spain's capital of design. And, of course, there is Les Rambles,
the city's most famous thoroughfare, where people gawk for hours
at performance artists, portrait painters, parrots on sale and the
parade of pedestrians.

This city spruced itself up considerably for the 1992 Olympic
Summer Games, a face-lift that is still paying off. Dozens of old
factories and seedy restaurants that blocked access to the waterfront
were torn down, creating a Mediterranean beach marvelous for
strolling and sunbathing. Near the Old Port are a new aquarium and
an IMAX theater, excellent diversions for those with kids in tow.

After 40 years in which Franco repressed Barcelona, the Catalan
language and the culture of the region, this proud city has strained to

make Catalan culture flourish again. Scores of townspeople dance the traditional Sardana on Sunday mornings in front of the 14th-century Cathedral. In 1995, the city opened the Barcelona Museum of Contemporary Art, a glistening white sun-drenched building designed by the American Richard Meier. The museum, at 1 Plaça dels Angels, (34-93) 412-0810, is open Monday, Wednesday, Thursday and Friday 11 a.m. to 7:30 p.m., Saturday 10 a.m. to 8 p.m.; Sunday 10 a.m. to 3 p.m. Admission: $4, $2 on Wednesday.

best of times

The city enjoys a warm Mediterranean climate year-round; rainfall can be heavy.

Barcelona is a city that loves to party. Toward the end of February, there is the spirited Carnival celebration with fireworks and parades. On April 23, the city marks the Festival of St. Jordi (St. George) in a romantic way—men give roses to women and women give books to men, and the streets, in what has evolved into a publishers' festival, are filled with booths selling flowers and books.

On Sept. 24 comes what is perhaps the city's biggest celebration, the Festival of La Mercè, one of the patron saints of Barcelona. A parade begins at the church, Nostra Senyora de la Mercè, and snakes along the Rambles toward the harbor. There are fireworks, folk dancing, concerts and parades of gegants and caps grossos (giants and big-headed figures). One unusual feature is the fire race in which Barcelonans run through small fires.

The most important cultural event each summer is the Barcelona Summer Festival, known as the Grec. From June 24 to the end of July, the city explodes with music, dance and theater performances, with a focus on the avant-garde.

From October to December each year, Barcelona sponsors the International Festival of Jazz, where visitors can drop in on jam sessions at the Harlem Jazz Club or see famous musicians at the city's gorgeous Palau de la Música; information (34-93) 232-6754.

what to see

Many bold-colored paintings and sculptures by Joan Miró, the Catalan artist who died in 1983, are on display at the Miró Foundation, a museum on Montjuïc overlooking Barcelona. The foundation, on the Plaça de Neptú, (34-93) 329-1908, is open Tuesday to Saturday 10 a.m. to 7 p.m., Thursday until 9:30 p.m., and Sunday until 2:30 p.m. Admission: $4.25.

The Picasso Museum, 15-23 Montcada, (34-93) 319-6310, fills

five medieval palaces with one of the world's most extensive collections of Picasso's early works, particularly from the years 1895 to 1904, when he lived in Barcelona. Open Tuesday to Saturday 10 a.m. to 8 p.m., Sunday 10 a.m. to 3 p.m. Admission: $3.75.

After years of renovation, the National Museum of Catalan Art, which served as the National Palace in the 1929 World's Fair, has reopened. The museum, in Montjuïc Park, has a spectacular collection of 12th- and 13th-century frescoes and altarpieces moved from remote churches in the Pyrenees. Call (34-93) 423-7199. Open Tuesday to Saturday 10 a.m. to 7 p.m., Thursday until 9 p.m., and Sunday until 2:30 p.m.; $4.25.

The Gothic Quarter resembles a maze, with surprises wherever one turns. On torrid summer days, the Cathedral's well-shaded cloister, with its cool stone and many plants, is the perfect escape. The romantic should not miss two well-preserved squares: the Plaça del Pi, known for its cafes and guitar-strumming troubadors, and the Plaça de Sant Felipe Neri, an oasis of serenity with a gentle fountain.

The Museum of the History of the City, housed in a 14th-century mansion on Plaça del Rei, (34-93) 315-1111, is full of wonders, including excavations of Roman ruins. Hours: Tuesday to Saturday 10 a.m. to 2 p.m. and 4 to 8 p.m., Sunday 10 a.m. to 2 p.m. Admission: $3.75.

A five-minute walk from the museum is the soaring, stark Church of Santa María del Mar, on Plaça de Santa María, a 14th-century structure with spectacular nave and columns. Unfortunately, its ornate decorations were destroyed during the Spanish Civil War.

Those thirsting to see Gaudí works can buy a $3.20 Ruta de Modernisme pass at the Center of Modernism, 41 Passeig de Gràcia, (34-93) 488-0139, a turn-of-the-century mansion designed by Lluís Domènech i Montaner with breathtaking murals and a florid stained-glass wall. The pass provides half-price admission to 10 Modernist buildings, including the Temple of the Sagrada Familia, at 401 Mallorca, (34-93) 455-0247, the vast still-unfinished church that Gaudí worked on for 43 years before his death in 1926. He is buried in the crypt. Open daily 9 a.m. to 8 p.m.

Gaudí lovers should not miss Güell Park, on Carrer Olot, an unfinished work that he designed to be a model community. It has a brilliantly colored, serpentine mosaic bench, an outdoor hall of stately columns and two guardhouses inspired by the story of Hansel and Gretel. Open daily from 10 a.m. to 7 p.m.

Although the dance floor often does not start rocking until 1 a.m., La Paloma, at 27 Tigre, (34-93) 301-6897, a century-old dance hall with lavishly painted rococo walls and ceiling, is worth a look anytime. Open Thursday to Sunday. Admission: $4.25.

where to stay

Two single beds are customary in Barcelona, so those who prefer a double bed should ask for one. Prices below do not include the 7 percent tax.

BUDGET: A block from the Cathedral, the Regencia Colón, 13 Sagristans, (34-93) 318-9858, fax (34-93) 317-2822, is a hospitable 55-room hotel with doubles at $88.

With doubles costing just $48, the 40-room Hotel Jardí, 1 Plaça Sant Josep Oriol, (34-93) 301-5900, fax (34-93) 318-3664, is a bargain, with many rooms facing the romantic Plaça del Pi and Plaça Sant Josep Oriol.

MODERATE: With many rooms facing the Cathedral, the Hotel Colón, 7 Avenida de la Catedral, (34-93) 301-1404, fax (34-93) 317-2915, a charming, classical 147-room establishment, is ideally situated. Doubles are $141.

The elegant Duques de Bergara, 11 Bergara, (34-93) 301-5151, fax (34-93) 317-3442, in a handsome Modernist mansion near the Plaça Catalunya, the city's main square, recently expanded to 150 rooms when its owners bought an adjacent building. Doubles cost $144.

LUXURY: The Ritz, opened by Cesar Ritz in 1919, embodies Old World elegance with its marble columns, stately restaurants and well-appointed rooms. Near the fashionable Passeig de Gràcia, the 161-room Ritz, 668 Gran Via, (34-93) 318-4837, fax (34-93) 318-0148, charges $241 for a double room. The thick carpets, antiques and landscapes on the walls bespeak opulence.

Boasting more modern elegance is the Hotel Claris, in the converted 19th-century Vedruna Palace, also near the Passeig de Gràcia. The 120-room hotel at 150 Pau Claris, (34-93) 487-6262, fax (34-93) 215-7970, has a Japanese garden, rooftop pool, a gallery of Egyptian artifacts and a lounge with fifth-century Roman mosaics. Doubles, at $229, come in various styles, including postmodern, some with plush leather chairs, some with cherry furnishings. Many have saunas and whirlpool baths.

where to eat

For a spectacular view of the Mediterranean and equally impressive seafood, Cal Pinxo is the place to go. Situated in Barceloneta, an up-and-coming neighborhood originally built for fishermen's families, this restaurant, at 124 Baluard, (34-93) 221-5028, has excellent paella, sea bass (lubina) and esquexada, a seafood salad full of olive oil and cod. Try a bottle of Yllera, a smooth red wine from Old Castile. Dinner for two, with wine, costs about $65.

A popular place for business executives and artists is Senyor Parellada, a bright yellow room filled with plants. The restaurant, at 37 Argenteria, (34-93) 310-5094, has excellent hake with donostiara sauce, containing olive oil, butter and lemon, and anglerfish with burnt garlic. Dinner for two, with wine: $65.

Widely considered one of the best tapas bars in a city famous for tapas, Cal Pep, 8 Plaça de les Olles, (34-93) 310-7961, has seafood galore. At night, there are often lines for the bustling marble bar, but it is worth the wait. Try the succulent baby squid (chipirones), the grilled shrimp, the mussels and the spinach with garbanzo beans and garlic. Dinner for two: $60, with wine.

Budget-minded tourists might try Agut, 16 Gignás, (34-93) 315-1709, with a $6.70 lunch menu with entree, wine and dessert included. At night, menus are à la carte. The vegetable pie with tomato sauce is tasty, as are the filet of hake with Provençal sauce and the lasagna with escalivada, a mixture of grilled peppers, eggplant and onions. Dinner for two, with wine: $50.

The $5.35 lunch menu is a stunning bargain at El Convent, in a converted medieval convent, at 3 Jerusalem, (34-93) 317-1052, just behind the colorful Boquería food market. Appetizers include lentil salad, baby squid salad and asparagus with garlic mousse.

vital statistics

POPULATION (1998): City 1,505,581

HOTEL: Room for one with tax $166.50

DINNER FOR ONE: With tax and tip but not drinks $19.85

TAXI: Upon entry $1.57; Each additional kilometer 55 cents; From the airport $8.38

CAR RENTAL FOR A DAY: Midsize car with unlimited free mileage $83.27

FOR MORE INFORMATION: Telephone: (34-93) 304-3232; Web: www.bcn.es/english/ihome.htm

Sources: Runzheimer International, Tourist Office of Spain, local businesses

Berlin

A "heart transplant," but will it work?

Brandenburg
Gate, Berlin

EVE SCHAENEN
Eve Schaenen is a journalist and former resident Berlin.

These days, when Berliners talk about their city, the question is always the same, accompanied by a sweeping gesture toward the crane or bulldozer inevitably positioned nearby: "You think it will work?"

For the visitor interested in urban development, contemporary architecture or, indeed, world history, Berlin is a veritable candy store for the mind. All over town the city's physical past is being confronted, restored, reshaped or at times obliterated to make way for the 21st-century capital.

There is the newly transplanted heart at Potsdamer Platz, with the steel and glass towers of Sony and Daimler-Benz. The area was the commercial center of prewar Berlin—but it was also the site of Hitler's bunker, of the wall and the mined no man's land behind it. There is the Reichstag, birthplace of the Weimar democracy in 1918, but also the setting for the infamous fire used by the Nazis to seize power in 1933. Refashioned by Sir Norman Foster, the British architect, the building once again houses the German Parliament.

On a less monumental scale, there is the old Jewish quarter in the Mitte district. Due to conflicting claims, much of the area was off limits to investors after the wall fell, resulting in a squatters' paradise and a flourishing subculture that left its mark in the neighborhood's trendy galleries, clubs and restaurants.

Yet all this is just the sideshow. For in reclaiming its status as government capital, Berlin is determined to reclaim its 1920's role as cultural capital of Europe. The city boasts three state-subsidized opera houses, five symphony orchestras and three ballet companies. Some 15,000 seats are available nightly for concerts and musical theater.

best of times

With an impressive array of high- and pop-cultural events throughout the year, there is really no bad time to visit Berlin. Summer tends to be muggy and less culturally active, so those with a special affinity for dance, film, jazz, opera or theater may be advised to plan a trip around one of the many top-notch festivals.

The annual arrival of the Berlin Film Festival, or Berlinale, in February adds color to an otherwise gray Berlin winter. Temperatures in February tend to be cold and damp, with little snow and still less sun. Based at the Potsdamer Platz, the Berlinale might be less glamorous than its counterparts in Cannes and Venice, but it is unbeatable in terms of breadth of films. Telephone (49-30) 259 200.

Once spring arrives, the city blossoms. May is a perfect time to visit, especially if one is a lover of good German-language theater. The Berlin Theater Festival takes place during the first three weeks of the month when the weather is generally mild and showcases the work of both established and exciting new directors; (49-30) 254 890.

The Berlin Festival Weeks, started in 1949 as a means to reacquaint Berliners with developments in the arts they had been isolated from during World War II, has since developed into one of the city's most distinguished events. Running through September, a month often marked by a warm altweiber summer, the Festival Weeks feature performances in music, dance and theater; (49-30) 254 890.

If the annual Berlin Jazz Festival in November has one flaw, it is that it is too short. Held each year on a long weekend at the beginning of the month, the jazz festival draws a mixture of big names and critical favorites from the world of contemporary jazz; (49-30) 254 890.

Other festivals of note include Dance in August at the Hebbel Theater, (49-30) 259 004 27, and the Jewish Cultural Festival in mid-November, (49-30) 2839 230.

what to see

The best way to immerse oneself in the rhythm of Berlin is to step into its noisy unfinished center. Emerge from the Potsdamer Platz S-Bahn station to a sky filled with 30 cranes, lifting, swiveling, loads dangling.

A short walk into the heart of the old Jewish quarter leads to the Hackeschen Hofe, 40-41 Rosenthaler Strasse, eight connecting Jugendstil buildings and courtyards that successfully combine the public life of cafes, galleries, clubs and fashion boutiques with private housing.

Two museums opened in June 1998. The Picture Gallery at the Kulturforum, 8 Matthai Kirchplatz, (49-30) 2090 5555, unites some 1,000 masterworks of European painting, an encyclopedic collection divided in two for the past half-century by the exigencies of war and the wall. The understated building relies almost exclusively on natural overhead light. Open Tuesday through Friday 10 a.m. to 6 p.m., weekends from 11 a.m. to 6 p.m. Admission: $3.80.

The Allied Museum, in the former American military movie theater at 135 Clayallee, offers a multimedia depiction of the history of Berlin and the Allies. Among the items on display are an original raisin bomber from the Berlin airlift, the Checkpoint Charlie house and a piece of the wall. Open daily except Wednesday, 10 a.m. to 6 p.m.; (49-30) 818 1990. Admission: free.

An unprecedented influx of young people, many of them from former West Germany, is affecting a demographic revolution in Prenzlauer Berg, Berlin's traditionally working-class neighborhood just north of the city's historic center. Since the wall fell, the neighborhood has witnessed a turnover of 50 percent. Bars, cafes, Tuscan food—the classic harbingers of metropolitan gentrification—have arrived in full force. And yet the magnetic force the neighborhood exerts on its newest residents appears to emanate less from the spanking newness than from the crumbling remains left between the cleared spaces, the psychic pull of Germany's swiftly fading physical past: war-wounded facades, dark courtyards, coal heating. Grayness.

where to stay

BUDGET: Situated in trendy Kreuzberg directly over the Marheineke market hall, the 16-room Gasthaus Dietrich Herz, 15 Marheineke Platz, (49-30) 693 1173, offers clean, no-frills accommodations with front-row seats for one of Berlin's liveliest street scenes. Rooms have private bath and shower; some have balconies overlooking the Platz. Doubles including breakfast: from $69 to $81.

Specializing in families with small children, the 31-room Hotel-Pension Wittelsbach, 22 Wittelsbacherstrasse, 10707, (49-30) 864 9840, fax (49-30) 862 1532, devotes a floor to fairy-tale-inspired doubles and suites, complete with castle- or fort-shaped bunk beds and a gingerbread house in the corridor. There is a small playground. Doubles including breakfast: from $104; $145 for a four-person family room.

MODERATE: The Bleibtreu Hotel, 31 Bleibtreustrasse, (49-30) 884 740, fax (49-30) 884 74444, is hidden in an artfully designed courtyard just off western Berlin's toniest shopping street, the Kurfurstendamm. The 60 quiet rooms feature Italian designer furniture in natural materials. Doubles, including breakfast: from $164 on weekends, $197 weekdays.

LUXURY: The 204-room Four Seasons, 49 Charlottenstrasse, (49-30) 20338, fax (49-30) 2033 6166, opens onto one of the city's most impressive imperial squares, the Gendarmenmarkt, with its twin cathedrals and concert hall. The oak paneling and marble fireplace in the corner dining room suggest traditional opulence, while the fitness room and technologically equipped business centers comply with more modern needs. Doubles: from $228 to $315.

The Kempinski Hotel Bristol Berlin, 27 Kurfurstendamm, (49-30) 884 340, fax (49-30) 883 6075, remains a grande dame among Berlin hotels, with 301 traditionally luxurious rooms on the Kurfurstendamm. The breakfast buffet, served in a sunny winter garden, is one of the finest in town. Doubles with breakfast: from $231.

where to eat

Situated in the house where Rahel Varnhagen conducted her famous literary salon in the 1790's, Vau, at 54-55 Jagerstrasse, attracts an elegant business crowd with its contemporary classic interior, exceptional service and haute cuisine. The four- and six-course menus (at $51 and $109) feature seasonal specialties, such as sautéed langoustines on white beans and summer truffles. A three-course dinner for two with wine starts at $116. Vau's special lunch offer, any dish on the menu for $11.60, has become an insider institution. Reservations, at (49-30) 202 9730, are necessary. Both lunch and dinner are served.

With its blood-red velvet settees and live piano music, Die Mowe, 1 Palais am Festungsgruben, (49-30) 201 2029, recalls the sophisticated salon ambience of prewar Berlin. A generous seasonal salad can be followed by roast duck with kohlrabi purée.

Dinner for two with wine is roughly $80. Monday night is "Art Enjoyment," a changing program of musical entertainment with a thematic three-course meal for $35. Reserve ahead. Dinner only.

Schwarzenraben, across from the Hackeschen Hofe, 13 Neue Schonhauser Strasse, (49-30) 2839 1698, serves Italian fare in a cool beige setting with a heaping side order of attitude. Assorted cold grilled vegetables or pheasant pâté (each $10.40) make good starters. The piatti di mezzo—such as baby lamb chops in red wine sauce with summer vegetables ($13.85)—are large enough for a main course. Dinner for two with wine starts at about $80. Lunch and dinner.

Berlin is renowned for its breakfast culture; indeed, many cafes serve breakfast to late risers well into the afternoon. In an 1885 villa with idyllic garden seating, Cafe-Wintergarten im Literaturhaus, 23 Fasanenstrasse, (49-30) 882 5414, offers six breakfast specials ranging from basic Milchkaffee and croissants ($4.90) to house-smoked salmon and champagne ($15.60), plus many à la carte selections. Kamala, 69 Oranienburger Strasse in Mitte, (49-30) 283 2797, serves inexpensive and delicious Thai food. The $8.40 lunch includes soup and a main dish. The underground restaurant is small; you may have to share a table.

There is a German saying: Everything has an end—only the wurst has two. The standing tables at the Currywurstbude, 195 Kurfurstendamm, are crowded with business people and shoppers sampling Berlin's preferred fast food. The classic Currywurst is $1.80.

vital statistics

POPULATION (1999): City 3,400,000

HOTEL: Room for one with tax $158.50

DINNER FOR ONE: With tax and tip but not drinks $24.10

TAXI: Upon entry $2.70; Each additional kilometer 95 cents; From the airport to Kurfurstendamm $13.50; From the airport to Mitte $27.00

CAR RENTAL FOR A DAY: Midsize manual shift car with unlimited free mileage $61.00

FOR MORE INFORMATION: Telephone: (49-30) 250 025; Web: www.berlin-tourism.de

Sources: Runzheimer International, German National Tourist Office, local businesses

Boston

New wealth brings new glitter,
but tradition is still cherished

Boston,
Massachusetts

DEBORAH WEISGALL
Deborah Weisgall often writes on art and
culture in the Boston area.

These days, conservative Boston seems newly alive and bur-
geoning, even brash. The grove of cranes that marks the Big
Dig, one of the most expensive highway-construction projects in
American history, looks like exotic willows orange with sap. The
project involves moving the Central Artery underground to recon-
nect downtown to the harbor that was the source of its early wealth.

Boston's current money comes from high tech, venture capital
and money management, and this fresh green cash is reseeding the
town, spiffing up its fabled shabbiness. In the financial district,
around Post Office Square, glass towers cast sharp shadows over
narrow streets, once cow paths. Beside them, restored 19th-cen-
tury buildings seem to cringe at their new neighbors' scale.

Despite its renewed affluence, the city cherishes tradition.
Boston's Puritan founders hardly disapproved of wealth, only of its
public display. Facades remain austere, if freshly painted, the luxury inside private.

The life of the mind continues to flourish. John Updike, Sue

Miller, Robert Parker and James Carroll are among the writers who choose to live and work here.

best of times

Boston's seasons seem to turn on an academic calendar. Fall is a season of beginnings, a time to wander the brick sidewalks in Cambridge with returning students, watch crews compete at the Head of the Charles Regatta the third weekend in October, and partake of the city's rich culture. My favorite event is the Boston Symphony's opening Friday-afternoon concert at the end of September. Boston's great ladies sit resplendent, if a bit faded, in the same seats their grandmothers occupied.

December, although it's dark by 4 p.m., is a lovely time; Boston's venerable choral groups present their Christmas concerts; the Christmas Revels, a compendium of traditional songs and dances, are a hometown institution. First Night, the nationwide New Year's Eve festival, with elaborate ice carvings, a parade and dozens of performances, began here in Boston.

In sweet, capricious spring, the Museum of Fine Arts celebrates May with Art in Bloom, the Public Gardens burst with tulips, the Red Sox return to glorious old Fenway Park, whose days might be numbered, and the Boston Marathon draws hordes of runners.

In late May and early June, proud families book hotels a year in advance for their kids' commencements. During the summer, towns ringing Boston, such as Concord and Lexington, or Gloucester and Salem, might prove more attractive than the city. But the spectacular Fourth of July fireworks choreographed to the Boston Pops concert on the Esplanade are worth a journey.

what to see

The city boasts several prominent art museums, including the Isabella Stuart Gardner Museum, 280 The Fenway, (617) 566-1401; the Fogg Art Museum in Cambridge, 32 Quincy Street, (617) 495-9400; and the Museum of Fine Arts, 465 Huntington Avenue, (617) 267-9300.

The Freedom Trail, a strip of bricks embedded in Boston's sidewalks, is still worth following to the main sights, beautiful even apart from their historic associations: Faneuil Hall, the Old State House, Old North Church. A good starting point is Boston Common, where an information booth has trail maps.

A recent book, *The Literary Trail, a Guide to Greater Boston's Newest Trail,* suggests self-guided tours of sites connected with

Boston writers, including the Longfellow House in Cambridge, Louisa May Alcott's Orchard House and Nathaniel Hawthorne's Old Manse in Concord, and Henry David Thoreau's reconstructed cabin at Walden Pond. Organized by the Boston History Collaborative, the guide sells for $4.95 at local bookstores or it can be ordered by calling (617) 574-5950.

Boston is not far from the country, and there is a bike path that begins in Arlington, 10 minutes northwest at Route 95 and extends west 10 miles to Bedford, passing plenty of places to stop and refuel. A one-block detour leads to the Lexington green, where the Revolutionary War began.

An inviting multi-use trail in the Minuteman National Historical Park stretches five and a half miles from Lexington to Concord—along boardwalks through marshes and across ancient fields—giving a sense of what the countryside was like two centuries ago. Open dawn to dusk. Information: (978) 369-6993.

The Society for the Preservation of New England Antiquities owns many properties around Boston. Their headquarters, the 18th-century Harrison Gray Otis house, designed by Charles Bulfinch, is at 141 Cambridge Street. In Lincoln, 15 miles west of the city, the Gropius House, 68 Baker Bridge Road, built by the founder of the Bauhaus movement, is a compact marvel of minimalist design, and the elegant 18th-century Codman House is close by. Information: (617) 227-3956.

Boston has its share of interesting shopping opportunities. Alan Bilzerian, who has shops at 34 Newbury Street and 1241 Centre Street in Newton Centre, is a passionate fashion visionary. The cashmere, silk and merino knitwear designed by his wife, Be, and made in Italy is exquisite (and will set you back $200 to $600); (617) 536-1001.

At Formaggio Kitchen, (888) 212-3224, a small but formidable establishment at 244 Huron Avenue in Cambridge, the selection of cheeses is seductive (pecorino di Pienza gran riserva is $17.95 a pound), the fresh pasta ($3.50 a pound) is tender, and the selection of oils and vinegars distills the best of the Mediterranean. The poet Louise Gluck mentions Formaggio in her poems; the place itself is an ode to food.

where to stay

BUDGET: A group called Bed and Breakfast Associates Bay Colony, (888) 429-7568, fax (781) 449-5958, is a booking service for inns in the city and suburbs. Doubles: from $90 to $175. A Victorian town house in the South End, with two guest rooms, each with private bath, garden-level kitchen, full breakfast and parking, costs $99 to $160.

MODERATE: In Cambridge, the Inn at Harvard, 1201 Massachusetts Avenue, (800) 458-5886, fax (617) 492-4896, is quiet and well-appointed with traditional cherry furniture and colors of peach, cream and gray. For visiting scholars, it's just half a block from the Fogg Art Museum and Widener Library. It has 113 rooms and a restaurant in its atrium. Rooms from $189.

The Sheraton Commander, 16 Garden Street, Cambridge, near Harvard, (800) 535-5007, fax (617) 868-8322, has 175 rooms. Doubles start at $199, depending on occupancy and season.

LUXURY: The Ritz-Carlton, Arlington and Newbury Streets, (617) 536-5700, fax (617) 536-1335, where Louis the trumpeting swan bunked in E. B. White's *The Trumpet of the Swan,* is synonymous with Boston. Its doormen seem to know everything about the city, and many of the 275 rooms have a view of the Public Garden. The décor is French provincial, with original art on the walls. Doubles: from $445.

The Four Seasons, which also faces the Public Garden at 200 Boylston Street, leavens the serious luxury of its 288 pastel rooms—three phones with two lines, one-hour pressing of clothes—with a sense of humor. Children and pets are invited (there are 24-hour room service menus for each and dog-walking). Doubles: from $560; (617) 338-4400, fax (617) 423-0154.

The smaller Eliot Hotel, 370 Commonwealth Avenue, features all suites, with English-style antiques and pastel colors, two dual-line phones and faxes. Doubles from $395 for the 95 suites. Reservations: (800) 443-5468, fax (617) 536-9114.

where to eat

Be sure to call for reservations well ahead on weekends at Radius, Michael Schlow's restaurant at 8 High Street in Boston's business district. It's worth the effort—informal but sleek, and the menu includes confit of pork and a terrine of veal cheeks, sweetbreads and asparagus. The menu changes monthly. Dinner for two with wine: $120; (617) 426-1234.

In Waltham, Il Capriccio, 888 Main Street, offers consistently sumptuous northern Italian food cooked by Richard Barron, with an extraordinary list of Italian wines—many of them hard to find outside of Italy—collected by co-owner Jeannie Rogers. The wild mushroom soufflé is a classic, the veal chop (in a variety of ways) irresistible. Dinner for two: $110. Reservations (at least two weeks in advance for a weekend) at (781) 894-2234.

In Stephanie's on Newbury, a clubby bar and skylit dining space at 190 Newbury Street, (617) 236-0990, Stephanie Sidell serves sophisticated American cooking, big salads, grilled fish and chicken. For comfort food, try the rosti. Dinner for two: $70.

At Aujourd'hui, 200 Boylston Street, in the Four Seasons, everything—the service, the view of the Public Garden, the exquisite food—is perfectly orchestrated. Try anything, from the vegetarian tasting menu to chocolate soufflé. Dinner for two: $150; (617) 451-1392.

The Hi-Rise Bread Company, 208 Concord Avenue in Cambridge, is addictive, with some of Boston's best bread, fruit pies and brioche. Soups and sandwiches make a great lunch; roasted free-range chicken ($12) and quiche provide dinner. Sandwiches average $7, soup from $2.50 to $6, breads $3 to $8; (617) 876-8766.

vital statistics

POPULATION (1998 estimate): City 555,447; Metro area 3,289,096

HOTEL: Room for one with tax $239.50

DINNER FOR ONE: With tax and tip but not drinks $27.00

TAXI: Upon entry $1.50; Each additional mile $2.10; From the airport $18.00

CAR RENTAL FOR A DAY: Midsize car with unlimited free mileage $61.50

FOR MORE INFORMATION: Telephone: (888) 733-2678; Web: www.bostonusa.com

Sources: Runzheimer International, U.S. Census Bureau, local businesses

Brussels

Home to NATO and the European Union, and filled with delightful quirks

Guild Houses, Brussels

ERIC SJOGREN

Eric Sjogren is a journalist who lives in Brussels.

The Grand'Place, one of Europe's most splendid and theatrical squares, is the real heart of Brussels and draws visitors and residents alike. The sidewalk cafes overflow with people from April until well into fall.

Dominated by a Gothic Town Hall with a slender belfry—looking better, thanks to a recent scouring, than it has for the past 500 years—and surrounded by Baroque guild houses adorned with gilded statuary inspired by Greek mythology, it makes a stately backdrop for a multitude of events, including jazz concerts, bird markets, folklore dancing, historical processions and Christmas fairs.

The Christmas market features stalls from all the European Union member states, for don't forget that Brussels considers itself the Capital of Europe, home to both the European Union and NATO. An inevitable consequence has been the conversion of one residential area after another into high-rise cityscapes. But Brussels remains at heart a provincial city, and its inhabitants continue to find expression for their quirky individuality—in town houses, for instance, with results ranging from the odd to the spectacular, or in private gardens and public parks. A walk down an unfamiliar residential street is a pleasure that many Bruxellois treat themselves to from time to time.

best of times

May through September are the most popular months for visiting Brussels, with temperatures ranging from mid-60's to low 70's.

For 10 days from the end of April, the Royal Greenhouses at the Palace of Laeken are open to the public. The enormous Art Nouveau extravaganza covers almost four acres of plants and trees in luxuriant bloom. Information: (32-2) 513-8940.

The Queen Elizabeth International Music Competition in May, one of the world's toughest, features young pianists, violinists and singers in successive years. If you want to hear a real ovation, be at the Palais des Beaux-Arts, 23 rue Ravenstein, in the wee hours of the night the winner is proclaimed. (32-3) 507-8220.

For pomp and circumstance, no event can match the annual Ommegang, staged in early July in the highly theatrical setting of the Grand'Place. It is a copy of a 1549 procession in honor of the Holy Roman Emperor Charles V, born and raised in Belgium. The magnificently dressed lords and ladies of the court are portrayed by aristocrats, some playing their forebears. There is also lots of entertainment, including flame throwers, acrobats and Breughelian dancers. Tickets for grandstand seats can be ordered from the Ommegang, 180 rue des Tanneurs; (32-2) 512-1961, fax (32-2) 502-6835.

The Tapis de Fleurs, or Flower Carpet, is a biennial event, next scheduled for 2002. The Grand'Place is covered for a display with hundreds of thousands of flowers, put in position in a single afternoon to preserve their freshness. The 15th-century Town Hall is decorated with flowers and opened so that visitors can admire the flower carpet from its balconies.

what to see

The Grand'Place isn't the only square in town worth visiting. The upmarket Grand Sablon, off the Rue de la Régence, is home to fashionable antique dealers, art galleries, boutiques, cafes and restaurants. Next to the Notre Dame du Sablon, antique dealers and booksellers set up their stands, rain or shine, all day Saturday and Sunday morning. Across the street, the Petit Sablon offers a delightful haven in the form of a beautifully manicured public garden. The wrought-iron gate is topped by 48 statuettes representing different crafts, carrying the tools of their trade. They're not all obvious; the tallow maker, for instance, carries a bottle and a dead goose.

The new Musical Instruments Museum (M.I.M.) has moved its vast collections into an extravagant Art Nouveau building from 1899, originally designed for the Old England department store. From here you enter the adjoining building, where 1,400 instruments from all over the world are displayed. When you approach one, you hear music featuring that instrument, thanks to headphones equipped with an infrared device. The museum is at 2 rue Montagne de la Cour (off the Place Royale), (32-2) 545-0130. Open daily (except Monday) 9:30 a.m. to 5 p.m.; weekends from 10 a.m.; Thursday until 8 p.m., followed by a concert. Admission: $3.40.

Along most any Brussels street, but especially in the boroughs of St.-Gilles and Ixelles, you will notice the remarkable variety of architecture. It is the legacy of the Art Nouveau movement, which flourished at the beginning of last century. Its progenitor was Victor Horta, whose home, now a museum, illustrates his ability to create a sense of opulence and spaciousness in a limited area. The Horta Museum, 25 Rue Americain (32-2) 537-1692, is open daily except Monday, 2 to 5:30 p.m. Admission: $2.95 during the week, $5.80 on weekends.

The preference of chocolate gourmets in this city of great chocolate has switched from milk or white chocolate to ever-darker cacao in search of the pure chocolate taste. Three chocolatiers are ahead of the rest in this pursuit: Wittamer (6 Place du Grand Sablon), past masters at fresh-cream pralines, $8.50 for 250 grams; Galler (44 rue au Beurre near the Grand-Place), whose Extrème is 70 percent cacao, $7 (250 grams); and a newcomer, Pierre Marcolini (39 Place du Grand Sablon), where you can taste before you buy from a flowing chocolate fountain, $9 (250 grams).

where to stay

Reduced rates are often available on weekends and from mid-July to the end of August.

BUDGET: Hotel Welcome, 5, rue du Peuplier, (32-2) 219-9546, fax (32-2) 217 1887, proudly claims to be Brussels' smallest hotel, but the six rooms offer most of what anyone might need, including king-size beds. The small inconveniences (no elevator) are made up for by the youthful enthusiasm of the owners, Michel and Sophie Smeesters. Breakfast room and restaurant. Doubles: from $59 to $93 (no weekend rates).

The Galia, 15-16 Place du Jeu du Balle, (32-2) 502-4243, (32-2) 502-7619, right on the flea market, is not for the fainthearted but has its own kind of jaunty charm. The elevator is slow but gets you there, and the 24 rooms are small but all have showers. There's a lively, skylighted tavern behind the reception. Doubles: from $43 to $64 (no weekend rates).

MODERATE: Le Dix-Septième, 25 rue de la Madeleine, (32-2) 502-5744, fax (32-2) 502-6424, in a 17th-century house, is a tasteful haven. The 30 rooms, all different, feature wooden floors, Oriental carpets, exposed beams. Excellent service. Doubles start at $160, buffet breakfast included.

Manos Residence, 102 Chaussée de Charleroi, (32-2) 537-9682, fax (32-2) 539-3655, consists of two art-filled town houses. Nine of the 38 rooms are reached by a spiral staircase to the fourth floor (which connects with the other, elevator-equipped section). The breakfast room and bar open onto extensive gardens. Doubles with bath cost $188; suites are a bargain at $308.

LUXURY: Le Meridien, 3 Carrefour de l'Europe, (32-2) 548-4211, fax (32-2) 548-4080, has an undeniable Parisian chic, reflected in the smartness of the 224 red, green or blue rooms, the round marble lobby with its chandelier, and the restaurant, l'Épicerie, whose Mediterranean-flavored cuisine matches the colorful Limoges china. Doubles cost $318, not including breakfast.

Radisson SAS, 47 rue du Fossé-aux Loups, (32-2) 219-2828, fax (32-2) 219-6262, has a young, can-do spirit, and the 281 spic-and-span rooms come in four styles. The greenery-filled atrium is a pleasant oasis. Doubles: from $295.

where to eat

Unless otherwise indicated, restaurants are closed Saturday at lunchtime and Sunday, and for two weeks in July or August.

Le Bistrot du Mail, 81 rue du Mail, (32-2) 539-0697, is a cozy, casual place with oxblood-red walls where most of the clientele are regulars. Diners generally stray in late, 9 to 9:30 p.m. We loved the sea scallops with caramelized endives, the roast turbot with asparagus and potatoes crushed in olive oil, and lamb from the Pyrenees. Lunchtime regulars go for the plat du jour at $7.85. Dinner for two with wine: about $90.

Le Passage, 13 avenue J. &. P. Carsoel at the Place St. Job in Uccle, a 20-minute cab ride from downtown, (32-2) 374-6694, is my favorite neighborhood restaurant; Michelin handed it a star in 2000. The décor is simple but the cuisine highly inventive: swordfish carpaccio, lasagna of roast salmon and langoustines, lightly curried caramelized apple. Dinner with wine for two is $100. Prix fixe menus are bargains: a two-course lunch, $14; four-course dinner, $29.

For a budget meal, a good choice is 't Kelderke, in a subterranean brick vault at 15 Grand-Place, (32-2) 513-7344, open daily from noon to 2 a.m. The plat du jour is an unbeatable $6.70. Stoemp—a potato and vegetable mash—with sausages and other Brussels specialties served in generous portions is the featured dish. Two can dine in style for $45, or half that with a bit of care.

Comme Chez Soi, 23 place Rouppe (32-2) 512-2921, the 75-year-old luxury bistrot, earned its third Michelin star years ago. The owner and chef, Pierre Wynants, believes in enlightened nepotism and has promoted his son-in-law, Lionel Rigolet, to share top billing with him. Critics rave that the younger man's perfectionism matches the father-in-law's. One old favorite, sole with a Riesling mousseline and tiny, sweet shrimps, is always on the menu. An à la carte dinner for two can easily come to $191; the fixed-price lunch costs $46, and dinner menus start at $78. Closed Sundays, Mondays and all of July.

At Le Pain Quotidien, 4 Grand-Sablon, (32-2) 513-5154, a very democratic bakery–snack bar, a big communal table welcomes all. It opens for breakfast at 8, serving delicious croissants, and offers open-face sandwiches on great, crunchy bread ($3.50 to $8.80) and salads ($8.25 to $11) until 7 p.m. A glass of wine costs $2.35, a beer $1.90.

vital statistics

POPULATION (1999): City 1,250,000

HOTEL: Room for one with tax $243.00

DINNER FOR ONE: With tax and tip but not drinks $29.50

TAXI: Upon entry $3.00; Each additional kilometer $1.00; From the airport $30.00

CAR RENTAL FOR A DAY: Midsize manual shift car with unlimited free mileage $91.67

FOR MORE INFORMATION: Telephone: (32-2) 548-0461; Web: www.brusselsdiscovery.com

Sources: Runzheimer International, Belgian Tourist Office, local businesses

Cairo

Assaulting the senses and inspiring the imagination

Ibn Tulun Mosque, Cairo

DOUGLAS JEHL
Douglas Jehl is a former chief of the Cairo bureau of *The Times*.

At once maddening and alluring, Cairo is a city for the tenacious. Beyond its noise and heat and traffic lie much to be discovered, but too many visitors leave content with a glimpse of the Great Pyramids, reached via tour bus.

It is, famously, not an easy city to navigate. Language can be a barrier, unless you have a guide. Policemen seem to be everywhere, but most drivers pay them no heed, and their presence can bring reminders of terrorism past, though there have been no attacks on Westerners since 1997, and the threat posed by Islamic militants seems to have all but disappeared.

Certainly, no visit would be complete without pilgrimages to the Pyramids and the Sphinx—awe-inspiring, though the city of 16 million has now reached their very edge—and to the Egyptian Museum, where Pharaonic treasures are displayed by the roomful, though often without signs. But Egypt's history only began with Pharaohs. And to sample some of the rest, it is wisest to plunge in, experiencing the chaotic streets that lead some foreign residents to say they love Cairo and hate it, usually on the same day.

The city's old market, the Khan al-Khalili, assaults the senses with the exhilarating jumble of a Middle East bazaar, where the shouts from donkey carts and the glimmer of gold shops compete for attention with the pungent smells of cumin heaped into the spice stalls. Beyond the tourist haunts, full of trinkets, lie back streets where ordinary Cairenes buy and sell, in timeless scenes that recall the novels by the Nobel Prize-winning author, Naguib Mahfouz. Here, buildings are centuries old, and narrow streets give way to mosques and Christian churches that date back far longer, to the early days of the two religions.

In Zamalek, home to many embassies, stylish galleries sit side by side with antique shops crammed with ornate furnishings, and more traditional merchants: the cobblers, knife sharpeners, rug menders and the poultrymen, whose live wares squawk from side-walk cages. Along the Nile, young couples walk hand in hand, gal-abeyas juxtaposed against Armani and mobile phones. Alongside stream black-and-white Fiat taxis, held together mostly with a prayer, and also, and increasingly, the Mercedes Benzes and BMW's favored by the nouveau riche entrepreneurs relishing an easing-up of government control.

best of times

To avoid mind-numbing heat, visit Cairo between October and April, when mild, dry weather presents a gentler face. Beware mid-summer, when anything more than a dip in the hotel pool can seem an oppressive chore.

On breezy days, escape the chaos of the city with a felucca ride on the Nile. Boatmen and their traditional sailboats can be hired from their docks on the western side of the river, near the Meridien Hotel.

To experience Cairo at its most pious, visit during the Muslim holy month of Ramadan, whose timing varies according to the Islamic calendar but which in 2001 will begin in November. At night, after a daytime fast, the city has a festive air.

what to see

At Al-Ghuri Palace, in an old part of the city, whirling dervishes perform the dances of the al Mawlawia, a medieval offshoot of Islam that has now all but disappeared. The 70-minute show is per-formed each Wednesday and Saturday in the former reception hall of the 15th-century palace. Performances start at 9 p.m. and are free; it is wise to show up at least 30 minutes early for a seat. Information: (20-2) 510-0823.

The Gayer-Anderson Museum, next to the Ibn Tulun Mosque, (20-2) 364-7822, provides a tantalizing glimpse into a traditional Islamic home. In adjoining 16th- and 17th-century Arabic-style houses, the museum displays furniture and keepsakes. But its real wonders include magnificent mashrabiya windows and the enclosed galleries used by women of the household to peer unseen into gatherings limited to men. Open daily 8 a.m. to 4 p.m. Admission: $5.50.

A walk through Old Cairo helps one appreciate the city's count-less sects and the layers upon which it is built. A starting point, the Hanging Church (or El Muallaqa), is under renovation, but remains accessible to visitors and is a thriving center for Egypt's Coptic Christians. Rebuilt in the 10th century, it dates from 600 years earlier and is supported by the remains of a Roman fortress. Free admission; open Sunday and Friday 11:30 a.m. to 5 p.m., other days 9 a.m. to 5 p.m.

Not far away is the Ben Ezra Synagogue, a smallish building that is the city's oldest surviving house of Jewish worship. It was built in 1115 where an earlier Coptic church once stood; the site also has ancient associations for Jews. The synagogue's treasures include a Torah on gazelle skins from the fifth century B.C. Open daily 9 a.m. to 4:30 p.m.; free admission.

Also nearby is the mosque of Amr Ibn al-As, built in 642, just 10 years after the death of the prophet Mohammed. It is the oldest mosque in Africa. It has an enormous open court surrounded by four arcaded walkways adorned with Byzantine wood carvings. Admission $1.80; open daily from 9 a.m. to 5 p.m. except (like most mosques) during Friday prayers.

The Khan al-Khalili can be a shopper's trove, even though the sheer number of small shops can sometimes make it seem an exhausting maze. The alleys and stairways contain less touristy wares, such as antique copper and old Bedouin jewelry. Often, the best items are at the bottom of a merchant's sack. Something more easily found is a cartouche, usually a pendant in gold or silver with the wearer's name in Pharaonic hieroglyphics. One established artisan, Mihran Garbis Yazejian—whose custom work in gold begins at about $90 and takes at least four days—is at 8 Khan al-Khalili, (20-2) 591-2321.

No visitor should miss the Great Pyramids of Giza. But for a less crowded glimpse of ancient Egypt, visit the tombs and pyra-mids at Saqqara and Dashour, an hour's drive south of central Cairo, which attract a fraction as many tourists. Car and driver for a four-hour round trip should cost less than $50; admission, $6.

where to stay

BUDGET: Good lodging in the heart of Cairo can be found at the 55-room Windsor Hotel, 19 al-Alfi Street; telephone (20-2) 591-5810, fax (20-2) 592-1621. A former British officers' club built at the turn of the century, it retains its old-fashioned charm. A small, somewhat plain double with breakfast and tax is $39.

MODERATE: On the crowded Nile island of Zamalek, home to many embassies, is the Flamenco Hotel, 2 El Gezira El Wosta Street, (20-2) 340-0815, fax (20-2) 340-0819, with 157 comfortable and clean rooms and suites overlooking the river. Doubles: $85 plus 19 percent tax and service.

Nearby, the 117-room, European-style President Hotel, 22 Taha Hussein Street, (20-2) 341-6751, fax (20-2) 341-1752, offers relative quiet, a homey atmosphere with traditional furnishings and good food. Doubles: $70, including breakfast and tax.

LUXURY: The Marriott, Saraya al-Gezira, Zamalek, (20-2) 340-8888, fax (20-2) 340-6667, was originally a palace built in 1869 for Empress Eugenie of France. Its well-equipped but unremarkable guest rooms are housed in two modern towers overlooking the Nile. But the well-restored public rooms provide a stunning setting for restaurants and bars. There are tennis courts, a pool and a health club. Doubles: $120, plus 19 percent tax and service.

The Mena House, Pyramids Road, (20-2) 383-3444, fax (20-2) 383-7777, in the shadow of the Giza Pyramids, is a former royal lodge that has grown to 525 rooms, with a golf course, tennis courts and a spectacular pool. In the best (and priciest) accommodations, an Old World spirit endures, with towering ceilings and antiques. Doubles in the original palace cost $250 plus 19 percent tax and service. A view of the Pyramids is $30 extra but worth it. Rooms in the newer wings are cheaper, but only a few have a view of the Pyramids.

where to eat

In the Khan al-Khalili, the Naguib Mahfouz restaurant, 5 Seket al-Badistan, (20-2) 590-3788, is an easy first foray into Egyptian cuisine, including shorbat al-ads, or lentil soup, grilled pigeon and, afterward, the bubbly waterpipe known as shisha. (The tobacco is so mild that even nonsmokers may enjoy a puff.) Lunch for two with fresh juice is about $30; no alcohol is served. Open daily 10 a.m. to 2 a.m. and, during Ramadan, until 3:30 a.m.

Felfela is a budget institution. The restaurant features grilled chicken, kebabs and local favorites like shakshouka, fava beans mashed with tomatoes, eggs and butter. Dinner for two with local Stella beer is about $17. The original restaurant (it has several branches) is at 15 Hoda Shaarawi Street, a 10-minute walk from Tahrir Square; (20-2) 392-2833.

Christos, just across from the Giza Pyramids on Pyramids Road, (20-2) 383-3582, specializes in grilled seafood. Diners can choose among fish, shrimp and squid (a combination is $11) and between indoor tables and a rooftop terrace with a dazzling view of the monuments. Lunch for two, with Egyptian salads and a bottle of Egyptian wine, is about $40.

On top of the Cairo Nile Hilton, the Rotisserie Belvedere, Corniche El Nil, (20-2) 578-0666, offers impressive cooking and a spectacular view. Carrot soup with ginger ($5) and filet of lamb with thyme-infused confit ($17) are examples of a fresh, modern style. With a good South African wine, dinner for two is about $120.

Les Trefles, Corniche El Nil, across from the World Trade Center, (20-2) 579-6511, is among Cairo's most expensive and romantic restaurants. Like the outstanding French cuisine, the atmosphere is European, with elegant décor and a terrace that overlooks the Nile. Offerings include a salad of fresh salmon, marinated with dill ($16), and sliced duck with grape sauce ($17). With a bottle of French wine, pricey in Egypt, dinner for two is about $150.

vital statistics

POPULATION (1998): City 16,000,000

HOTEL: Room for one with tax $199.00

DINNER FOR ONE: With tax and tip but not drinks $20.95

TAXI: Upon entry $1.00; Each additional kilometer 30 cents; From the airport $17.50

CAR RENTAL FOR A DAY: Midsize car with unlimited free mileage $47.50

FOR MORE INFORMATION: Telephone: (877) 773-4978; Web: www.egypttourism.org

Sources: Runzheimer International, Egyptian Tourist Authority, local businesses

Cape Town

Many comforts, certainly, but also many
reminders of a difficult history

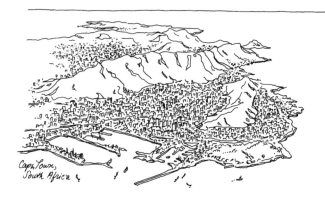

HENRI CAUVIN

Henri Cauvin is a correspondent in
The Times's Johannesburg bureau.

Cape Town has long been the destination of choice for overseas
tourists traveling to South Africa looking for luxury and comfort. But there's more for them to find: the lessons of a city central
to the country's history, from the arrival of white settlers more than
three centuries ago to the imprisonment of Nelson Mandela more
than three decades ago.

Framed by imposing Table Bay Mountain, Cape Town is a
charming spectacle of nature. The surrounding region offers still
more stunning sights, from the lush wine country just to Cape
Town's north to the mountains of the Cape Peninsula, heading
south from Cape Town toward the continent's southern tip.

Home to many of the country's best restaurants and a short
drive from the region's world-famous wineries, the city allows
gourmands to indulge in an array of cuisine. From Portuguese and
French to African and Indian, the diversity of fine restaurants
reflects those who've made their homes here.

Typically Cape Town is pleasantly warm in the summer (though
it does become decidedly hot on occasion), and comfortably cool

during the winter (though it can become chilly, even cold, for stretches).

Crime is not as serious a problem as in South Africa's biggest city, Johannesburg, and extra effort is made to protect tourists. But in a country with some of the highest crime rates in the world and a poorly trained, understaffed national police service, one must always travel with care and caution.

best of times

December and January are the most popular and most crowded months, which means that they are also the most expensive months to visit. Affluent South Africans celebrating the Christmas holiday and Europeans and North Americans eager to escape the cold of the Northern Hemisphere winter, flock to the city. The Cape to Rio Yacht Race, (27-21) 421-1354, and the J&B Met, (27-21) 700-1600, a leading horse race, both of which are usually staged in January, are among the other big events early in the year.

By February, March and April, the holiday crowding has begun to thin out, but the weather is still quite warm. The North Sea Jazz Festival, (27-21) 418-5614, modeled after one in the Netherlands, kicked off in March 1999.

Also staged around this time of year are two of the country's biggest sporting events. The Cape's big annual bike race, which takes more than 30,000 riders over a 65-mile course, (27-21) 685-6551, is usually run in March. The Two Oceans Marathon, (27-21) 671-9407, which takes in some of the region's most striking scenery, is run in March or April.

The wine harvest typically begins in late March or early April, and the wineries usually sponsor a number of events to celebrate.

July and August are usually the coolest months, but for anyone accustomed to the winters of New York or Boston or Washington, the weather probably won't feel bad at all. There is still a lot to do, and it's often easier and cheaper to do it.

As winter wraps up and summer begins, October and November offer the Cape Town International Film Festival, (27-21) 419-2885, showcasing films from South Africa and from overseas.

what to see

The two oceans provide miles of majestic coastline. If it's really hot, try the beaches on the Atlantic Ocean—Clifton and Camps Bay Beaches are close to town but crowded. Sandy Bay, farther south, is popular with nudists; and Blouberg Beach, up north, is popular with surfers. Indian Ocean beaches, on the other side of the peninsula, offer warmer water and lots of choices.

At Robben Island, former political prisoners lead tours of the buildings, including the cellblock that housed Nelson Mandela. The tight schedule does not allow for much reflection or exploration. Amenities are limited (as is the selection of food). Call (27-21) 419-1300; admission: $16.

A number of outfits offer guided visits to some of the Cape's townships. Grassroute Tours is one, with its tour of Khayelitsha, a sprawling area southeast of Cape Town. Although useful reality checks after the splendor of much of the Western Cape, the tours are somewhat scripted. We visited a school and saw the students sing and dance, which was at once very sweet and very sad, because these performances, which are done in part to draw donations, take them away from schoolwork. The cost is $25, plus donations to some of the places you visit; (27-21) 424-8480.

The towns of Franschhoek, Paarl, Pniel, Stellenbosch and Wellington are the centers of the Western Cape winelands, and a day trip to one or two is a chance to take in some of South Africa's most memorable landscapes. The Winelands Tourism Association, 194 Main Road in Paarl, (27-21) 872-0686, fax (27-11) 872-0534, is a good starting point.

The Two Oceans Aquarium, (27-21) 418-3823, is on the waterfront. Seeing the sharks in the predator exhibit is thrilling (feeding time is 3:30 p.m.). General admission is $5.40 for adults, $2.85 for children.

The District Six Museum, 25 Buitenkant Street, is a glimpse into a neighborhood that was one of Cape Town's most vibrant until the apartheid regime declared it a white area in 1966, forced out its 60,000 residents and razed their homes. A memory cloth features notes from former residents recounting tales of the community. Admission is free; (27-21) 461-8745.

where to stay

BUDGET: If you don't want to pay for a room in the luxurious Mount Nelson but want to be close enough to pop over for high tea, the Cape Swiss, Kloof and Camp Streets, (27-21) 423-8190, fax (27-21) 426-1795, in the Gardens neighborhood, is an option. Its 44 very basic rooms are a short walk from a host of interesting restaurants, including two attached to the hotel, a pub and a Vietnamese place. Doubles: $74.

The Don Suite Hotel, 249 Beach Road in Sea Point, (27-21) 434-1083, fax (27-21) 434-4808, is close to the water but away from the busy Victoria and Alfred Waterfront. This branch of a local chain offers comfortable rooms with kitchenettes. But only 10 of the 27 rooms look out on the water. Rates range from $64 to $93.

MODERATE: Barely two years old, the 546-room Holiday Inn, 1 Lower Buitengragt, (27-21) 409-4000, fax (27-21) 409-4444, is several blocks closer to the waterfront than some of the downtown hotels, but the surrounding area is still a work in progress. The standard rooms feature cherrywood night tables and headboards, and matching desks with modem ports. Doubles: $122.

The Victoria Junction, Somerset and Ebenezer Roads, (27-21) 418-1234, fax (27-21) 418-5678, is one of the city's newer mid-priced hotels. Part of the local Protea chain, it has a movie-studio theme, and takes its cue from the Paramount and the Royalton in New York. Instead of suites, it has 24 lofts, or duplex rooms. Its 148 standard rooms are small but comfortable, and the modern furnishings make good use of the space. The location, several blocks from the heart of the business district, isn't bad, but walk out the front door, and you're staring at an auto repair shop. Doubles: $68 to $123.

LUXURY: Just a few years old, the elegant 329-room Table Bay, at Quay 6 on the Victoria and Alfred Waterfront, (27-21) 406-5000, fax (27-21) 406-5767, has established itself among the country's best. While all rooms are said to look out on either Table Mountain or the Atlantic Ocean, some of the views from the lower floors are not great. The rooms themselves feature handsome oak furnishings and marble bathrooms. Doubles are $355 through March and $267 April through September.

One of the country's most lavish hotels, the 226-room Mount Nelson, 76 Orange Street, (27-21) 483-1000, fax (27-21) 424-7472, continues to draw affluent guests who are enchanted by its cozy grandeur and eager to return to favorite rooms (each is a bit different). Doubles: $418.

where to eat

Simply Salmon, 2 Park Road, (27-21) 424-1100, a comfortable, subdued spot on the ground floor of an old Victorian cottage in the Gardens neighborhood, specializes in salmon. Try the Scottish salmon in honey, soy, sesame oil and Thai red curry. Non-fish platters include chicken, lamb, ostrich and a tasty beef fillet in peppercorn sauce. Dinner for two with wine: $75.

Portuguese food is popular in South Africa, and with branches in Cape Town and four other places, Vilamoura is among the most popular purveyors. The Cape Town outlet, at the Promenade and Victoria Road, (27-21) 438-1850, is on two floors overlooking the beach in Camps Bay. From the balcony, diners enjoy the setting sun on one side and Table Mountain on the other. The menu features lots of seafood, including mussels and oysters among the starters, langoustines, shrimp and codfish among the entrees, along with chicken peri-peri, a grilled chicken butterflied and marinated in an olive-oil-based chili sauce. Dinner for two with wine: $60.

For chicken peri-peri on the cheap, the Portuguese-influenced chain Nando's is the place. It's not exactly fast food (there are real plates, with real silverware), but it is quick and inexpensive, with 21 outlets around the city. A family of four can eat for $12.

The Africa Cafe, 108 Shortmarket Street, (27-21) 422-0221, is a downtown outpost of a popular suburban spot that serves traditional African dishes in communal style. Several countries are represented in the décor, as well as on the menu, from Kenyan irio patties—stuffed with spinach, potato and peas—to Senegalese stuffed papaya filled with curried chickpea salad and red pepper sauce. The prix fixe menu is $12.70 each, with wines $6.35 to $23.

Indian cuisine is another favorite, and Annapurna, 42 Hans Strydom Avenue, (27-21) 418-9020, is one of several good options. The menu features a tasty lamb saagwala (strips of lamb cooked in puréed baby spinach), along with lots of other lamb dishes and an assortment of fish, chicken and vegetable dishes. Dinner for two with wine: $30.

vital statistics

POPULATION (2000): City 4,200,000

HOTEL: Room for one with tax $66.00

DINNER FOR ONE: With tax and tip but not drinks $41.00

TAXI: Upon entry 28 cents; Each additional kilometer $1.03; From the airport $18.00

CAR RENTAL FOR A DAY: Midsize car with unlimited free mileage $64.80

FOR MORE INFORMATION: Telephone: (27-21) 426-4260; Web: www.cape-town.org

Sources: Runzheimer International, South African Tourist Board, local businesses

Casablanca

The muezzin's call resounds through a languid, romantic city that Bogie made famous

Hassan II mosque, Casablanca

JOSEPH B. TREASTER

Joseph B. Treaster is a financial news reporter for *The Times*.

Of all the gin joints in all the towns in all the world, Ingrid Bergman had to walk into Humphrey Bogart's in Casablanca. And ever since, Casablanca has been a romantic place somewhere out there in the imagination of millions of Americans.

In real life, Casablanca, the biggest city and main port of Morocco, is intensely romantic—faded, languid and vaguely decadent. Yet if you ask residents, they will most often tell you that their city is just another disagreeable metropole with too many people and too many cars and that you'd be far better off setting out for the more authentic Morocco—Marrakesh and Fez, say.

Residents of Casa, as they call it, seem hardly to notice that they are living in an Art Deco museum, with some austere French Colonial buildings mixed in. To them, the muezzin's soulful call to prayer is as ordinary as the sunrise. And the daily tide of veiled women and desert tribesmen, and others in tatters, jeans and the latest designer stuff, barely merits a glance.

Casablanca, which was a small town when the French made it the commercial capital of their protectorate in 1912, is clearly not ancient. And it is not entirely Moroccan in body and soul. But none of that makes it mundane. It is a whitewashed city of sidewalk cafes and fine restaurants with bazaars where you can bargain for carpets and hand-painted plates.

An enduring modern legend is that Bogie never set foot in Casablanca (the movie was shot in Hollywood). But his most recent biographers, A. Sperber and Eric Lax, say it isn't so. According to them, Bogie dropped by in 1943, shortly after the Allied landing in Morocco and the release of the movie.

best of times

Unlike some of the other cities in Morocco, there is no overwhelming event that would justify a trip to Casablanca. Often, what draws travelers is the city's mystique, which must rank close to that of Timbuktu.

At the dawn of the new millennium, even as the government was taking steps to provide formal protection for some of Casablanca's Art Deco and French Colonial architecture, some tourist officials were still steering visitors to the International Festival of Sacred Music in Fez, usually held in May or June, and the National Festival of Folk Arts—mainly regional music and dance—in Marrakesh in June.

The sensible thing is to go to Fez and Marrakesh, but to spend a day or two in Casablanca. As romantic as the other cities may seem, they are to a large extent managed for tourists; Casablanca has the advantage of being a real place with real Moroccans focused mainly on living Moroccan lives.

Americans and Europeans seem to find Casablanca most comfortable in the spring and fall when the temperatures are usually in the 70's. But the city is washed by a wonderful Atlantic breeze so that even in the summer—when Fez and Marrakesh are sweltering—it rarely gets hotter than the low 80's. If there is going to be rain (and, to the distress of the farmers beyond the city, that is never certain), it will probably be in the winter. Otherwise, you're usually stuck with brilliant blue and white ceramic skies.

what to see

The Art Deco architecture of Casablanca is so plentiful that you don't have to work at seeing it. A relaxed way to take in some and enjoy the street life is to stroll east along Mohammed V Boulevard from the Place des Nations Unies in the heart of the city, by the Old Medina with its landmark clock tower, wandering off on side streets when the fancy strikes. Turn down the Rue Mohammed

Qori, for example, and you'll find the Rialto Theater, whose interior has been renovated in modern style. It presents first-run films and live performances in its 1,000-seat auditorium.

At the Place Mohammed V, the post office, the police prefecture and the Palace of Justice are examples of the neo-Mauresque style of French architects in the 1920's and 1930's, rich with arches, columns and tiles.

At the north end of the quiet, thickly wooded League of Arab Nations Park on Boulevard Hachidi is Paul Tornon's Sacred Heart Cathedral, closed for years, but a towering 1930's Art Deco wonder of soaring stone spires that El Greco might have dreamed up.

Another of the city's great visual delights is the Corniche, the oceanfront boulevard that looks out on the freighters and derricks in the port, the remains of an old fortress, the towering Hassan II Mosque, nightclubs, hotels and miles of beaches and rolling surf. At the vast, somewhat scruffy public beaches, packed with humanity, young men gallop along the water's edge chasing soccer balls. But at private beach clubs like the Miami, which charge a few dollars to enter, the standard is more Monaco than Mecca, and foreigners and less traditional Arab women take the sun in bikinis by half a dozen sparkling swimming pools.

Neither of Casablanca's two main bazaars comes close to the teeming maze of passageways of the one in Marrakesh. But the one in the walled Old Medina, which dates from the 18th century and is across from the Hyatt Regency, is a working market with lots of practical goods, like bargain shirts and shoes.

One of the complaints about Casablanca is that it has no museums. But the Hassan II Mosque, opened within the last decade, comes pretty close to filling that gap. Its angular minaret, visible throughout the city, soars 60 stories and its interior is a tour de force of craftsmanship: walls and ceiling covered with mosaic tiles, intricately carved wood and stucco. Three-story-high Venetian crystal chandeliers—among the few imports in the mosque—are virtually swallowed up beneath the 180-foot-high vaulted ceiling, one of the high-tech features. It slides open and, when the wind picks up, the two halves are quietly closed by computers. The mosque has electrically warmed marble floors. There are several tours daily for visitors.

The hot spots on the Corniche don't even open until near midnight. Most nights at most places, the pricey drinks ($7.50 for a beer, $11 for the best scotch) are the only admission charge. The Fandango, at the Rue de la Mer Egee-sur La Corniche, (212-2) 39-85-08, and Le Cafconce, at 10 Rue de la Mer Adriatique, (212-2) 94-42-33, are pleasantly decorated villas with soft lighting and the easy feel of a friend's home. If Bogie were operating in Casablanca today, the Fandango might be his place.

where to stay

Room rates often turn out to be negotiable, and some of the least expensive hotels are charming.

BUDGET: The Hotel Bellerive, on the ocean drive, a few doors from Hotel de la Corniche, is an Art Deco gem with 35 commodious rooms with high ceilings, 14 of them with small sitting areas looking out to sea over a terrace cafe, a park and a good-sized pool. Doubles are about $45; (212-2) 39-14-09, fax (212-2) 39-34-93.

Across Place des Nations Unies from the Old Medina is the 80-year-old Hotel Excelsior, at 2 Rue el Amraoui Brahim, (212-2) 20-02-63. It has 60 rooms and a lovely curving stairway leading up from the dark-wood lobby. The rooms are large and clean, but expect no frills except breakfast in doubles for $30.

MODERATE: The Hotel Idou Anfa, with 220 rooms in plain, European modern, at 85 Boulevard d'Anfa, (212-2) 20-01-36, fax (212-2) 20-00-09, makes up in efficiency what it lacks in ambience. Though the switchboard is not geared for computers, there is cable television in every room. Views from the high floors sweep across the city to the sea. Doubles are $86.

Out at the beach, 15 minutes from downtown, double rooms at the 51-room Hotel de La Corniche, with its angular Art Deco concrete and marble and gold trim, cost $58; (212-2) 36-10-11, fax (212-2) 39-11-10.

LUXURY: The Royal Mansour at 27 Avenue de l'Armee Royale, (212-2) 31-30-12, fax (212-2) 31-48-18, offers spacious doubles from $225 and a five-room suite from $3,570. Managed by the French Meridien chain, this 182-room hotel boasts a spectacular arched entrance, a soaring pillared lounge and mosaic-tiled corridors.

And at the 251-room Hyatt Regency, on the Place des Nations Unies, (212-2) 26-12-34, fax (212-2) 22-01-80, doubles start at about $230. The rooms are big, with contemporary furnishings, and amenities include a pool and a fitness center.

where to eat

The best Moroccan food is served in Arabian Nights-style restaurants, with colorful inlaid tiles, filigreed stucco and, sometimes, fountains. Menus feature tagines, stews of lamb or chicken with olives, prunes, lemons and onions; incredible pastries called pastillas, stuffed with cinnamon, pigeon and almonds and topped with powdered sugar; and the national dish, couscous—steamed cracked-wheat semolina, usually with raisins and chickpeas, and piled high with lamb, chicken or vegetables.

Perhaps the best of these restaurants is Al-Mounia, at 95 Rue du Prince Moulay-Abdallah, (212-2) 22-26-69. There, dinner for two with a bottle of Moroccan wine is about $65.

In the same price range is the excellent Ryad Zitoun, at 31 Boulevard Rachidi, (212-2) 22-39-27. The restaurant features the simple rose-colored walls typical of Marrakesh rather than the ornate local style.

For about $45, two can dine on grilled shrimp and fillets of local fish under the ceiling fans of the Taverne du Dauphin, at 115 Boulevard Houphouet-Boigny, within sight of the main entrance to the port; (212-2) 27-79-79.

The proprietors of Restaurante Au Petit Poucet, with its white tablecloths, crystal sconces and gauzy curtains in the shade of one of the arcaded sidewalks downtown at 86 Boulevard Mohammed V, boast that Antoine de St.-Exupery was a regular when he flew airmail around North Africa. There is a fixed lunch and dinner menu, with soup, a choice of steak, chicken or fish, dessert and a cocktail for an astounding $9 each; (212-2) 27-54-20.

vital statistics

POPULATION (1994): City 3,094,202

HOTEL: Room for one with tax $65.00

DINNER FOR ONE: With tax and tip but not drinks $20.00

TAXI: Upon entry 13 cents; Each additional kilometer 73 cents; From the airport $18.27

CAR RENTAL FOR A DAY: Midsize car with unlimited free mileage $80.00

FOR MORE INFORMATION: Telephone (in Casablanca): (212-2) 36-47-08; Web: www.tourism-in-morocco.com

Sources: Moroccan National Tourist Board, Moroccan Ministry of Tourism, local businesses

Charleston

The Civil War, an earthquake and a hurricane
can't keep it down

Charleston

TRIP DuBARD

Trip DuBard, who lives in South Carolina, has written about travel
(among other subjects) for a variety of publications.

Charleston's grace is its breeze, an ocean offering that caresses residents and urges visitors on to greater exploration. The breeze emphasizes that this is a city for walking, not for touring while encased in a car or bus.

This is a city that has endured, and today there is a feeling not just of having survived, but of recovering with panache. Occupied by the British during the Revolutionary War, Charleston later was the site of the first shots of the Civil War. Still struggling from that war's devastation, the city was struck by an earthquake in 1886 that affected much of downtown.

The South's economic malaise left Charleston remarkably unchanged for decades, and that lack of massive urban redesign led the way to its renaissance as a tourist destination today. Still, Hurricane Hugo almost wiped all that away in 1989, and the Charleston Naval Base lowered its flag for the last time in 1996, ending a nearly 95-year history that created 26,000 jobs at its peak.

But Mayor Joseph Riley's leadership over more than two decades has seen hundreds of millions of dollars in new investments revive Charleston's central market along with the King Street retail district. A new Waterfront Park provides harbor vistas, and in 2000 the new South Carolina Aquarium opened.

best of times

Spring in Charleston is not just a season, it's a performance, too. Flamboyant red azaleas, fragrant white magnolias and Spanish moss sway to and fro. At the height of the season, the Historic Charleston Foundation sponsors its hugely popular Festival of Houses and Gardens. It features interior tours of more than 100 private homes and many gardens, capped by an oyster roast at beautiful Drayton Hall Plantation. For information, contact (843) 722-3405.

Spoleto's 17 days at the end of May and beginning of June decorate the city with internationally acclaimed artists. More than 100 performances of opera, chamber music, theater and dance—as many as 10 a day—are scheduled. Information: (843) 722-2764.

Concurrent with its big brother, Piccolo Spoleto spotlights Southeastern talents at locations citywide. Contact (843) 724-7305.

Perhaps one reason the Spoleto Arts Festival is so embraced is that it serves as the grand farewell before the long, sullen days of summer, when residents retreat into air-conditioned oases.

Fall brings better weather and more offerings, including the Candlelight Tour of Houses and Gardens, conducted by the Preservation Society of Charleston, generally in September and October. Similar to the spring tour, homes, gardens and churches are open in the evening. Contact (843) 722-4630.

Also in the fall, the city's restaurateurs sponsor Taste of Charleston. Details: (843) 577-4030.

The mild winter features the migration of thousands of wildlife-art enthusiasts who arrive in February for the Southeastern Wildlife Expo. One of the largest shows of its kind, the expo features thousands of nature paintings, photographs, sculpture and crafts for sale. Contact (843) 723-1748.

what to see

A good starting point is the visitor center, at 375 Meeting Street. A 12-foot-square model of the city orients visitors, while a slide show provides social and historical background. Receptionists pair visitors with walking, carriage and boat tours, hotel rooms, show tickets and plantation tours. For information, call (800) 868-8118.

Charleston's small buildings, hidden gardens and compact historic district encourage street-level exploration, on your own or with a tour. Choose from carriage rides ($10 to $15 for 45 minutes) or walking tours (about $12 for two hours), either generic or specializing in subjects like architecture, Civil War history or gardens.

The Charleston Heritage Passport is one ticket good for the Gibbes Art Museum, the Nathaniel Russell House (serene gardens and a stunning unsupported interior elliptical staircase), the Edmondston-Alston House and the plantations of Middleton Place and Drayton Hall. The passport is $29 for adults, $19 for children. Call (843) 556-6020.

Of these, Drayton Hall, on Route 61 about 25 minutes west of downtown, is especially noteworthy. Built in 1738, this Georgian Palladian masterpiece is the only Ashley River plantation to have survived the Civil War untouched. It remains architecturally unchanged—no electricity, water or other modern conveniences—and barren of furniture.

The South Carolina Aquarium, opened in the spring of 2000, is an exploration of the state's streams, lakes and bays. And, almost as an afterthought, it offers the best views yet of Charleston Harbor. Start amid the second floor's mountain waterfalls and make your way to the Piedmont, Coastal Plain, Coast and Ocean Exhibits, observing sea turtles and a myriad of fish, crabs and rays. The aquarium is at 100 Aquarium Wharf and is open daily. Hours vary throughout the year. Admission: $14 for adults, less for children and seniors; (843) 720-1990.

The Waterfront Park offers an oasis to those with tired feet. Between the Battery and Market areas, the park includes inviting fountains (go ahead and cool your feet) and wide bench swings. Sit back and watch freighters slip away to begin their trans-Atlantic voyages. Open 6 a.m. to midnight.

You may wish to end the day at the Library Bar atop the Vendue Inn, 19 Vendue Range, (843) 577-7970, extension 410, open noon to 10 p.m., no cover. There, reflect on Fort Sumter standing guard over a harbor full of returning sailboats, freighters and skiffs. Then, in the fragrant dusk breeze, try to count Charleston's steeples as the sun turns clouds of combed cotton shades of russet, pink and purple.

where to stay

For help in finding a room, contact the Charleston Area Convention and Visitors Bureau at (800) 868-8118, or Historic Charleston Bed and Breakfast, (800) 743-3583.

BUDGET: Days Inn, centrally situated at 155 Meeting Street, (800) 329-7466, fax (843) 723-5361, offers 124 basic motel rooms beginning at $139 for a double, but daily specials can push that below $100.

MODERATE: The 226-room Francis Marion Hotel, (843) 722-0600, (800) 433-3733, fax (843) 723-4633, is at 387 King Street. The lobby, with its Greek Revival architecture, chandeliers and thick carpets, evokes a European grandeur popular when it opened in 1924. Doubles begin at $109 Sunday to Thursday, $129 Friday and Saturday.

The Holiday Inn Historic District, 125 Calhoun Street, (877) 805-7900, fax (843) 805-7700, has 126 recently renovated rooms, coffeemakers, hair dryers and data ports. Doubles start at $139.

Close to good restaurants and Waterfront Park, the Lodge Alley Inn, 195 East Bay Street, (800) 845-1004, fax (843) 722-1611, took 18th-century warehouses, mixed plush burgundy carpets with plank floors, and created large rooms featuring 18th-century reproductions, minibars and free valet parking. Doubles begin at $130.

LUXURY: In the heart of the historic district, Charleston Place, 130 Market Street, (843) 722-4900, (800) 611-5545, fax (843) 722-0728, remains the city's most expensive address. The 440 spacious rooms are furnished with antique reproductions, and the lobby with a 12-foot-wide crystal chandelier. Doubles begin at $210.

where to eat

Charleston's East Bay Street has several well-regarded restaurants, among them Slightly North of Broad, at 192 East Bay Street; (843) 723-3424. Playing on its antiestablishment name (South of Broad is Charleston's most prestigious residential address), SNOB's open kitchen, elaborate wrought-iron decorations and chandeliers, and brick walls attract diners to its Maverick Grits, with shrimp, scallops, smoked sausage and country ham ($7.75). Dinner for two with wine: $65.

Nearby is Blossom Café at 171 East Bay Street; (843) 722-9200. The same owners run another good restaurant nearby (Magnolia's), but here they highlight New American cuisine using local seafood and produce. Enjoy the funky interior or the patio as you try handmade pasta with Carolina crab ravioli, and shrimp and scallop risotto. Also recommended: the Wasabi rubbed grilled tuna loin, with fresh scallions and pepper slaw. Dinner for two with wine: $70.

Opened in 1996, Hominy Grill quickly won accolades for its casual atmosphere, good prices and even better down-home food. Situated in an old house at 207 Rutledge Avenue a short walk from touristy Charleston, the restaurant features a quirky menu with chicken-fried steak, mashed potatoes with mushroom gravy and one vegetable; a fried-green-tomato B.L.T.; and grilled soft-shell crab with baked-cheese grits. Open for breakfast, lunch, dinner and a Sunday brunch; (843) 937-0930. Dinner for two: $40.

You may hear it as "G and M" or "Fast and French," probably because that's easier to pronounce than Gaulart et Maliclet (go-LAHR AY mahl-ee-CLAY), 98 Broad Street, (843) 577-9797. Breakfast, lunch and dinner featuring fresh baguettes and cheeses in sandwiches, salads, soups and fondues are served to as many as 35 guests seated at the irregularly shaped black-topped counter. Dinner for two with wine: about $25.

Louis Osteen, a renowned chef who once ran the elegant restaurant in the Charleston Place Hotel, has moved into his own place, Louis's, just down the street at 200 Meeting Street; (843) 853-2550. His light, fun, refined new location prides itself on crusted salmon in sweet brown butter, grilled tenderloin filets and Black Angus strip steaks with blue-cheese sauce.

One of the best dining experiences in Charleston is the Peninsula Grill, 112 North Market Street, (843) 723-0700, in the Planter's Inn at the corner of Market and Meeting Streets. Try their bourbon-grilled jumbo shrimp, seared lamb or marinated pork chop. With velvet-covered walls near a garden courtyard, the Peninsula Grill is a lovely setting in the heart of downtown. Dinner for two with wine: $110.

vital statistics

POPULATION (1998 estimate): City 87,044; Metro area 541,159

HOTEL: Room for one with tax $123.00

DINNER FOR ONE: With tax and tip but not drinks $29.20

TAXI: Upon entry $3.00; Each additional mile $1.25; From the airport $21.00

CAR RENTAL FOR A DAY: Midsize car with unlimited free mileage $58.50

FOR MORE INFORMATION: Telephone: (800) 868-8118; Web: www.charlestoncvb.com

Sources: Runzheimer International, U.S. Census Bureau, local businesses

Chicago
A home of great architecture expands outward and upward

Sears Tower, Chicago

BRENDA FOWLER

Brenda Fowler is the author of *Iceman: Uncovering the Life and Times of a Prehistoric Man Found in an Alpine Glacier.*

A decade ago, Chicago's downtown was confined to a milewide swath of Lake Michigan shoreline that stretched from the gleaming shops of Michigan Avenue in the north to the steps of the Field Museum in the south. But catalyzed by the cheery economy, urban activity is bursting out every which way.

Old redbrick factories along the western edge of downtown are being converted into residential lofts, galleries, restaurants and clubs; vacant lots with views of the skyline are being built up; and small stretches of the Chicago River, which sneaks almost unnoticed right through the city center, are being cleaned up.

Chicago is expanding upward, too. At the touristic epicenter, hoteliers are building atop older structures. And, in a city of tall buildings, the architectural firm Skidmore, Owings & Merrill has announced plans to reclaim for Chicago the title to the tallest building in the world, with a 1,550-foot building called 7 South Dearborn to be done by 2004.

Those who look upon such development with skepticism can find comfort in the unchanging waters of Lake Michigan, whose shores are lined for miles with well-kept, if occasionally crowded, paths for bikers and pedestrians of various speeds and styles.

best of times

For information on upcoming events, call the Mayor's Office of Special Events at (312) 744-3370.

You can get a lesson and then dance under the stars to live bands during the free Chicago Summer Dance program, which typically runs Thursday to Saturday evenings, and Sunday afternoons, from mid-July to mid-September in Grant Park at the Spirit of Music Garden, 601 South Michigan Avenue, (312) 742-4007. Each session begins with a free hourlong lesson in the style of dance—everything from zydeco to klezmer to salsa—that suits the performing band. Sunday always features ballroom dancing

From September through May the Chicago Symphony Orchestra, Symphony Center, 220 South Michigan Avenue, performs under the direction of Daniel Barenboim. Tickets: (312) 294-3000.

The University of Chicago Folk Festival of Traditional Music, Mandel Hall, 1135 East 57th Street, usually presents more than a dozen concerts, as well as dance and instrument workshops with the performers, over three days in late January or early February. General information: (773) 702-9793; tickets (available in January): (773) 702-7300.

The Steppenwolf Theatre Company, 1650 North Halsted Street, (312) 335-1650, whose ensemble includes John Malkovich and Gary Sinise, typically performs five shows between September and August.

The Art Institute of Chicago, 111 South Michigan Avenue, (312) 443-3600, has an excellent permanent collection of 19th-century French painting, including many works by Renoir and Picasso, and opens new temporary exhibitions each month. Tuesdays are free.

Throughout the summer the Chicago Cubs play day and evening games at Wrigley Field, 1060 West Addison Street, an intimate ballpark built in 1914. Unreserved bleacher seats cost $6 until May 18, and rise to $15 for the rest of the summer. Box seats go for $25. Call Ticketmaster at (800) 347-2827, or (312) 831-2827 inside Illinois. Tickets are also sold at the ballpark.

what to see

The Chicago Architecture Foundation's 90-minute river cruise offers a relaxing introduction to the city's architecture. Boats depart from the southwest corner of the Michigan Avenue bridge.

Hours and schedule vary by season. Cost: $21. To buy tickets in advance (recommended), stop at the dock during tour hours, or at the Chicago Architecture Foundation at 224 South Michigan Avenue, (312) 922-3432, or 875 North Michigan Avenue, (312) 751-1380, or call Ticketmaster at (312) 902-1500.

On a clear day, you can see across Lake Michigan to Michigan from the 94th-floor observatory in the obelisk-like John Hancock Center, 875 North Michigan Avenue, the city's second-tallest building after the Sears Tower. Open daily 9 a.m. to midnight; (888) 875-8439. Admission: $8.75.

The excellent interactive displays at the Peggy Notebaert Nature Museum, a contemporary building of soaring skylights and prairie stone that opened in October 1999, show how implicated humans are in what we commonly refer to as nature. At the water lab, visitors can make it rain on the 40-foot-long model of an urban river, and then test how human interventions like sewer systems affect its flow. The various exhibits incorporate living organisms such as butterflies, snakes and plants with a few well-placed artifacts, such as Charles Darwin's microscope. The museum is at 2430 North Cannon Drive; (773) 755-5100. Admission: $6.

The neighborhoods of Wicker Park and Bucktown, which join up at the gritty intersection of North, Damen and Milwaukee Avenues, are home to Mexican and Polish immigrants, artists and, increasingly, young urban professionals. The main streets are dotted with restaurants, cafes, thrift shops and expensive boutiques that sell vintage furniture and clothing. Robin Richman, 2108 North Damen, (773) 278-6150, sells quirky vintage and new women's clothing and accessories like beaded pocketbooks; Red Hen Bread, 1623 North Milwaukee, (773) 342-6823, sells pastries and breads.

Though several galleries at the Oriental Institute Museum, housed in a building designed in a sort of Art Deco Gothic style on the campus of the University of Chicago, 1155 East 58th Street, (773) 702-9520, are closed for renovation, the small Egyptian Gallery reopened last year. The exhibit begins with an imposing quartzite statue of King Tutankhamen that dates to about 1334 B.C. The displays on the four different scripts used by ancient Egyptians are especially enlightening. Free.

where to stay

BUDGET: The Willows, 555 West Surf, sits on a quiet tree-lined residential street on the city's near north side. The 55 rooms, with data ports and bathrobes, are done in mauve, pink and light green.

Afternoon tea is served in the pretty lobby. A standard double room costs $149; (773) 528-8400, fax (773) 528-8483.

MODERATE: The lovely Hotel Burnham, 1 West Washington Street, is in the former Reliance Building (1894), right in the middle of the Chicago Loop. Floors 7 to 15 preserve the feel of a distinguished old office building: the floors are the original terrazzo (carpeted down the middle to reduce noise); the doors to the rooms are inset with large frosted panes of glass (lined on the other side with a mirror). Many of the 122 rooms, elegantly done in gold and dark blue, have a chaise longue nestled in the bay window. Rates are $185 to $230; (877) 294-9712, fax (312) 782-0899.

When it was built in 1925, the Allerton Crowne Plaza, 701 North Michigan Avenue, then known simply as the Allerton, was the tallest building in Chicago, with 24 floors. Miraculously, considering that it's in the center of the downtown shopping district, the views are still panoramic from many of the recently renovated hotel's 443 rooms, which are decorated in yellows, golds, flowers and plaids. Rates from $169 to $199; (312) 440-1500, fax (312) 440-1819.

In the lobby and bar of the House of Blues Hotel, 333 North Dearborn, India meets Morocco meets New Orleans meets Tibet; the music is from the Andean highlands, and the smell is of incense. The artful clashing of cultures and colors continues into the bar, where patrons lounge among pillows under fringed canopies. Rooms are decorated in bright colors and fabrics. The hotel has a bowling alley, and is also adjacent to the House of Blues. Rates for the 367 rooms run from $149 to $289; (877) 569-3742, fax (312) 923-2442.

LUXURY: The venerable Drake, 140 East Walton Place, occupies the intersection of Lake Shore Drive and North Michigan Avenue. Each afternoon, to the strains of a live harp, ladies and gentlemen take tea in the Palm Room off the lobby. The hotel's 537 rooms are appointed with traditional furnishings and color schemes, some with splendid views of Lake Michigan. Rates: $239 to $295; (800) 553-7253, fax (312) 787-1431.

where to eat

The view from a loft table up through the industrial, ridge-shaped skylight at the restaurant called mk, 868 North Franklin, (312) 482-9179, almost makes a predusk dinner reservation, say 5:30 p.m., sound like a cool idea. In any case, if you delay making your reservation at this minimalist restaurant on the edge of downtown, 5:30 p.m. is what you will get. Michael Kornick's contemporary

American menu has included such selections as a roast rack of lamb, garlic flan, roasted plum tomatoes and mint. The desserts are hard to forget, notably one titled "three banana, new banana, vol. III," described as banana malt semifreddo, banana coffee cake and butterscotch sauce. Dinner and wine for two: $125.

Large parties, families and young couples seem to prefer Wishbone, 1001 West Washington; (312) 850-2663. The décor is airy and bright; the food, Southern home-style with dishes like Hoppin' John (black-eyed peas with rice and cheese), baked bone-in-ham, shrimp and grits. Dinner and wine for two: $30. The restaurant has a branch at 3300 North Lincoln Avenue, (773) 549-2663.

Rambutan, a Filipino-American restaurant at 2049 West Division Street, (773) 772-2727, serves original appetizers such as ukoy, crispy shrimp fritters battered with sweet potatoes and cassava; main courses such as coriander-crusted barbecue beef; and, for dessert, the buko cream tart, with coconut and sliced bananas in a chocolate-cookie crust. Bring your own wine or beer. Dinner for two: $40.

L'Olive, 1629 North Halsted Avenue, (312) 573-1515, a quiet restaurant with perfectly dimmed lighting, serves Moroccan specialties like the appetizer grilled spinach with roasted peppers and spicy olives and the main course tagine zitoun, baked chicken with olives and preserved lemon. Dinner and wine for two: $70.

The Taco and Burrito House, 1548 West Fullerton Avenue, (773) 665-8389, with a counter and a few tables, makes a steak burrito worth driving out of one's way for. Dinner for two without wine: about $12.

vital statistics

POPULATION (1998 estimate): City 2,802,079; Metro area 7,939,351

HOTEL: Room for one with tax $185.00

DINNER FOR ONE: With tax and tip but not drinks $28.40

TAXI: Upon entry $1.60; Each additional mile $1.40; From the airport $28.00

CAR RENTAL FOR A DAY: Midsize car with unlimited free mileage $78.00

FOR MORE INFORMATION: Telephone: (800) 226-6632; Web: www.choosechicago.com

Sources: Runzheimer International, U.S. Census Bureau, local businesses

Copenhagen

A lot to see in a compact package

CORINNE LaBALME

Corinne LaBalme writes frequently
about cultural events in Europe.

Contradictions are to be expected from a city that nurtured both Hans Christian Andersen and Soren Kierkegaard. With its low skyline, pedestrian streets and lush gardens, Copenhagen's sober, old-fashioned facade hides a city that is surprisingly rich in historic sites and tourist activities. Although this diminutive capital can be crossed on foot in a few hours, most visitors will need more than one week to explore Copenhagen's treasures. And with a 10-mile bridge-tunnel connection to Malmo inaugurated in July 2000, budget extra time for a side trip to Sweden.

Founded in the 12th century, Copenhagen was nearly destroyed on several occasions, most notably by a fire in 1795 and the 1807 British bombardments during the Napoleonic wars. For this reason, the city's prevailing architectural style dates from the early 19th-century neo-Classical period, with some exceptions like the 16th-century Stock Exchange, the Renaissance-style Rosenborg Slot castle, and the Baroque Marble Church. Danish Modern thrives with two dazzling avant-garde projects unveiled in 1999:

the dramatic Black Diamond addition to the Royal Library on the Christianbrygge waterfront and the shimmering, glass-sheathed Danish Design Center at 27 HC Andersens Boulevard.

Increased exhibition space may be the one thing that museum-heavy Copenhagen didn't need. The crowded roster includes the imposing Statens Museum for Kunst (Danish National Gallery), 48-50 Solvgade, (45) 33 74 84 94; the Ny Carlsberg Glyptotek art museum, 7 Dantes Plads, (45) 33 41 81 41; the Hirshsprung Collection (see below); the City Museum with its newly expanded Kierkegaard room, 59 Vesterbrogade, (45) 33 21 07 72, and the Rosenborg Summer Palace, Ostervolgade 4A, (45) 33 15 32 86, where the crown jewels are displayed.

Shoppers should spend at least one afternoon exploring the fancy boutiques on the Stroget, the vast pedestrian avenue in the center of town. And getting to know the city means at least one break for smoerrbrod, Danish open-face sandwiches topped with herring, shrimp or eggs, in a waterfront cafe in the newly-gentrified Nyhavn district.

best of times

February is the coldest month of the year, with average temperatures well below zero, but summer heats up appreciably. In late June, the four-day Roskilde Rock Festival, Northern Europe's answer to Woodstock, takes place 30 minutes outside town.

When the world-famous Copenhagen Jazz Festival opens in the second week of July, there are balmy nights for roughly 450 concerts, many held outdoors. Schedules are available in May at (45) 33 93 20 13.

Open-air performances of the Copenhagen International Ballet Festival take place in the university gardens of suburban Frederiksburg for two weeks in early August. Information: (45) 39 90 15 00. Immediately afterward, the opera-ballet season in Copenhagen's Royal Theater, Det Kongelige Teater, revs up and continues through early June. Information: (45) 33 69 66 66.

In even-numbered years, the biennial Golden Days Festival, late August through early September, celebrates Copenhagen's rich cultural history from 1800-1850 with a series of concerts, exhibits and architectural tours.

In mid-November, the first Julebryg, high-proof Christmas Beer, arrives from the city breweries in ceremonial horse-drawn carts, and the shopping-feasting-party pace becomes frenetic. Tivoli amusement park reopens in late November with a traditional

Christmas Market and ice rink. Danes celebrate Christmas Eve at home, but the colorful Santa Parade, with floats and music, takes place a month earlier on Nov. 25.

what to see

For fans of the Vikings, the classic Nordic quest begins at Copenhagen's National Museum, 10 Ny Vestergade, (45) 33 13 44 11, where runestones, jewelry, weapons and mummified remains of Viking graves are displayed with clear English explanations. The delicate Sun Chariot sculpture is one of the museum's major Bronze Age artifacts. Open Tuesday to Sunday 10 a.m. to 5 p.m. Admission $4.70 for adults, children free.

Those who don't get enough Nordic lore here will find Viking home life is brilliantly recreated at Trelleborg, a reconstructed 10th century village on the remains of an ancient fortress 62 miles southwest of Copenhagen at Trelleborg Alle, Hegninje/Slagelse, (45) 58 54 95 06. Visitors can model chain-mail armor and watch live demonstrations of Viking crafts. From April 1 to Oct. 30, open daily 10 a.m. to 5 p.m.; From Nov. 1 to March 30, open daily from 1 p.m. to 5 p.m. Admission $4.10 for adults, children $2.35.

Despite busloads of camera-toting admirers, the Little Mermaid appears justifiably disconsolate at being seated in the harbor across from an oil-storage silo on the north edge of town. Nearby, the relatively unknown Danish Resistance Museum in Churchill Park, (45) 33 13 77 14, details daily life in Denmark from 1940 to 1945. Open Tuesday to Saturday 10 a.m. to 4 p.m. and Sunday 10 a.m. to 5 p.m; after Sept. 16, Tuesday to Saturday 11 a.m. to 3 p.m. and Sunday 11 a.m. to 4 p.m. Free.

The Hirshsprung Collection, 20 Stockholmsgade, (45) 35 42 03 36, reopened in March 2000 after a year's renovation. The collection of 19th-century Danish painting and sculpture that belonged to the tobacco baron Heinrich Hirshsprung is housed in a neo-Classical-style mansion filled with furniture from the homes and studios of the artists. Open Thursday to Monday 11 a.m. to 4 p.m. and Wednesday 11 a.m. to 9 p.m. Admission: $3; children free.

The 21-acre Tivoli amusement park, 3 Vesterbrogade, (45) 33 15 10 01, has enchanted visitors since 1843 with its lavish flower gardens, outdoor concerts, fanciful pavilions and numerous restaurants. Rides include the Chinese-inspired Panda Tower for children, and the scary Valhalla Funhouse. Open April 14 to Sept. 24 and Nov. 17 to Dec. 23. Admission: $4.55 to $5.75 for adults; children $2.35 to $3.

where to stay

BUDGET: A cheerful children's playroom and an enclosed outdoor patio adjoin the dining room at Ibsen's Hotel, 23 Vendersgade, (45) 33 13 19 13, fax (45) 33 13 19 16, in a residential district near the lush Botanical Gardens. Most of the 118 rooms display clean, no-frills Scandinavian design, although top-of-the-line suites have more ambitious décor and kitchenettes. The generous buffet breakfast is included in the room price. Doubles: $131 to $156.

MODERATE: The conveniently situated 51-room Hotel Danmark, 89 Vester Voldgade, (45) 33 11 48 06, fax (45) 33 14 36 30, between Tivoli and the National Museum, offers a friendly welcome and uncluttered, traditional décor with bold colors. The typically tiny, spotless bathrooms have built-in hair dryers. The private garage ($9.40 a day) is a bonus. Doubles: $137.

Near the Amalienborg Palace, the 366-room Copenhagen Admiral Hotel, 24-28 Toldbodgade, (45) 33 74 14 14, fax (45) 33 74 14 16, is housed in an 18th-century granary with atmospheric barrel-vaulted hallways. Harborside rooms offer views of cruise ships and sailboats. And although rooms derive great charm from 200-year-old rough-hewn pine beams, the landmark wooden infrastructure means no air-conditioning. Amenities include a nightclub and sauna. Doubles: $128 to $164.

LUXURY: The gracious Hotel d'Angleterre, 34 Kongens Nytorv, (45) 33 12 00 95, fax (45) 33 12 11 18, was built in 1755 in the Grand Hotel tradition. Its 124 rooms are decorated in a variety of styles, some with sumptuous canopy beds with French provincial textiles. The hotel has two restaurants, Internet access from rooms and an indoor pool and spa. Doubles: $287 to $449.

While far smaller in its dimensions, the 84-room Nyhavn 71, 71 Nyhavn, (45) 33 43 62 00, fax (45) 33 43 62 01, exudes considerable antique charm. Its pint-size rooms, with exposed beams and colorful textiles, are squeezed into an 1804 warehouse on a scenic stretch of waterfront with views of the old naval base. Work is under way on a 44-room annex. Doubles: $187 to $224.

where to eat

The sleek, minimalist dining room in the Royal Library's new Black Diamond wing, 1 Soren Kierkegaards Plads, (45) 33 47 49 49, offers some of the city's most sophisticated cuisine. The menu includes grilled catfish paired with succulent Norwegian lobster, and superb smoked Baltic salmon with dill and scrambled eggs. Waterfront views are sensational at sunset, so ask for a window table. A three-course dinner for two with a modest bottle of wine is $113.

In an upscale neighborhood of power brokers and power shoppers, Cafe Zeze, 20 Ny Ostergade, (45) 33 14 23 90, serves eclectic European fare, like lamb filets topped with shiitake mushrooms and an exotic vegetarian pasta laced with coconut cream and hot chili pepper. Dinner and Tuborg for two in this streamlined bistro is $45.

Tourism has tamed the once disreputable Nyhavn waterfront, and open-air restaurants have ousted tattoo parlors and brothels. At Nyhavns Faergekro, 5 Nyhavn, (45) 33 15 15 88, the all-you-can-eat lunch buffet with 10 varieties of Scandinavian herring for $11 is one of the best seafood bargains in Copenhagen. The famous fish cakes with remoulade sauce or smoked lamb sandwiches, both $5.60, also make a fine light lunch. At dinner, there is a fixed-price two-course menu for $19.

High ceilings and leaded-glass windows lend a lofty look to Cafeen I Nikolaj, 12 Nikolaj Plads, (45) 33 11 63 13, which serves down-to-earth Danish fare in a deconsecrated church site. The creamed seafood chowder is superb, and the classic lunch combinations of herring, smoked eel, shrimp or salmon tartare never disappoint. Two for lunch will spend $35. It is open for dinner from spring through summer with an expanded menu that includes steak tenderloin or lemon sole. Dinner for two with wine: $75.

The Stroget takes its festive ambience from street mimes and musicians. At Cafe Europa, 1 Amagertorv, (45) 33 12 04 28, the outdoor tables are tantalizingly close to the Royal Copenhagen and Georg Jensen showrooms. An oversized Danish sandwich topped with marinated artichoke, sun-dried tomato, roasted eggplant and fresh basil costs $8. A glass of wine or beer is $3.50. (No reservations.)

vital statistics

POPULATION (1999): City 491,000; Metro area 1,800,000

HOTEL: Room for one with tax $206.00

DINNER FOR ONE: With tax and tip but not drinks $27.40

TAXI: Upon entry $2.75; Each additional kilometer $1.03; From the airport $16.85

CAR RENTAL FOR A DAY: Midsize car with unlimited free mileage $116.33

FOR MORE INFORMATION: Telephone: (45) 70 22 24 42; Web: www.woco.dk

Sources: Runzheimer International, Danish Tourist Board, local businesses

Dallas

Home of the cosmopolitan cowboy

Dallas, Texas

KATHRYN JONES AND ALLEN R. MYERSON

Kathryn Jones contributes to *The Times* from Dallas.
Allen R. Myerson, an editor of business news for *The Times,*
is a former Dallas bureau chief for the newspaper.

No longer does the State Fair of Texas in Dallas feature tattooed ladies and, as in the early 1970's, H. L. Hunt, then probably the world's wealthiest man, hawking his HLH Gastro-Majic indigestion pills. But each fall, you can ride a 212-foot-high Ferris wheel, witness the judging of the champion Brahman bull or Angora goat and marvel at Big Tex, the fair's 52-foot-tall, bilingual, waving icon.

Even for this business capital's most polished executives and subtle lawyers, the state fair is a chance to pile the kids into the Chevy Suburban and play the rube. And for visitors, it's a glimpse back at the rural underpinnings of this state's history.

If the State Fair of Texas remains proudly, perennially provincial, Dallas and its neighbor, Fort Worth, have no lack of sites and events attesting to their yearning to be considered cosmopolitan. And Fort Worth is host to one of the world's leading competitions for concert pianists.

Further evidence of this suburbanized city's cosmopolitan strivings is an 11-mile rail line. The trains began rolling in June 2000, but they go nowhere near the two major airports, where even taxis are sometimes scarce. Visitors should reconcile themselves to being in the Sunbelt and, if possible, rent a car.

best of times

The best times to visit the Dallas area are spring and fall. During the summer, newspapers keep running counts of consecutive 100-degree days. Winters are mild and virtually snowless but bland, as lawns with grass tough enough to survive the summer turn brown by Christmas.

Come March, the Dallas area blossoms again. Go for a drive or walk through Highland Park, a wealthy island suburb near downtown, to see the azaleas. Or visit the Dallas Arboretum, (214) 327-4901, on the south short of White Rock Lake, for its annual Dallas Blooms celebration.

Once every four years, in late May and early June, the world's best young pianists converge on Fort Worth for the Van Cliburn International Piano Competition, named in honor of the pianist who collected his Tchaikovsky Competition prize in Moscow and came home to Fort Worth. The concerts take place at the Nancy Lee and Perry R. Bass Performance Hall, a modern Beaux-Arts monument, with 48-foot-high trumpeting angels in Texas limestone. A full schedule of concerts, ballets and plays keeps the hall busy when the pianists aren't in town.

Fall brings the State Fair of Texas, (800) 375-1839, one of the largest, most heavily attended such festivals in the nation. It fills the 277-acre Fair Park near downtown, whose Art Deco monuments include the Cotton Bowl, from the last weekend of September through the third week of October. Outdoor concerts, on a plaza where listeners generally stand or dance rather than sit, feature some of the nation's leading country-and-western and Latino performers. Admission is $10 for adults, $6 for those older than 60 or children under 4 feet tall; free for children under age 2 and for everyone on Thursday. Rides and the abundant food cost extra. Hours are 10 a.m. to 10 p.m., but not all exhibits are open as long.

Fall also brings football. As much cultural as sporting events, home games of the Dallas Cowboys usually sell out well in advance. Any remaining tickets, sold only in pairs, are available through Ticketmaster, (214) 373-8000. Several hotels in Irving, the suburb where the Cowboys play in Texas Stadium, have packages that include two tickets, transportation to the game and a night's lodging for $199 to $349. Call (800) 247-8464.

Dallas's live-music scene picks up in September and October at the Smirnoff Music Center, an amphitheater in Fair Park. Ticket prices vary with location—the cheapest are on the lawn, where concertgoers can take their own blankets or chairs.

The Dallas Symphony Orchestra, (214) 692-0203, conducted by Andrew Litton, presents a full season of concerts in the I. M. Pei-designed Morton H. Meyerson Symphony Center, 2301 Flora Street.

what to see

Many people still associate Dallas with President Kennedy's assassination in 1963. On any given day, visitors dot the grassy knoll downtown at Dealey Plaza and gaze up at the former Texas School Book Depository. The Sixth Floor Museum at Dealey Plaza, 411 Elm Street, (214) 747-6660, takes its name and location from where Lee Harvey Oswald fired the fatal shots. It sensitively depicts Kennedy's life and assassination with film clips, photographs and records. Open 9 a.m. to 6 p.m. daily. Admission, with an audiotape guide, is $10 for adults; $8 for those 65 or older, students and children; and free for children under age 6.

For a different view of history, the Conspiracy Museum, 110 South Market Street, (214) 741-3040, explores conspiracy theories related to the assassinations of John F. Kennedy, Robert Kennedy, Martin Luther King and Abraham Lincoln with exhibits and memorabilia. The museum, operated by self-styled "assassinologists," is open daily 10 a.m. to 6 p.m. Admission is $7 for adults, $6 for seniors and students, $3 for children 9 to 12 and free for children under age 9.

Dallas's status as a modern business capital is more a result of its beginnings as a mercantile and financial hub than of its role as a center of the cattle industry, although cattle drives cut through downtown as recently as the 1850's. Now there's a permanent cattle drive in bronze—the "Trailing Longhorns" sculpture at Pioneer Plaza at Young and Griffin streets, where 40 bronze longhorn steers appear to be stampeding down a hill, driven by three cowboys on horseback.

Dallas has three concentrations of clubs, lounges and live music hangouts: downtown's West End, the Deep Ellum neighborhood east of downtown and lower Greenville Avenue. Poor David's Pub, 1924 Greenville Avenue, (214) 821-9891, is a fixture on the local music scene, with an eclectic mix of live music. Covers range with the featured band from zero to $25.

A new attraction in Fair Park is the Women's Museum: An Institution for the Future, a permanent project (in association with the Smithsonian) that chronicles women's contributions in science, politics, the arts and other fields through computer displays and more traditional exhibits. Admission: $5 for adults, $4 for those under age 12 and $3 for seniors and students.

where to stay

BUDGET: The Clarion Inn, 7138 North Stemmons Freeway, (214) 461-2677, fax (214) 461-2678, is a 10-minute drive from downtown. The hotel's 62 rooms are furnished simply but comfortably, and have small refrigerators. The standard double rate, $79 weekdays and $69 weekends, includes breakfast.

MODERATE: The recently renovated redbrick Melrose Hotel, 3015 Oak Lawn Avenue, (800) 635-7673, fax (214) 521-2470, built in 1924, has 184 rooms in a charming older neighborhood between downtown and the exclusive Highland Park area. Doubles start at $149 for weekends and $219 weekdays. The high-ceilinged rooms are equipped with antique-style furnishings and minibars.

For a bed-and-breakfast that is centrally situated 15 minutes from downtown but secluded, the Courtyard on the Trail, (214) 553-9700, fax (214) 553-5542, is near scenic White Rock Lake. The three rooms—a suite with a sitting room, a room with Southwestern décor, and a room with a king-size bed and a marble bathroom—have French doors leading to a pool or garden. Prices range from $110 to $155.

LUXURY: The Mansion on Turtle Creek, 2821 Turtle Creek Boulevard, (800) 527-5432, fax (214) 528-4187, routinely draws the rich and famous. The nine-story hotel is built around a terracotta-colored Spanish Colonial mansion that serves as the restaurant. All 141 rooms have chaises longues, love seats and French doors that open onto private balconies. The standard rate is $440 to $530, with discounts based on dates and availability. The Mansion on Turtle Creek restaurant, (214) 526-2121, pioneered upscale Southwestern cuisine (with tortilla soup and lobster tacos). A three-course dinner for two with modest wine is at least $200, but a $20 prix fixe three-course lunch was recently added.

The Adams Mark Hotel, 400 North Olive Street, (800) 444-2326, fax (214) 922-0308, on the eastern edge of downtown, is Texas's largest hotel. Its 1,844 eclectically decorated rooms contain sitting areas and armoires, and are within walking distance of the Museum of Art, the Meyerson Center and the financial district. Standard doubles: $210.

where to eat

At Star Canyon, 3102 Oak Lawn Avenue, (214) 520-7827, the chef, Stephan Pyles, puts a spicy spin on Texas favorites like fried catfish and rib-eye steak—served under a mound of thin fried onion rings encrusted with ground chilies. Reservations are a must. Dinner for two, with wine, is about $150.

Ciudad D.F., 3888 Oak Lawn Avenue, Suite 135, (214) 219-3141, is one of the best of a growing number of restaurants that offer Mexico City-style cuisine in a sophisticated setting. Specials include duck flautas and ravioli stuffed with cheese and poblano chilies with vanilla-bean shrimp. Dinner for two, with wine or margaritas, is about $90.

Gloria's, 3715 Greenville Avenue, (214) 874-0088, is a favorite for its colorful atmosphere and Latin American cuisine, including Salvadoran dishes like banana-wrapped tamales stuffed with chicken and a full Mexican menu. Dinner for two, with beer or a margarita, about $35.

For funky atmosphere, head south across the Trinity River to Tillman's Corner, 324 West Seventh at Bishop, (214) 942-0088, a big informal space furnished with 1950's knickknacks. Chicken breast grilled with lime and cilantro with stir-fried vegetables and black-bean and corn salsa is excellent; specials, like grilled scallops over angel hair pasta, are reliably good. Dinner for two with wine, about $60.

One of the cheapest and best meals in Dallas is barbecue, and there are many good spots throughout the city. Peggy Sue BBQ, 6600 Snider Plaza (near Southern Methodist University), (214) 987-9188, has lean, sweet ribs, brisket and turkey, good vegetables and delicious fried pies. A meal for two with beer is under $25.

vital statistics

POPULATION (1998 estimate): City 1,075,894; Metro area 4,802,463

HOTEL: Room for one with tax $147.50

DINNER FOR ONE: With tax and tip but not drinks $30.05

TAXI: Upon entry $2.00; Each additional mile $1.60; From the airport $26.00

CAR RENTAL FOR A DAY: Midsize car with unlimited free mileage $73.00

FOR MORE INFORMATION: Telephone: (800) 232-5527; Web: www.dallascvb.com

Sources: Runzheimer International, U.S. Census Bureau, local businesses

Denver

World-class attractions in the gateway to the Rockies

State Capitol Building, Denver

JAMES BROOKE

James Brooke was the Rocky Mountain bureau chief of *The Times* from 1995 to 1999.

World renowned for skiing, Colorado actually draws more tourists in summer than in winter. In the past, Denver was often a pit stop on the family driving vacation. But today it sparkles with world-class attractions, meriting at least a weekend stopover before tackling the Rockies.

One of the latest attractions, Colorado's Ocean Journey, an aquarium with 300 species of fish and mammals, opened in June 1999. The aquarium is part of an ongoing investment in stadiums, museums and an amusement park that is giving downtown Denver one of the nation's most exciting urban cores.

For visitors who seek low-key summer excitement, the metro area offers 450 miles of bicycling and jogging trails, which vary from paths meandering along creek banks to steeper pitches promising mountain workouts. Always a city with a leafy feel, Denver has increased its park space by 50 percent in the 1990's, up to 6,000 acres.

One summer, I took two of my sons to Roxborough State Park, just out of view of downtown. Nearing a stream at dusk, we startled a brown bear about 40 yards away, who reared high on her hind legs to protect her cub. Farther down the trail, we watched two coyotes chase a fox across a meadow, and then stalk, in vain, a pregnant doe. On the way back, we spotted the bear family again and crossed the path of a (benevolent) skunk.

best of times

Outdoorsy visitors will quickly discover the burning power of the Colorado sun. Denver has a skin-killer combination: more sunny days than San Diego, and 24 percent more ultraviolet radiation than sea-level beaches. Summer visitors learn quickly to slather on sunscreen. Otherwise, temperatures in the 80's and little or no humidity make summer uniquely pleasant. In winter, Denverites often enjoy snow without the drawbacks, as the strong sun will often burn off a morning snowfall by evening.

Not surprisingly, Denver is host to some of the nation's grandest gatherings of the American West's first peoples. During the first three weeks in January, Denver is home to the National Western Stock Show and Rodeo, for more than 90 years the world's premier stock show and one of the nation's largest rodeos. Cowboys stomp through town and remind all newcomers of Denver's cow-town roots. Information: (303) 297-1166.

In March, over 700 dancers and musicians from 70 Native American tribes assemble for the Denver March Powwow, one of the nation's largest powwows. For three days the Coliseum showcases authentic arts and crafts, dance performances and tribal food specialties; (303) 934-8045.

Around the Fourth of July, as sidewalks start baking, 200 jury-selected artists from across the United States display glass, jewelry, watercolor, photography and sculpture at the Cherry Creek Arts Festival, which is considered one of the nation's top arts-and-crafts exhibitions; (303) 355-2787.

In October, downtown Denver turns frenetic faux Bavarian during the Great American Beer Festival, the largest beer bash in the United States. Over 1,700 beers compete for medals, as stouts, lagers, ales and local brews come to be tested; (303) 447-0816.

what to see

Denver's human carnival flows through Lower Downtown, bounded by 14th and 20th Streets and Wynkoop and Larimer Streets, a redbrick historic district that has passed, in less than a decade, from skid row to LoDo.

LoDo's 80 restaurants have made it the city's dining center and its art galleries, antique stores, comedy clubs, sports bars, historic buildings and the Tattered Cover Bookstore make it a stroller's paradise, day or night.

A natural extension to a LoDo exploration is a stroll along the milelong pedestrian mall on 16th Street. Crowds flock to the Denver Pavilions, an outdoor urban mall with 15 movie screens and restaurants like Wolfgang Puck Grand Cafe, Hard Rock Cafe and Cafe Odyssey. Just west of the mall, a two-block stretch of Larimer Street offers boutique shopping in century-old buildings.

Denver has no beach, but the new aquarium is a pretty good stand-in. Built on Water Street, Ocean Journey is part of an amusement district that includes the Children's Museum and Six Flags Elitch Gardens, Colorado's largest amusement park. Ocean Journey, 700 Water Street, features the ecology of two rivers, the Colorado and the Kampar River of Indonesia. If the kids aren't impressed by the Mexican sharks, maybe they will be intrigued by the Sumatran tigers in the "rain forest." Ocean Journey is open daily in summer 9 a.m. to 6:30 p.m. and 10 a.m. to 6 p.m. after Labor Day. Tickets, sold in advance, cost $14.95 for adults, $12.95 for ages 13 to 17 and over 65, and $6.95 for ages 4 to 12. Information: (303) 561-4450.

The Children's Museum of Denver, 2121 Children's Museum Drive, (303) 433- 7444, is open daily from 10 a.m. to 5 p.m. with interactive exhibits, including a giant musical maze and a year-round ski slope. A renovation completed in autumn 2000 added a wing geared to literacy and the under-4 set, based on new research that shows this age group should be presented with written words even earlier than previously thought. Admission is $5, $2 for ages 1 and 2, and $3 ages 60 and up.

Six Flags Elitch Gardens, (303) 595-4386, at Elitch Circle and Speer Boulevard, offers more than 48 rides, including the Boomerang coaster, and a water park. Through Labor Day, the park is open 10 a.m. to 10 p.m. daily. Admission costs $28 for anyone 48 inches and taller, $14 for those under four feet and is free for those under 4 years old.

The Denver Art Museum, 100 West 14th Avenue Parkway, is on the eastern edge of Denver's new gallery neighborhood, the Golden Triangle, and is open 10 a.m. to 5 p.m., except Wednesday, when it closes at 9 p.m., and Sunday, when it opens at noon. It is closed Monday. Admission is $4.50 for adults and $2.50 for those over age 65, children over 6 and students; (303) 640-2793.

Also downtown, the Denver Center Theater Company, a 1998

Tony Award winner for regional theater, is based at the Denver Performing Arts Complex, which includes nine stages and 9,200 seats. Tickets: (303) 893-4100 or (800) 641-1222.

where to stay

BUDGET: Connected by a sky bridge to the Brown Palace, the Comfort Inn Downtown, 401 17th Street, (800) 237-7431, fax (303) 297-0774, has 229 rooms, with room rates starting at $89.

Near the Cherry Creek shopping and dining area is the Fairfield Inn Cherry Creek, 1680 South Colorado Boulevard, (303) 691-2223, fax (303) 691-0062. It offers an indoor pool, free breakfast and 170 rooms in a 10-story building. Rooms start at $79.

MODERATE: Hotel Teatro opened in 1999 in the lovingly restored 1911 Tramway Tower, across Arapahoe Street from the Denver Performing Arts Complex at 1100 14th Street. Drawing on the theatrical wealth of its neighbor, Teatro's décor features stage props, commedia masks and, in the rooms, old photographs of stage productions. Each of the 116 rooms has caller-identification telephones, high-speed Internet access and a printer, scanner and fax. Room rates range from $129 to $255; (303) 228-1100, fax (303) 228-1101.

Right on the Mall, Courtyard by Marriott, 934 16th Street, (888) 249-1810, fax (303) 571-1141, has opened in a wonderfully refurbished 1883 department store. Away from the buzz of the street, the Courtyard offers a spacious lobby and 177 rooms, with doubles for $152 during the week, and sometimes half that on weekends.

LUXURY: The Queen Bee of Denver hotels has long been the Brown Palace, a venerable, century-old Victorian landmark with a breathtaking nine-story atrium at 321 17th Street; (303) 297-3111. All its 235 rooms (starting at $265) are furnished with antiques.

Hotel Monaco, 1717 Champa Street, (800) 397-5380, fax (303) 296-1818, vies for the title of Denver's hippest hotel. Decorated in a mix of Art Deco and contemporary, the main lobby, in the renovated 1917 Railway Exchange building, has a reception desk patterned after a steamer trunk and a brightly hand-painted geometric ceiling that soars 23 feet. Each of the 189 rooms has a CD player, and guests can request a pet goldfish. The rates start at $155 for a double and $195 for a suite.

where to eat

Serious about Italian food, Barolo Grill, 3030 East Sixth Avenue, (303) 393-1040, sends its staff to northern Italy for two weeks every year to sharpen its Tuscan, Piedmontese and small-country-inn menus. Dinner for two, with wine, is about $75. Closed Sunday and Monday.

Radek R. Cerny, a New York transplant, is the chef at two popular new restaurants, Papillon Cafe, 250 Josephine Street, (303) 333-7166, and Radex, 100 East Ninth Avenue, (303) 861-7999, which specialize in pasta and seafood. Dinner for two with wine is about $100 at Papillon and about $75 at Radex.

For the visitor, the high-end restaurant that offers the best sense of place is The Fort, 19192 Highway 8, Morrison, (303) 697-4771, a replica of an 1840's adobe fur-trappers' trading post. The menu features such delights as Taos Pueblo–style trout ($18), elk medallions in Montana huckleberry sauce ($27.50) and buffalo steaks ($33 to $37).

For a quiet meal in a relaxed French bistro setting, Aubergine Cafe, 225 East Seventh Avenue, (303) 832-4778, stands out for its food and service. The menu changes often; a standout appetizer one month was lettuce salad with persimmon, walnuts, goat cheese and champagne vinaigrette for $7; sautéed skate wing with capers, sherry vinegar, lemon aioli and pommes frites cost $18. Closed Monday.

The Wynkoop Brewing Company is in the heart of LoDo, at 18th and Wynkoop Streets, (303) 297-2700. Despite its large size, Wynkoop offers an intimate feel, breaking up a turn-of-the-century industrial space with indoor dining nooks, outdoor tables, a basement comedy club and an upstairs pool hall. The food is good and affordable: mango barbecue chicken breast, a pint of Rail Yard Ale and a chocolate cream tartlet come to about $20.

(Elizabeth Heilman Brooke, a freelance writer and James Brooke's wife, contributed to this article.)

vital statistics

POPULATION (1998 estimate): City 499,055; Metro area 1,938,642

HOTEL: Room for one with tax $132.50

DINNER FOR ONE: With tax and tip but not drinks $29.75

TAXI: Upon entry $1.60; Each additional mile $1.60; From the airport $43.00

CAR RENTAL FOR A DAY: Midsize car with unlimited free mileage $67.50

FOR MORE INFORMATION: Telephone: (800) 233-6837; Web: www.denver.org

Sources: Runzheimer International, U.S. Census Bureau, local businesses

Dublin

Temple Bar, a riverside neighborhood,
symbolizes the new glamour

O'Connell Bridge, Dublin

EMILY LAURENCE BAKER

Emily Laurence Baker is an American journalist living in London.

During the past decade, Dublin, once a gloomy, provincial city, has become Europe's darling. The economy is booming, and Dublin now is a regular on lists of top 10 destinations.

Helping to fuel the attraction is the redevelopment of Temple Bar, a once neglected riverside neighborhood that has become the city's new cultural quarter. Artistic venues include the Arthouse, a multimedia center; Temple Bar Music Center; the Ark, a cultural spot for children; the Irish Film Center and the Gallery of Photography. There are also numerous oversized pubs that attract English bridal parties on weekends.

The area, a small network of streets on the south bank of the river just west of O'Connell Bridge, is new and lively but still has the feel of engineered revival.

To experience the more enduring charm that distinguishes the city, stroll through St. Stephen's Green on a Sunday afternoon to see Dubliners at play. Take a walk past brightly painted Georgian doors with fan arches in the Merrion Square area. Stop for a late-afternoon pint at The Palace in Fleet Street or across the river at The Dockers'.

Even in Temple Bar it's still possible to drop in on an impromptu session of fiddles and flutes at Oliver St. John Gogarty's.

best of times

Unfortunately, rain, or at the very least, a gray sky, is likely during a Dublin visit. The driest, sunniest weather is usually in July and August, while December tends to be the wettest month.

Two distinctly Dublin annual events occur in the spring. The St. Patrick's Festival is a multiday celebration during which city center streets are closed off for dancing, singing and general merrymaking, as well as a big parade on March 17; telephone (353-1) 676-3205 for more information.

Fans of the novel *Ulysses* will want to be in Dublin for Bloomsday on June 16, the day in which the novel takes place in 1904. The city pays homage to James Joyce with readings, lectures, pub talks and other activities with actors in period costumes.

There's an opportunity to witness a very local celebration during the Liberties Festival, usually held for one week in early July. Residents of the Liberties, one of Dublin's oldest neighborhoods, near Christchurch Cathedral, celebrate their heritage with parades, live music in pubs and church concerts; (353-1) 454-1465.

In early August, the Kerrygold Horse Show is on for about four days at the grounds of the Royal Dublin Society in Ballsbridge, about one mile south of the city center. Kerrygold, also known as the Dublin Horse Show, is not only an important international competition, but also a major Dublin social event. Ticket information: (353-1) 668-0866.

what to see

Ceol, a visitor attraction at Smithfield Village, a new residential and commercial development off Arran Quay, (353-1) 817-3820, tells the history of Irish music in an impressive modern setting. Children will enjoy the many interactive exhibits, including the chance to dance a jig in front of large screens showing dance videos. Open Monday through Saturday 9:30 a.m. to 6 p.m., Sunday 10:30 a.m. to 6 p.m. Admission is $5.10 for adults, $3.90 for those ages 7 to 12.

The Musical Pub Crawl leaves from Oliver St. John Gogarty's at 52 Fleet Street in Temple Bar nightly at 7:30 from the first Friday in May through the last Saturday in October. Two musicians perform songs and give an overview of Irish musical history during a two-and-a-half-hour tour of four pubs. In November, February, March and April, the walk takes place on Friday and Saturday only. Tickets are $8.60. More information: (353-1) 478-0193.

The Literary Pub Crawl is led by two actors who perform scenes by Dublin's famous playwrights and novelists. The two-and-a-half-hour walk among four pubs leaves nightly at 7:30 as well as Sundays at noon from The Duke, on Duke Street, from Easter through Oct. 31. From November to Easter, the walk takes place on Thursday through Sunday evenings as well as Sunday at noon. Tickets are $8.45 for adults and $7.15 for students and seniors. More information: (353-1) 670-5602.

Tickets and information for these and other pub crawls are also available at the Dublin Tourism Center, Suffolk Street (no telephone information; walk-ins only).

The Book of Kells, the intricate illuminated manuscript of the Gospels made around 800, is one of the biggest draws in Dublin. It is displayed in the Old Library at Trinity College, College Green; (353-1) 608-2320, along with exhibits that show how illuminated manuscripts were painstakingly crafted. Open Monday to Saturday 9:30 a.m. to 5 p.m.; Sunday from 9:30 a.m. to 4:30 p.m. June to September, and noon to 4:30 p.m. October to May. Admission is $5.85 for adults, $5.20 for students and senior citizens, free for children under 12.

On the southeast corner of Merrion Square, Dublin's finest Georgian square, No. 29 Lower Fitzwilliam Street, (353-1) 702-6165, has been restored to its original décor, and looks as it did when it was home to a well-off 18th-century family. Visitation is by guided tour only, which takes about 40 minutes, including a saccharine introductory video. Open Tuesday to Saturday 10 a.m. to 5 p.m., Sunday 2 to 5 p.m. Closed Mondays and the two weeks before Christmas. Admission is $3.25 for adults, children under 16 free.

where to stay

Hotels fill up quickly in Dublin, especially at the lower end of the price scale.

BUDGET: There are no frills but plenty of character and a friendly welcome at the Clifton Court Hotel, 11 Eden Quay, O'Connell Bridge, Dublin 1, (353-1) 874-3535, fax (353-1) 878-6698, a 30-room guesthouse overlooking the River Liffey. Bathrooms are closet-sized, with showers but no tubs. The bar has Irish music nightly. Doubles are $92, including Continental breakfast; ask about specials for stays of more than one night.

The Townhouse of Dublin, 47-48 Lower Gardiner Street, (353-1)

878-8808, fax (353-1) 878-8787, a guesthouse just north of the river, has 80 rooms. Standard doubles, which have a bathroom shared among four rooms, start at $78; luxury doubles with private bathroom start at $104. Rates include full Irish breakfast. Ask about midweek specials from October to June.

MODERATE: Behind the locked gate of 31 Leeson Close, (353-1) 676-5011, fax (353-1) 676-2929, Noel Comer, his wife, Deirdre, and their dog, Homer, offer a friendly welcome. The guesthouse has a total of 20 rooms, 5 of which are in the basement of two modernized 19th-century coach houses. White brick walls and tile floors contribute to a cozy, informal atmosphere. Across the leafy courtyard is a Georgian town house with 15 rooms that fronts on Fitzwilliam Place. Breakfast is served family-style in the upstairs conservatory of the coachhouse. All bedrooms have private bath. Double rooms are either $122 or $143, including a hot breakfast.

The seven rooms at the Grey Door, 22-23 Upper Pembroke Street, (353-1) 676-3286, fax (353-1) 676-3287, offer a homey stay in gracious Georgian style, and the hotel dining room is one of Dublin's finest restaurants. All rooms have bathrooms with both showers and tubs. Doubles are $124 a night Monday through Thursday, $110 a night Friday through Sunday if you stay at least two consecutive nights. On weekdays Continental breakfast is $6.50, hot Irish breakfast $9; on weekends one's choice of breakfast is included in the room rate.

LUXURY: Crystal chandeliers and muted elegance abound at the Shelbourne Dublin, a Meridien Hotel, 27 St. Stephen's Green, (353-1) 676-6471, fax (353-1) 661-6006. There are 190 rooms, many of which overlook the Green. Doubles start at $267 plus a 15 percent service charge. Breakfast is extra: $17 (Continental) and $20 (cooked).

Buswells Hotel, Molesworth Street, (353-1) 676-4013, fax (353-1) 676-2090, is near major museums. The refurbished 70-room hotel caters to business travelers but has a pleasant Old World feel. Standard doubles are $203, including cooked breakfast.

where to eat

Dublin restaurants have become increasingly cosmopolitan, but Conrad Gallagher still stands out for his creative Mediterranean-influenced cuisine. His restaurant, Peacock Alley, in the Fitzwilliam Hotel, St. Stephen's Green West, (353-1) 478-7037, is white-wall stark with windows overlooking St. Stephen's Green. Entrees include char-grilled guinea fowl with saffron risotto and pan-roasted red mullet with eggplant stew and coconut and curry emulsion. Dinner for two with wine, about $155. Lunch and dinner Monday through Saturday, closed Sunday.

Another hot spot is the casual Mermaid Cafe, 69-70 Dame Street, (353-1) 670-8236. The kitchen produces sophisticated eclectic fare using lots of local ingredients, including chicken and parma ham Kiev with creamed corn or grilled aubergine (eggplant) with ricotta and sweet chili relish. Portions are huge. Dinner for two with wine is about $80. Dinner nightly, lunch Monday to Saturday, brunch on Sunday.

For Irish classics, Gallagher's Boxty House, 20-21 Temple Bar, (353-1) 677-2762, is the place, with fine boxty (stuffed potato pancakes) and hearty stews. It's likely you'll share a long table when it's busy. No reservations, but after 5 p.m. (2 on weekends) you can call for a time to come in. Dinner for two with wine, about $45.

Families will feel comfortable at Elephant and Castle, 18 Temple Bar, (353-1) 679-3121, a popular diner-style eatery that is a branch of the establishment in New York. The simple but good food is centered on hamburgers, omelets and spicy chicken wings. Dinner for two with wine starts around $45.

vital statistics

POPULATION (1998): City 481,854; Metro area 952,892

HOTEL: Room for one with tax $207.00

DINNER FOR ONE: With tax and tip but not drinks $27.75

TAXI: Upon entry $1.70; Each additional mile $1.00; From the airport $17.00

CAR RENTAL FOR A DAY: Midsize car with unlimited free mileage $66.00

FOR MORE INFORMATION: Telephone: (353-1) 605-7700; Web: www.visitdublin.com

Sources: Runzheimer International, Irish Tourist Board, local businesses

Florence

Exquisitely designed piazzas and
small-town friendliness

Ponte Vecchio,
Florence

PAULA BUTTURINI

Paula Butturini is a journalist who lives in Paris.

Florence is, perhaps more than any other spot in Italy, a city of
beautifully ordered spaces. Medieval and Renaissance men
ignored the traces laid down by ancient Rome and made their own
rules, turning Florence, in its circle of hills, into an architectural
jewel. The city's narrow streets open suddenly onto broad, expan-
sive piazzas, which provide breathing spaces of exquisite design,
encouraging one to emerge from the cool, private shadows of gray
back alleys into powerful sunlit vistas.

Florence may stupefy a visitor with its artistic and architectural
richness, but thanks to human proportions and harmony of design,
it never loses its human feel. A surprising number of Florentines
get around by bicycle, but walking is still the best way to see the
city, especially now that pedestrian zones have reduced traffic in
some central areas to an almost tolerable level. Ask for help finding the right bus and someone will probably take you in hand till
you reach your destination.

best of times

May can be magical in Florence. The nights are still cool, the days still free of summer's baking heat. Spring rains encourage the city's celebrated irises to bloom, and the hordes of visitors that traditionally inundate Florence at Eastertime have usually tapered off a tad to a nearly manageable level.

Florentines enjoy gathering in the Piazza del Duomo on Easter Sunday for the Scoppio del Carro (Explosion of the Cart). An antique cart led by four oxen and accompanied by a parade of costumed participants winds into the cathedral square before the 11 a.m. Mass. Before Mass ends, a dove-shaped device is lighted and sent on a wire from the high altar to the cart outside, which explodes in fireworks upon contact, sending the dove hurtling into the sky. The closer the dove gets to the altar during its flight, the more fruitful the year will be.

Maggio Musicale, the city's celebrated May music festival, normally runs through May and June, and annually brings world class performers to the Tuscan capital. Tickets can be purchased at the box office, Teatro Communale, 16 Corso Italia. For information and advance bookings, telephone (39-055) 211158 Tuesday to Saturday 10 a.m. to 1 p.m. and Tuesday to Friday 2 to 4:30 p.m.

May visitors can also take advantage of the city's annual International Iris Competition, which usually runs for about two and a half weeks. The competition, which is free, takes place on a hillside overlooking the city above the Arno, near Piazzale Michelangelo. It is open daily 10 a.m. to 12:30 p.m. and 3 to 7 p.m.

Florence attracts legions of visitors, so many that the city center seems to run out of sidewalk space for them all during the high season, early spring through late fall. For visitors seeking a quieter look at the city's medieval and Renaissance treasures, the best time to visit may be during the worst of winter, mid- to late January. Gray, raw, drippy days can be a relatively small price to pay for the chance to study Botticelli's "Birth of Venus" or Cimabue's famed Crucifix in the absence of elbowing throngs.

what to see

The Uffizi Gallery is in the midst of a major renovation that has already transformed what is considered to be Italy's most important museum. New wings have been opened for exhibitions and another wing, containing the precious Contini Bonacossi collection, is open to the public on Wednesday and Friday. A new entrance is also planned. The Uffizi Gallery, 6 Loggiato degli Uffizi;

(39-055) 294883, is open Tuesday to Saturday 8:30 a.m. to 6:50 p.m., Sunday and holidays until 7 p.m.; closed Mondays and Christmas, New Year's Day and May 1. Admission: $5.50.

After trekking through the Uffizi and the nearby Palazzo Vecchio, after traversing the Ponte Vecchio to see the Raphaels and Titians in the Pitti Palace, after recrossing the Arno to see the Baptistry and Brunelleschi's red-tiled cupola on the Duomo, after walking to the Galleria dell'Accademia to see Michelangelo's "David"—in short, after visiting one too many of the city's astounding collections of museum treasures—the best antidote is an escape to the hills that surround Florence.

You don't have to leave the city to appreciate the view. The No. 13 bus (tickets 70 cents) will take you from the main train station to Piazzale Michelangelo, a broad lookout on the left bank of the Arno that offers a panorama of the entire city. Another antidote is an evening stroll through Florence's beautiful squares. To wander into the gracefully arched loggias of Piazza della Santissima Annunziata is always a comfort. Piazza della Signoria, Piazza Santa Croce, Piazza di Santa Maria Novella: each is unique, each worth visiting, especially at night when tourist traffic has dwindled and the street lights play along the rooftops.

where to stay

From April through October, Florence teems with tourists, so it is advisable to book lodgings in advance. Visitors arriving without reservations can go to the main train station, the Stazione Santa Maria Novella, and stand in the generally long line at the hotel-finding kiosk; telephone (39-055) 282893. There is a commission of $2 to $7, and you must pay the first night's rate at the kiosk. Unless otherwise specified, prices are for high season: April through June and September and October.

BUDGET: The Hotel Hermitage, 1 Vicolo Marzio, (39-055) 287216, fax (39-055) 212208, is a few steps from the Ponte Vecchio and has a spectacular roof terrace that overlooks the Arno and the red-tiled roofs of the city. A pleasantly furnished double costs $186, including breakfast, which is served on the terrace in warm weather. Most of the 28 smallish rooms have showers rather than baths.

The Pensione Annalena, 34 Via Romana, (39-055) 222402, fax (39-055) 222403, is across the Arno, just five minutes from the Pitti Palace. The pensione, on the second floor of a building without an elevator, has 20 small, eclectically decorated rooms. A double with breakfast costs $127.

MODERATE: The 102-room Pullman Hotel Astoria-Palazzo Gaddi, 9 Via del Giglio, (39-055) 2398095, fax (39-055) 214632, must have the most dramatic breakfast room in all of Florence, an ornate hall with a gloriously frescoed ceiling, painted in 1596 by Luca Giordano. Double rooms cost $290, including breakfast.

Travelers seeking less rarefied lodgings in old pensione style can try the 100-year-old Hotel Tornabuoni Beacci, 3 Via dei Tornabuoni, (39-055) 212645, which occupies the top floors of a 15th-century building. Doubles cost $182, including breakfast. The 28 rooms are quirkily furnished in typical pensione eclectic style.

LUXURY: The Hotel Helvetia and Bristol, 2 Via dei Pescioni, (39-055) 287814, fax (39-055) 288353, is in Florence's historic center. Built in the late 1800's, the 49-room hotel reopened in 1990 after a three-year restoration aimed at re-creating the ambience of the days when the hotel regularly drew such guests as Stravinsky, Pirandello, de Chirico and Eleanora Duse. Doubles: from $315 to $395; add $18 a person for Continental breakfast.

For updated elegance in a quiet, parklike setting, the Hotel Regency, 3 Piazza Massimo D'Azeglio, telephone and fax (39-055) 245247, is an apt choice. The 34-room hotel is at the edge of a formal, tree-filled square and only a 10-minute stroll from Santissima Annunziata, arguably the city's most beautiful piazza. Double rooms, including breakfast, cost $316.

where to eat

Most Florentines would choose beans, accented with a dribble of fruity, light green olive oil, over pasta. Simply grilled or roasted meats are a Tuscan specialty, and all over Italy a T-bone steak is known as a fiorentina, cut from Italy's best beef cattle, the Chianina. Most restaurants close in August.

Enoteca Pinchiorri, 87 Via Ghibellina, (39-055) 242777, is rated the city's best. A meal for two can start with homemade pasta with squid and zucchini flowers in a garlic sauce, followed by sea bass in a crust of sea salt accompanied by eggplant with mozzarella and dry tomato sauce and olives. For dessert, try cake with mascarpone and licorice ice cream. About $114 per person without wine. Closed Sunday and Monday, and at lunch on Tuesday. Reservations required.

Lo Strettoio, 7 Via di Serpiolle, (39-055) 425 0044, offers a splendid view of Florence from its sweeping terrace on the hills to the north. A former olive oil press, the restaurant still has the original wooden strettoio, or olive press, in the center of the long, vaulted dining room. The menu changes almost daily to reflect seasonal specialties. A meal for two, of homemade pasta with ricotta cheese and aromatic herbs and tomato, followed by veal stuffed with artichokes and finishing with a mocha torte, costs $73, including wine. It's $15 to $20 by taxi from the city center. Closed Sunday and Monday. Reservations required.

One of the best places to sample Tuscan beef or veal is Trattoria Sostanza-Troia, 25 Via del Porcellana, (39-055) 212691, which has been serving charcoal-cooked meats since 1869. After ordering a fiorentina or lombata di vitello, a thick veal chop from a milk-fed calf, you can watch through the open kitchen doorway as the chef slices your meat to order. A meal for two, including wine, costs $45 to $64. Reservations are requested. Closed Saturday and Sunday.

At Trattoria Cibreo, 118 Via dei Macci, (39-055) 234 1100, the chefs explore old regional recipes predating pasta's appearance in Tuscany. The trattoria is attached to a much more expensive restaurant of the same name. A meal for two at the trattoria, which might start with a ricotta cheese torte and chicken, be followed by veal meatballs and end with a light Bavarian cream, costs about $45, including wine. Closed Sunday, Monday and usually January 1 to 8.

The best way to beat the generally high cost of dining in Italy is to eat standing at a bar; sit at a caffe table and prices double. The Caffe Giacosa, 83 Via dei Tornabuoni, (39-055) 239 6226, offers tiny sandwiches and rice-and-mozzarella balls (arancini), and tasty desserts. A sandwich and arancino, followed by coffee and a slice of torta delizia, costs about $10 for two. Closed Sunday.

vital statistics

POPULATION (1999): City 376,760

HOTEL: Room for two with tax $88

DINNER FOR ONE: With tax and tip but not drinks $23

TAXI: Upon entry $2.04; Each additional kilometer 67 cents; From the airport $13.60

CAR RENTAL FOR A DAY: Midsize car with unlimited free mileage $80.50

FOR MORE INFORMATION: Telephone: (39-055) 247814 or (39-055) 234 6286; Web: english.firenze.net

Sources: Italian Statistics (ISTAT), Tourism Research Center, local businesses

Geneva

Don't wait for ski season to see this beautifully landscaped lakeside city

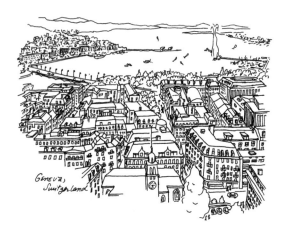

ELIZABETH OLSON

Elizabeth Olson writes for *The Times* from Switzerland.

While Geneva is widely known as a way station for skiers going to the Alps, the lovely city on western Europe's largest lake is at its best during the warmer months. At the first hint of tolerable weather, residents and tourists alike cluster around the immaculately manicured flower clock and marvel at the 460-foot column of water that is Geneva's best-known landmark. Visible from all around the city, the Jet d'Eau spews 132 gallons into the sky each second from its location on the lake's southern shore.

Or they venture onto Lake Geneva, known to the Swiss as Lac Leman, in sailboats or larger commercial vessels, which include four Belle Epoque steamboats. These stop at nearby picturesque villages such as Yvoire in France, or go far up the lake to Montreux to the fairy-tale Château de Chillon of Lord Byron's poem.

Walking and cycling paths lead past some magnificent architecture, including the 14th-century Maison Tavel with its tower, the oldest house in Geneva; the Gothic houses on the Old Town's main street, the Grand' Rue, and the cathedral of St.-Pierre, which dates to the 12th century.

The city as a nature preserve can be explored on boats that ply the Rhone River between April and November. Starting at Pont de L'Île, Quai de Moulins, the mouettes (long, low covered boats) glide quietly for about two and three-quarters hours, passing ducks, swans and gray herons, which live in abundance along the forested river, where hunting is banned.

best of times

Geneva hosts both local and international events year-round, most at the Palexpo Center, near the airport. Winter's end is marked when the Jet d'Eau is turned on, an event that happens within days of the International Motor Show, which draws some 700,000 visitors to see the latest futuristic technology.

If deluxe items attract, Geneva is the site of an annual international luxury watch exhibition featuring the latest examples of the country's top-flight watch industry. That is followed every spring by the International Fair for Books, Press and Multimedia, which features books and magazines from around Europe, as well as online publications.

Shortly afterward, the city is host to the yearly International Exhibition of Inventions, New Techniques and New Products, with 1,000 new inventions from dozens of countries. Those intrigued with the new can attend the International New Rose Contest, in June, where a gold rose is offered as the first prize.

For the sports-minded, Geneva is the site in June of Europe's biggest inland sailing race, with more than 650 competing boats.

Music lovers will feel quite at home in Geneva, which has musical events sprinkled throughout the year, beginning with a festival of contemporary music in March. Concerts take place in the parks in Geneva's Old Town frequently during the summer months. Music is the centerpiece of the Fêtes de Geneve, when the entire lakeshore becomes a huge festival with shows, concerts, parades and fireworks.

The best-loved event in Geneva's year is the Escalade, which is a celebration complete with period costumes of the city's heroic defense against the efforts of the Duke of Savoy to seize the town by surprise on Dec. 11, 1602.

what to see

The most charming part of Geneva is its Old Town. Start at the Place du Bourg-de-Four, with its 18th-century fountain decorated with flowers, little bistros with tables spilling out to the street and tony shops. As long ago as Roman times, the square was a gathering place, with markets held there. City dwellers came to collect drinking water, brought by aqueduct from nearby mountains. The area is also where John Calvin spoke during the Protestant Reformation.

The Old Arsenal, with five cannons tucked under its arcades opposite the Town Hall, is a favorite climbing and picture-taking spot. The old Geneva artillery once protected the city ramparts. Seized by Austrians in 1813, the cannons were returned in 1923. The arsenal features some mosaics dating from 1949 depicting important chapters in Geneva's history, among them the arrival of Julius Caesar in 58 B.C. and the welcoming of Huguenot refugees during the Reformation.

Geneva's hilly streets may be daunting for some. An easy way to cover them is by mini-train, which departs the Place Neuve and winds through the Old Town. The mini-trains also transport people to sites around the lake. Go to the Quai de Mont-Blanc for trains leaving for the Right Bank circuit, which takes about 40 minutes and includes the Botanical Gardens, several international institutions and parks as well as lake views. Service starts April 1. Round-trip fare: $4.60 for adults, children $3.25; (41-22) 781-0404.

A stroll down to the Rhone leads to the remains of the 13th-century Tour de L'Île constructed to protect the city against the Savoyards. Only the tower was spared after several fires damaged it. Restored in 1897, it is topped by a clock. At its base is a bronze statue of a hero of Geneva's independence, Philibert Berthelier, who was tortured and beheaded there in 1519.

About three minutes away is the splendid Forces Motrices, built in 1886 in the industrial style as a hydroelectric plant, but renovated recently for use as a theater.

where to stay

BUDGET: Families who want a glimpse of rural Swiss life within close range of Geneva can try a gite, or farmhouse. The nearest one to Geneva, 15 minutes from downtown, is Chez Jacques Imobersteg, 74 Route de Coudres, in Celigny, a small house that sleeps up to six and overlooks the farm; $53 to $67 a day. Reservations: (41-31) 329-6623.

A charming budget choice (and perhaps the only budget hotel overlooking the Rhone) is Hôtel des Tourelles, 2 Boulevard James-Fazy; (41-22) 732-4423, fax (41-22) 732-7620. The 23 rooms in this family-operated establishment feature modern décor and new prefabricated baths. Four turreted rooms face the water. Doubles: from $80.

Another budget alternative is the freshly renovated eight-room Hôtel de la Cloche, 6 Rue de la Cloche, (41-22) 732-9481, fax (41-22) 738-1612, near the train station. Its large, yellow double rooms with bath start at $80.

MODERATE: The 51-room Hôtel Strasbourg-Univers, 10 Rue Pradier, (41-22) 906-5800, fax (41-22) 738-4208, is well situated near the train station. It has a fresh feel, with rooms in a light green and mustard color scheme. This Best Western has Internet, modem and fax connections in each room and double-glazed windows for quiet. Doubles begin at $127.

The Hôtel Eden, 135 Rue de Lausanne, (41-22) 716-3700, fax (41-22) 731-5260, is a favorite for visitors to the United Nations nearby. For those who can't be separated from e-mail and the Web, each of the 54 rooms—done up in cheerful blue plaid—is connected to the Internet. It overlooks a park by the lake. Doubles start at $167, with breakfast. Its restaurant is open weekdays.

LUXURY: For Old World appeal, there's the Beau Rivage, 13 Quai du Mont-Blanc, (41-22) 716-6666, fax (41-22) 716-6060, with a fountain gurgling in the lobby. Its 97 rooms, radiating from an atrium, have elegant modern baths and stained-glass windows. One historical suite honors "Sissi," the Empress Elizabeth of Austria, a hotel patron who was assassinated nearby a century ago. Founded in 1865, the family-owned hotel has two restaurants. A double room starts at $347.

The 253-room Hôtel President-Wilson, 47 Quai Wilson, (41-22) 906-6666, fax (41-22) 906-6667, caters to business clientele with a conference center, but still has a resort-in-the-city feel with a pool and grill, two restaurants and Clarins spa. Many of the plush rooms, done in understated neutrals, overlook the lake. Doubles: from $353.

where to eat

To sample a Geneva institution, try the Mère Royaume, 9 Rue de Corps-Saints, (41-22) 732-7008, which may be the only restaurant to glorify someone who spilled soup. There are two floor-to-ceiling stained-glass windows celebrating a local woman who, in 1602, dumped a cauldron of soup on a Savoyard invader. Dinner for two, with a good Swiss wine, such as Yvorne, Clos de Georges 1996, runs $160. Specialties are veal ($27) and bass in pastry ($29). There's a splendid dessert cart. Closed Sunday, dinner only Saturday.

A Rhone River boat outing can culminate with a wonderful

meal at the Café de Peney, part of the nearby deluxe Château Vieux restaurant and hotel, (41-22) 753-1755, which is just steps away from the boat stop. The cafe's colorful floor tiles make the décor. A lunch for two, with lobster ravioli, fish in risotto, lamb chops and choice of dessert is $60, plus wine.

A less costly Geneva institution is Brasserie Lipp, 8 Rue de la Confédération, (41-22) 311-1011, a lively place for good food, especially fish. Starting in springtime, it serves a Geneva specialty: perch filets from the lake. Dinner for two from $50.

For lunch, Les Fous de la Place, 21 Rue de la Corraterie, (41-22) 310-5340, recently offered a hearty plat du jour of chicken, rice and green beans for $10. Red mullet for two with wine was $53. Patrons are asked not to smoke cigars or pipes. Closed Sunday and Monday.

A good budget choice is Café des Bains, 26 Rue des Bains, (41-22) 321-5798, where a diverse clientele samples bistro food, including pasta dishes ($12). Dinner for two with wine: from $40. Closed weekends.

Students and artists flock to Café Gallay, 42 Boulevard St. Georges, (41-22) 321-0035, with its wooden tables and bistro atmosphere. A typical dinner of mussels and french fries for two averages $35. Closed Sunday.

vital statistics

POPULATION (1999): City 180,000; Canton 400,000

HOTEL: Room for one with tax $242.50

DINNER FOR ONE: With tax and tip but not drinks $20.45

TAXI: Upon entry $3.54; Each additional kilometer $1.52; From the airport $18.40

CAR RENTAL FOR A DAY: Midsize car with unlimited free mileage $76.00

FOR MORE INFORMATION: Telephone: (41-22) 909-7000; Web: www.geneva-tourism.ch

Sources: Runzheimer International, Swiss National Tourist Office, local businesses

Hong Kong
The colonial era is officially over, but the transition may take a while

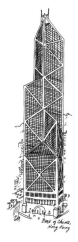

MARK LANDLER

Mark Landler is chief of the Hong Kong bureau of *The Times*.

It has been several years since this former British colony reverted to Chinese rule. But some locals are still startled when they see the words "Hong Kong, China" on a television report or travel brochure.

Old habits die hard, and Hong Kong is in the midst of an awkward transition from colonial outpost to Chinese metropolis. The outward trappings of empire have been largely effaced (only the Royal Hong Kong Yacht Club still preserves the Royal in its English name). Inwardly, however, Hong Kong has not completely thrown off its heritage as a Crown Colony in the exotic East.

The Hong Kong Tourist Association still promotes the territory's residual British flavor as well as its Chinese characteristics and its cosmopolitan atmosphere as the most international city in Asia. Hong Kong's most eagerly awaited tourist attraction is neither Chinese nor British. It is a Walt Disney theme park, scheduled to open in 2005 on Lantau Island, west of Hong Kong.

The Asian economic crisis of the late-1990's compounded Hong Kong's identity crisis by slowing its capitalist heartbeat. But with the economy bouncing back, the city is reverting to the gaudy celebration of wealth that characterized it during the go-go years.

Indeed, if you walk the streets, Hong Kong feels like its old self. It throbs with the energy of 7 million people—buying, selling, or chatting on their ubiquitous cell phones. Victoria Harbor remains a dazzling tarantella, as ferries, barges, cruise ships, and the odd sampan dodge and weave past each other.

Kai Tak Airport, with its legendary rooftop-skimming landings, was closed in 1998, but the new Hong Kong International Airport has won raves from passengers. With its soaring marble-and-glass terminal and a flawlessly efficient high-speed rail link to Kowloon and Central, the airport is a powerful reminder that Hong Kong is, above all, a city that works.

best of times

Fall and winter are the best seasons to visit Hong Kong. Sunny skies and brisk temperatures make the city a wonderful place to explore by foot, or from a ferry chugging through the surrounding waters. Hong Kong's climate is tropical, which means stifling, humid summers. From July through November, typhoons occasionally slam the territory, flooding streams and rattling windows.

The first major event of the year is the Chinese New Year's parade, which occurs in January or February, depending on the Chinese lunar calendar. Colorful floats and vibrant lion dancers parade past thousands of onlookers. At night, spectacular fireworks light up the harbor.

In March, rugby players from around the world converge on Hong Kong Stadium to compete in the Rugby Sevens tournament. Beer flows freely in the raucous grandstand.

In June, the annual Dragon Boat Festival fills up the city's bays and coves with decorative boats. With 22 oarsmen on each boat and a dragon scowling from every prow, this Chinese version of crew is a colorful display and a fun way to spend an afternoon. The races are held in several places, but the most popular viewing spot is at Stanley, on the south side of Hong Kong Island. Admission is free.

In November, the focus shifts 38 miles across the Pearl River delta, to Macao. This former Portuguese colony, which also recently reverted to Chinese sovereignty, hosts one of Asia's most popular Formula III races, the Macao Grand Prix. Drivers navigate the serpentine streets, which are lined with ultramodern high-rises and charming colonial buildings in Portuguese pastels.

what to see

The cheapest and best way to see Hong Kong is on a Star Ferry. These redoubtable green-and-white vessels ply the choppy waters of Victoria Harbor every 5 to 10 minutes between 6:30 a.m. and 11:30 p.m. The view from the upper deck is one of the wonders of the world, with Victoria Peak hulking behind a glittering skyline, and the manta-ray roof of the new Hong Kong Convention Center. Ferries serve Tsim Sha Tsui in Kowloon and Central and Wanchai in Hong Kong. Adult fare: 30 cents.

Debark on either side of the harbor, and several fabulous shopping centers beckon, in one of the few cities where shopping is a form of sightseeing. Although Hong Kong is no longer the mecca for bargains it once was, the shopping centers are vast, the stores are dazzling and you can buy everything from haute couture to herbal medicine.

Among the most spectacular shopping centers is Harbor City in Kowloon, a complex adjacent to the Star Ferry terminal that encompasses four shopping malls with 700 stores; it is open daily 9:30 a.m. to 9 p.m. On the Hong Kong side, Pacific Place has 150 upscale stores, open 10:30 a.m. to 8:30 p.m. daily.

If you steer clear of the big malls, you can still find bargains in hole-in-the-wall places, like camera shops along Stanley Street, antique stores on Hollywood Road and souvenir stalls at the Stanley market.

The Hong Kong Museum of History, in Tsim Sha Tsui, Kowloon, is free. Hours are Monday to Thursday and Saturday 10 a.m. to 6 p.m., Sunday 1 to 6 p.m., closed Friday; (852) 2724-9042.

While Hong Kong's skyline is its signature, the natural landscape is its unsung glory. The territory sprawls across 236 islands, some of which are accessible by ferry and offer a different slice of Hong Kong. Among the most charming is Lamma Island, a funky retreat southwest of Hong Kong Island popular with backpackers. The waterfront is lined with seafood restaurants and feels vaguely Mediterranean. A ferry sails from Central to Sok Kwu Wan on Lamma Island every 70 minutes. Better yet, you can take a junk from the Aberdeen fish market—a trip that is an evocative throwback to Hong Kong's fishing-village past.

where to stay

BUDGET: Garden View International House at 1 Macdonnell Road, (852) 2877-3737, fax (852) 2845-6263, sits in the foothills of Victoria Peak, overlooking the colonial governor's mansion. The

130 rooms are a steal at $62. The hotel is affiliated with the Y.W.C.A., whose gym and pool in the hotel are open to guests.

Nearby is the Bishop Lei International Guest House, 4 Robinson Road, (852) 2868-0828, fax (852) 2868-1551. Also in the hills above Central, it has 203 compact but tidy rooms. Doubles go for $165. A shuttle bus offers hourly service to Central, the Star Ferry and Pacific Place.

MODERATE: The Excelsior Hotel at 281 Gloucester Road, (852) 2894-8888, fax (852) 2576-7715, has Victoria Harbor at its feet and the teeming shops of Causeway Bay in its backyard. Rooms in this large hotel (887 rooms) are nothing special, but there is a coolly modern Asian fusion restaurant on the top floor. Doubles: $180 to $205, including breakfast.

On the Kowloon side, the Hyatt Regency at 67 Nathan Road, (852) 2311-1234, fax (852) 2739-8701, boasts faux antique furnishings, superb restaurants and an intimate lobby. The 723-room hotel is steps from the hectic Tsim Sha Tsui shopping district. Standard doubles start at $130.

LUXURY: Hong Kong's finest hotels are temples of sybaritic living, with service that leaves Westerners slack-jawed. The pinnacle, perhaps, is the Regent, on the waterfront in Kowloon, at 18 Salisbury Road, (852) 2721-1211, fax (852) 2739-4546. The 602 rooms are tasteful and muted—an oasis of calm looking out on the clamorous cityscape. Rates are $303 to $342 for doubles.

On Hong Kong Island, the Mandarin Oriental is a dowager queen. The exterior of this 542-room landmark, at 5 Connaught Road, Central, (852) 2522-0111, fax (852) 2530-0180, could use a scrubbing, but the service is faultless, with a staff-to-guest ratio of 2 to 1. Its Chinnery Bar is so colonial you'll wonder if the handover ever happened. Doubles, with breakfast, range from $232 to $348.

where to eat

The aristocrat of restaurants is Fook Lam Moon, 35 Johnston Road in Wanchai. Since 1972, this temple of Cantonese cuisine has catered to Hong Kong's wealthiest and most discriminating diners, with impeccable renditions of delicacies like shark's fin soup and sliced abalone. For those who blanch at $60 for a bowl of soup, there are less pricey specialties like roasted pigeon with spicy salt and deep-fried crispy chicken. Dinner for two, with wine but without the soup, will cost about $150. Reservations are necessary: (852) 2866-0663.

One of the city's best seafood restaurants is Victoria City

Seafood in the Sun Hung Kai Center in Wanchai, east of Central. Seafood specialties, like deep-fried prawns at about $8.40, are celebrated. Other dishes—like roast suckling pig ($7)—are marvelous, too, though appetizers are small and wine is expensive. Dinner for two with a bottle of wine is about $165. Reservations are a must, at (852) 2827-9938.

For a Cantonese feast, try Yung Kee, a celebrated restaurant that occupies five floors at 32-40 Wellington Street in Lan Kwai Fong, the nightlife district. The house specialty is roast goose, sold by the hundreds every day, but still succulent, at $15. Shark's fin soup is an extravagant delicacy, at $17 a bowl. With the soup, dinner for two is about $130; (852) 2523-2343.

Just up the street, at 77 Wellington, is Mak's Noodles, a local institution for wonton soup and noodles. The tacky orange and green Formica doesn't detract from the plump wontons. Two bowls for $6.50 are a perfect snack during a trip to nearby shops; (852) 2854-3810.

No trip to Hong Kong is complete without dim sum, and City Hall Restaurant, at Edinburgh Place, offers the quintessential experience. The cavernous dining room echoes with the clanking of trolley carts, bearing bite-sized treats like steamed pork buns and shrimp dumplings. Lunch for two is $25; (852) 2521-1303.

vital statistics

POPULATION (2000 estimate): City 6,900,000

HOTEL: Room for one with tax $263.50

DINNER FOR ONE: With tax and tip but not drinks $34.20

TAXI: Upon entry $1.92; Each additional kilometer 90 cents; From the airport $48.00 (to Hong Kong Island, including tolls); $38.50 (to Kowloon, including tolls)

CAR RENTAL FOR A DAY: Compact car with unlimited free mileage $90.00

FOR MORE INFORMATION: Telephone: (852) 2807-6543; Web: www.hkta.org

Sources: Runzheimer International, Hong Kong Tourist Association, local businesses

Honolulu

The gateway to Oahu

Iolani Palace, Honolulu

JOCELYN FUJII

Jocelyn Fujii, author of *Under the Hula Moon*
and other books on Hawaii, lives in Honolulu.

If you must be stricken with jet lag, let it be in Honolulu. The longest nonstops in America fly by Diamond Head and Waikiki to land on a runway by the ocean in the capital of Hawaii, some 5,000 miles from the East Coast. Passengers who left terra firma on the East Coast 10 hours earlier disembark to balmy air scented with tuberose and plumeria and views of Diamond Head from the airport concourse.

In Waikiki, their hotels are on or near a white-sand beach where surfers and outrigger canoes dot the horizon and Mai Tais with real orchids are always within reach. Even in the dense honky-tonk that is Waikiki, there is always a gleam in the visitor's eye.

Those who venture beyond Waikiki to windward Oahu, the North Shore, and the eastern point of Makapuu will see why Oahu is Hawaii's most underrated island. With about 120 miles of sandy coastline, rain forests atop the Koolau Mountains, and top-notch restaurants and museums, there is a full plate here for culture and recreation addicts.

best of times

Except for sparse rainy spells in the winter and muggy days in late summer, good weather is a given. Temperatures in the 70's and 80's and ocean temperature averages that vary only 5 degrees throughout the year are the norm. That makes Honolulu a year-round attraction where nature's rhythms are measured by such things as the seasonal appearance of jasmine (spring), mangoes (summer), high surf and whales (winter).

From mid-November to mid-December, all eyes turn to the ocean, if not to the big-wave pros in the Vans Triple Crown of Surfing in Haleiwa, then for the humpback whales that visit island waters every winter.

On May 1, at the annual Brothers Cazimero Lei Day concert at the Waikiki Shell, the lei-bedecked audience is as much of a show as the hula and Hawaiian music.

From Thursday to Sunday in mid- to late July, jazz buffs throng to the Hawaii International Jazz Festival for licks by the likes of Linda Hopkins and Ernie Watts at the Hawaii Theater, a 1922 Beaux-Arts fantasy. July is also a time for hula. On the third Sunday, drums, chant and native dance fill the sprawling grounds of Moanalua Gardens at the Prince Lot Hula Festival.

Come September, Hawaiian pageantry reaches its peak when the two-month, 54-year-old Aloha Festivals, Hawaii's largest statewide event, kicks off with a Royal Court and giant block parties downtown and in Waikiki.

In the last week of October going into November, Honolulu goes Gallic with the balls, art shows and citywide offerings of the French Festival. On its heels the first two weeks in November, celluloid rules when the Hawaii International Film Festival features Asian, Pacific Islands and American films throughout the state.

what to see

Trees nearly 150 years old shade the grounds of Foster Botanical Garden, 50 North Vineyard Boulevard, (808) 522-7065, 14 acres at the edge of downtown Honolulu that are a living museum of exceptional and endangered plants from tropical regions worldwide.

In Pearl Harbor, the U.S.S. Missouri Memorial, (808) 423-2263, features guided or self-guided tours of the battleship, which was restored by volunteers and is docked at the 450-acre Ford Island. You can climb between the decks of the "'Mighty Mo'" and peer into officers' cabins, where shoes are placed neatly beside bunks, as if in a time warp. Admission: $14 for adults, $7 ages 4 to 12; $14 for a guided tour.

In Kahuku on the North Shore, the James Campbell National Wildlife Refuge, managed by the Federal Fish and Wildlife Service, is open Thursday from 4 to 5:30 p.m. and Saturday 3 to 4:30 p.m. for guided tours of the wetlands. This refuge was designed to help the recovery of four endangered species: the black-necked Hawaiian stilt, Hawaiian moorhen, Hawaiian coot and Hawaiian duck. The tours are free and offered August 1 through February 15, when the stilts aren't nesting; reservations are necessary: (808) 637-6330.

The Kaena Point Natural Area Reserve—the most remote point on Oahu, reached by hiking from the western Waianae coast or Mokuleia on the North Shore—is fertile viewing grounds for tropical birds, native vegetation and, if you're lucky, the occasional monk seal. The point is about two and a half miles from the ends of both the Farrington Highway and Route 930 in Mokuleia. The hikes aren't difficult but bring water to counter the heat.

Hawaiian Waters Adventure Park, on 29 acres in arid west Oahu, is attracting even resolute beachgoers. The park, (808) 945-3928, with inner-tube slides, a 60-foot water slide and artificial waves on a sandless beach, is 35 minutes from Waikiki, at 400 Farrington Highway in Kapolei, Exit 1 on the H-1 Freeway heading west. Admission is $30 for adults, $20 for ages 4 to 11 and $10 for 60 and older.

where to stay

BUDGET: Starbucks and Kenneth Cole are next to the lobby of the Outrigger Islander Waikiki, 270 Lewers Street, (800) 688-7444, fax (808) 924-5755, in a busy area only five minutes from the beach. The 287-room hotel is convenient for those who want to stay in the thick of shopping and night life. Doubles cost $159 to $179.

The open-air lobby, lava-rock walls and luxuriant tropical foliage of the Hawaiiana Hotel, (808) 923-3811, fax (808) 926-5728, are a testament to the best features of pre-resort Hawaii. On a side street at 260 Beachwalk Avenue, about a five-minute walk from the beach, this Waikiki treasure was built in 1956, as was the koa table in the lobby. Trade winds carry the scent of plumerias across the two pools. There are 93 rooms with kitchenettes in two walk-up buildings. Rates, at $85 to $190, are less than they were in 1994, and there are discounts for weekly rentals. Renovations have added fresh carpets, upholstery and bedding in some suites.

MODERATE: In Waikiki, the Royal Garden Hotel, 440 Olohana Street, (800) 367-5666, fax (808) 946-8777, is a marvel of marble inside and out. It's a 15-minute walk from Waikiki Beach. Two good restaurants, two attractive pools, foliage and 220 tastefully decorated (though not spacious) rooms are among its attractions. Doubles: $130 to $600.

LUXURY: The Halekulani, 2199 Kalia Road, Honolulu, (800) 367-2343, fax (808) 926-8004, remains the darling of Honolulu, unfailingly gracious in its attention to detail. In plush rooms with lanais, three phones and all the comforts (an individual toaster is supplied with room service), you can see Diamond Head even from the bathtub in some of the 456 units. The House Without a Key, the hotel's informal outdoor cafe, is the favorite place for sunset Mai Tais and hula under a 100-year-old kiawe tree. It also has two swank oceanfront restaurants, Orchids and La Mer. Rates: $310 and up.

Five miles from Waikiki, in an upscale residential area, the Kahala Mandarin, 5000 Kahala Avenue, Honolulu, (800) 367-2525, fax (808) 739-8800, is away from the crowds of Waikiki, with hotel balconies that look over the mountains, golf course or the ocean, and tasteful rooms with grass-cloth walls and four-poster beds. Some of the 371 rooms look over a lagoon where dolphins leap and spin. Rates: $295 and up.

where to eat

George Mavrothalassitis, formerly of Halekulani's La Mer and Seasons at the Four Seasons Resort Wailea, opened his own restaurant, Chef Mavro, (808) 944-4714, and immediately became a culinary star of Honolulu. The restaurant, at 1969 South King Street near Waikiki, is elegant and welcoming, with three-tiered prix fixe menus with or without wine pairings. Mr. Mavrothalassitis produces such wonders as ahi tartare with caviar, and onaga (red snapper) baked in Hawaiian-salt crust, served in a subtle seaweed infusion. Prix fixe menus cost $48, $59 and $79 without wine; the four-course menu with wine is $77. Closed Monday.

On the western edge of Waikiki in the Doubletree Alana Waikiki Hotel, 1956 Ala Moana Boulevard, (808) 946-3456, Padovani's Bistro and Wine Bar has a dress code, a French-Mediterranean menu, bamboo floor, Frette table linens and Riedel stemware. Philippe Padovani's sautéed fresh shrimp with mushroom polenta, clam-corn chowder with ogo (local seaweed), and Hawaiian chocolate desserts are among the offerings. Upstairs, the wine bar serves 48 wines by the glass (the cellar has over 500 labels). Dinner for two with wine is about $160; prix fixe menus, $45 and $85 a person.

In contrast to the hushed tones of Padovani's, Alan Wong's Restaurant, on the fifth floor at 1857 South King Street, (808) 949-2526, is a lively, informal dining room marked by elegant culinary touches. Dine next to an open kitchen, or in a glassed-in terrace with mountain and street views. Specials include the famous ahi cake and warm California roll made of warm Kona lobster instead of rice. Mr. Wong should get a medal for his rose apple sorbet. Dinner for two with wine: $130 to $170.

Across town, in Kahala, the Olive Tree Cafe, (808) 737-0303, claims a covey of regulars for its Greek and Mediterranean fare. Order at the counter (no reservations or written menu) near the tiny open kitchen and sit at a table indoors or out. Savas Mojarrad's offerings include excellent marinated mussels, hummus and fresh fish souvlakis in a yogurt-dill sauce. Seven different spices form the secret of the syrup for the baklava, ambrosial and light as air. Dinner for two: about $25, plus whatever bottle of wine you bring.

For shrimp scampi in very casual surroundings, head for the North Shore and the graffiti-covered Giovanni's Aloha Shrimp Truck, (808) 293-1839. Parked on the Kamehaneha Highway next to the sugar mill in Kahuku, about an hour's drive from Waikiki, Giovanni's serves grilled shrimp, shrimp scampi and hot-and-spicy shrimp. Shaded by a tarp, the plastic tables have plumeria center-pieces. All dishes cost $11.

vital statistics

POPULATION (1998 estimate): City 395,789; Metro area 872,478

HOTEL: Room for one with tax $129.50

DINNER FOR ONE: With tax and tip but not drinks $30.85

TAXI (rates may vary by company): Upon entry $2.00; Each additional mile $2.00; From the airport $22.00

CAR RENTAL FOR A DAY: Midsize car with unlimited free mileage $41.00

FOR MORE INFORMATION: Telephone: (800) 464-2924; Web: www.gohawaii.com

Sources: Runzheimer International, U.S. Census Bureau, local businesses

Houston

Get off the highways and you'll find world-class arts institutions

JIM YARDLEY

Jim Yardley is chief of *The Times*'s Houston bureau.

Famous as a city without zoning, Houston is a sprawling metropolis, laced with highways as serpentine as ant tunnels, a place so vast that popular myth holds that a motorist can drive for an hour at 55 miles an hour and never get from one end of the city to the other.

Is it true? Probably not. But the city's sprawl tends to obscure just how much is actually going on there. Houstonians will have you know it's a pretty cool town. An array of world-class fine arts institutions is clustered in the city's oak-lined Museum District, and a revived downtown cultural and restaurant district is a short walk from the new high-tech, old-style ballpark of the Houston Astros, Enron Field. There is great theater and the highly regarded Houston Ballet at the Wortham Center, Texas at Smith Street, (713) 523-6300. Houstonians love to eat out, and the restaurant scene ranges from fine Vietnamese food to Texas barbecue.

There are green, lush neighborhoods and fine parks for walking. And there is shopping, most famously in the Galleria area. But the real attraction is the people, a big-talking, big-hearted bunch who have managed to ignore a hot, sticky climate and build the fourth-largest city in the country.

best of times

The best time to visit Houston is anytime but summer, which stretches from June through September. Then the heat and humidity give way to mild temperatures and clear skies as the rest of the country is gripped by winter. It is sweet revenge.

One of the best annual attractions is the Houston International Festival, a funky street festival in April that celebrates world culture with hundreds of concerts and an array of food and shopping booths. The highlight is the Art Car Parade, in which scores of cars transformed into zany works of art meander through downtown, competing for prizes.

For gardening enthusiasts interested in touring some of the biggest mansions in Texas, the city's prestigious River Oaks neighborhood opens its gates for a springtime blizzard of red, pink and white azaleas in the annual Azalea Trail. Included in the tour is Bayou Bend, the mansion and gardens of legendary Houston philanthropist Ima Hogg.

Winter is a great time for art lovers to tour the Museum District. Anyone in town for the holiday season should visit the historic old Heights neighborhood for "Lights in the Heights," when Victorian houses are festooned with decorations and lights. And for lovers of hot blues and hot weather, the Juneteenth Blues Festival is one of the premier showcases for rural and urban blues.

what to see

Opened in 1965, the Houston Astrodome, the world's first indoor baseball and football stadium, was once considered the Eighth Wonder of the World, but now it is almost empty. For anyone interested in examining one of the emblems of its era, the Dome, on Kirby off the intersection with Loop 610, is worth a tour ($4).

Enron Field, the new home of the Houston Astros, signals not only the return of baseball but, city leaders hope, a rebirth of the city center. With a retractable roof, a grass field and a design inspired by old ballparks, Enron should appeal to traditionalists turned off by the Astrodome. Yet on those unbearably hot days and nights, the team can close the roof and turn on the air-conditioning. Tickets: $5 to $29, (713) 627-8767.

The city's other great shrine of the 1960's is far from obsolete. Space Center Houston, 1601 NASA Road One, is about 25 miles southeast of the city off I-45. With 200,000 square feet devoted to NASA and the history of space travel, the Space Center lets visitors pull on space helmets, touch moon rocks and pretend, through computer simulation, to retrieve a satellite. There are Mercury, Gemini and Apollo capsules and daily IMAX films. Open 10 a.m. to 5 p.m. weekdays, to 7 p.m. weekends. Admission: $13.95, $9.95 ages 4 to 11; (800) 972-0369.

One of the city's most popular attractions is the Houston Museum of Natural Science, 1 Hermann Circle Drive, particularly its arching Cockrell Butterfly Center. Admission, $4; (713) 639-4629.

With the spring 2000 opening of its new Audrey Jones Beck Building, the Museum of Fine Arts, 1001 Bissonnet, vaulted from the 30th-largest museum in the country to the sixth. Tickets are $5; (713) 639-7300. Open Tuesday, Wednesday and Saturday 10 a.m. to 7 p.m.; Thursday and Friday, 10 a.m. to 9 p.m.; Sunday, 12:15 to 7 p.m. The Contemporary Arts Museum, 5216 Montrose Boulevard, (713) 284-8250, is open Tuesday to Saturday, 10 a.m. to 5 p.m.; Thursday, 10 a.m. to 9 p.m.; Sunday, noon to 5 p.m. Free.

The Holocaust Museum Houston, 5401 Caroline Street, (713) 942-8000, covers Jewish life in Europe from Hitler's rise to the liberation, and includes a film of survivors in the Houston area recalling their Holocaust experiences. The smokestack-shaped building was designed by Ralph Appelbaum, who did the Holocaust Museum in Washington. Hours: Monday to Friday, 9 a.m. to 5 p.m.; Saturday and Sunday, noon to 5 p.m.; free.

The Menil Collection, at 1515 Sul Ross, occupying a gray clapboard building designed by Renzo Piano, is considered one of the world's leading private fine arts institutions, with a highly regarded permanent collection, particularly strong in Byzantine, African, Surrealist and contemporary art. Free. Information: (713) 525-9400.

For a day trip, head south along I-45 and within an hour you will hit Galveston and the Gulf of Mexico. There are miles of beaches, the historic downtown Strand (a Texas-style slice of New Orleans with restaurants, shops and nightclubs) and lovely Victorian neighborhoods. Or drive northwest an hour to mall towns like Brenham and get a taste of the bluebonnet season, when wildflowers fill the pastures. The flowers are best until the beginning of May. For more information, contact the Greater Houston Convention and Visitors Bureau, 901 Bagby, Houston, Texas 77002; (800) 446-8786.

where to stay

BUDGET: Near the Museum District and Rice University, the 284-room Holiday Inn Hotel and Suites, 6800 Main Street, offers suites from $89 to $149 on weekdays, $59 to $130 on weekends; (713) 528-7744, fax (713) 528-6983.

MODERATE: In the center of the Museum District, the Warwick Hotel, 5701 Main Street, with 308 rooms decorated in a traditional style, recently completed a major renovation and expansion that includes a new patio and restaurant facing the Museum of Fine Arts. Doubles are $159 to $259 on weekdays, $129 on weekends; (800) 670-7275, fax (713) 526-0359.

LUXURY: Downtown, the 399-room Four Seasons, 1300 Lamar, is one of the city's most elegant and most expensive establishments. Recently renovated in a traditional European style, the hotel has a heated outdoor pool, a newly refurbished health club, a whirlpool and a gift shop. Doubles are $315 on weekdays, $155 and up on weekends; (713) 650-1300, fax (713) 652-6220. A short walk from Enron Field.

Another downtown possibility, the 350-room Doubletree Hotel, 400 Dallas at Bagby, (713) 759-0202, fax (713) 752-2734, is less expensive than the Four Seasons but still very nice. Doubles are $195 on weekdays and $119 on weekends.

Tucked beside Memorial Park and set on 18 wooded and landscaped acres, the Houstonian Hotel Club and Spa, 111 North Post Oak Lane, (800) 231-2759, fax (713) 680-2992, was once the official address of former President George Bush. In the style of a Texas hunting lodge, with a 30-foot fireplace, the hotel is decorated in rich earth tones and tapestry fabrics. It has a Mediterranean-style restaurant. The day spa is very popular. Doubles: $229 on weekdays, $139 to $179 on weekends.

where to eat

Many of the best restaurants in Houston are in the Montrose area, including several clustered along Montrose Boulevard near the Museum District. Neither overly fancy nor overly casual, Boulevard Bistrot, 4319 Montrose, (713) 524-6922, attracts artists, society types and just about everybody else with its eclectic menu. The pistachio-crusted salmon filet is superb; the walnut and sage polenta stack with a portobello mushroom and oven-roasted tomato is a delicious appetizer. Dinner for two with wine: about $80.

Nearby, the Sierra Grill, 4704 Montrose, (713) 942-7757, offers entrees ranging from a lime jalapeño pasta with grilled shrimp to an Australian rock lobster to Sonoma Liberty duck with seared foie gras and red wine sauce. The split-level dining room with antique wood tables is decorated in a Southwestern motif. Dinner for two with wine: about $100.

One of Houston's most popular Vietnamese restaurants is Kim Son, 2001 Jefferson, (713) 222-2461, with a large, no-nonsense dining room and an enormous menu that includes Vietnamese fajitas, black pepper crab and some of the best spring rolls in town. Open Sunday to Thursday until midnight, Friday and Saturday till 3 a.m. Lunch for two: about $25; dinner for two with drinks: $35.

For terrific authentic Mexican in a casual setting, try El Tiempo, 3130 Richmond, (713) 807-1600, specializing in mesquite-grilled chicken, beef and pork in fajitas and carnitas, as well as lobster tails, jumbo shrimp, quail and baby back ribs. Dinner for two with drinks: about $55.

There is great barbecue all over town. Here are three choices: Luling City Market Bar-B-Q Restaurant and Bar, 4726 Richmond, (713) 871-1903; Pizzitola's Bar-B-Cue, 1703 Shepherd, (713) 227-2283; and Goode Company Barbeque, 5109 Kirby, (713) 522-2530. At all three, dinner for two with beers is about $25.

vital statistics

POPULATION (1998 estimate): City 1,786,691; Metro area 3,931,688

HOTEL: Room for one with tax $178.50

DINNER FOR ONE: With tax and tip but not drinks $30.25

TAXI: Upon entry $1.50; Each additional mile $1.50; From the airport $32.00

CAR RENTAL FOR A DAY: Midsize car with unlimited free mileage $81.00

FOR MORE INFORMATION: Telephone: (800) 446-8786; Web: www.houston-guide.com

Sources: Runzheimer International, U.S. Census Bureau, local businesses

Indianapolis

With a long tradition of thrift, it finds
plenty of new uses for its old buildings

DOUGLAS WISSING

Douglas Wissing is a writer and consultant in Bloomington, Indiana

When 19th-century German immigrants joined the Southern Uplanders and flinty New Englanders already on the prairie at Indianapolis, the city's thrifty, conservative character was forged. Hoosiers still tend to make do and reuse, gently stitching new ideas onto old.

The architecture of downtown Indianapolis today is like a Hoosier quilt, with pieces of the old backed by brand-new fabric. Even the heralded Conseco Fieldhouse, home of the National Basketball Association Indiana Pacers, harks back to 1920's high school gyms—a retro temple to basketball, comfortable as an old sock with warm brick and tiled walls, and girders and trusses that cast nostalgic shadows across the crowd. But with comfortable seating, great sight lines and globally influenced food, from smoked salmon martinis to Thai coconut-marinated pork with peanut sauce, the fieldhouse, between Delaware and Pennsylvania Streets at Georgia Street, epitomizes today's fast-paced, affluent Indy.

In the mid-1970's, civic leaders determined to remake the city, using amateur sports as a tool. Since then Indianapolis has invested

$400 million in athletic facilities, attracting millions of people to a pulsing downtown now filled with bars, restaurants and theaters.

best of times

Auto racing and basketball put Indianapolis on the map and continue to do so. Each Memorial Day weekend the Indianapolis Motor Speedway thunders with the sound of the Indianapolis 500. Since 1994 the Speedway also has been host to the Brickyard 400 Nascar Winston Cup race in early August, the first major racing event other than the Indy 500 at the Speedway since 1911. And now the only Formula One race in the United States, the SAP United States Grand Prix, winds through a new track on the Speedway grounds, bringing Indy a touch of continental sporting sophistication. Contact (317) 484-6700; www.indy500.com.

As the crocuses push through the rime of early springtime, Indiana is deep in basketball frenzy, and Indianapolis is clearly roundball crazy too. The venerable Hinkle Fieldhouse, site of tiny Milan's fabled 1954 state championship that inspired the movie *Hoosiers,* resounds to the Girls High School State Basketball Finals in early March. The Boys High School State Basketball Finals erupts in late March at the Conseco Fieldhouse. Information: (317) 846-6601. The Indiana Pacers also play at the Conseco Fieldhouse. Call (317) 239-5151 for tickets.

With lavish corporate and community support, the initial 1999 Indy Jazz Festival became an instant success. The 2000 festival, held on the third weekend of June, featured more than 90 jazz, blues, funk, soul and gospel artists. Information at (800) 983-4639, www.indyjazzfest.org

The Indiana State Fair in mid-August is the quintessential Indiana experience, a carnival of Hoosierness with midway rides, country music, and blue-ribbon livestock and foods. Contact (317) 927-7500.

what to see

Monument Circle is the axis of downtown, as it has been since 1902 when the Soldiers' and Sailors' Monument was built. On the east and west sides of the monument, fountains cascade from two huge statuary groups, representing war and peace. The five-block stretch of Meridian north of the circle introduces the visitor to one of Indiana's great exports: Bedford limestone. Many of the big downtown buildings are faced with this stone—as are the Empire State Building, Rockefeller Center and a good part of prewar midtown Manhattan. The Meridian corridor's monumental structures include the Indiana War Memorial Plaza between Michigan and Vermont Streets and, at No. 650, the mammoth Scottish Rite Cathedral.

Nearby, at 450 West Ohio Street, (317) 232-1882, the Indiana Historical Society contains exhibits on Indian culture and famous Midwesterners like Amelia Earhart, Abraham Lincoln and Eugene Debs. A jukebox in the Cole Porter Room offers music from Indiana songwriters Porter, Hoagy Carmichael, Michael Jackson and John Mellencamp. Closed Monday; free.

In March 2000, the National Collegiate Athletic Association National Headquarters, part of the White River State Park at 700 West Washington Street, (317) 917-6222, opened its interactive Hall of Champions, a Michael Graves-designed tribute to the champions in 22 sports from fencing to football. Tickets are $7 for adults, $5 ages 3 to 11.

The Medal of Honor Memorial is made up of 27 curving glass walls 7 to 10 feet high meandering along the Central Canal's north bank in White River Park. The walls are etched with the names and branches of service of the nation's 3,432 medal recipients, and details of their heroism.

The Indiana Repertory Theater performs in the majestic 1927 Spanish-Baroque Indiana Theater at 140 West Washington Street; (317) 635-5252. The Indianapolis Symphony Orchestra is the headline tenant in the ornate Hilbert Circle Theater, 45 Monument Circle; (317) 639-4300.

At the Indianapolis Museum of Art, 1200 West 38th Street, (317) 923-1331, you will find the largest collection of Turner watercolors and drawings outside Britain, and fine Neo-Impressionist, Chinese and Japanese collections. Admission is free.

An adobe Southwestern-style building at 500 West Washington Street houses the Eiteljorg Museum of the American Indian and Western Art, (317) 636-9378, with works by Western artists like Georgia O'Keeffe and Frederic Remington, and a collection of Indian artifacts. Closed Monday. Admission: $5 for adults, $2 for students and children.

Broad Ripple is a small canal-side neighborhood north of downtown, where the cozy streets are lined with boutiques, cafes and nightspots. Young hipsters crowd the Eden dance club, 6235 North Guilford Avenue, (317) 475-1588 (cover charge $2 to $3) and the Patio, 6308 Guilford, (317) 253-0799 ($2 to $4). The Vogue, 6259 North College Avenue, (317) 255-2828, is the grand-daddy of Broad Ripple's music scene and draws graying boomers along with young folk; admission: from frcc to $20. Thc funky Alley Cat Lounge, 6267 Carrollton Avenue, (317) 257-4036, is a late-night warren with a good jukebox and pool tables.

The Indianapolis Motor Speedway, West 16th Street and Georgetown Road, (317) 484-6747, claims to be the capital of auto racing, and few would argue. The museum contains several winning cars from the Indy 500, including the first from 1911, and a sparkling collection of pre-World War II racing trophies from Europe. Open 9 a.m. to 5 p.m.; $3.

where to stay

BUDGET: Two hotels are generic plain-vanilla, though fairly new and clean. The 80-suite Ramada Limited Waterbury Hotel, 108 North Pennsylvania Street, (317) 614-1400, fax (317) 614-1401, is in the historic Fletcher Trust building. Suites are $79, including Continental breakfast.

The other, the Hampton Inn Downtown, 105 South Meridian Street, (317) 261-1200, fax (317) 916-1985, offers 180 rooms near the Circle Centre mall. Rates: $99 to $119.

MODERATE: Two bed-and-breakfasts in the Victorian Old Northside neighborhood evoke an Indiana of long ago. The Stone Soup Inn, 1304 North Capitol Avenue, (317) 639-9550, is a rambling Colonial Revival structure with a trove of Mission-style decorative arts. The seven rooms range from $75 to $125.

The neighboring Looking Glass Inn, 1319 North New Jersey Street, (317) 635-8832, is more formal, with Victorian and Empire furnishings. The six rooms are $95 to $125.

LUXURY: Europe comes to the Midwest at the 99-room Canterbury Hotel, 123 South Illinois Street, (800) 538-8186, fax (317) 685-2519, a favorite of visiting celebrities and a warm refuge of French and English-style furnishings, with white-on-white damask wall coverings. Rooms are $155 to $175.

The Westin Indianapolis, 50 South Capitol Avenue, (317) 262-8100, fax (317) 231-3928, is a sprawling 573-room hotel noted for its service. Many rooms offer views of downtown, and wound-up sports fans can unwind at the fitness center with pool, workout equipment and whirlpool. Doubles: $259.

where to eat

St. Elmo Steak House, 127 South Illinois Street, (317) 635-0636, began serving steaks in 1902. The place was redone in 1996, but the original tin ceilings and thrum and clatter of happy diners remain. The meat may be a touch less tender than in the old days (filet mignon remains the most reliable cut), but the tuxedoed staff still sets the standard for service. The shrimp cocktail is legendary for the tear-producing sauce made with fresh horseradish. Dinner for two with wine: about $150.

Four generations of Hoosiers have sat at the Formica tables at Shapiro's Delicatessen Cafeteria, 808 South Meridian Street, (317) 631-4041, for the mountainous corned beef and pastrami sandwiches—which, with drinks and the fabled desserts, will cost under $30 for two.

The Rathskeller, 401 East Michigan Street, (317) 630-4569, open since 1898, is one of Indianapolis's oldest restaurants. Muse on Indiana's German heritage while supping on Jaeger schnitzel (breaded pork loin with a wild mushroom sauce) and fishbowls of beer. Kurt Vonnegut's grandfather designed the looming German-Austrian Hapsburg-style building. Dinner for two with beer and dessert is a bargain at $50.

Something Different, 4939 East 82nd Street, (317) 570-7700, is a New American restaurant in a contemporary setting. Dishes like fig maple glazed venison loin with a morel flan, chestnut pesto and choucroute are well prepared. The wine list contains several fine values. Dinner for two with wine and dessert is $150.

You may feel as if you're in an episode of *Father Knows Best* at Hollyhock Hill, 8110 North College Avenue, (317) 251-2294, where families congregate for superb fried chicken and mashed potatoes with milk gravy in a soothing urban setting of the early 1960's, with murals of hollyhocks and crisp white trellises. Tabs for two seldom reach $60.

At the 1928 Fountain Square Theater, 1105 Prospect Street, (317) 686-6010, the old-time soda fountain looks as if Ricky Nelson could show up at any moment. It has duck pin bowling for $18 an hour. The Fountain Room jumps to rockabilly ($4 to $6 cover charge), and a Fountain Burger Deluxe is $4.50. The ballroom offers Friday-night swing dances ($7).

vital statistics

POPULATION (1998 estimate): City 741,304; Metro area 1,519,194

HOTEL: Room for one with tax $149.50

DINNER FOR ONE: With tax and tip but not drinks $22.05

TAXI: Upon entry $1.25; Each additional mile $2.00; From the airport $18.00

CAR RENTAL FOR A DAY: Midsize car with unlimited free mileage $64.50

FOR MORE INFORMATION: Telephone: (800) 323-4639; Web: www.indy.org

Sources: Runzheimer International, U.S. Census Bureau, local businesses

Istanbul

Legendary sights live up to their hype,
but the quiet little districts fascinate, too

Hagia Sophia,
Istanbul

STEPHEN KINZER

Stephen Kinzer is a former chief of the Istanbul bureau of *The Times.*

This is the city of sultans and harems, long the seat of an immense empire, described over the centuries as the pole to which the world turns, the envy of kings, city of the world's desire. In one tribute, the Ottoman poet Nedim wrote: "O city of Istanbul, priceless and peerless! I would sacrifice all Persia for one of your stones!"

Dozens of guidebooks catalog the splendid palaces, mosques, museums and countless other wonders that evoke the glories of the Byzantine and Ottoman Empires. Istanbul's legendary attractions live up to their reputations. In front of imposing sites like the Topkapi Palace or Hagia Sophia are guides displaying government-issued licenses. Some of these guides are erudite historians who have quit low-paying jobs as university professors and now offer wonderfully insightful private tours.

But there is another side to Istanbul, one that many visitors miss. Although this is a huge city with more than 12 million residents, it is also a city of neighborhoods. Until as recently as half a century ago, the city that is now Istanbul was a series of self-enclosed quarters and villages, each with its own identity. As the city gobbled up these places, many of them lost their character. But more than a few retain some distinctive flair; they make wonderful places to explore.

best of times

The warm weather arrives early, and from April through October much public life is outdoors. This is the ideal time to discover marvelous old neighborhoods, take a boat ride along the Bosporus and dine under the warm sun or evanescent starlight.

Istanbul's status as the only city in the world that lies on two continents is more than simply a geographical curiosity. When the climate turns irresistible, as it does early each spring, visitors can pick almost any neighborhood, step out of a taxi and sense the extent to which this city combines the cosmopolitan flair of Western capitals with the exotic flavor of the East. It is overcrowded, noisy, unclean and chaotic, but highly dramatic and exciting.

what to see

The core of Istanbul may roughly be divided into four sections, each with its own personality and undiscovered neighborhoods. The oldest is Eminonu, the former Muslim quarter centered around major monuments like the Hagia Sophia, Blue Mosque and Topkapi Palace. Across the Galata Bridge from Eminonu is the city's most vibrant borough, the formerly Christian quarter now known as Beyoglu, much of which is in the midst of an exciting revival.

North of these areas lie the Bosporus villages to which wealthy Istanbul residents used to decamp in summer. Many of these villages still boast handsome wooden mansions called yalis that overlook the magnificent waterway. The fourth and perhaps least-visited section of Istanbul is the Asian side of the Bosporus, bursting with urban life and dotted with mosques, Ottoman pavilions and other jewels.

Be sure to take at least one stroll along Istiklal Caddesi, the pedestrian boulevard that runs through the heart of Beyolgu. Here you can eat cheaply at cafeteria-style Turkish restaurants, sip strong coffee in tradition-shrouded cafes, and buy porcelain and other handicrafts. When you arrive at the far end of the boulevard, near Tunel Square, walk another couple of blocks to the 650-year-old Galata Tower and climb to the top for one of the city's most spectacular views. Adjacent to Tunel Square, at 15 Galip Dede, is a 500-year-old monastery of the Mevlevi Brotherhood, known to Westerners as whirling dervishes. The dancers perform their entrancing ritual for the public on the last Sunday of each month at 3 p.m. Admission is $4.75; (90-212) 245-4141.

One of my favorite neighborhoods is Asmalimescit (pronounced ahs-mal-eh-MEZ-jit), a postage-stamp piece of the sprawling Beyoglu borough. It is within walking distance of the Galata Tower. Asmalimescit fell into disrepair when Greeks and Jews who lived there left at midcentury, but it is being turned into a vibrant community by some of Turkey's leading artists. It has dozens of galleries and studios, along with cafes, restaurants and funky shops selling antiques, used books, maps and prints, photographs and even artifacts from Ottoman courts. To find it, start on Istiklal Caddesi, turn onto Asmali Mescit Sokak and then onto Sofyali Sokak, the quarter's main street.

On the Asian side of the Bosporus, Uskudar is famous for its mosques, and Kadikoy is a colorful mix of shops, markets and faces. The Asian side is best reached by ferries that leave from docks called Eminonu Iskele and Besiktas Iskele.

Many visitors overlook the splendid 14th-century frescoes and mosaics at the Church of St. Savior in Chora, now the Kariye Museum, on Kariye Camii Sokak in the Edirnekapi section. This ensemble of Byzantine works, depicting scenes from the Bible and the life of Jesus, is among the world's finest. Open 9:30 a.m. to 4:30 p.m. except Wednesday; $3.35.

Few tourists miss the Topkapi, but not all realize that Istanbul's Archaeological Museum, which is predictably full of delights, is on the same site. Among its treasures is the magnificent late-fourth-century Alexander Sarcophagus, depicting the victory of Alexander the Great over the Persians. It is open daily except Monday, 9:30 a.m. to 4:30 p.m.; (90-212) 520-7740. Admission: $4.85.

Istanbul's music scene has become sophisticated. The AFM Kerem Gorsev Jazz Bar is at 61 Abdi Ipekci Caddesi, wedged into a neighborhood of trendy cafes, restaurants and boutiques in Nisantasi, not far from Taksim Square. It is run by Mr. Gorsev, a gifted jazz pianist. Cover charge is $15 standing, $19 seated. Music starts at 10:30 p.m. weekdays, 11 p.m. weekends, reservations advisable; (90-212) 231-3950.

In Asmalimescit, the artistic quarter, a club called Babylon, at 3 Seyhbender Sokak, (90-212) 292-7367 or 252-5167, features top-quality music from Turkey and abroad. Shows start around 9:30 p.m. on weekdays, 11 p.m. on weekends; $9 to $15.

where to stay

BUDGET: Good choices close to Beyoglu include the 85-room Bristol, (90-212) 251-3855, fax (90-212) 252-6117, where doubles are $60; and the 84-room Grand Hotel Halic, (90-212) 252-6980, fax (90-212) 249-7066, with its own Turkish bath. Doubles: $70.

MODERATE: Kybele, 35 Yerebetan Caddesi, (90-212) 511-7766, fax (90-212) 513-4393, close to major sights, is a lovely 16-room inn with rich carpets, framed calligraphy and hanging lamps. Doubles: $75.

The Merit Antique, 226 Ordu Caddesi, (90-212) 513-9300, fax (90-212) 512-6390, is in the Laleli district of Eminonu, across from the imposing Laleli Mosque. It has 274 modern rooms, a pool and a health club, and may be the only hotel in the world with Chinese, Turkish and kosher restaurants. Rates: $125.

Adjacent to the Asmalimescit quarter is the Richmond Hotel, 445 Istiklal Caddesi, (90-212) 252-5460, fax (90-212) 252-9707, with 106 modern rooms and a new restaurant with Bosporus views. Doubles: $190.

LUXURY: Of the dozen first-class hotels in Istanbul, the two best-loved are probably the 315-room Ciragan Palace Kempinski on the shore of the Bosporus far from the center, and the Four Seasons, with 65 rooms in the old city by the Hagia Sophia. The Ciragan Palace, 84 Ciragan Caddesi, (90-212) 258-3377, fax (90-212) 259-6686, has rooms with Bosporus views from $420, lower in winter. The Four Seasons, 1 Tevkifhane Sokak, (90-212) 638-8200, fax (90-121) 638-8210, has reduced winter rates through March, with doubles from $250.

where to eat

No one can claim to have dined like a Turk without spending at least one evening in a meyhane, a traditional drinking house. At meyhanes one normally does not order a main course but works through an intimidating variety of mezes—appetizers that range from cheeses and salads to bubbling stews cooked in small earthenware pots. Everything is washed down with raki, the potent anise-flavored national drink. One popular meyhane is Yakup 2, 35 Asmalimescit in Beyoglu, (90-212) 249-2925, which serves some of the best boreks—rolled pancakes stuffed with cheese, spinach and other delicacies. Two people can stuff and intoxicate themselves at such places for around $40.

Around the corner from Yakup, the Refik restaurant, 10 Sofyali Sokak, (90-212) 243-2834, is an institution. The portly white-haired gentleman who sits outside in the summer and just inside the door in winter is Refik himself, the quarter's unofficial mayor. You can feast on small plates of cold vegetables (eggplant and stuffed cabbage are especially popular), then move on to grilled lamb or fish. Dinner for two with raki: about $45.

For first-class kebabs and fresh salads, try Tike, at 1 Haci Adil Caddesi in Levent, 4 Aralik in Second Levent, a residential area above the European side of the Bosporus, (90-212) 284-8479. It is a fine grill house built around a garden in a renovated villa. Dinner for two with wine is about $60.

Istanbul is a fish lover's paradise, and several of its neighborhoods, like Yesilkoy, are known for their concentrations of fine seafood restaurants. The best place in Yesilkoy for both fresh fish and lively atmosphere is Hasan Balikcilar, 8 Rihtim Sokak. Reservations necessary; call (90-212) 573-8300. Point to the fish you want, or ask your waiter to send over what's best that day. Dinner for two with wine or raki is $75.

Turkish cuisine at bargain prices is the attraction at Tarihi Sultanahmet Koftecisi, at 12A Divanyolu Caddesi, (90-212) 513-1438. It is small and bustling. A family of four can feast on thick soup, koftes (minced and grilled lamb), salad and helva, a sweet dessert made from semolina, for $18.

For adventurous eaters, Sayan, at Yildiz Posta Caddesi, 46-47 Ayyildiz Sitesi in Esentepe, (90-212) 211-3089, is open 24 hours a day. Kebabs are on the menu, but why bother with pedestrian fare when you can have cow's stomach soup, sheep's intestines or—my favorite—sheep's head soup, complete with head. A meal for two (no alcohol served) is $18.

vital statistics

POPULATION (1999 estimate): City 12,000,000

HOTEL: Room for one with tax $209.00

DINNER FOR ONE: With tax and tip but not drinks $22.55

TAXI: Upon entry 60 cents; Each additional kilometer 50 cents; From the airport to Taksim $12.00; From the airport to Sultanahmet $10.00

CAR RENTAL FOR A DAY: Midsize car with unlimited free mileage $71.00

FOR MORE INFORMATION: Telephone: (90-212) 293-8619; Web: www.tourism.gov.tr

Sources: Runzheimer International, Turkish Government Tourist Office, local businesses

Jerusalem

Jews, Christians and Muslims coexist in a stunning setting

DEBORAH SONTAG

Deborah Sontag is the chief of the Jerusalem bureau of *The Times*.

The typical tourists in Jerusalem fill their days with official sites because, from the Yad Vashem Holocaust memorial to the al-Aksa Mosque, there is so much history to be seen. But the real, throbbing, conflicted city often gets overlooked.

Jerusalemites like to appreciate their hilltop city in two ways: by rising above it, in the perpetual search for the best view, and by plunging deep inside its diverse neighborhoods. To listen to locals describe the special light of the city as it glances off the white stone buildings is to hear a rhapsody of affection; to watch them argue city politics over a pile of figs in the marketplace is to see a different, more complicated kind of passion.

Perhaps the most engaging way to stand above the city and at the same time explore the line between East and West, ancient and modern, is to walk the turreted ramparts of the Old City's walls. They offer both panoramic vistas and glimpses into the private workaday world within.

Stand at the Damascus Gate, above the market where old women sell bunches of mint, and work your way around. From within the Old City, it is hard sometimes to see beyond the tourist stalls and the pesky, would-be guides. But when, from the walkway, you peer inside at the strings of laundry hanging like necklaces between satellite dishes, you realize that this is a small, teeming metropolis—40,000 people, Jews, Christians and Muslims, packed together, a unique social experiment in a stunning setting.

best of times

Winters, from November to March, are cool and damp, with occasionally warm and brilliant days. Locals find the winter clouds a relief from the unrelentingly blue skies of the summer season that builds to a crescendo of glaring sun and intense heat in July and August. Jerusalem, while very hot and dry during the summer days, is high enough to cool down at night. Weather-wise, April and May are the nicest months, warm and green and wildflowery.

Since all three Abrahamic faiths claim the city as holy, religious holidays shape Jerusalem's calendar, from Rosh Hashanah to Ramadan to Easter. On major Jewish holidays, public transportation shuts down, as do all stores and most restaurants.

Secular holidays include Holocaust Memorial Day, Fallen Soldiers Memorial Day and Independence Day, all in the spring. Late spring and early summer bring two cultural highlights, the Israel Festival of the Performing Arts, which is nationwide, and the International Film Festival at the Cinémathèque in Jerusalem, (972-2) 672-4131.

In late July, international crafts are on display at the Arts and Crafts Festival in the Sultan's Pool. Leading musicians from around the world play at the International Chamber Music Festival in September.

what to see

After walking on the walls of the Old City (the fee is $3), try plunging beneath. The tunnels under the Western Wall can be toured with a guide. The tour, winding through ancient aqueducts and quarries, explores the underground remains of the Temple Mount, as excavated so far. Call (972-2) 627-1333 to reserve; English tours ($4) are usually at 2 p.m.

Emerging from down below, you are at the Western Wall, a moving religious experience for some and for others a fascinating glimpse of the ultra-Orthodox in swaying prayer—or, on the Sabbath, in joyful song and dance.

There is almost too much to absorb in the Old City, not only the clash of different cultures—Armenian, Jewish, Christian and Muslim—but also of commerce and faith. On the Via Dolorosa, where you often see Christian pilgrims dragging a giant crucifix through the Stations of the Cross, you can also sample the most delicious hummus in the city. You can buy the latest Reeboks in the Muslim quarter, then ascend to the Dome of the Rock, where Islamic prayer and music mingle inside the gilded octagonal structure. The excellent Tower of David Museum, near the Jaffa Gate, (972-2) 626-5333, gives a great overview of Jerusalem's history, with artifacts, holograms, videos and dioramas. It is open Sunday to Thursday 10 a.m. to 5 p.m., Friday and Saturday until 2 p.m. Admission $6.20.

Try investigating neighborhoods, too. Wander the German Colony, near the railway station, with its boutiques, wine shops, art cinema and sushi bar, to get a taste of fairly affluent secular Jerusalem. Or venture, respectfully and modestly dressed, into Mea Shearim to see the modern-day version of an old shtetl. Walk up Agrippas Street to the Shuk, or Mahane Yehuda open-air market, where you can buy olives or apricots, or—in the wee hours— pub-hop in the Russian compound.

Keo, 25 Emek Refaim in the German Colony, sells delicate, modern hand-crafted jewelry ($20 to $75) by local artisans. In the Old City, at 14 Al-Khanka in the Christian Quarter, (972-2) 628-2074, Kevork Kahvedjian sells excellent old photographs ($20 each) taken by his father, Elia, during the British mandate days. Palestinian Pottery, 14 Nablus Road near Damascus Gate, (972-2) 628-2826, sells Armenian pottery (go figure) and brilliantly colored and whimsical tiles for $3 to $10 each.

where to stay

BUDGET: To stay inside the walls of the Old City at night is a real treat, and the 30-room Austrian Hospice, a hidden pearl at 37 Via Dolorosa, provides an inexpensive way to do so. Rooms are spare but nice, and each has a full bath. The garden is relaxing, and the chapel is beautiful. The rooftop offers a commanding panorama of Jerusalem. Double rooms, tax included, are $76; (972-2) 627-1466, fax (972-2) 627-1472.

MODERATE: The Y.M.C.A. soars above King David Street, and the lobby boasts vaulted ceilings with exquisite tiles and local woodwork. Its 56 guest rooms are small but attractive, more like a hotel than a hostel, and each has a private bath. There is also an indoor pool, outdoor running track and gym. Doubles with breakfast cost

$145 a night, including tax (pricey, but then so is Jerusalem); (972-2) 569-2692, fax (972-2) 623-5192.

The 217-room Prima Kings Hotel, at 60 King George Street, is very comfortable, with clean, standard, fully equipped rooms. Request one with a view; it will have a balcony facing south and will not cost extra. Doubles are $206 with breakfast; (972-2) 620-1201, fax (972-2) 620-1211.

LUXURY: The American Colony Hotel, 1 Nablus Road, East Jerusalem, (972-2) 627-9777, fax (972-2) 627-9779, is an elegant, genuinely Middle Eastern hotel. Its 84 rooms are a refuge from the bustle, but within walking distance of the Damascus Gate. A bar is set in romantically lighted gardens. Some rooms are modern, some "pasha style," appointed with antiques beneath a tiled, star-filled ceiling. There is a small, pleasant pool area. The loudspeaker of a neighboring mosque issues regular, loud calls to prayer. Doubles: from $212, including a lavish breakfast.

One of the newest luxury hotels in town is the 381-room Jerusalem Hilton, 7 King David Street; (972-2) 621-1111, fax (972-2) 621-1000. Rooms are sleek, ample and wonderfully suited for business travelers. Doubles: from $370, with breakfast.

where to eat

There is only a handful of fine restaurants in Jerusalem, but many pleasant ones in great settings, and some genuinely funky, dirt-cheap places in colorful neighborhoods.

Many consider Arcadia, in an alleyway off 10 Agrippas Street, (972-2) 624-9138, to be the city's all-around class dining establishment. Set in an elegant old stone house with courtyard, it offers inventive cuisine that makes good use of local ingredients. For starters, there's a pumpkin soup, delicately spiced with oranges, cinnamon and cayenne pepper, or a cold vegetable terrine that layers goat cheese with eggplant, dried tomatoes, grilled peppers and swiss chard; for entrees, red mullet filet on a bed of white beans; and for dessert, a fig tart filled with almond cream. Dinner for two with wine is $125.

Darna, 3 Horkenos Street, (972-2) 624-5406, is a strikingly beautiful Moroccan restaurant, and its ornate casbahlike décor, with materials and workers from Morocco, a former enemy of Israel, is a culinary dividend of the peace process. Costumed waiters offer gracious service to Western-style tables or low-slung banquettes piled with colorful pillows. The cuisine combines savory and sweet flavors. Specialties include the traditional pastilla, a flaky pastry filled with chicken and almonds, and tagines (stews) of meat, fish or chicken cooked with fruits or vegetables. Dinner for two with wine is $100; a sampling menu is $43 each.

From Cacao's, the restaurant at the Cinémathèque, 11 Hebron Road, (972-2) 671-0632, the views of the Old City walls are lovely. Salads, homemade pasta and salmon are prepared in many ways. Dinner for two with drinks is $37.

At 4 al-Zahara Street in East Jerusalem, the National Palace Hotel's rooftop restaurant serves excellent Middle Eastern food, from salads to shish kebabs. Expect to pay $34 for a complete meal for two, including soft drinks; (972-2) 627-3210.

Cap a stroll through Mea Shearim with a crispy ball of fried chickpeas at Shlomo Felafel, in the heart of the neighboring Bukharan Quarter on David Street. It is the oldest felafel stand in Jerusalem. The present proprietor is the third-generation Shlomo. He sells two balls for 25 cents; for splurgers, an oversized Iraqi-style pita with felafel, assorted salads and tehina sauce is $3.

Lina's, on the Via Dolorosa before the fifth Station of the Cross, qualifies as a hole-in-the-wall. But its hummus, at $1.75 to $2, is the best.

vital statistics

POPULATION (2000 estimate): City 700,000

HOTEL: Room for one with tax $196.00

DINNER FOR ONE: With tax and tip but not drinks $36.05

TAXI: Upon entry $1.90; Each additional kilometer 7 cents; From Ben-Gurion airport $40.00

CAR RENTAL FOR A DAY: Midsize car with 250 free kilometers $87.00

FOR MORE INFORMATION: Telephone: (972-2) 625-8844; Web: www.goisrael.com

Sources: Runzheimer International, Israel Ministry of Tourism, local businesses

Las Vegas
It never sleeps and never stops changing

BRETT PULLEY
Brett Pulley is a former national correspondent for *The Times*.

For the many people planning to visit Las Vegas since hearing that it had become family oriented, with plenty of affordable fun for the young and old, time may be running out. The place seems to be in a perpetual state of transformation, and the casino companies that built the amusement parks and Disneylike attractions in the early 1990's have now set their sights on more upscale tourists, building luxury hotels and casinos with couture shops and restaurants operated by world-renowned chefs.

Redefining itself is what keeps Las Vegas fresh and keeps people returning—especially with casino gambling available all around the country. From its gangster beginnings, to its martini-drenched Rat Pack age, its Elvis era, its Sin City days and its most recent family-friendly years, this other city that never sleeps also never stays the same.

The cheap buffets and modestly priced rooms are still here—as is the Liberace Museum—but the new Bellagio Hotel and Casino, which tries to combine high cost and high culture, may change all of that. With an estimated $300 million in paintings and sculptures on display at Bellagio, suddenly everyone's an art expert.

best of times

Las Vegas receives more than 33 million visitors each year, with enough indoor events to maintain a steady flow even during the 100-degree summer months.

The Las Vegas Convention Center, the largest single-level meeting facility in the United States, is home to the Antiques Roadshow in September and the Motor Trend International Auto Show in November.

Las Vegas is also home to two annual PGA Tours, the Invensys Classic in October and the Senior Classic in April. Call (702) 242-3000.

The Las Vegas Philharmonic, founded in 1999, now holds a Fourth of July concert at Hills Park, complete with fireworks.

The Bite of Las Vegas Food Festival is the city's largest annual food festival. It takes place at Lorenzi Park, just northwest of the strip, every October. Call (702) 451-0344.

The Las Vegas International Mariachi Festival, held annually in September since 1990, is now at Mandalay Bay and features more than three and a half hours of music. The show starts at 8 p.m. and costs between $35 and $75. Contact Mandalay Bay at (877) 632-7400.

what to see

Bellagio, at 3600 Las Vegas Boulevard South, is full of attractions. Outside it looks like an Italian village and has an eight-acre lake with more than 1,000 illuminated fountains. In the evening, the water jets up to 240 feet in the air, choreographed to popular music. The show is free and performed every half hour from 5 p.m. until midnight Sunday through Friday, and 2 p.m. to midnight on Saturday. Information: (702) 693-7111.

Inside the hotel is the Bellagio Gallery of Fine Art, with a small but blue-chip selection of works by Monet, Renoir, Picasso, van Gogh, Pollock and de Kooning, among others (the works can be purchased, so the lineup can change without notice). The gallery is open daily 9 a.m. to 11:30 p.m. (children are allowed from 9 to 11 a.m. only). Admission is $12, and includes a recorded tour. Information: (888) 488-7111. The wait to enter the gallery is made much more bearable by the fact that the line passes through a breathtaking conservatory and botanical garden. Lines are shortest later at night.

Another piece of Italy has come to the Strip. Afternoons and evenings at the Venetian, 3355 Las Vegas Boulevard South, the bell inside the 315-foot-high reproduction of the Campanile rings on the hour. A canal winds through the shopping mall, whose centerpiece is a reproduction of Renaissance-era St. Mark's Square, and for a fee visitors can ride with singing gondoliers. Along the streets, costumed characters like Napoleon, Casanova and Marco Polo will give live performances. The mall is open 10 a.m. to 11 p.m. Sunday to Thursday and till midnight Friday and Saturday; (702) 733-5000.

At the Mirage, 3400 Las Vegas Boulevard South, the Secret Garden of Siegfried & Roy is a little jewel of a zoo with the white tigers and lions that appear (and disappear) in the illusionists' show. The garden is very small, but the magnificent rare creatures seem content to wrestle in a desultory fashion and paddle in their pool. Behind the garden at the Dolphin Habitat (included in the $10 admission fee), cackling cetaceans toss a beach ball back and forth with visitors. Open 11 a.m. to 5:30 p.m. When the garden is closed, on Wednesday, admission to the Dolphin Habitat is $5.

The word "bizarre" has been applied to Las Vegas more than once. Now "bazaar" has entered the local lexicon, too, with the opening of Desert Passage, a shopping mall with a Middle Eastern theme. It is connected to the Aladdin Resort and Casino, Las Vegas's newest megaresort, which added 2,567 rooms to the city's inventory when it reopened on August 17, 2000, across Las Vegas Boulevard from Bellagio. The 130 stores and 14 restaurants are set amid Moorish archways, authentic antiques and other Moroccan décor, all of it aimed at making shoppers think they are strolling in the markets of Tangier, Fez and Marrakesh. The stores are open daily from 10 a.m. to midnight, although the restaurants and nightclubs will operate later.

To get back to reality, head 55 miles northeast of the city to the 35,000-acre Valley of Fire State Park. Open from sunrise to sunset, the early-morning and late-afternoon sunlight here intensifies the red of the sandstone formations. From Las Vegas, take I-15 north to Highway 169. Admission is $5 a car. Information: (702) 397-2088.

From the observation deck of Hoover Dam, about 25 miles south of Las Vegas on Highway 93-95, you can peer 700 feet down to the Colorado River. Tours (35 minutes) are conducted from 8 a.m. to 5:15 p.m. daily; $8 for adults, $7 ages 62 and up, and $2 for children 6 to 16. Information: (702) 293-8367.

where to stay

Room rates are unpredictable in Las Vegas. Trips organized at the last minute or during convention weekends usually aren't great deals.

BUDGET: The Quality Inn, 377 East Flamingo Road, (800) 634-6617, fax (702) 369-6911, is less than a mile from the Strip and has its own casino. All 318 rooms have wet bars, refrigerators and coffeemakers. Doubles start at $60 on weekdays, $100 on weekends.

The 800-room Maxim Hotel, P.O. Box 1990, (800) 634-6987, fax (702) 735-3252, lacks character but meets basic requirements. It is at 160 East Flamingo Road, across from Bally's. Doubles from $59.

Right on the Strip near the Riviera, the 351-room La Concha Motel, 2955 Las Vegas Boulevard South, (702) 735-1255, fax (702) 369-0862, is a funky 50's-style place with the world-weary air one expects in a Las Vegas motel. Rooms here are perfectly adequate. Rates: from $48.

MODERATE: Unlike the city it's named after, New York–New York Hotel and Casino, 3790 Las Vegas Boulevard South, (800) 693-6763, fax (702) 740-6920, is medium priced. A 47-story version of the Empire State Building is at the heart of the "skyline," and the property includes such other scaled-down Gotham landmarks as a 300-foot-long Brooklyn Bridge. The 2,033 hotel rooms and suites have an Art Deco theme. Doubles: $50 to $300 on weekdays, $90 to $400 on weekends.

LUXURY: Still one of the most recognized names on the Strip is Caesars Palace, 3570 Las Vegas Boulevard South, (800) 634-6661, fax (702) 731-7172. This giant hotel and casino has plenty of Las Vegas nostalgia and nouveau extravagance. The newest tower brought the total of rooms and suites to 2,471. All of the rooms have marble baths. Doubles: $79 to $450.

Bellagio, 3600 Las Vegas Boulevard South, (702) 693-7111, fax (702) 693-8585, is luxurious in every detail, from its grand lobby to its Mediterranean-style pool area with six pools. The 3,005 deluxe rooms and suites, all with marble bathrooms, have sweeping views. Standard doubles from $159 to $459, and suites from $375 to $1,400.

where to eat

Celebrity chefs from around the country have opened restaurants in the new luxury casinos and shopping malls over the last few years. Among the most popular is Emeril's, at the MGM Grand, 3799 Las Vegas Boulevard South, (702) 891-7374. Emeril Lagasse serves up Creole cooking, specializing in fish, and a seafood bar. Lunch and dinner are served daily in the wide-open, somewhat noisy dining room. A three-course dinner for two with wine will cost about $125.

At least one big-name newcomer to this city's restaurant scene has struck out on its own, unattached to any new casino projects. Smith & Wollensky, the famous New York steakhouse, has opened a branch at 3767 Las Vegas Boulevard South, across from the Monte Carlo, that copies the look of the original, inside and out; (702) 862-4100. Lunch and dinner are served daily, with a three-course meal for two with an inexpensive wine costing about $150.

For a more affordable lunch or a late dinner, try the Noodle Kitchen at the Mirage, 3400 Las Vegas Boulevard South, (702) 791-7111. The service is fast and the menu includes Chinese noodles, barbecued meats and poultry, and rice porridge. A meal for two, with drinks, will cost about $30.

Main Street Station's Triple 7 restaurant and brewery, downtown at 200 North Main Street, (702) 387-1896, is a nice change from buffets for about the same price. Dinner specials, including grilled fish, meats, and seafood, cost about $10. The microbrews cost $2.95 for a 16-ounce glass, or $4.95 for a sampler of 5 ounces of each of the five brews.

The graveyard-shift steak special is another dying tradition. Binion's Horseshoe Coffee Shop, 128 Fremont Street, (702) 382-1600, is hanging on with a worthy $4.99 version (a 10-ounce New York strip steak, baked potato, salad and rolls) served from 11 p.m. until 7 a.m.

vital statistics

POPULATION (1998 estimate): City 404,288; Metro area 1,321,546

HOTEL: Room for one with tax $140.50

DINNER FOR ONE: With tax and tip but not drinks $23.20

TAXI: Upon entry $2.20; Each additional mile $1.60; From the airport $17.50

CAR RENTAL FOR A DAY: Midsize car with unlimited free mileage $56.00

FOR MORE INFORMATION: Telephone: (702) 892-7575; Web: www.lasvegas24hours.com

Sources: Runzheimer International, U.S. Census Bureau, local businesses

Lisbon

The excitement returns to where it all began:
along the Tagus River

Tower of Belém
Lisbon

MARVINE HOWE

Marvine Howe, a former correspondent for *The New York Times*,
lives in Virginia and Portugal.

Gradually, this sedate Old World capital has gained an exciting new dimension along its waterfront. It's as though the center of gravity had shifted from the city's time-worn hills back to the great silvery Tagus River, where it all began.

Lisbon has become a major cruise port. The 12-mile littoral from Belém to the ethereal new Vasco da Gama Bridge has been spruced up and in places totally renewed. Seedy warehouses, dilapidated tenements and abandoned factories have been reconstituted as museums, cafes, restaurants, discos and shops or replaced by grassy esplanades and mosaic promenades.

This intense renewal effort began barely a decade ago, when Mayor João Soares, then a city councilman, pierced the riverside commuter train tracks with viaducts and overpasses. First, the West Side was gentrified with new restaurants and cultural institutions. Then the Alcântara docks were rehabilitated as a center of nightlife. But the major challenge was the transformation of the ugly industrial zone on the East Side into a welcoming home for

Expo 98, and its integration as a vibrant part of the city—a work still in progress.

Lisbon received a surge of visitors in the spring of 2000, when it took its six-month turn as capital of the European Union. And again, as the starting point for annual pilgrimages to Fatima on May 12 and 13, when Pope John Paul II came to honor the beatification of two of the three children (the third is still living), said to have witnessed the Virgin Mary there in 1917.

best of times

Graced with a mild Atlantic-Mediterranean climate, Lisbon is a year-round destination. Summers are usually long, hot and dry, relieved by sea breezes; winters often rainy and cool— never freezing. The most appealing season is spring, when the jacaranda is in full bloom and it is sheer delight to stroll along the city's shady mosaic walks.

Lisbon's cultural season runs from October through May and competes favorably with European counterparts. Besides a world-class museum, the Calouste Gulbenkian Foundation, Avenida de Berna 45, (351) 21-793-5131, fax (351) 21-793-7296, presents a varied program of concerts and dance, with leading international performers. The Belém Cultural Centre, Praça do Imperio, (351) 21-361-2400, fax (351) 21-361-2560, offers a rich choice of drama, art shows, ballet and concerts all season long. And there's classic opera at the exquisite gilt 18th-century São Carlos Opera House, 9 Rua Serpa Pinto, (351) 21-346-5914, fax (351) 21-343-0613.

Every June 12 to 30, Lisbon celebrates its favorite saints, Anthony, John and Peter, with a religious procession, parade, street music, dancing and grilled sardines.

A new annual event is the Festival of Fado—Portuguese blues— in early February. Another attraction is the Oceans Festival: fireworks, parades and nautical exhibits from mid-August for two weeks.

Not to be forgotten are Lisbon's suburbs. The Sintra Music Festival stages a repertory of romantic music in churches, palaces and parks from July to September. Also in summer, there is the Estoril Coast Music Festival, an International Handicraft Fair, tennis, golf and windsurfing tournaments.

what to see

The most dazzling approach to Lisbon is by sea. The Transtejo ferry line runs daily two-hour guided tours from the Parque das

Nações to Belém. They leave from Terreiro do Paço at 11 a.m. and 3 p.m. Tickets cost $14.25 for adults, less for children.

Although Lisbon has Roman roots, much of the Baixa, or downtown, was rebuilt after the earthquake of 1755. The city's main gateway is Terreiro do Paço, a vast mosaic square framed by 18th-century gold-colored government buildings facing the river. A triumphal arch leads to a handsome grid of banks, offices and shops, now largely a pedestrian area with open-air cafes.

The oldest neighborhoods hug the hills, with the Moorish São Jorge Castle towering over the city. Inside the ramparts, an exhibit provides a thumbnail sketch of Lisbon's history, and a giant periscope offers spectacular views of the city and river. Open daily 9 a.m. to 9 p.m.

From the castle, it's an easy stroll downhill through the old Moorish quarter of Alfama, a maze of cobblestone alleys, stairways and modest houses with iron balconies, flowers and fluttering laundry. Near the base of the hill, the 12th-century Sé (cathedral), with romanesque towers and gothic chapel, is open daily 10 a.m. to 5 p.m., except Sunday and holidays.

Around the corner, the new Fado and Guitar Museum at 1 Largo do Chafariz de Dentro, gives an introduction to Lisbon's special music. Open daily 10 a. m. to 6 p.m., except Tuesday. Admission: $2.15.

On the opposite hill, the Chiado, a fashionable shopping area devastated by fire in 1988, has been restored. The centerpiece is the Armazéns do Chiado, an old department store converted into an upscale shopping center with fabulous views.

The adjacent Bairro Alto used to be a working-class neighborhood with bars and taverns, where many fado singers like Amália Rodrigues, who died in 1999, got their start. The fado houses have been gentrified, as has much of the old neighborhood. Café Luso, 10 Travessa da Queimada, is in the vaulted cellars of a 17th-century palace. An evening of dinner, folk dancing and fado costs $55 to $70 for two. Open from 8 p.m.; (351) 21-342-2281.

On the western edge of the city, the monuments of Belém mark the site from which Vasco da Gama and other navigators set out to discover new worlds. The Tower of Belém and Jerónimos Monastery, 16th-century masterpieces, have undergone major repairs. The Monument of the Discoveries, a stylized caravel, was built in 1960 to honor the 500th anniversary of Prince Henry the Navigator's death.

Until Expo 98, the National Azulejo Museum, in the Madre de Deus Monastery, 4 Rua Madre de Deus, was a cultural oasis in the industrial zone on Lisbon's East Side. This exceptional collection of religious and secular decorative tiles is open 10 a.m. to 6 p.m. except Tuesday morning and Monday. Admission: $2.15.

The Parque das Nações, as the Expo 98 area is now called, is open free daily 9:30 to 1 a.m., till 3 a.m. Friday and Saturday. The Oceanarium, one of Europe's finest aquariums, is still the main attraction. It is open daily 10 a.m. to 6 p.m. Admission: $7.15 for adults, $3.80 for children and seniors.

A popular addition to the parque is the Vasco da Gama shopping center with a variety of restaurants and cafes; Sunday fairs (10 a.m. to 7 p.m.) on the northern waterfront near the restaurant area have alternating themes: stamps and coins, then street art, antiques and secondhand books.

where to stay

BUDGET: Hotel Miraparque, 12 Avenida Sidónio Pais, (351) 21-352-4286, fax (351) 21-357-8920, overlooks Parque Edward VII. The 100 rooms have minibars, satellite television, air-conditioning, homey flowered curtains and chenille bedspreads. Doubles, with breakfast, are $69.

MODERATE: Off the Avenida da Liberdade, the Lisboa Plaza, 5 Travessa Salitre, (351) 21-346-3922, fax (351) 21-347-1630, combines modern comforts—double-glazed windows, air-conditioning, modem jacks—with traditional charm, like large marble bathrooms and decorative tiles. It has 112 rooms furnished in sunny pastels. A double is about $128, including a copious American breakfast buffet.

The Orion Lisboa is a modern apartment-hotel in the former Eden Theater, 24 Praça dos Restauradores, (351) 21-321-6600, fax (351) 21-321-6666, in the center of town. Behind the splendid Art Deco façade, 75 studios and 59 apartments all have kitchenettes with microwave, refrigerator and dishwasher, and air-conditioning. A studio is $78, an apartment $93.

LUXURY: The Avenida Palace, 123 Rua Primeiro Dezembro, (351) 21-346-0151, fax (351) 21-342-2884, is a grand hotel in the heart of the city, with spacious foyer and salons, brocaded walls and crystal chandeliers. All 82 rooms are equipped with effective soundproofing and air-conditioning and decorated in classic elegance. A double with breakfast is $170.

Formerly a private mansion, Hotel da Lapa, 4 Rua do Pau da Bandeira, (351) 21-395-0005, fax (351) 21-395-0665, is on a hill in the elegant diplomatic quarter. It has a richly decorated lobby and banquet hall, and the 94 spacious rooms are tastefully done.

The large balconies overlook lush gardens with a fountain and pool. A double is $270.

where to eat

The latest word in riverside restaurants has no sign and an unlikely name: O Bica do Sapato (The Shoe Tap), Avenida Infante D. Henrique, Cais da Pedra; (351) 21-881-0320. The inspiration of three well-known Portuguese restaurateurs who have the actor John Malkovich as a partner, Bica combines a terrace cafeteria, upscale restaurant and sushi bar in four renovated warehouses. The restaurant specializes in New Portuguese cuisine (fresh and organic), like grilled squid with artichokes. Dinner for two with wine is about $55.

A Travessa, 28 Travessa das Inglesinhas, (351) 21-390-2034, with red-tile floors, whitewashed walls and local art, is near Parliament. Specialties include bacon-wrapped dates and grilled turbot encrusted in salt to preserve the juices. Dinner for two with a good wine: $55.

Originally situated across from the Presidential Palace, Nobre was widely considered to have the best food in town. When it moved to the Expo marina, its faithful clientele followed. The new Nobre, Edificio Nau, Marina Expo 98, (351) 21-893-1604, has kept its standards with refined dishes like sea bass meuniere aux fines herbes. Open daily except Sunday evening. Dinner for two with wine is about $75.

António Clara, also called Clube de Empresários, 38 Avenida da Republica, (351) 21-799-4280, is in a charming old mansion near the bull ring. The atmosphere is elegant, with damask curtains, silk-covered chairs, silver under-plates and an attentive staff. French cuisine, like chateaubriand bearnaise, dominates. Dinner for two with wine: around $65.

For family fare, the best bargain is Bonjardim, 11 Travessa Santo Antao, downtown off the Avenida da Liberdade. The décor is simple and rustic, and tasty roast chicken, salad, French fries and an earthenware jug of wine for two runs about $10.

vital statistics

POPULATION (1998 estimate): City 1,000,000; Metro area 3,326,00

HOTEL: Room for one with tax $140.50

DINNER FOR ONE: With tax and tip but not drinks $25.65

TAXI: Upon entry $1.50; Each additional 170 meters 6 cents; From the airport $6.50

CAR RENTAL FOR A DAY: Midsize manual shift car with unlimited free mileage $127.00

FOR MORE INFORMATION: Telephone: (351) 21-361-0350; Web: www.atl-turismolisboa.pt

Sources: Runzheimer International, Portuguese National Tourist Office, local businesses

London

The focus returns once again to the River Thames

SARAH LYALL AND PAMELA KENT

Sarah Lyall reports for *The Times* from London.
Pamela Kent works in *The Times*'s London bureau.

London has never been short of attractions to lure tourists from the ceremonial Changing of the Guard at Buckingham Palace. But in recent years new attractions have switched the focus of activity to the River Thames. One of the most popular attractions is the London Eye, the 450-foot Ferris wheel on the South Bank at Westminster Bridge that rotates very slowly, allowing passengers to appreciate stunning views for 25 miles in every direction. Shakespeare's Globe, the replica of the original wooden-O theater, which opened in 1997, plays to packed houses throughout its season from May to September, and in 2000 opened a permanent exhibition in the underGlobe.

Improved boat services on the Thames enable passengers to visit sites from Greenwich in the East where the National Maritime Museum and Royal Observatory are located, to Hampton Court Palace in the West. In between are the Design Museum; Vinopolis, devoted to wine; the new Tate Modern; the South Bank Arts Center; and Somerset House, home to the Courtauld collection of

Art and the Gilbert Collection of decorative arts. And for walkers and cyclists, there is the new Thames Path.

best of times

In winter, and inclement weather, visitors can duck into the galleries and museums, or choose a play, concert, opera or one of many other forms of indoor entertainment. When the sun shines, there are parks and other open spaces. Among them are the Royal Parks that surround Buckingham Palace: St. James's with its central lake; Green Park; and Hyde Park, which contains the new Princess Diana Memorial Garden for children.

The only time that London closes down for tourists is December 25 and 26 and New Year's Day, when residents retreat to their homes for traditional family celebrations. Many hotels offer Christmas packages, which usually have to be booked well in advance.

In late March, the Oxford and Cambridge Boat Race features crews from the two universities racing four and a half miles along the Thames from Mortlake to Putney in a tradition dating from 1829. Best viewing points are Putney and Chiswick Bridges, the Dove Inn at 19 Upper Mall, Hammersmith, and the Ship Inn at Ship Lane, Mortlake.

The Chelsea Flower Show, late May, is at the Royal Hospital grounds, London SW3. Information: (44-207) 7649-1885. Tickets, $35 to $38, must be bought in advance.

During an eight-week period from mid-July to mid-September, the BBC Henry Wood Promenade Concerts, Royal Albert Hall, Kensington Gore, offer 70 orchestral performances with a wide variety of composers. Programs ($6) are available from May at (44-1232) 325672; information, (44-207) 7765-5575. Tickets from $4.25 to $85.

In November, the Lord Mayor's Show is a tradition from the 13th century. The Lord Mayor travels a round trip from Mansion House in the financial district, leaving at 11 a.m. via St. Paul's Cathedral and the Royal Courts of Justice in the Strand. His gilded coach is followed by a parade with more than 6,000 participants and over 140 colorful floats, military bands and units of the armed services. At 5 p.m. there is a spectacular fireworks display on the Thames between Blackfriars and Waterloo Bridges.

what to see

The Victoria and Albert Museum includes a collection of 300,000 photographs, with works by Edward Steichen, Nan Goldin, Henri

Cartier-Bresson and Irving Penn. Open Monday, noon to 5:45 p.m.; Tuesday to Sunday 10 a.m. to 5:45 p.m. Admission is $8.50 for adults, $5 for seniors; free for students, children and the disabled, and from 4:30 to 5:45 p.m. The museum is on Cromwell Road; (44-207) 938-8500.

It has been derided as an instant monument to outdated architecture, but the British Library at 96 Euston Road is worth visiting for its first-rate exhibitions. Among other treasures, it houses Shakespeare's First Folio of 1623 and a Gutenberg Bible, printed circa 1455. Open Monday, Wednesday, Thursday and Friday 9:30 a.m. to 6 p.m.; Tuesday to 8 p.m.; Saturday 9:30 a.m. to 5 p.m., and Sunday 11 a.m. to 5 p.m. Admission is free; (44-207) 412-7000.

The Royal Observatory in Greenwich, southeast London, is the site of the prime meridian, which marks Greenwich Mean Time— ground zero of world time. The observatory is in Greenwich Royal Park near the Maze Hill rail station (trains run from Charing Cross and London Bridge Stations). Open 10 a.m. to 5 p.m. daily. Admission is $10 for adults, $8 for seniors; children under 16 and students get in free; (44-208) 858-4422.

Watch the desert locusts swarm and marvel at the microscopic nematodes in the Micrarium, which calls itself the tiniest zoo in the world. All this and more is going on at the Web of Life, the celebration of biodiversity at the London Zoo. Admission to the zoo, which is open daily from 10 a.m. to 4 p.m., is $15 for adults, $13.50 for seniors and students, $12 for children 4 to 14, and free for those 3 and under. The zoo is in Regent's Park; (44-207) 722-3333.

Dresses worn by Diana, the Princess of Wales, are on display at Kensington Palace, part of a permanent collection that includes some of the Queen's clothes. Tickets are $16 for adults, $12 ages 5 to 16 and $13 for students and senior citizens. The palace, in Kensington Gardens, is open daily from 10 a.m. to 4 p.m; (44-207) 376-2858.

where to stay

BUDGET: Newly refurbished, the Park Hotel, 64 Belgrave Road, SW1V 2BP, (44-207) 834-3118, fax (44-207) 834-9328, is close by Victoria Station and not far from Buckingham Palace. There are 18 rooms, and doubles start at $105, with tax and full breakfast.

The Kingsway Hotel, at 27 Norfolk Square, W2, (44-207) 723-5569, fax (44-207) 723-7317, is in a quiet square that has the advantage of being just south of Paddington Station, where you might catch a train, and just north of Hyde Park. It has 35 rooms. Doubles start at $114, with tax and full English breakfast.

MODERATE: The Portobello Hotel, 22 Stanley Gardens, W11 2NG, (44-207) 727-2777, fax (44-207) 792-9641, is in an oasis of quiet (and trendiness) in bustling Notting Hill. It's a 24-room town-house hotel that aims to feel more like a private home; its furnishings and décor make it cozy and relaxed. Doubles start at $217, including V.A.T. and full breakfast.

LUXURY: St. Martins Lane, 45 St. Martins Lane, WC2 4HX, (44-207) 300-5500, fax (44-207) 300-5501, in Covent Garden is one of Ian Schrager's high-concept hotels. It has 204 rooms and 6 bars and restaurants, and is particularly proud of its "witty and ironic" touches, including the garden gnomes in the lobby (you sit on their hats). Rooms have floor-to-ceiling windows, and when you flick a switch, the light, and your room, changes color. Double rooms start at $397, plus V.A.T.

My Hotel, 11-13 Bayley Street, Bedford Square, WC1B 3HD, phone and fax, (44-207) 667-6000, aims to offer calmness and tranquillity through, among other things, an adherence to feng shui. Guests in the 76 rooms specify in advance what kind of music they like; each is assigned a "personal contact" who is supposed to make it unnecessary to talk to any other staff member. The hotel has modern rooms, and it offers a variety of exotic beauty treatments. Double rooms start at $262, plus V.A.T.

where to eat

Le Gavroche, 43 Upper Brook Street, W1, (44-207) 408-0881, has been around forever (well, 33 years), but has successfully made the transition to the modern age. The classic French food is exquisite— if stratospherically expensive—and the atmosphere is empowering rather than intimidating. Specialties include an appetizer of lobster mousse wrapped in spinach, with caviar and champagne butter sauce, and a main course of mignonette of beef with briskets in red wine sauce. Dinner for two, with wine, costs about $340; there's a minimum of $100 a person. Closed on weekends.

At St. John, a restaurant that proudly offers "nose-to-tail eating," appetizers include roast bone marrow and parsley salad; for a main course, try the smoked Gloucester Old Spot pork chop, with boiled potatoes and homemade chutney. Dinner for two with wine: about $100. The restaurant is at 26 St. John Street in Clerkenwell, East London, EC1M 4AY; (44-207) 251-0848.

It's not hard to imagine what's cooking at Fish!, in a hip glass box of a building south of the Thames on Cathedral Street in Borough Market, SE1. Start with a plate of smoked salmon or some potted shrimp, and then choose from a selection of whatever's fresh. Dinner for two, with wine, comes to about $100; (44-207) 234-3333.

Lola's, in the Mall Building, Camden Passage, 359 Upper Street, Islington, N1, (44-207) 359-1932, is a lively fixture for cool residents and a theatrical crowd fueled by the Almeida Theater nearby. Appetizers include a bitter leaf salad with French beans, poached egg and pancetta; main courses include grilled quail with figs, Parma ham, rosemary and mashed potatoes. Dinner for two, with wine, comes to about $120.

The Asian-fusion food at Itsu, 118 Draycott Avenue, SW3, (44-207) 584-5522, slides past you on a conveyor belt: everything from little bits of sushi to grilled chicken with green soba noodles. The dishes cost $4.25 to $6 each, which may come to about $60 for dinner for two. But who's counting? Itsu is open from noon to 11 p.m. daily except Sunday, when it closes at 10 p.m.

It's in tourist-friendly Piccadilly, but the buffet-style restaurant at the Royal Academy of Arts, (44-207) 287-0752, offers more than convenience. There are salads and sandwiches, cold dishes like poached salmon, and hot choices that always include homemade soup, meat or fish, and a vegetarian dish. Lunch usually costs about $30 for two, with a soft drink. The restaurant serves breakfast from 10 to 11:45 a.m. and tea with cakes from 2:45 to 5:30 p.m. On Friday night there's a candlelight supper with fancier food and live music.

vital statistics

POPULATION (2000 estimate): Greater London 7,000,000

HOTEL: Room for one with tax $332.00

DINNER FOR ONE: With tax and tip but not drinks $37.60

TAXI: Upon entry $2.00; Each additional kilometer $1.45; From the airport $54.00

CAR RENTAL FOR A DAY: Midsize car with unlimited free mileage $80.00

FOR MORE INFORMATION: Telephone: (44-870) 608-2000; Web: www.londontown.com

Sources: Runzheimer International, British Tourist Authority, local businesses

Los Angeles

Downtown (yes, there is such a place)
is on the rise again

TODD S. PURDUM

Todd S. Purdum is chief of the Los Angeles bureau of *The Times*.

Even natives love to deride Los Angeles as a city without a downtown. Or more accurately as a city with several, from City Hall to the office towers and mall of Century City, to the beach at Santa Monica 15 miles away. But the Democratic National Convention in 2000 put the spotlight back on the city's original downtown, where it began and prospered until its center of gravity started shifting steadily westward more than 70 years ago.

The skyline lacks an iconic landmark. Streets are often all but deserted at night, and the district is crisscrossed by freeways whose ramps make navigating its vertiginous one-way streets tricky for the uninitiated.

But downtown is, in fact, experiencing what city officials and real estate titans hope will amount to a comeback, and nothing symbolizes those aspirations better than the spanking new Staples Center. Downtown can still seem a long hike from the luxury canyons of Beverly Hills and Brentwood, and it is only one slice of the bubbling pie that is Los Angeles, but an intrepid visitor could find plenty to do there.

From the kitschy-quaint shops of Olvera Street, the brick arcade that was the site of the original Spanish pueblo of Los Angeles, to the Deco-Mission-style grandeur of Union Station, to Little Tokyo, to the bustling multiethnic buzz of the Grand Central Market, with its butchers and greengrocers stretching from Broadway to Hill Street, downtown can be a vital place. For better or worse, it remains the city's seat of high culture, with theater, opera and symphonies at the Los Angeles Music Center and a gaggle of museums.

best of times

Los Angeles summers are not what one might think: temperatures in the low 80's, dry air and infrequent rainfall make it one of the more pleasant times to visit. Winters aren't much worse—temperatures range from the high 40's to high 60's—but it is the rainiest time of year.

The city's many ethnic communities contribute to a busy calendar of annual festivals. In late January to late February, depending on the year, there's the Chinese New Year Festival and Parade, with a carnival and the Golden Dragon Parade; (213) 617-0396. Cinco de Mayo brings two spring events, the A.T.&T. Fiesta Broadway, on Broadway between First Street and Olympic Boulevard in late April, (310) 914-0015; and Celebrate Cinco 2000, with a carnival, Mexican folkloric dances and food in early May at El Pueblo de Los Angeles Historic Monument, (213) 628-1274.

Summer means that the Los Angeles Philharmonic moves to the Hollywood Bowl, and there is no more elegant place for a cool California evening with a box supper and a bottle of wine in seats with flip-up tables. Most performances are at 7:30 or 8:30 p.m.; (323) 850-2000.

Nisei Week Japan, in Little Tokyo in mid-August, offers Japanese folk dancing, food, music and martial arts; (213) 687-7193. The African Marketplace and Cultural Faire includes hundreds of crafts experts and vendors in Rancho Cienega Park, in late August and early September; (323) 734-1164.

Las Posadas is a candlelight procession on Olvera Street that reenacts the journey of Mary and Joseph to Bethlehem, in mid- to late December; (213) 628-3562. And celebrities, floats and marching bands turn out for the Hollywood Christmas Parade, along Hollywood and Sunset Boulevards between Van Ness and Highland in early December; (323) 469-8311.

what to see

For a bird's-eye view from Bunker Hill, the downtown cluster of office towers, try Angels Flight, a two-car funicular railway built in 1901 to connect the commercial heart of the city to the Victorian residential enclave above. Recently restored, it climbs a 315-foot incline to the modern financial district built in the 1960's and 70's where the Victorian homes once stood, in a quaint reminder of the city's relative youth and phenomenal growth. Fare: 25 cents.

Not far away, at the grand old Union Station, is the terminus of Los Angeles's newly completed 17.4-mile subway, at nearly $5 billion the most expensive subway in American history. Troubled by more than a decade of construction delays and cost overruns, the subway opened its final link in the summer of 2000, and at last offers some worthwhile destinations just a short ride from downtown: Hollywood Boulevard, and Universal Studios in North Hollywood. The trains are clean and quiet and the stations spectacularly decorated, with tile murals at one stop and lighting that mimics a stage set at another. The fare is $1.35 (cheaper for weekly passes).

The Grand Central Public Market, 317 South Broadway at West Third Street, is one of the few places in all of Los Angeles where the city's rich polyglot population can be seen in all its diversity. Downtown office workers and immigrants from virtually every country mingle amid the cheery, vital bustle of old-fashioned food stalls, butchers and fishmongers. Enter hungry, and you'll be full when you leave.

No building downtown is more beautiful than the Los Angeles Central Library, 630 West Fifth Street, between Grand and Flower, a 1930 Byzantine-Moorish-Egyptian-Roman landmark with a modern addition. The restored reading rooms are beautiful, and a new auditorium is host to a lecture series and special events; (213) 228-7000.

The Japanese American National Museum, which opened a major new building in 1999 next to the Geffen at 369 East First Street, is the nation's only museum dedicated to the Japanese experience in the United States. It is housed in two structures, a 1925 Buddhist temple and the new 85,000-square-foot pavilion by Gyo Obata, which houses, among other rotating exhibits, a reconstructed barracks from a World War II internment camp for Japanese-Americans; (213) 625-0414.

where to stay

BUDGET: Within walking distance of all civic-center attractions, the Miyako Inn and Spa, 328 East First Street, offers simple, spare guest rooms, all equipped with minibars and safes. The spa has four whirlpools, and there's karaoke in the lounge. Rates in the 174 rooms are $107 to $139; (800) 228-6596, fax (213) 617-2700.

MODERATE: The New Otani, 120 South Los Angeles Street, a mecca for Japanese businessmen and tourists, is a convenient, attractive downtown perch with an elegant garden and a reputation for good service. The 434 rooms include three Japanese-style suites, in the heart of Little Tokyo. Shiatsu massage and sauna are available in the spa. Rates: $180 to $250; (800) 421-8795, fax (213) 622-0980.

The Los Angeles Marriott Downtown, 333 South Figueroa Street, was formerly a Sheraton. Renovated two years ago, this 14-story convention hotel has a crisp, clean feel, and is near the Music Center. Rates: $199 to $350, with weekend packages as low as $119; (800) 321-2211 or (213) 617-1133, fax (213) 613-0291.

LUXURY: The Biltmore, 506 South Grand Avenue, the grande dame of downtown, was the largest hotel west of Chicago when it opened in 1923, and has undergone several renovations in recent years. Its elegant lobby and bar are the place to see and be seen. As typical for hotels of its age, guest rooms can be tiny, but the public spaces, with Moorish touches and coffered ceilings, will let you pretend you're Douglas Fairbanks or Mary Pickford. The 620 rooms and 63 suites start at $150, depending on availability; (800) 245-8673, fax (213) 612-1546.

The Wyndham Checkers Hotel, 535 South Grand Avenue, is a boutique outpost convenient for business travelers. Its 173 rooms and 15 suites can be smallish. But it is among the classiest places downtown, and it has a rooftop pool. Rates: from $199; (213) 624-0000, fax (213) 626-9906.

where to eat

Routinely ranked as one of the best seafood houses in this seaside town, the Water Grill, at 544 South Grand Avenue, is all curving wood and cozy booths. Its ice-cold, honest martinis make the perfect foil for the towering platters of fresh, chilled shellfish stacked on crushed ice. Grilled, baked or sautéed, the fish is the freshest around, from Pacific tuna tartare to Dungeness crab cakes to a chowder of Manila clams. Dinner for two $150, with a moderately priced wine. Reservations: (213) 891-0900.

Joachim Splichal is among the reigning imperial chef-entrepreneurs of Los Angeles (perhaps best known for Patina and his bevy of Pinot brasseries), and his latest entry is a traditional American steakhouse, Nick and Stef's, named for his two sons, in the Wells Fargo Center at 330 South Hope Street. In a sleek urban setting, with a glass-walled aging chamber displaying cold hunks of meat sitting on racks, waiters make Caesar salad tableside and serve up strips, filets, rib-eyes and Porterhouses grilled, juicy and thick. Biggest complaint: the side dishes are much less impressive. But the lemon meringue pie is the kind your grandmother made. Dinner for two, with wine: $150; (213) 680-0330.

The Original Pantry Cafe, 887 South Figueroa Street, a short walk north of the Staples Center, is a local institution, owned by Mayor Richard J. Riordan. It never closes and is the place to go for breakfasts, steaks, chops and baked goods. A greasy spoon and proud of it. Dinner for two is about $30, but go for breakfast or lunch and it's even cheaper (and probably better); (213) 972-9279.

Philippe the Original, 1001 North Alameda Street, across from Union Station, claims to have invented the French dip sandwich. There's certainly no questioning the authenticity of this beloved spot, with its sawdust-covered floors, long bench tables and fabulous food. Don't miss the homemade tapioca. Lunch for two with fresh lemonade: $15. (213) 628-3781.

Hama Sushi, in the Japanese Village Plaza Mall at 347 East Second Street in Little Tokyo, is a highly reliable choice for sushi. Small and unpretentious, it is full of jovial chatter at lunch, and the fish is fresh and the service friendly. A meal of sushi runs about $15 to $20, and beer and sake are available. Call (213) 680-3454.

vital statistics

POPULATION (1998 estimate): City 3,597,556; Metro area 9,213,533

HOTEL: Room for one with tax $183.50

DINNER FOR ONE: With tax and tip but not drinks $32.35

TAXI: Upon entry $1.90; Each additional mile $1.80; From the airport $26.00

CAR RENTAL FOR A DAY: Midsize car with unlimited free mileage $60.50

FOR MORE INFORMATION: Telephone: (213) 689-8822; Web: www.lacvb.com

Sources: Runzheimer International, U.S. Census Bureau, local businesses

Madrid

The capital of a newly prosperous nation reflects that affluence

Plaza Mayor, Madrid

PENELOPE CASAS

Penelope Casas is the author of
Discovering Spain: An Uncommon Guide.

Spain was thrust onto the international stage in 1992 by the Olympics, the 500th anniversary of Columbus's voyage to America, a World's Fair and full membership in the European Community, and it has remained there ever since. Madrid, its capital, is at the epicenter of Spain's newfound prosperity and pride, reflected in a flood of upscale stores, hotels and restaurants, and in the overall rejuvenation of the city.

New hotels have opened and older ones have undergone major makeovers. The Palace Hotel is the talk of the town, restored to its turn-of-the-century glory while incorporating every modern amenity. Barajas Airport has been enlarged, and the pace of life has undoubtedly quickened.

best of times

Late spring and early fall—when the weather is generally fair, temperatures moderate, and Madrid is in full swing—are ideal times of year to visit the city. August should be avoided, since many shops and most of the city's best restaurants close for the month, Madrileños leave en masse for summer vacations and the heat is intense. Spring and fall have the added advantage of offering several annual events.

Although Holy Week, from Palm Sunday to Easter Sunday, may not be as spectacular as it is elsewhere in Spain, the solemn processions of richly adorned floats, accompanied by penitents as they wind their way through Old Madrid on the evening of Good Friday, are especially impressive.

May 8 marks the beginning of the Fiestas de San Isidro—patron saint of the city—and downtown streets are alive with throngs of strollers, who squeeze into tapas bars and pour out onto the sidewalks.

In the fall Madrid celebrates its Autumn Festival, which includes dance, film and theater. There is also a Jazz Festival that runs throughout the month of November. And the newly reopened and beautifully restored Teatro Real has brought opera back to Madrid, both in the spring and fall.

what to see

Within the so-called Golden Triangle formed by Madrid's three world-renowned museums, there is always something to entice visitors.

The Museo del Prado, Paseo del Prado, (34) 91-330-2800, is undergoing an overhaul to allow more of the thousands of masterpieces now in storage to be displayed. Hours: 9 a.m. to 7 p.m. Tuesday through Saturday, and 9 a.m. to 2 p.m. Sunday and holidays. Admission is $2.70. The Reina Sofía museum, 52 Santa Isabel, (34) 91-467-5062, concentrates on modern art ("Guernica" is on display there). It is open weekdays, except Tuesday, and Saturday from 10 a.m. to 9 p.m., and Sunday from 10 a.m. to 2:30 p.m. Admission is $2.70. The Museo Thyssen-Bornemisza, in the neo-Classical Villahermosa Palace, 8 Paseo del Prado, (34) 91-369-0151, was born six years ago when a private collection of some 800 masterpieces went on view. Open 10 a.m. to 7 p.m. except Monday; admission is $3.75.

The elegant 19th-century Royal Opera House (El Teatro Real), closed in 1925, reopened in 1997 after major renovations. Besides opera, the Symphony Orchestra also performs here. Information: (34) 91-516-0660, fax (34) 91-516-0651. And the Teatro Calderón, 18 Atocha, (34) 91-369-1434, fax (34) 91-360-0656, has its own opera season.

Madrid's flea market (El Rastro) is a lively place on Sunday morning. Vendors selling everything imaginable fill the Ribera de Curtidores and surrounding streets, and visitors jostle for position (beware: it is a pickpocket's joy). As noon approaches, tapas bars open—Los Caracoles, 106 Toledo, (34) 91-366-4246, is a classic, serving the traditional caracoles (snails) in paprika sauce.

The neo-Classical chapel Ermita de San Antonio de la Florida was painted in 1798 by Goya at the behest of King Charles IV. The frescoes in the dome depict marvelous scenes of a miracle in which St. Anthony of Padua brings a murdered man back to life to identify his assassin. The event is witnessed by the common people of Madrid, including beggars and prostitutes—a scandalous choice at a time when painting was devoted principally to aristocracy. The hermitage, which is also Goya's burial place, is at 5 Paseo de la Florida; (34) 91-542-0722. Open Tuesday to Friday, 10 a.m. to 2 p.m., and 4 to 8 p.m.; Saturday and Sunday, 10 a.m. to 2 p.m.; closed Monday and holidays. Admission is $1.60.

The 16th-century Monasterio de las Descalzas Reales, 3 Plaza de las Descalzas Reales; (34) 91-542-00-59, still inhabited by Poor Clares nuns, is a beautifully restored Renaissance palace that has an excellent collection of paintings, sculpture and tapestries. There is also a curious display of dolls and other toys that belonged to illegitimate royal offspring placed in the nuns' care. Open Tuesday to Thursday, 10:30 a.m. to 12:45 p.m. and 4 to 5:45 p.m.; Sunday and holidays 11 a.m. to 1 p.m.; closed Mondays and Friday afternoons. Admission: $3.75 for adults, $1.60 for ages 5 to 16.

El Retiro park, once the grounds of a 17th-century palace built for Philip IV, used to be somewhat formal. Today joggers, street performers, strollers, cyclists and frolicking children vie for space. A typical Sunday for many Madrileños means renting a rowboat on the Great Lake. The formal flower beds, wide avenues, majestic statuary and fountains have all been preserved.

where to stay

BUDGET: Inexpensive hotels with character and adequate facilities are hard to come by in Madrid. An exception is the Carlos V, 5 Maestro Victoria, (34) 91-531-4100, fax (34) 91-531-3761, a comfortable family-run hotel with 67 rooms on a pedestrian street in the heart of downtown. Doubles are $88.

Also good is the 79-room Ópera Hotel, 2 Cuesta de Santo Domingo, (34) 91-541-2800, fax (34) 91-541-6923, in a lovely location facing the Royal Palace and the Royal Opera House. Doubles are $96.

MODERATE: The Reina Victoria Hotel, 14 Plaza Santa Ana, (34) 91-531-4500, fax (34) 91-522-0307, is a 201-room historic hotel with classical décor in subdued colors. Its location on Santa Ana Square, a place that hums with tapas bars in the evenings, is ideal. Doubles: $120.

The Gaudí Hotel, 9 Gran Vía, (34) 91-531-2222, fax (34) 91-531-5469, is on the main avenue downtown, in a recently restored building in the turn-of-the-century style made famous by the Catalan architect Antonio Gaudí. Its 88 rooms embody comfortable good taste. Doubles: $149.

LUXURY: The ideally situated 440-room Palace Hotel, 7 Plaza de las Cortes, (34) 91-360-8000, fax (34) 91-360-8100, has become the most sought-after reservation in Madrid. The rotunda with its stained glass cupola is a fine spot to relax over a drink and observe the comings and goings. Doubles are $337.

On Madrid's most fashionable boulevard, convenient to shopping and museums, is the Villa Magna, 22 Paseo de la Castellana, (34) 91-587-1234, fax (34) 91-575-9504, a coolly elegant 182-room hotel sheathed in white marble, luxuriously decorated in early-19th-century style and surrounded by gardens. Doubles: $358.

where to eat

These restaurants (but not the tapas bars), unless otherwise noted, close for Saturday lunch and all day Sunday.

Tomás Herranz, the creative chef of El Cenador del Prado, 4 Prado, (34) 91-429-1561, never overlooks traditional dishes from his mother's kitchen. A meal at his stylish restaurant, which looks like an outdoor garden, might begin with anchovy alioli toasts followed by exceptional charcoal grilled hake on a bed of eggplant purée with essence of black olive. Desserts like raspberries in spun-sugar cobwebs are works of art. A four-course prix fixe menu of $19 a person, without wine, must be ordered for everyone at the table. Dinner for two with wine: about $65.

Although Posada de la Villa, 9 Cava Baja, (34) 91-366-1860, is a large multistory restaurant, the beamed ceilings and rustic Castilian furnishings give this 17th-century inn in Old Madrid a cozy warmth. Its most splendid dish is fork-tender baby lamb, roasted in full view in a wood-burning brick oven. About $65 for dinner for two.

La Trainera, 60 Lagasca, (34) 91-576-8035, in the stylish Salamanca district, is at the top of the list for seafood. The ideal meal begins with a glistening fresh shellfish vinaigrette or sweet grilled shrimp, both in portions large enough for two, and proceeds to outstanding, lightly egg-coated hake (merluza à la romana) or equally good oversized grilled sole. A dessert tart of trout and custard is a specialty. By skipping expensive shellfish, two people can eat wonderfully for about $95. Open Saturday for lunch and dinner.

The delightful terrace of La Terraza, 15 Alcalá, (34) 91-521-8700, is closed unless weather permits, but the dining room is elegant and the food extraordinary. It is within the Casino de Madrid, a private club in a magnificent turn-of-the-century building. A tasting menu at $48 a person, with 10 dishes, is excellent. On the regular menu, you might begin with tapas like sardines with raspberry vinegar and quail legs in soy sauce, then try sweet-sour venison or hake with chestnuts, onions and wild mushrooms. A meal for two with house wine is $110.

For a relatively light, early and inexpensive meal, stop in at 19th-century Lhardy, 8 San Jerónimo, (34) 91-522-2207, and serve yourself sherried consommé from a silver tureen, a glass of sherry, ham and chicken croquettes, and tea sandwiches. Pay on the honor system as you leave.

You can eat in a similar style at any of the hundreds of tapas bars all over the city, where a lunch or dinner for two with a glass of wine or beer usually costs under $20. Mallorca, 6 Serrano, (34) 91-577-1859, serves excellent sandwiches and savory pastries, and near La Puerta del Sol, La Trucha, 3 Manuel Fernández y González, (34) 91-429-5833, specializes in Andalusian-style fried fish.

vital statistics

POPULATION (1998): City 2,881,506

HOTEL: Room for one with tax $193.50

DINNER FOR ONE: With tax and tip but not drinks $22.60

TAXI: Upon entry $1.00; Each additional kilometer 50 cents; 66 cents (Zone B—outlying areas); From the airport $15.18

CAR RENTAL FOR A DAY: Midsize car with unlimited free mileage $83.27

FOR MORE INFORMATION: Telephone: (34) 91-540-4010; Web: www.munimadrid.es

Sources: Runzheimer International, Tourist Office of Spain, local businesses

Melbourne

Blessed by a Victorian gold rush and immigrants' multicultural influences

SUSAN GOUGH HENLY

Susan Gough Henly is a freelance photojournalist who lives in Melbourne.

Forged with gold-rush money at the height of the Victorian era, Melbourne is graced with grand public buildings, tree-lined boulevards and decorous parks. While it may be the most British of Australian cities, it also is one of the world's largest Greek cities, and has a sizable Vietnamese quarter, neighborhood markets that rival those in Paris, and a palm fringed waterfront akin to Venice Beach, California. Decades ago, Italian immigrants brought espresso to its cafes. Today its restaurants are sophisticated and multiethnic, drawing from the rich surrounding farmlands, vineyards and coastal waters.

Trams still rattle along the middle of streets on the way to distinctive neighborhoods that ring the city center: fashion-conscious South Yarra, funky St. Kilda by the bay, the terrace houses of Albert Park, retro Fitzroy and the bargain-shopping haven of Richmond, to name a few.

The people here are generally easygoing, but when it comes to sports—be it Aussie Rules football, the Melbourne Cup horse race, the Australian Grand Prix auto race or the Australian Open tennis tournament—they display a rare fanaticism. Long before Sydney, Melbourne was the first Australian city to be host to the Olympic Games, in 1956.

Melbourne's theater and live-music scenes are among the most vibrant in the country, and the National Gallery of Victoria has one of the strongest art collections in the Southern Hemisphere.

best of times

Situated on the southern tip of the vast Australian continent, the city is known for offering all four seasons in one day. It all depends on whether the wind is blowing hot from the desert or frigid from the Antarctic. That said, probably the most pleasant times to visit are in the spring and autumn, which are also when most of the festivals take place.

The Australian Open Tennis tournament focuses the world on Melbourne Park (near the site of the 1956 Olympic Games) in the last 10 days of January, and the Qantas Australian Grand Prix, first round of the Formula One championship auto racing season, takes place in early March.

The Melbourne Food and Wine Festival occurs over a three-week period from mid-March through early April in a number of different venues around the city.

Most of April is reserved for the Melbourne Comedy Festival, and the Melbourne Festival, with a diverse offering of music, dance, drama and art exhibitions, takes place over three weeks in October and November.

During the Spring (horse) Racing Carnival, from late October through early November, the highlight is the Melbourne Cup, which is run on the first Tuesday in November. It is the only horse race in the world that merits a public holiday.

what to see

Melbourne encompasses a range of architecture and shopping. For each of its major east-west streets there is a bustling lane in between worth exploring. Stop by the 19th-century Old Treasury Building, State Houses of Parliament, and the elaborate Princess Theater on Spring Street and wander into the nearby Fitzroy Gardens. Collins Street offers the most interesting and upscale shopping. Check out the ornate Block's shopping arcade (No. 282). Slip into Flinders Lane for the galleries; several specialize in Aboriginal art.

Little Bourke Street is in the heart of Chinatown. Free city-circle trams (painted burgundy and gold) run every 10 minutes and pass many of the major sights, taking about 40 minutes to make the circuit.

With almost 1,000 merchants in a series of landmark buildings at the corner of Elizabeth and Victoria Streets, the Queen Victoria Market is a multicultural food mecca and a good place to pick up picnic fare. Trading hours are Tuesday and Thursday 6 a.m. to 2 p.m., Friday 6 a.m. to 6 p.m., Saturday 6 a.m. to 3 p.m., Sunday 9 a.m. to 4 p.m. Two-hour tours ($9.60 or $11.50) are offered Tuesday, Thursday, Friday and Saturday mornings. Bookings are essential: (61-3) 9320-5822.

The Melbourne Museum, (61-3) 8341-7777, which opened late in 2000, is designed to promote public debate on issues relating to the natural environment, new technology and other changes in society. The museum, beside the historic Royal Exhibition Building in Carlton Gardens, will incorporate Bunjilaka, the Aboriginal Center; a Children's Museum; a study center called InfoZone to provide information access for the public; a living environment called the Forest Gallery and education facilities. Admission: $7 adults, $18 families.

The Melbourne Aquarium, Queen's Wharf Road and King Street, (61-3) 9620-0999, offers a floor-to-ceiling coral reef, a 360-degree fishbowl, acrylic tube tunnels, and an opportunity to feed stingrays in the Mangrove Swamp and see fierce sharks. There are also deep-sea simulator rides. An adult ticket is $12.40, a child's ticket is $6. Open daily 9 a.m. to 9 p.m. in January, to 6 p.m. February to December.

Melbourne's tranquil Royal Botanic Gardens, bordering the Yarra on Alexandra Avenue, offer a diverse selection of native and imported plants. Highlights include the rain forest walk, the eucalypts and the fern gully (where you may hear flying foxes making a racket in the trees). A delightful teahouse sits beside one of the lakes. Free tours depart from the National Herbarium (F Gate) at 11 a.m. and 2 p.m. Sunday to Friday; (61-3) 9252-2300.

where to stay

BUDGET: The Avoca Bed and Breakfast, 98 Victoria Avenue, (61-3) 9696-9090, fax (61-3) 9696-9092, is one of a row of double-story Victorian terrace houses in the delightful inner-city suburb of Albert Park. Guests stay in one of three charming rooms ($80 to $87), all with private bath and decorated in Laura Ashley-style prints, and indulge in full cooked breakfasts.

The Olembia Hotel, a restored 23-room Edwardian guesthouse at 96 Barkly Street, in beachside St. Kilda, (61-3) 9537-1412, fax (61-3) 9537-1600, is one of the best bargains around if you don't mind sharing one of the black-and-white tiled bathrooms. Guests can enjoy the pleasant living areas and also cook their own meals in the kitchen. The small, very clean rooms are $22 single, $32 double.

MODERATE: The Hotel Lindrum, 26 Flinders Street, City, (61-3) 9668-1111, fax (61-3) 9668-1199, is a modern boutique hotel located in the heart of the city. The intimate bar, billiard room and restaurant have the air of a private club and the 53 softly lit high-ceilinged rooms, decorated in olives, beiges and browns, offer a spare elegance. Doubles start at $121.

Across the architectural spectrum, the Tilba Hotel, on the corner of Toorak Road West and Domain Street, South Yarra, (61-3) 9867-8844, fax (61-3) 9867-6567, is an Edwardian gem, with 18 rooms and suites, all with private bath and individually decorated in period furniture. Doubles: $90 to $125, including Continental breakfast. The front parlor has chess and backgammon and a cozy fire in cool weather.

LUXURY: Sheraton Towers Southgate, 1 Southgate Avenue, (61-3) 9696-3100, fax (61-3) 9626-4110, is a five-star hotel in the popular Southbank shopping and dining precinct on the Yarra River. The 386 rooms are decorated in neutral tones and exude a comfortable elegance. Doubles start at $193.

Built in 1883, the Windsor Hotel, at 103 Spring Street across from Parliament House, (61-3) 9633-6000, fax (61-3) 9633-6001, is the only grand hotel of the Victorian era remaining in Australia. Painstakingly restored, the hotel offers 180 rooms and suites with overstuffed armchairs, 12-foot ceilings, cream marble bathrooms and huge walk-in closets. Doubles start at $224.

where to eat

Circa, The Prince, in The Prince Hotel, 2 Acland Street, St. Kilda, (61-3) 9536-1122, is Melbourne at its most chic. The white leather banquettes and dramatic designer curtains and spare courtyard set the tone. The British chef, Michael Lambie, offers seared scallops with potato salad and truffle oil before an entree such as bouillabaisse with saffron potatoes and rouille, a garlicky sauce, and a caramelized pear tarte tatin for dessert. Dinner for two with wine is around $110.

In a grand basement space decorated in chocolate tones, Langton's, 61 Flinders Lane, (61-3) 9663-0222, is a popular high-end bistro with an excellent wine list. Chef Philippe Mouchel, who trained under the legendary Paul Bocuse, offers French classics with strong flavors delivered in delicate portions. Start with an orange- and cardamom-infused fish soup with rouille and parmesan cheese followed by a duck medley "pot au feu," and, perhaps, a waffle served with chocolate ice cream and chocolate sauce. Dinner for two with wine runs around $80.

In a sleek, narrow dining room in the basement of the Adelphi Hotel, Ezard, (61-3) 9639-6811, is edgy and polished and offers some of the most interesting and multi-influenced food in the city. Try the gratinated potato gnocchi with blue cheese, shaved pear and toasted walnuts for an appetizer and, for the main course, seaweed and dashi salted, seared yellowfin tuna with wasabi and sour cream mash, preserved cucumber and pickled ginger juice. Mandarin, coriander and gin sorbet with citrus fruits and pistachio wafer make a tangy end to the meal. Dinner for two with wine, $72.

Donovan's at 40 Jacka Boulevards, St. Kilda, (61-3) 9534-8221, is in a converted bathhouse on the beach. It offers a stylish but comfortable atmosphere with colorful pillows and rustic knick-knacks. The food is bistro bold, with an emphasis on char-grilled fish and meats, plus Italian-inspired appetizers and excellent pastas and risottos. Dinner for two, with wine: $72.

Jim's Greek Tavern, 32 Johnston Street, Collingwood, (61-3) 9419-3827, is a festive taverna with generous, delicious plates of dips and grilled seafood and lamb. The octopus is a specialty. This is a bring-your-own restaurant whose diverse clientele brings everything from great Aussie reds to beer. Dinner for two is $36.

Pellegrini's, 66 Bourke Street, City, (61-3) 9662-1885, has a long counter, a menu fixed in brass on the wall and one table—for groups—in the kitchen. Have the classic minestrone soup, lasagne and a grapefruit granita and perfect caffe latte. Nothing updated or trendy, Pellegrini's is timeless but more alive than any number of sleek newcomers. Dinner for two, without wine: $17.

vital statistics

POPULATION (2000): City 3,321,700

HOTEL: Room for one with tax $184.00

DINNER FOR ONE: With tax and tip but not drinks $18.20

TAXI: Upon entry $1.58; Each additional kilometer 65 cents; From the airport $15.56

CAR RENTAL FOR A DAY: Midsize car with unlimited free mileage $28.30

FOR MORE INFORMATION: Telephone: (66-3) 775-2000; Web: www.visitmelbourne.com

Sources: Runzheimer International, Australian Tourist Commission, local businesses

Mexico City

Intense, chaotic, creative, crisis-ridden

BARBARA BELEJACK

Barbara Belejack is a journalist based in Mexico City.

On a weekday night in a hard-luck neighborhood not far from Mexico City's main plaza, Paquita la del Barrio sings to her fans in a crowded restaurant. With perfect phrasing, she enunciates her lyrics as though they were declarations of universal truths. "I deserve better than you," she sings as the audience roars its approval. "I'm going to squash you like a bug."

In the Colonia Guerrero, her barrio, Paquita is something of a patron saint. But her following also extends to the city's most exclusive neighborhoods. Whatever they may mean to her legions of fans, her songs of heartbreak and revenge, defeat and defiance also evoke the love-hate relationship many have with the city itself, a place of enormous intensity, energy and creativity—as well as chaos, crisis and crime.

The crime has captured the headlines. The problem is real enough—a product of economic crisis, the growing disparity of income and the global criminal networks. But there is also an element of sensationalism, particularly on the part of Mexican television, which for decades presented a sanitized, Soviet-style image of daily life.

Travelers to Mexico City need to be cautious and savvy, but not paranoid. Skip the Volkswagen taxis that prowl the capital streets and call a radio taxi (such as Servicio Taxi-Mex, 5519-7690; Tax-Radio, 5566-7266; or Taxi Radio Mex, 5574-3520), or ask for the nearest reliable sitio, or taxi stand. Unfortunately, the pirate cabdrivers who force passengers to withdraw money from A.T.M.'s—referred to in local slang as secuestro expres, or kidnap express—aren't likely to go away soon.

best of times

Semana Santa, the week before Easter, is vacation time throughout Latin America, which makes this one of the best times of the year to fully appreciate the nation's capital. Millions of residents flock to the beach, but the city's museums and markets remain open. As the week progresses traffic comes to a halt; on Good Friday the megalopolis turns into a walker's paradise. Should you plan to visit, stick to the city itself. Normally pleasant getaways, such as Tepoztlan or Valle de Bravo, are filled with escaping residents of Mexico City .

The Catholic Church commemorates All Saints' and All Souls' Day on November 1 and 2, but in Mexico, the holiday is known as Day of the Dead. According to tradition, the spirits of departed ancestors return to earth at this time. In recent years, Halloween has begun to take its toll, but in Mexico City, Día de los Muertos (November 2) is still a time for families to visit cemeteries, prepare ofrendas, or altars, and enjoy traditional pan de muertos sweet bread. The city's cultural centers outdo themselves in creating ofrendas that are true works of art, with the most elaborate at the Museo Dolores Olmedo Patiño, Avenida Mexico 5843, Colonia La Noria, Xochimilco, (52-2) 5555-1016; Tuesday to Sunday, 10 a.m. to 6 p.m.

what to see

To catch up on the past two millenniums of Mexican history, the Zócalo, or Plaza de la Constitución, is a good place to begin. Depending on when you visit, the whim of officials and a complex web of competing interest groups, the Zócalo may be filled with street vendors, striking students or protesters, or it may be squeaky clean and eerily tranquil. The National Palace with its famous Diego Rivera murals (open weekdays 9 a.m. to 5 p.m; admission free with photo ID), the Templo Mayor, the ruins of an Aztec ceremonial site and the San Ildefonso museum are all adjacent.

Also in the Zócalo is the city's Cathedral, a blend of Gothic,

Baroque and neo-Classical styles, begun in 1573, finished 250 years later and now in the midst of a major restoration to prevent it from sinking. Open daily 10:30 a.m. to 2:30 p.m.

The delegacion, or borough, of Coyoacán in the south of the city (it's best to go by taxi) is a popular destination with capital residents as well as those on the Frida Kahlo circuit. The cornflower-blue house where Kahlo was born, lived and worked is at 247 Londres, Colonia del Carmen. It contains personal effects, a pre-Hispanic art collection, Kahlo paintings and works of other artists. The spectacular, cheerful kitchen remains decorated as it was when Kahlo lived here with her husband, Diego Rivera. Open Tuesday to Sunday, 10 a.m. to 5:45 p.m.; $2.

Coyoacán is also home to some of the city's finest bookstores and restaurants, as well as great people-watching opportunities in Plaza Hidalgo. The market (at Allende and Abasolo Streets), open daily 10 a.m. to 6 p.m., is one of the best in the city. You can wander through aisles of fruit and vegetables, or enjoy a cheap meal at a counter restaurant. Seafood cocktails are $2.75 and $5, fresh-squeezed orange juice $1 and two quesadillas $1.

The Museo Mural Diego Rivera, at Balderas and Colon, Colonia Centro, (52-5) 512-0754, contains 17 incomplete works by Diego Rivera. The works, owned by Rivera's grandchildren, are in various stages of completion, and are seen as important for a study of the techniques Rivera used in his various phases. Open Tuesday to Sunday, 10 a.m. to 6 p.m. Admission: $1.

And those seeking a respite from big-city bustle may find a welcome alternative in the Parque Ejidal San Nicolás Totolapán, a cool, crisp pine forest in the far south of the city. The land belongs to the largest ejido, or communal farm, in the city, with a population of 13,000. The residents have created a well-organized, well-maintained park open to hikers, bicyclists or campers. Horses and guided tours available. For information, call Pedro Rivera, (52-5) 630-8935.

where to stay

BUDGET: There's no sign announcing Casa González, 69 Rio Sena, Colonia Cuauhtemoc, (52-5) 514-3302, a renovated mansion across from the British Embassy on a quiet street two blocks from the Paseo de la Reforma. Doubles range from $23 to $53, plus 17 percent value-added tax (referred to as IVA), and the 22 clean, bright rooms with 1950's décor are definitely a step up from Centro Histórico budget hotels; no credit cards. Family-style meals are served in the dining room ($4 to $9.50).

MODERATE: The Hotel de Cortés, 85 Avenida Hidalgo, (52-5) 518-2181, fax (52-5) 512-1863, bills itself as the city's oldest hotel, tracing its history to Augustinian friars. It's been operating as a hotel since the 1940's, across from Alameda Park. Its 29 rooms face an interior patio restaurant decorated with plants, trees and caged birds. Both single and double rooms cost $84 plus IVA.

The big advantage of the 77-room Hotel Polanco, 8 Edgar Allan Poe, Colonia Polanco, telephone and fax (52-5) 280-8082, is its proximity to Chapultepec Park. Its bright, well-lighted rooms cost $67, including IVA, for a double.

The Hotel Majestic, 73 Madero, Colonia Centro, (52-5) 521-8000, fax (52-5) 512-6262, built in 1895, faces onto the Zócalo and is part of a complex of portals and stores opposite the National Palace, with a rooftop terrace restaurant. The 85 rooms, with colonial-style furniture, are $88 plus IVA.

LUXURY: Hotel La Casa Vieja, 45 Eugenio Sue, Colonia Polanco, (52-5) 282-0067, fax (52-5) 281-3780, is an exclusive 10-suite inn close to Polanco shopping, restaurants and museums. Rates: from $250 up to $715 for the presidential suite.

where to eat

Leave the Condesa neighborhood for a week or two, and a new restaurant is sure to open while you're gone: it's one of the most popular restaurant and cafe districts.

La Sabia Virtud, 134B Tamaulipas, (52-5) 211-8416, a small cafe with a few outdoor tables, specializes in poblano (from the state of Puebla) cuisine. The chalupitas San Francisco appetizer, small tortillas with mashed beans, cheese and either pork or chicken, is $2.75, the mole poblano and the mole verde $6 each. Dinner for two with wine: about $25.

Matisse, 260 Amsterdam, (52-5) 264-5853, serves Mexican and international cuisine—squash blossom soup, beef tenderloin with mushrooms—in a restored mansion with an outdoor terrace across from the Parque de Mexico. A meal for two with wine: $30 to $35.

In the Centro Histórico, La Casa de las Sirenas, 32 Guatemala, (52-5) 704-3345, behind the Cathedral, serves Mexican and international food in a colonial building with stained glass windows and a creaky, winding wooden staircase. There's a terrace and a downstairs tequila bar. Specialties include cilantro soup, squash blossom crepes, beef tips in chipotle sauce, huachinango (red snapper) and duck. Dinner for two with wine: $40.

In Coyoacán, El Tajín, 687 Miguel Angel de Quevedo, (52-5)

659-4447, serves seafood from Veracruz and Yucatecan specialties based on the recipes of Doña Alicia Ojeda de Gironella, one of Mexico's finest chefs. It is about 10 minutes from the main plazas of Coyoacán, in the Centro Cultural Veracruzano complex. Open daily 1 to 6:30 p.m. Dishes include shrimp in tamarind sauce and a fish fillet prepared in banana leaf tamal with nopales and mushrooms. Dinner for two with wine, $45.

vital statistics

POPULATION (1995): City 8,500,000; Metro area 20,000,000

HOTEL: Room for one with tax $224.50

DINNER FOR ONE: With tax and tip but not drinks $17.55

TAXI (Sitio cabs): Per hour $4.82; From the airport $8.57

CAR RENTAL FOR A DAY: Midsize car with unlimited free mileage $46.00

FOR MORE INFORMATION: Telephone: (52-5) 250-0123; Web: www.mexico-travel.com

Sources: Runzheimer International, go2mexico.com, local businesses

Miami

Beautiful people and
beautiful weather

MIREYA NAVARRO

Mireya Navarro is a former Miami bureau chief of *The Times*.

Visitors have made Miami–Dade County the second most popular destination in Florida in recent years after Orlando, and not just because of the weather. With an average maximum temperature of 83 degrees and an average minimum of 69 degrees during the year, there is so much sunshine that a light sweater or jacket is a necessity for the indoors because of universal air-conditioning that is often set too high.

But Miami has also worked hard for its image, successfully making tourists forget the bad news about hurricanes, riots and political corruption by enticing them with new toys and playgrounds. A new basketball arena, new upscale and convention hotels and expansions at the port and airport have all been part of a building boom that is meant to solidify the area as a sophisticated cosmopolitan destination.

Alongside the boutique Art Deco hotels of Miami Beach there are hotels like the 800-room Loews Miami Beach Hotel. Near the arena where the National Basketball Association Miami Heat play, a new Performing Arts Center will rise by autumn of 2002 for fans of ballet and opera.

Ultimately, however, officials must realize that the weather is the draw. If not, why would even Miami International Airport have a sundeck?

best of times

Helping to start the new year in mid-January is Art Deco Weekend along Ocean Drive in Miami Beach, a celebration of artifacts and antiques along the oceanfront strip of restaurants and bars. Visitors do not need to stray far to see the whimsical 20th-century architecture that has made South Beach famous and stands as a testament to preservation efforts. For information, call (305) 672-2014.

The Miami International Boat Show and Strictly Sail in February is one of the largest boat and marine accessories shows in the country, with more than 2,300 boats on exhibit and free rides on a variety of craft. The show, which is celebrating its 60th anniversary in 2001, takes place at three sites: the Miami Beach Convention Center, the Bayside Marketplace and Sealine Marina in Miami. Information: (305) 531-8410.

Miami's Hispanic community puts on the best block party in town every March with the Calle Ocho Festival, which attracts hundreds of thousands of people to SW 8th Street between 4th and 27th Avenues in Little Havana to sample performances from top salsa bands and eat the food of Latin America. Of Cuban roots, the event has increasingly become a showcase for the area's diverse Latino population. Information: (305) 644-8888.

The Italian Renaissance Festival in March turns the Vizcaya Museum and Gardens at 3251 South Miami Avenue in Miami into 15th-century Italy and a playground for more than 200 costumed characters. The Festival is also an ideal way to experience the magnificence of the sprawling mansion at the edge of Biscayne Bay, which was fashioned after the villas of Veneto. Information: (305) 250-9133, extension 2250.

In November, the Fairchild Tropical Garden at 10901 Old Cutler Road in Coral Gables holds its Ramble, a garden festival with more than 15,000 plants for sale, from herbs to fruit trees. There is also food, music, exhibits and activities for kids. Information: (305) 667-1651.

what to see

The Miami Seaquarium at 4400 Rickenbacker Causeway, the bridge that leads to Key Biscayne, has added an exploration program that allows visitors (children must be at least 52 inches tall) to touch, kiss and swim with dolphins for $125 ($32 for observers). The price includes a towel and snacks as well as admission to the aquatic park's marine-life exhibits and shows, which otherwise costs $21.95 for adults, $16.95 for children 3 to 9, plus tax. Reservations, at (305) 365-2501, are required for the dolphin exploration program, which is offered twice a day Wednesday through Sunday. The park is open daily 9:30 a.m. to 6 p.m. Information: (305) 361-5705.

After swimming with the animals, you can talk with them at Parrot Jungle and Gardens at 11000 Southwest 57th Avenue in Miami, (305) 666-7834. The collection of exotic birds, monkeys and other animals is spread out in a setting of tropical trees and flowers, and there are shows with trained birds. Admission is $14.95 for adults, $9.95 ages 3 to 10, plus tax. Open daily 9:30 a.m. to 6 p.m.

A shuttle service, the Electrowave, now operates along Washington Avenue in Miami Beach's South Beach section late into the night to transport revelers among hotels, restaurants and bars, for 25 cents a ride.

A 15-mile tour through Everglades National Park's Shark Valley, about 40 miles west of downtown Miami on Highway 41, offers a glimpse of the expanse of marshlands and wildlife, including alligators and wading birds, in the Everglades. (The area sits in a slough whose waters feed the Shark River farther south.) Admission is $10 a car. Two-hour tram tours, from 9 a.m. to 4 p.m. every hour on the hour, cost $9.30 for adults, $5.50 for those age 12 or younger. Reservations, (305) 221-8455, are recommended for the tram tours in winter through April. Bike rentals, from 8:30 a.m. to 3 p.m., are $4.25 an hour. Shark Valley itself is open 8:30 a.m. to 6 p.m.

where to stay

BUDGET: The 247-room Hotel Riande Continental, 146 Biscayne Boulevard, (800) 742-6331, fax (305) 532-7689, is in the heart of downtown Miami's shopping district and across from Bayside Marketplace, the shopping and entertainment mall by Biscayne Bay. Most rooms have two double beds; all have small refrigerators. Doubles are $140.

MODERATE: A block away, the 28-room La Flora Hotel at 1238 Collins Avenue, (877) 523-5672, fax (305) 538-0850, is one of the collection of intimate boutique hotels in the Art Deco district. Rooms are decorated with soft tones and Art Deco-style furniture.

The lobby has the original terrazzo floor. Doubles: $149 to $179 with Continental breakfast. The hotel also has a business center in a 12-seat conference room.

Fairwind Hotel and Suites, 1000 Collins Avenue in Miami Beach, (305) 531-0050, fax (305) 531-0565, has 48 newly reno-vated rooms, 17 of them suites with full kitchen and dining area. An outdoor bar and inexpensive restaurant allow for people watch-ing in the heart of South Beach. Doubles: $75 to $125. Quadruple occupancy for suites: $125 to $175.

LUXURY: Ian Schrager's Delano, 1685 Collins Avenue, (800) 555-5001, fax (305) 674-6499, has added a beach "village" with tents that offer massages and spa treatments, fitness classes, and food and drink to sunbathers. The oceanfront hotel has all-white décor and geometric furniture. Doubles: $220 to $400.

The Hotel, 801 Collins Avenue in Miami Beach, (305) 531-2222, fax (305) 531-3222, an Art Deco building with three stories and 52 rooms in the heart of South Beach, has had an exquisite restoration by the fashion designer Todd Oldham. Green, blue and gold predominate in guest rooms, which have custom-designed furniture. Doubles: from $195 to $345 May through October, and $275 to $405 November through April.

where to eat

In many restaurants, particularly in Miami Beach, a tip (generally 15 percent) is included in the bill.

On Lincoln Road, a pedestrian boulevard of cafes, shops, street musicians and galleries, Balans, 1022 Lincoln Road, (305) 534-9191, is a neighborhood hangout with reliable food at reasonable prices. Main courses include an excellent herb-crusted Chilean sea bass ($17.95) and sesame-crusted tuna ($15.95). The menu also has salads and sandwiches. A three-course dinner for two with wine costs about $65. Open 8 a.m. to midnight Sunday through Thursday, until 1 a.m. on Friday and Saturday.

For Cuban fare and the latest in exile-politics gossip, there is Versailles Restaurant, 3555 Southwest Eighth Street in Little Havana; (305) 444-0240. Combination plates include El Clasico, a heap of roasted pork, ground beef stew, sweet plantains, white rice and black beans, ham croquettes, yucca and tamal pie for $10.95. A meal for two with wine costs less than $45. Open 8 a.m. to 2 a.m. Monday through Thursday, until 2 a.m. on Friday and 4 a.m. on Saturday, 9 a.m. to 2 a.m. on Sunday.

Red Fish Grill in Matheson Hammock Park at 9610 Old Cutler

Road in Coral Gables, (305) 668-8788, is out of the way but worth the trip for its setting at the edge of Biscayne Bay. You can sit outside, under palm trees and stars. Entrees include sautéed snapper with red wine grape sauce, shallot mashed potatoes and vegetables ($21.50). Reservations are suggested. Dinner for two with a modest wine runs about $80. Dinner only; closed Mondays.

A tropical courtyard is the setting for Wish at The Hotel at 801 Collins Avenue in Miami Beach, (305) 674-9474. The menu has a variety of seafood, with exotic herbal sauces, using ingredients from Asia, the Southwest and the Caribbean. Entrees include marinated grilled portobello mushrooms ($18.50) and crispy-skin yellow-eye snapper ($26.50). The executive chef is Andrea Curto, a recent winner of a *Food & Wine* magazine award. A meal for two with wine comes to about $80.

Ortanique on The Mile, at 278 Miracle Mile in Coral Gables, (305) 446-7710, serves Caribbean-inspired dishes such as jerk chicken penne pasta ($15) and pan-sautéed Bahamian black grouper marinated in teriyaki and sesame oil with an orange liqueur and rum sauce ($26.) Dinner for two, with wine: about $70.

vital statistics

POPULATION (1998 estimate): City 368,624; Metro area 2,152,437

HOTEL: Room for one with tax $156.50

DINNER FOR ONE: With tax and tip but not drinks $24.60

TAXI: Upon entry $1.50; Each additional mile $2.00; From the airport to South Beach $24.00

CAR RENTAL FOR A DAY: Midsize car with unlimited free mileage $51.00

FOR MORE INFORMATION: Telephone: (305) 539-3000; Web: www.tropicoolmiami.com

Sources: Runzheimer International, U.S. Census Bureau, local businesses

Montreal

Talk of separatism abates, and a growing self-confidence replaces it

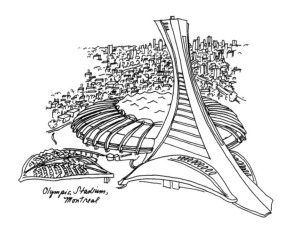

Olympic Stadium, Montreal

JAMES BROOKE

James Brooke is the Canada bureau chief of *The Times*.

This bubble of Latin culture, the world's second-largest French-speaking city, after Paris, has drawn Americans since the days of Benjamin Franklin. Promoting itself as "Paris without jet lag," Montreal can now throw in "without the long ride from the airport." All commercial air traffic now goes to Dorval International Airport, a 15-minute cab ride from downtown, as opposed to the 40-mile ride from Mirabel, the old airport.

As Americans reserve Montreal hotel rooms at the fastest clip since the Expo 67 World's Fair, they will discover an attitude change here. Montreal is on the economic rebound as investors finally accept the "French fact." With a huge concentration of college students, Montreal is churning out a French-speaking middle class. With the French language more dominant in Montreal than it has been since the 1760's, separatism is on the back burner and Quebecers are increasingly self-confident and outward looking.

best of times

Montreal is at its finest in summer, when "festival fever" grips the city and sidewalk cafes spring up like flowers. The season kicks into high gear with the Canadian Grand Prix each June. The Formula One event takes place on Île Notre-Dame, a man-made island across from the old Port. Information and tickets: (514) 350-0000.

The Montreal Jazz Festival, usually starting at the end of June, offers hundreds of concerts, most of them free, largely in and around Place des Arts downtown. Information: (888) 515-0515.

Join the television executives looking for hot comedians at the Just for Laughs festival in July. Stand-ups and troupes from around the world perform in French and English, and many of the 1,500 shows are free on outdoor stages along Rue St.-Denis. For information, call (514) 845-3155.

Fireworks set to music is the theme of the Benson & Hedges International Fireworks Competition on 10 nights in July, over the old World's Fair grounds on Île Ste.-Hélène. Among the competitors are Japan, Germany, Italy and the United States. Information: (514) 872-6222.

July finishes and August begins with the Lesbian and Gay Pride celebration, with attendance expected to hit half a million for the Pride Parade on the last day. Information: (514) 285-4011.

Montrealers go indoors when temperatures drop, and art galleries, theaters and orchestras save their finest offerings for the fall and winter months. For information on exhibitions and events, call (514) 844-5400.

The city's cozy jazz clubs are particularly appealing after a day spent ice-skating in the Old Port or cross-country skiing on the Lachine Canal. The new Winter High Lights Festival, held from mid-February to early March, celebrates Montreal's enviable cultural and gastronomic heritage with events at more than 100 restaurants, theaters and museums across the city. Free light shows are held each night of the festival at the Place des Arts. Information: (514) 288-9955 or (888) 477-9955.

what to see

The delights of a Montreal summer require footwork: strolling centuries-old blocks and streets, inspecting architectural details, reading historic plaques, window shopping on streets lined with antiques shops, or sipping an allongé coffee at a sidewalk cafe. The best neighborhoods for walks are Vieux-Port, the Old Port section where the city began life 358 years ago; the Rue St.-Denis restaurant, cafe and shopping streets; and Rue Ste.-Catherine, the shopping and entertainment district.

For $13.50, the Montreal Museum Pass allows holders to visit 21 museums over two days. A good place to start is just off the docks in the Old Port section. The new Pointe-à-Callière Montreal Museum of Archaeology and History, Place Royale at Rue de la Commune, offers visitors a good background on the city's development, starting with a fast-paced, Monty Python–style bilingual multimedia show on Montreal's history. The tower provides a bird's-eye view of Old Montreal and the St. Lawrence River. Open 10 a.m. to 6 p.m. Tuesday to Friday, 11 a.m. to 5 p.m. weekends; (514) 872-9150. Admission: $5.75 for adults, $2 ages 6 to 12.

If you need a break from the heat (yes, it can happen even in Montreal), slip into the cool and soothing, robin's-egg-blue interior of Notre-Dame Basilica, about three blocks up the hill from the history museum, at 110 Rue Notre-Dame West. This graceful Gothic Revival church was believed to be the largest religious edifice in North America when it opened in 1829. The architect, a New Yorker named James O'Donnell, was so taken with its soaring, gold-leaf interior and stained-glass windows depicting the history of Montreal that he converted to Catholicism in order to be buried there. Admission is $1.35.

The Montreal Botanical Garden, 4101 Sherbrooke East, one of the world's largest, hits full bloom in late June. With 21,000 species of plants, the gardens sprawl over 30 acres, ranging from formal European gardens, to a Chinese pavilion in the style of the Ming Dynasty, to a 16-acre arboretum and 10 exhibition greenhouses. Admission: $6.45 for adults, seniors and students $4.75, ages 6 to 17 $3.20; (514) 872-1400.

After stopping to smell the roses, you may desire more vigorous activity. There's bicycling along an eight-mile lighted, paved path from René Lévesque Park to the Père Marquette Promenade, a route that passes by the Lachine Rapids. Bikes can be rented at any of several kiosks in the Old Port.

where to stay

Rooms can be scarce during major festivals, and high demand caused by the strength of the United States dollar will also make rooms hard to find.

BUDGET: At the junction of the busy bar, restaurant and boutique scene, at the corner of Rue Ste.-Catherine and Rue Crescent, the Comfort Suites, 1214 Rue Crescent, (514) 878-2711, fax (514) 878-0030, offers 96 simple, comfortable rooms, each with balcony. Doubles: $80 to $112.

One block to the east, the Novotel, 1180 Rue de la Montagne,

(514) 861-6000, fax (514) 861-0992, has slightly higher priced rooms on a street lined with boutiques and restaurants. The 227 rooms have bright, modern décor, and there is a fitness center. Doubles: $87 to $135.

MODERATE: With 487 spacious rooms, the Holiday Inn Montreal-Midtown, 420 Sherbrooke Street West, (514) 842-6111, fax (514) 842-9381, is a good bet during the peak season. Many of the rooms have views along Sherbrooke, Montreal's Fifth Avenue. Doubles are $114 to $150.

For the charm of Old Montreal, the Auberge du Vieux-Port, 97 Rue de la Commune East, (888) 660-7678, fax (514) 876-8923, is a late-19th-century stone building converted to a hotel. The 27 neo-Classical rooms, in great demand, have brass beds, stone or brick walls, and large casement windows overlooking the port docks. Doubles are $129 to $179, including full breakfast.

LUXURY: The Ritz-Carlton Montréal, 1228 Sherbrooke West, (514) 842-4212, fax (514) 842-4907, the 88-year-old empress of Montreal's Golden Mile, has just emerged from a renovation that added luster to its marble bathrooms, to its rooms appointed with antiques, and to its piano bar and delightful garden restaurant. The turn-of-the-century ambience melds nicely with two-line phones in the 229 rooms. Doubles are $288.

The largest of half a dozen inns to open in historic buildings in old Montreal in recent years, the Auberge Bonaparte, 447 St.-Francois Xavier, (514) 844-1448, fax (514) 844-0272, offers views of Montreal's historic heart from many of its 30 individually decorated rooms. On a quiet side street, the Bonaparte has an excellent restaurant of the same name. Doubles: $98 to $132.

where to eat

It used to be said that, after language and politics, food was the favorite topic of conversation in Quebec. But now, judging by the expanding waistlines of the graying separatist leaders, food may be winning out.

My introduction to the sensuous culinary delights of Montreal came one winter when a waitress at Toque instructed me to place a chunk of warm foie gras on my tongue and feel it dissolve around the sides. In an unpretentious setting on Montreal's restaurant row, Toque, 3842 Rue St.-Denis, (514) 499-2084, is near the top of the city's dining pyramid. Giving Québécois products a new spin, the chef, Normand Laprise, serves maple-syrup-glazed quail as an appetizer, and roasted saddle of lamb with butternut squash and fiddlehead ferns among the main courses. Dinner for two, with wine, was $150. Reservations are essential.

Within walking distance of the Sherbrooke Street hotels is an old favorite for a quiet romantic dinner by the fireplace, Chez la Mère Michel, 1209 Rue Guy, (514) 934-0473. As flute music warbled, we had lobster soufflé Nantua and tournedos bearnaise. Dinner for two, with wine, was $142.

In heavily French-speaking East Montreal, Laloux is an elegant restaurant popular with the business crowd at lunch. It is run by an expatriate French chef, André Besson, and is at 250 Avenue des Pins East, (514) 287-9127, on a quiet street far from the tourist flow. Laloux offers veal escalope with dried apricots, almonds, muscat wine sauce and linguini, or poached red snapper with white wine, à la mandarine, and crispy vegetables. Dinner for two, with wine: $68.

An affordable place in the Old Port neighborhood is Stash's Café, 200 St.-Paul West, (514) 845-6611, a Polish restaurant with a Warsaw counterculture air. Ensconced behind thick stone walls with views of pedestrian traffic, Stash's offers four-course menus for $13 to $16.50. Specialties include zurek (a white borscht), wild boar, and strudel.

Pino, 1471 Rue Crescent, (514) 289-1930, with a heavily Italian menu, is strategically perched on a second-floor corner, with tables placed by the curving windows for people-watching along Rue Ste.-Catherine. Calamari with garlic butter, a three-cheese green pasta and beers came to $36 for two.

(Susan Catto, a Canadian researcher for *The New York Times,* contributed to this article.)

vital statistics

POPULATION (1999): City 1,000,000; Metro area 3,428,500

HOTEL: Room for one with tax $99.00

DINNER FOR ONE: With tax and tip but not drinks $19.00

TAXI: Upon entry $1.69; Each additional kilometer 83 cents; From the airport $18.00

CAR RENTAL FOR A DAY: Midsize car with unlimited free mileage $35.09

FOR MORE INFORMATION: Telephone: (800) 363-7777; Web: www.tourism-montreal.org

Sources: Runzheimer International, Statistics Canada, local businesses

Munich

Big festivals,
but lots of stunning architecture, too

JOHN TAGLIABUE

JOHN TAGLIABUE is a *Times* correspondent in Paris.

There is more, of course, to Munich than the sights, sounds and smells of Christmas, the raucous and rousing merriment of Fasching, the Bavarian variety of Mardi Gras, and the drunken revelry of Oktoberfest. The city also has some of Europe's finest museums, and picturesque neighborhoods, like the old Bohemian quarter in Schwabing, invite exploration.

When snow begins to fall, Alpine ski resorts lie at the city's doorstep. From early summer into the autumn, Alpine pastures invite hikers, and picturesque Bavarian lakes, like the Ammersee, Starnberger See, Tegernsee and Chiemsee are easily accessible by car or train.

best of times

Spring and summer bring the most favorable weather, but it's almost worth skipping Munich at its most seasonable to enjoy its big blowouts.

Come in December, and you'd think this was the place that invented Christmas. And in some ways, you'd be right. After all, didn't the Christmas tree arise from the medieval German custom of draping evergreen branches in the home with sausages and apples? And doesn't our image of Santa Claus stem largely from the pen of Thomas Nast, the 19th-century political cartoonist who was born in Germany? One of Germany's most endearing Christmas customs remains the Christmas Market, outdoor fairs where ornaments, toys and gingerbread burden stalls, and the bracing perfume of sizzling sausages and mulled wine laces the cold air. German cities vie for the loveliest Christmas Market, and certainly Munich is a leading contender. Christmas in Munich is also a time for music, when musicians perform the "Christmas Oratorio" by Bach and churches resound with carols.

On the opposite pole from the Christmas market is rousing Fasching, which begins just after the New Year and ends on the eve of Ash Wednesday, when the women who tend the stalls at the Viktualienmarkt, the city's vast outdoor food market, perform their traditional Fasching dance.

In April and May, Munich celebrates the Frühlingsfest, or spring festival, at the Theresienwiese (a scaled-down version of the better known Oktoberfest, which takes place on the same site), and the Auer Dult, a weeklong mix of Coney Island and flea market that always starts on the last Saturday in April.

In years ending in even numbers (the next is the spring of 2002), there is the Biennale, a festival of contemporary music and theater at the Philharmonie am Gasteig and the Muffathalle.

Each year in July, the Bayerische Staatsoper stages the Opernfestival, which always ends July 31 with Richard Wagner's "Die Meistersinger von Nürnberg."

August brings the Sommerfest, at the Olympiapark, the site of the 1972 Olympic Games, featuring nightly concerts with live rock and jazz bands, eating and drinking, and sporting contests in events like rowing, climbing and mountain biking.

From mid-September to the first Sunday in October, of course, there is the infamous Oktoberfest, with its enormous beer tents, amusement rides and rivers of beer, beginning with a festive parade of beer brewers and beerhall waiters accompanied by colorful floats and brass bands.

what to see

A quick walk through the center of town leads to some of Munich's most magnificent rococo churches, among them the Asamkirche, the Church of St. Peter (or Peterskirche) and the Holy Ghost Church.

Of these, the Asamkirche is the most splendid. Situated along Sendlingerstrasse, it is officially named for St. John of Nepomuk, the 14th-century Czech martyr, but is better known by the name of Asam, for the brothers, star architects and sculptors of the Bavarian rococo. The interior, which should be viewed in the early morning, when light streams in the enormous facade window, is an explosion of decorative splendor.

The Peterskirche, the oldest in Munich, contains a magnificent rococo altar and statuary, and its upper reaches, until recently hidden by scaffolding, now feature the re-creation of 18th-century ceiling frescoes by the artist Johann Baptist Zimmermann that were destroyed in World War II. Entry is free.

A short walk from the Peterskirche is the Spielzeugmuseum, or Toy Museum, on several floors that are reachable by a narrow, twisting stairway of a tower in the Old Town Hall. It features a delightful collection of 19th- and 20th-century playthings, with wood-carved figurines and windup Popeyes; the Barbie dolls include first-generation models from the 1950's. Tickets: $2.30 for adults, 40 cents for children; (49-89) 271-1969.

Another fascinating place for young and old is the Deutsches Museum of science and technology, 1 Museumsinsel on an island in the Isar River. There are hundreds of exhibits, many of them mechanical, that illustrate mining and steel making, bridge building and computer technology. Press a button and watch a car being assembled. Admission: $5.50; (49-89) 21791.

where to stay

BUDGET: The Pension Agnes, 58 Agnesstrasse, about a 10-minute walk from a subway stop, has 26 rooms spread over several floors of an old walkup on a tree-lined side street. Doubles: $54 to $60; (49-89) 123-9450, fax (49-89) 123-9450.

The Hotel am Goetheplatz, 33 Waltherstrasse, at the Goetheplatz subway stop on a line to Marienplatz, offers 20 simply decorated rooms that look out onto a tree-lined square. Doubles: $60 to $90; (49-89) 530-306, fax (49-89) 5303-0624.

MODERATE: Given Munich's excellent subway system, you don't have to stay downtown. But if you do, one choice is Hotel am Markt, at 6 Heiliggeiststrasse, a narrow lane behind the Church of the Holy Ghost. It offers 30 recently renovated, but small, rooms, and not all have bathrooms and showers. Doubles: $51 to $79; (49-89) 225-014, fax (49-89) 224-017.

In the center of town, and slightly more expensive, is the Hotel

Excelsior, in the pedestrian mall at 11 Schutzenstrasse, which has 113 rooms comfortably furnished in a vaguely Alpine style. Doubles: $181 to $200; (49-89) 551370, fax (49-89) 5513-7121.

LUXURY: The Hotel Vier Jahres zeiten, at 17 Maximilianstrasse amid elegant stores and restaurants, is the queen of Munich hostelry. A five-minute stroll from the neo-Classical opera house and former residence of the kings of Bavaria, it has 318 sumptuous rooms with equally splendid bathrooms. Doubles: $245; (49-89) 21250, fax (49-89) 2125-2000.

Elegant, yet with more rustic Bavarian flavor, is the Bayerischer Hof, 2-6 Promenadeplatz, with Alpine antiques in its hallways and 409 rooms. Doubles: $287 to $407; (49-89) 21200, fax (49-89) 212-0900.

where to eat

Bavaria is largely pork-and-potato territory, which doesn't mean that it cannot be done imaginatively and tastefully. It is also serious beer country, and the favorite is Weissbier, a flavorful, cloudy type of brew taken in bulbous tankards of at least a half-liter in size. Many restaurants have the character of beer halls, with noise, bonhomie and often music.

Elegant fare can be enjoyed a stone's throw from the Viktualienmarkt, the city's large food market, at Grune Gans, which seats about 30 in a homey, dark wood atmosphere at 5 Am Einlass. Dinner for two—a first course of light potato pancakes with caviar of trout in creme fraiche followed by roast pheasant, cranberry sauce and champagne kraut, and by a desert of crepes filled with apple ragout—comes to about $90 with wine. Reservations required. Closed Sundays; (49-89) 266- 228.

In the shadow of the Cathedral, at 9 Frauenplatz, is the justifiably well-know Nurnberger Bratwurst-Glockl am Dom, a cozy place with dark wood walls and pewter plates that specializes in delectable pinky-sized sausages from Nuremberg, charcoal-grilled and served with steaming sauerkraut. A meal for two of beef broth with whole egg yolk and a platter of six sausages with sauerkraut, washed down by a glass of beer or white wine, comes to about $33; (49-89) 220 385.

One of the best-known restaurants for dressing up basic Bavarian ingredients is the cozy Weinhaus Neuner, at 8 Herzogspitalstrasse, in warm and inviting rooms that have served as an inn for four centuries. A meal might begin with homemade blood wurst on creamed sauerkraut with a truffle sauce, followed by venison calf filet in juniper flavored cream sauce with red cabbage, cranberry sauce and freshly prepared potato noodles. Dinner for two, with wine: $105. Reservations are recommended; (49-89) 260-3954.

Some of Munich's best cooking is Italian, given the city's proximity to northern Italy. La Grotta, 24 Schraudolphstrasse, is a bright little place on the edge of the lively Schwabing neighborhood. Dinner for two with wine—consisting of shrimp and chanterelle mushrooms, followed by grilled scampi, and profiterole for desert—costs about $72; (49-89) 271- 6363.

For a totally different experience with the whole family, try the Movenpick Marche Restaurant, at 19 Neuhauser Strasse, which offers a big assortment of fresh fish, meat, sausages and pizza, served cafeteria-style. Lunch or dinner for two, with beer or wine, comes to about $18; (49-89) 230-8790.

Most fun, however, is to drop by the Viktualienmarkt. A variety of stalls offer freshly prepared Bavarian specialties, like leberkas, a flat liver patty, or the deservedly famous weisswurst, plump white veal sausages served with sweet mustard. Weisswurst for two, with a pretzel and beer, costs about $10.

vital statistics

POPULATION (1999): City 1,315,254; Metro area 2 million

HOTEL: Room for one with tax $210.00

DINNER FOR ONE: With tax and tip but not drinks $26.55

TAXI: Upon entry $2.50; Each additional kilometer $1.10; From the airport $50.00

CAR RENTAL FOR A DAY: Midsize car with unlimited free mileage $90.00

FOR MORE INFORMATION: Telephone: (49-89) 233-0300; Web: www.muenchen-tourist.de

Sources: Runzheimer International, Munich Tourist Office, local businesses

Napa and Sonoma

Lots of wine and
an abundance of the good life

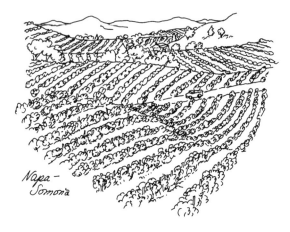

EVELYN NIEVES, JESSE McKINLEY
AND CHRISTOPHER HALL

Evelyn Nieves is chief of *The Times*'s San Francisco bureau.
Jesse McKinley writes about theater for *The Times*.
Christopher Hall contributes to *The Times* from San Francisco.

The Spanish Franciscan padres planted the first grapes in California in the late 18th century, but it took a 19th-century Hungarian immigrant named Agoston Haraszthy to spread the word that parts of the state—and Napa and Sonoma in particular—were ideally suited to the commercial production of wine. At his Buena Vista Winery, outside the town of Sonoma, Haraszthy's vines flourished even though he planted them on dry hillsides with no irrigation. One secret to his success: the Mediterranean climate of winter rains and summer warmth, with the Northern California twist of a summertime flow of marine air to keep things from getting overheated.

Haraszthy's efforts have borne fruit, as Napa and Sonoma are now among the world's premier wine-producing regions. In some ways, however, the two could not be more dissimilar. Where Napa is largely confined to a single crop in a single valley—which clogs with the cars of wine-tasting hordes during the summer and the fall crush—Sonoma is a sprawling, agriculturally diverse county with far-flung viticultural regions and a long coastline; where most of Napa's towns have the country-chic air of an idealized Tuscany or Provence, the funky and the fashionable seem to mix more freely in Sonoma.

Still, the good life can be had in either place. You can certainly find it while pampering yourself with a day of spa treatments or savoring an old cabernet and fine Euro-California cuisine at a big-name restaurant. But the true beauty of this impossibly blessed region is that the good life is just as easily experienced during an inexpensive vineyard picnic—feeling the sun on your face as you tuck into a tangy Sonoma chèvre, crusty bread and a fruity, young zinfandel.

best of times

The warm, sunny months of summer and early fall are a great time to see Napa and Sonoma—just ask any of the untold thousands who visit then. After the harvest, things begin to quiet down, and the charm of Napa and Sonoma is easier to appreciate. Although the winter and spring are showery and cooler, the vineyards appear at their most starkly beautiful then, as gnarled, leafless vines are silhouetted against emerald hills and brilliant, yellow carpets of wild mustard.

Throughout February and March, the Napa Valley Mustard Festival, (707) 259-9020, presents a series of cultural and culinary events, from art exhibitions to master-chef dinners. In June, the parties, tastings and bidding during the Napa Valley Wine Auction, (800) 982-1371, draw bon vivants from around the world, despite a ticket price in the low four-figures.

More democratic is August's Gravenstein Apple Fair, (707) 571-8288, in the Sonoma apple-growing town of Sebastopol. In September, redwood-shaded Guerneville in western Sonoma hosts the Russian River Jazz Festival, (707) 869-3940, where you can splash in the water while listening to cool riffs.

In October, the Wine Country's bounty is celebrated at the Sonoma County Harvest Fair, (707) 545-4203, in Santa Rosa.

wineries

There are more than 250 vineyards in the Napa Valley, and more than 190 in Sonoma County. Many of them offer tours and free samples.

The caves at Beringer Vineyards, 2000 Main Street, St. Helena,

(707) 963-4812, are just one of the reasons to see this winery, the oldest continuously operating one in Napa Valley. The 17-room Victorian Rhine House, on the National Register of Historic Places, features stained glass and ornate wood panels. Tours cost $5.

A relative newcomer to the Sonoma scene is the Viansa Winery, 25200 Arnold Drive (Highway 121), (707) 935-4700. Founded in 1990, Viansa is owned by Sam Sebastiani, a scion of the prominent wine family. The terraced, Italianate estate, on a hillside at the southern end of the Sonoma Valley, has sweeping views of the countryside and a specialty foods shop, the Italian Marketplace, on the premises. Wine tastings are free, and offered daily; picnicking and self-guided tours are also available.

And for sheer panache, the Niebaum-Coppola Winery in Napa is worth seeing. Owned by the filmmaker Francis Ford Coppola and his family, the estate, with a formal plaza and eucalyptus grove, has a permanent exhibition of old filmmaking gadgets (zoetropes) and winemaking tools (like stomping shoes). It's located at 1991 St. Helena Highway, Rutherford; (707) 963-9099.

what to see

The pleasures of Yountville, a picture-postcard town in the heart of the Napa Valley, include Vintage 1870, 6526 Washington Street, a winery converted into a mall of boutiques, and, next door, the Depot Gallery, an artists' collective. Yountville City Park, at Washington and Lincoln Streets, is a favorite spot for people-watching.

Petaluma, once described as the World's Egg Basket, still has chicken ranches, but it is becoming a destination for a downtown chock-full of antiques stores and boutiques. A good walking-tour brochure is available at the Petaluma Chamber of Commerce, 799 Baywood Drive, Petaluma, California 94952; (707) 762-2785.

Just as wines need careful handling, sometimes their purchasers do, too. A variety of spas can be found in and near Calistoga, the funky town built atop a boiling underground river. Nance's Hot Springs, 1614 Lincoln Avenue, (707) 942-6211, offers a hot-spring mineral bath, steam bath, black volanic mud bath and blanket sweat. One of every treatment, including a massage, costs $80. Indian Springs Spa, 1712 Lincoln Avenue, (707) 942-4913, includes a geyser-heated mineral swimming pool, as well as mud and mineral baths and massages. Treatments cost $65 to $150.

In addition to providing near-ideal weather, the area's dry, southerly breezes create fine conditions for all manner of aerial sport. Balloons Above the Valley, at 5091 Solano Avenue, in Napa, is one of the bigger companies of its kind, with balloons carrying anywhere from 8 to 16 passengers. After an hourlong flight, passengers receive a champagne breakfast. Flights are daily and cost $165 a person. Reservations are required. Call (800) 464-6824.

The Culinary Institute of America, at 2555 Main Street in St. Helena, is the West Coast affiliate of New York State's esteemed school. The institute—housed in a century-old stone building, originally the Christian Brothers' Greystone Cellars—has a gorgeous herb garden, an excellent kitchenware store and cooking demonstrations. Information: (707) 967-1010. Daily tours include cooking demonstrations on weekends. Fee: $2 on weekdays; $5 on weekends.

where to stay

BUDGET: The Village Inn, 20822 River Boulevard, (707) 865-2304, fax (707) 865-2332, in Monte Rio, an old beach town on the Russian River with a big faded "Vacation Wonderland" sign over the highway, is where the winter classic *Holiday Inn* was filmed. It is also funky and comfortable, with 10 rooms, with bathrooms, costing $65 to $140.

The Best Western Inn at the Vine, 100 Soscol Avenue, Napa, (707) 257-1930, fax (707) 255-0709, offers 68 rooms and loft suites with living rooms, a heated pool and whirlpool. Rates start at $110.

MODERATE: The Mount View Hotel, 1457 Lincoln Avenue, Calistoga, (707) 942-6877, fax (707) 942-6904, is a beautifully restored 1917 house decorated in country French style. Rates are $125 to $275, with a Continental breakfast served in the 29 rooms and 3 cottages.

Tall Timbers Chalets, off Highway 29 at 1012 Darms Lane, south of Yountville, (707) 252-7810, fax (707) 252-1055, is a nice change from the Victorian mansion bed-and-breakfasts that dot the valley. The eight country cottages, some with decks or porches, sleep four and cost $150.

LUXURY: The Madrona Manor, 1001 Westside Road, Healdsburg, (800) 258-4003, fax (707) 433-0703, is a Sonoma institution. The 1881 Victorian mansion and renovated outbuildings have 18 rooms and 4 suites, all decorated differently, some with antiques, most with fireplaces. Rates are $165 to $450, with breakfast.

One of the area's largest resorts is the 1,200-acre Silverado Country Club, a sprawling 19th-century estate with 23 tennis courts, 8 swimming pools and a pair of 18-hole golf courses. All of the Silverado's 312 suites are condominiums with fireplaces and

French-style furniture. The Silverado is at 1600 Atlas Peak Road, in Napa, (800) 532-0500, fax (707) 257-5425. Rates: $140 to $1,250.

where to eat

Tra Vigne, 1050 Charter Oak Avenue, St. Helena, (707) 963-4444, is a cozy trattoria in a landmark stone building. Its menu, regional Italian, offers interesting small plates of pastas and pizzas to complement its meats and fish. Dinner for two, including wine, is about $80.

Deuce, 691 Broadway, Sonoma, (707) 933-3823, is a clean, well-lighted place with both contemporary (grilled salmon with red bean chile, forbidden black rice and avocado salsa) and traditional (roasted pork loin) American food, featuring local produce and wines. Dinner for two, with wine, is about $70.

Pinot Blanc, at 641 Main Street in St. Helena, (707) 963-6191, is owned by Joachim Splichal, the Los Angeles–based chef. The restaurant has patio seating warmed by a wood-burning fireplace and an interior that suggests a 1940's bistro. The menu is playful and rich, with tasty items like "high cholesterol" foie gras and "towers" of ahi tuna. The wine list includes more than 300 wines. Dinner for two with a moderately priced bottle of wine is $95.

Brix, a restaurant and wine shop at 7377 St. Helena Highway in Yountville, (707) 944-2749, has an open kitchen and redwood details. The menu, described as Asian fusion, includes Korean quail with mango chili sauce, rack of lamb with peanut satay, and ahi tuna with wasabi aioli. Dinner for two with wine is about $100.

For lunch on the go, the Oakville Grocery, 7856 St. Helena Highway, Oakville, (707) 944-8802, is a delightful place to pick up a picnic. The wide variety of cheeses, spreads and breads complements the valley's bottled attractions, which are also sold here. A full bag of goodies for two runs about $40.

vital statistics

POPULATION (1998 estimate): Napa County 119,288; Sonoma County 433,304

HOTEL (High season weekend): Room for one with tax $200.00

DINNER FOR ONE: With tax and tip but not drinks $35.00

TRANSPORTATION: Airport transfer by van $18.00 (to Napa); $28.00 (to Sonoma)

CAR RENTAL FOR A DAY: Midsize car with unlimited free mileage $37.00

FOR MORE INFORMATION: Telephone: (707) 226-7459 for Napa, (800) 576-6662 for Sonoma; Web: www.napavalley.com, www.sonomavalley.com

Sources: Runzheimer International, Napa Valley Conference and Visitors Bureau, Sonoma Valley Visitors Bureau, U.S. Census Bureau, local businesses

New Delhi

A stately demeanor,
mixed with gritty reality

Humayon's Tomb,
New Delhi

CELIA W. DUGGER

Celia W. Dugger is co-chief of the New Delhi bureau of *The Times*.

If Bombay is India's New York City, then New Delhi is its Washington, a capital city with a staid provincial air that boasts broad, stately boulevards, grand vistas of awe-inspiring monuments and an abundance of bureaucrats and politicians. It is a place where the history of India—from the time of the Mughal emperors, through the British Raj, and into the post-independence era—is visible everywhere, like the layers of an archaeological dig.

The best way to get a feel for the city, particularly the buildings that were designed and laid out by the architect Edwin Lutyens during the Raj, is to hire a taxi (you'll have to ask for one with seat belts, since most have none). Be sure to take the majestic drive up to India Gate, the giant archway that is Delhi's Arc de Triomphe, a memorial to the 90,000 soldiers of the Indian Army who died in World War I. One of the spokes of the wheel of streets that spins out from India Gate, Rajpath, leads to Rashtrapati Bhawan, the official residence of the President of India, once the British Viceroy's house.

To step back in time, visit Shah Jahanabad, the city established by Emperor Shahjahan 350 years ago. Known today as Old Delhi, it is still a thriving, vital place. Walk through the vast interior of the Red Fort and its ill-kempt gardens or rent a bicycle rickshaw to take you through the narrow, clogged alleyways.

Anywhere you go, be prepared for the city's poor to jostle up against you. In the middle of busy streets, urchins, mothers holding naked babies and men with misshapen bodies knock on car windows, begging for a few rupees. Once out of official New Delhi, the jhuggis, or slums, sprawl outward from the highways.

best of times

Delhi's greatest annual events are its festivals. Republic Day on January 26 features a magnificent parade of soldiers, camels, brass bands and floats, with tickets available two weeks in advance. During Holi, the riotous spring festival that falls in February and March, people smear each other with colored powder and dump colored water on each other.

For Diwali in October, houses are illuminated with candles and lights, and shops selling Indian sweets and firecrackers spring up all over the city. Also in October, Dussehra celebrates the victory of Lord Rama over the demon king Ravana by exploding effigies of Ravana with firecrackers. The largest celebration takes place at the Ramlila grounds near Old Delhi.

what to see

Raj Ghat, the memorial to Mohandas K. Gandhi, father of the nation, is moving, not because of the simple petal-strewn marble platform but because of the pilgrims who touch it with reverence and emotion. With luggage balanced on their heads, they circle the memorial in a kind of mourning dance that has never ended since his assassination more than 50 years ago. It is set in a well-kept park east of the Red Fort, between the Ring Road and the Yamuna River.

Chandni Chowk, a shopping area from the Mughal era and still a thriving marketplace, has been spruced up. Here Delhiites buy everything from electrical appliances to deep-fried sweets at Jalebi Wala, an open-air shop where men squirt the pretzel-shaped treats called jalebis into vats of boiling oil.

Lodi Garden, next to the India International Center, is a lovely spot for a picnic or a stroll. Its tranquil, beautifully landscaped grounds are laid out around the tombs of the Lodi and Sayyid sultans who ruled north India in the 15th and 16th centuries.

The National Gallery of Modern Art, (91-11) 338-2835, near

India Gate on Rajpath, was once the Delhi residence of the Maharajah of Jaipur. Its bright, spacious galleries now house Indian and colonial art. Except for Mondays and holidays, the museum is open daily from 10 a.m. to 5 p.m. Admission is 12 cents.

The Crafts Museum, opposite the Purana Qila on Mathura Road, (91-11) 337-1641, a series of galleries in village huts, is a wondrous collection of the folk and tribal arts and crafts of India, which still provide a livelihood to more than 20 million people. Admission is free.

Delhi has many wonderful places to treasure-hunt. The prettiest is Santushti Shopping Complex in the Willingdon Air Force Camp, in Chanakyapuri, where elegant shops in white bungalows are set on a greensward along curving stone pathways. The shops sell clothing, crafts, jewelry and household objects. At Noorjehan a hand-painted scarf is $33. At Lotus Eaters, a silk and Pashmina shawl is $106.

Dilli Haat, Sri Aurobindo Marg, opposite the INA market, is a large, pleasant crafts market spread over six acres. The 62 stalls are arranged around a large, clean brick plaza. There is an admission charge of 12 cents. Here you can buy four sparkly arm bangles for $1.20 and a hand-painted sari from Bihar for $35. At the back of the plaza are stalls that sell snacks and meals from different regions of India that can be eaten at stone picnic tables.

where to stay

BUDGET: The Maharani Guest House, 3 Sunder Nagar, (91-11) 469-3129, is in one of the city's residential neighborhoods, close to the main Sunder Nagar market. This modest hotel is neatly kept, with its front lawn clipped like a mustache. The 24 rooms are spacious and air-conditioned. Mattresses on the wooden platform beds are on the thin side. A double room is $52, plus 10 percent tax.

Hotel Fifty Five, H-55 Connaught Circus, (91-11) 332-1244, fax (91-11) 332-0769, is a spare, air-conditioned hotel with a small terrace looking over the horn-tooting traffic that rushes past. Its 15 smallish rooms come with bathrooms and telephones, but no television. A double room costs $35, plus 10 percent tax.

MODERATE: The Ambassador Hotel, Sujan Singh Park, (91-11) 463-2600, fax (91-11) 463-8219, has pleasant, sunny rooms with window air-conditioning units. Near Khan market, a shopping center with everything from aspirin to books to handicrafts, the 88-room hotel has a cheerful coffee shop where people crowd the hand-painted yellow and blue tables. Double rooms cost $140 plus 20 percent tax.

Nirula's Hotel, L-Block, Connaught Circus, (91-11) 332-2419, fax (91-11) 335-3957, is a popular place near one of New Delhi's main shopping areas at Connaught Circle. The 28-room hotel has a lounge where light streams through large windows and a bustling coffee shop, and is next door to an ice cream parlor. The rooms are standard-issue, with central air-conditioning and showers. A double costs $68 plus 10 percent tax.

LUXURY: Delhi has a number of plush hotels, but perhaps the most elegant is the 290-room Oberoi New Delhi; (91-11) 436-3030, fax (91-11) 436-0484. It offers a gorgeous swimming pool; sybaritic health club; fancy Thai, Chinese and French restaurants; a 24-hour coffee shop that serves delectable Indian lunch buffets and beautifully decorated rooms. Doubles begin at $200 plus 20 percent tax.

The vaulted marble lobby of the 518-room Hyatt Regency Delhi, Bhikaji Cama Place, Ring Road, (91-11) 679-1234, fax (91-11) 679-1122, is brightened with lavish displays of fresh flowers. The hotel has a big pool and children's pool, tennis courts, a fitness center and the city's best Italian restaurant, La Piazza. It's fun to sip a Kingfisher beer and eat chips and salsa, Indian style, at the Polo Lounge, a wood-paneled bar. Doubles start at $250, plus 20 percent tax.

where to eat

Bukhara, at the Maurya Sheraton Hotel, Diplomatic Enclave, (91-11) 611-2233, is one of the most festive places to eat in Delhi. It is deservedly famous for its tandoori specialties from the Northwest Frontier provinces of India. The stone-clad walls are draped with carpets. Copper pots hang from wooden rafters. And guests, eating at wooden trestle tables with their fingers, consume platters of lamb, chicken and fish pomfret that have been marinated and roasted in the tandoor oven. A dinner for two with wine costs about $100.

Many Indian restaurants not based in the big hotels are very inexpensive by American standards. Moti Mahal, the famous old Indian restaurant on Netaji Subhash Marg, (91-11) 327-3011, serves tasty tandoori chicken, spicy lamb stews and buttery dal. Diners can eat outside and listen to live quawwali singing. Dinner for two, with beer (no wine is served), costs about $20.

Getting to Karim, Gali Kababiyan, Matia Mahal, near the Jama Masjid, (91-11) 326-9880, means wading through beggars, bicycle rickshaws and shoppers into the narrow, jam-packed alleyways of the old city. It is a raucous, smoky, exotic scene, a little like something out of an Indiana Jones movie. The restaurant is not air-conditioned and sells no alcohol, but the kebabs, tandoori meats and curried dishes are delicious. Dinner for two costs about $10.

The Sweets Corner, at 1 Sunder Nagar Market, (91-11) 461-9261, is a South Indian vegetarian restaurant that sells no alcohol. At the entrance is the Dosa Counter, where men at a griddle spread batter for the South Indian–style thin, crispy pancakes called dosa, then fill them with delectable spicy stuffings. It would take two people with very big appetites to spend more than $5 on dinner.

vital statistics

POPULATION (2000 estimate): City 9,300,000

HOTEL: Room for one with tax $293.00

DINNER FOR ONE: With tax and tip but not drinks $20.40

TAXI: Upon entry $1.00; Each additional kilometer 25 cents; From the airport $35.00

CAR RENTAL FOR A DAY: Midsize car with 80 free kilometers $84.00

FOR MORE INFORMATION: Telephone: (91-11) 332-0005; Web: www.tourindia.com

Sources: Runzheimer International, Government of India Tourist Office, local businesses

New Orleans

You could think you're in a foreign country,
but the tastes and sounds are uniquely its own

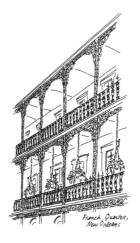

French Quarter,
New Orleans

FRANCES FRANK MARCUS

Frances Frank Marcus, a frequent contributor to *The Times,*
lives in New Orleans.

On damp early mornings in springtime when fog wraps the old colonial buildings in the French Quarter, you can believe you're strolling the narrow streets of a quiet town on the Mediterranean coast of Spain. But not for long. By late morning, with the sun warming, music all around and the scent of jasmine drifting over courtyard walls, you know you're in sultry Louisiana.

Winter hardly scrapes the city—though on occasion a quick cold spell will bruise the semitropical greenery or fade a camellia blossom—but the departure of cooler weather has little to do with the fun that follows. In New Orleans, a pestilence-ridden 18th-century outpost that defied the odds to become party heaven, it's accepted that every 10 minutes, there's fresh cause to frolic.

Thanks to the city's many first-rate restaurants, the seafood in the Gulf of Mexico and nearby lakes and swamps—rich in the ingredients for jambalaya, gumbo and shrimp remoulade—there is equal zest for dining out. In New Orleans, the latest lurid political scandal, another Louisiana specialty, is far less noteworthy than favorite spots to find the best fried soft-shelled crab, fried green tomatoes or Creole bread pudding.

best of times

Prime time is spring, when temperatures are mild and gardens blaze with color. The season's main events begin on a bookish note, in late March, with the celebration of Southern literature and a former resident, the Tennessee Williams–New Orleans Literary Festival, a gathering of scholars, authors and others paying homage to the writer who called New Orleans "one of the last frontiers of Bohemia."

The extravagance of festivals—rites of crawfish, as they are called here—owe their existence to hot rhythms or something as prosaic as new streets and sidewalks. Years ago, an astute former mayor placated constituents peeved by the lengthy amount of time those repairs took by approving a torrent of music known as the French Quarter Festival. In April, the festival's lively street party is a three-day weekend of jazz, rhythm and blues, ragtime, classical and Cajun music, zydeco and rock, accompanied by scores of booths serving regional food.

It's the warm-up for the 10-day blowout at the New Orleans Jazz and Heritage Festival in late April and early May. At the Fest, jazz and more—zydeco, Cajun, gospel, Afro-Caribbean and other beats—pour from a dozen stages at the Fair Grounds racetrack from morning until early evening and around town in clubs, cafes and concert halls at night.

Winters are temperate but the attractions are not, beginning with the Sugar Bowl in early January. Mardi Gras, the city's most spectacular street party, falls in February or early March. The floats begin rolling a week and a half before Fat Tuesday, when the city explodes with parades, music and screaming spectators, though in one way or another Carnival lasts all year.

what to see

New Orleans is a city for walkers and lovers of old streetcars. However you choose to get around you can see the graceful Creole architecture in the French Quarter, the waterfront where breezy promenades overlook the river that Mark Twain called the "crookedest" in the world, and the beautiful 19th-century houses in the Garden District. To skip the tacky commercial, sometimes rank, often outrageous district on Bourbon Street, head for the quieter areas near Esplanade Avenue. The St. Charles Avenue streetcars (fare $1.25) rattle between downtown and uptown, with stops along the edge of the Garden District and Audubon Park. The fare is $1.50 on riverfront trolleys, which do not go as far as the St. Charles line but do serve the French Quarter.

A Tennessee Williams tour and a tour touching on 65 other writers who were inspired by the city are led by a Williams scholar, Prof. Kenneth Holditch, who takes small groups on two-hour strolls around the Quarter. Mr. Holditch, emeritus professor of English at the University of New Orleans, runs Heritage Tours, 732 Frenchmen Street, (504) 949-9805. They begin from Le Petit Theatre at Jackson Square, and are conducted on demand. Tickets are $20 a person for a minimum of three people.

The city's passion for Carnival is clear in a new 16,000-square-foot exhibition of Mardi Gras regalia in the Presbytere, (800) 568-6968 or (504) 568-6968, a Louisiana State Museum facing Jackson Square. The elegant Spanish colonial building, dating to 1795, is filled with costumes, fake crown jewels, floats and other trappings. Closed Mondays. Tickets: $5.

More Mardi Gras sparkle can be found on Canal Street at the river, in Harrah's new palm-fringed casino, (504) 533-6000, with 100,000 square feet of gambling space enlivened by parades, floats and jazz.

Audubon Zoo, 6500 Magazine Street, (800) 774-7394, in Audubon Park, includes a recently expanded swamp section with its new white alligator exhibit. The zoo gate is a free shuttle bus ride—or a pleasant mile walk—from the park entrance on the St. Charles Avenue streetcar line. Hours vary by season. Tickets: $9 for adults, $4.75 ages 2 to 12.

In City Park, a landscape of lagoons and gnarled old oak trees, the New Orleans Museum of Art, 1 Collins Diboll Circle, (504) 488-2631, is open Tuesday to Sunday 10 a.m. to 5 p.m. Tickets: $6.

where to stay

Room rates are pegged to demand. The 11 percent hotel tax and the occupancy tax ($1 to $3 a night) are extra.

BUDGET: In the lower Garden District, the friendly St. Charles Guest House, 1748 Prytania Street, (504) 523-6556, fax (504) 522-6340, is popular with backpackers, Europeans and people who don't mind a patchy, flea market décor. Its 30 rooms, lacking telephones and television, occupy a row of four 19th- and early-20th-century houses. A cozy breakfast room overlooks a small oval pool and a deck with banana trees. Rooms with private bath: $65 to $125, with Continental breakfast.

MODERATE: In a quiet part of the French Quarter, Le Richelieu, 1234 Chartres Street, (800) 535-9653, fax (504) 524-8179, has an unusually helpful staff and 86 rooms, including 17 suites, decorated individually with traditional-style furnishings. A cafe overlooks a small pool in a courtyard. Rates: $95 to $170; parking included.

The Hotel Provincial, 1024 Chartres Street, (800) 535-7922, fax (504) 565- 3985, is on the National Register of Historic Places. It occupies five buildings with a total of 94 rooms and has a courtyard, three patios and a cafe. French Creole antiques and compatible reproductions decorate the rooms. Rates: $119 to $149.

LUXURY: The Omni Royal Orleans, 621 St. Louis Street, (504) 529-5333, fax (504) 529-7089, modeled after a grand 19th-century hotel, is a short walk from good restaurants and Royal Street antique shops. Beyond the arched windows and polished white marble in the lobby are 346 rooms, including suites, with coffeemakers and twice-daily housekeeping. The rooftop has a pool, a deck with scenic views and a small fitness center. Rates: $239 to $379.

The plush Windsor Court, 300 Gravier Street, (800) 955-5866, fax (504) 596-4513, is predictably British upper crust in flavor, an Orient Express hotel glowing with old paintings. The 324 units, including 266 suites, are decorated tastefully; most have balconies or bay windows with views of the city or the river. There is a 65-foot outdoor pool. Doubles: $230 to $400; suites: from $280.

where to eat

Prices include a modest-priced bottle of wine.

Since a redo in 1999 and the opening of a long-closed second floor, tables at Galatoire's, 209 Bourbon Street, (504) 525-2021, are easier to come by. It's now possible to make reservations upstairs, though some traditionalists prefer the minimally redecorated main dining room, still illuminated by bare bulbs attached to antique fixtures. On busy nights, the line for the first-floor room forms at the new upstairs bar, instead of on the sidewalk along Bourbon Street. On Fridays some diners celebrate noisily from lunch until dinner over platters of oysters Rockefeller, stuffed eggplant, creamed spinach, and hunks of butter on French bread as martinis and wine bottles come and go. Meal for two: about $80.

Beloved for its festive air and spiffed-up Creole cuisine, delicious turtle soup and grilled fish dishes, Commander's Palace, 1403 Washington Avenue, (504) 899-8221, occupies a turquoise-

and-white Victorian house in the Garden District. The sumptuous iconic dessert is bread pudding soufflé. Dinner for two: $150.

At Dick & Jenny's, 4501 Tchoupitoulas Street, (504) 894-9880, a popular new restaurant in an old cottage, the diners sit on mismatched chairs around tables covered with oilcloth, eating fried oysters, fried green tomatoes topped with crab cakes, and beef tournedos served with seared foie gras. Dinner for two: $75.

The fare at Irene's, 539 St. Phillip Street, (504) 529-8811, is rich country French and Italian, served in small, cluttered rooms. The menu includes shrimp and corn bisque and entrees like sautéed soft-shell crabs served over linguine tossed with crawfish tails, diced tomatoes, green onions and a light lobster sauce. Dinner for two: $65.

Louisiana Pizza Kitchen, 95 French Market Place, (504) 522-9500, sits on a corner behind the United States Mint in a vintage building with high ceilings. A pizza with shrimp or crawfish tails goes for $7.95, eggplant lasagna for $7.25. A meal for two: about $25.

vital statistics

POPULATION (1998 estimate): City 465,538; Metro area 1,309,445

HOTEL: Room for one with tax $152.00

DINNER FOR ONE: With tax and tip but not drinks $25.75

TAXI: Upon entry $2.50; Each additional mile $1.20; From the airport $24.00

CAR RENTAL FOR A DAY: Midsize car with unlimited free mileage $69.00

FOR MORE INFORMATION: Telephone: (800) 672-6124; Web: www.neworleanscvb.com

Sources: Runzheimer International, U.S. Census Bureau, local businesses

New York

A giant metropolis that should be explored one neighborhood at a time

Empire State Building, New York City

TERRY TRUCCO AND ANITA GATES

Terry Trucco writes frequently about travel. Anita Gates reviews
film, television and the theater for *The Times.*

New York, like any true metropolis, is a city of neighborhoods.
An excellent way to sample the city is to visit a neighborhood
you've never seen. Consider the meatpacking district, a collection
of warehouses in West Greenwich Village that is part trendy, part
industrial, where sides of beef hang next door to stylish boutiques
and restaurants. Or head north to Morningside Heights, buzzing
with sidewalk cafes and home to the architectural splendors of
Columbia University, Riverside Cathedral and the Cathedral of St.
John the Divine.

For all its contemporary energy, New York brims with history. A
great way to see something new is to look for something old.
Revolutionary War enthusiasts congregate at the tip of lower
Manhattan, home to Fraunces Tavern, where George Washington
addressed his officers, and Trinity Church, where Alexander
Hamilton rests beneath a stone pyramid.

Edith Wharton's gilded city comes alive in the gracious, cof-
fered-ceilinged rooms of the Frick Museum on the Upper East
Side and the polished woods of the Elsie de Wolf tearoom near

Gramercy Park. And if the Art Deco New York of old black-and-white movies quickens your heartbeat, tour the beautifully refurbished Radio City Music Hall.

best of times

New York is prettiest, and most bearable, in autumn and spring. But events, not weather, drive New York, so consider the social calendar when planning a visit.

The city revs up in fall, a season of openings. Museums often launch their biggest exhibitions, and though the new Broadway season officially starts on June 1, new plays and musicals rarely open before October. The best time to get tickets to hard-to-see shows is during January and February, the season's slowest months. For information on theater tickets: (888) 276-2392, or (212) 302-4111 in New York.

Among autumn favorites are the New York Film Festival at the Walter Reade Theater, beginning in late September, the New York City Marathon in early November, and the Big Apple Circus, the city's charming one-ring entertainment at Lincoln Center from late October through early January.

The New York City Ballet's exquisite *Nutcracker*, from November to the New Year at the New York State Theater, ushers in Christmas. The tree at Rockefeller Center is lighted in early December, and beautifully decorated trees sprout up throughout the city, notably at the Metropolitan Museum of Art, Lincoln Center and the American Museum of Natural History. And the Winter Antiques Show at the New York Armory brightens January.

Long seasons at Lincoln Center by American Ballet Theater and New York City Ballet announce the arrival of spring. Summer is alive with outdoor events. Look for Shakespeare in the Park and free concerts in Central Park, a blizzard of al fresco events at Lincoln Center, and dancing and Rollerblading under the stars at Chelsea Piers, on the Hudson at 23rd Street.

what to see

Like SoHo in the 1970's, the meatpacking district, a thin slice of the far West Village from Jane Street to 15th Street, is evolving swiftly, with galleries, restaurants and smart shops, like Jeffrey New York, 449 West 14th Street, sandwiched neatly between the butchers. The block-deep Chelsea Market, 75 Ninth Avenue between 15th and 16th Streets, is a New York-style mall of vendors.

The Bronx Zoo (or Wildlife Conservation Society Park, as it is officially known), Fordham Road and Southern Boulevard in the Bronx, continues to show off its Congo Gorilla Forest, an African rain forest habitat populated by 19 lowland gorillas. The zoo is open daily, Admission: $7.75, free Wednesday. Information: (718) 367-1010.

After a lengthy restoration, Grand Central Terminal is again one of the city's glories. Historians from the Municipal Art Society point out highlights, like the whispering gallery near the Oyster Bar, during free tours every Wednesday at 12:30 p.m., meeting at the information booth. The society also gives architectural tours of neighborhoods like Greenwich Village and the Flatiron District, priced from $10; (212) 935-3960.

The Metropolitan Museum of Art, Fifth Avenue at 82d Street, is open daily except Monday; suggested admission, $10. Information: (212) 535-7710. Just up the street is the Guggenheim Museum, Fifth Avenue at 89th Street. Closed Thursday; admission: $12; (212) 423-3500.

A visit to the Cloisters, the Metropolitan Museum's serene repository of medieval art in Fort Tryon Park in Washington Heights, offers a respite from the rest of Manhattan. Parts of five monastery cloisters are the backdrops for treasures like the restored Unicorn tapestries, a charming herb garden and dramatic views of the Hudson River. Staff members give talks on medieval life on Saturday at noon and 2 p.m. Open daily except Monday, with a suggested admission of $10; (212) 923-3700.

At the opposite tip of Manhattan, the chipper American Museum of Financial History, 28 Broadway at Bowling Green Park, offers walking tours of the Financial District, including a stop at the New York Stock Exchange, Friday at 10 a.m. for $15. Open Tuesday through Saturday. Suggested donation: $2. Information: (212) 908-4110.

The Rose Center for Earth and Space is so new that plenty of New Yorkers haven't gotten to it yet. Occupying the northern end of the American Museum of Natural History, with a separate entrance off 81st Street and Central Park West, the four-level center includes the new Hayden Planetarium, with a space show every half hour. Stroll into the main museum and commune with the dinosaurs. Suggested contribution for the Rose Center: $10 for adults, $7.50 for students and seniors, $6 for children. For the Rose Center, the space show and the American Museum of Natural History: $19 for adults, $14 for students and seniors, $11.50 for children. Information: (212) 769-5100. Advance tickets: (212) 769-5200. The space show is popular, so call a day or two ahead.

where to stay

BUDGET: It isn't easy, but it is possible to find a Manhattan hotel room for under $100. The Red Roof Inn chain has opened a property near Macy's Herald Square. The 17-story building, at 6 West 32nd Street, (212) 790-2700, fax (212) 790-2760, has 171 rooms for $89 to $329 a night, including Continental breakfast. There's an exercise room and a business center, cable TV, Web access, two-line telephones and hair dryers.

MODERATE: For visitors who want to be truly in the middle of everything, the Hilton Times Square opened in May 2000. At 234 West 42nd Street, (212) 840-8222, fax (212) 840-5516, it's surrounded by theaters. Every room has a view, since all 444, done in champagne tones, are on the 23rd floor or above. So does the sky lobby, facing north. Doubles begin at $325.

Decades ago, proper young ladies who came to New York to begin careers (including the young Grace Kelly) stayed at the Barbizon, at Lexington Avenue and 63rd Street, (800) 223-1020, fax (212) 223-3287, where gentlemen were never allowed above the lobby. These days, after a recent renovation, the Barbizon is a full-service 22-story hotel for both sexes, with a new look and contemporary furnishings. The 306 rooms start at $325 for a double and, for $15 extra, include use of a fitness club that takes up four floors. And Bloomingdale's is three blocks away.

LUXURY: The eight-story TriBeCa Grand, (212) 519-6600, fax (212) 965-3244, has bouncers to keep out the riffraff. The hotel isn't easy to find (2 Avenue of the Americas, at White and Church Streets, in this case). There's no sign or canopy—just the name on the Old World clock outside and, in tiny lettering, on the front door. The atrium lobby is a little dark, but all those fashionable people in the lobby bar ("continuous cocktails and cappuccino," the brochure says) may make up for that. Some are probably there to use the 98-seat screening room. The good-size rooms (by Manhattan standards) are decorated in earth tones, with high-tech amenities (from VCR to high-speed Internet access to printer). Rooms are $399 to $849.

For a real splurge, there's the Four Seasons New York, (212) 758-5700, fax (212) 758-5711, a skyscraper with 370 rooms and a marble lobby grand enough for ancient Egypt. The rooms are equally impressive (but not huge), with luxurious Italian marble bath-dressing rooms. The hotel is on 57th Street between Park and Madison Avenues, a great site for shopping, and doubles start at $615.

where to eat

AZ, 21 West 17th Street, (212) 691-8888, offers international fusion cuisine and great-looking Asian décor. Dishes include halibut in soy-ginger sauce, pork chops with prunes, and duck schnitzel. Three-course prix fixe dinner: $52. Reserve well ahead.

Guastavino's, 409 East 59th Street, (212) 980-2455, is Terence Conran's glamorous, huge new brasserie beneath the Queensboro Bridge, offering traditional bistro food like steak frites, a selection of caviars and more inventive dishes like lobster, corn and risotto timbale. There's a three-course lunch for $25 to $35; the prix fixe dinner is $65. The Conran's store is next door.

Métrazur, Grand Central Terminal, (212) 687-4600, gives diners one of the quintessential city views: the beautifully restored 1913 terminal in all its Beaux-Arts glory. The menu is Mediterranean-accented bistro fare: mushroom risotto, scallops with leeks, thyme-roasted halibut. Three-course pretheater dinner is $29.

Jack Rose, 771 Eighth Avenue at 47th Street, (212) 247-7518, offers an all-American menu in the theater district. Dishes include rosemary chicken, oysters Rockefeller and gigantic steaks. Dinner for two with wine: $80.

Half King, 505 West 23rd Street, (212) 462-4300, is a cozy new bar in Chelsea with a touch of star power. There's also a menu of upscale pub food, from burgers and fish and chips to lemon sole and lamb. Dinner for two, without wine: $40.

Fauchon, 442 Park Avenue, at 56th Street, (212) 605-0130, is finally here for New Yorkers who would rather be on the Place de la Madeleine in Paris. It's mainly an expensive little store, with slices of quiche ($5 each), a chocolaterie, a patisserie and Fauchon-brand teas, coffees and preserves. In a tiny, elegant salon du thè, afternoon tea is $28 a person.

vital statistics

POPULATION (1998 estimate): City 7,420,166; Metro area 20,126,150

HOTEL: Room for one with tax $322.50

DINNER FOR ONE: With tax and tip but not drinks $40.70

TAXI: Upon entry $2.00; Each additional mile $1.50; From LaGuardia Airport $15.50; From Kennedy Airport $30.00

CAR RENTAL FOR A DAY: Midsize car with unlimited free mileage $92.00

FOR MORE INFORMATION: Telephone: (212) 484-1222; Web: www.nycvisit.com

(NOTE: Hotel, dinner and car rental prices are for Manhattan.)

Sources: Runzheimer International, U.S. Census Bureau, local businesses

Orlando

A land of theme parks leads the way in entertainment innovations

SARA KENNEDY

Sara Kennedy is a journalist based in Tampa, Florida.

If competition breeds creativity, then the theme parks in and around Orlando are a case in point. They have some of the most imaginative ways for guests to spend their leisure time. Everything from a roller coaster that shoots its human cargo from the starting gate with all the subtlety of a missile launcher to a beautiful carousel based on the art of Dr. Seuss greet visitors to Orlando theme parks.

Vacationers will also find an entirely new park, SeaWorld's Discovery Cove, which opened July 1, 2000. It features a tropical, beachy setting populated with 10,000 fish and 300 birds. Guests can play with dolphins under the supervision of trainers, and enjoy leisurely swimming, snorkeling and sunning with smaller crowds and no lines, thanks to a planned daily limit of 1,000 patrons.

Orlando's theme parks, which in 1999 attracted more than 60 million visitors (up from 48.5 million in 1996), are trying to han dle the crush of crowds better. Discovery Cove's competitors are trying various ways to cut down waiting lines, a chief complaint of theme park customers.

Walt Disney World has Fastpass, in which guests may reserve a window of time later in the day for the park's 18 most popular attractions. When they return, they detour past regular lines to a separate entrance. Universal is testing a similar arrangement called Fast Track.

best of times

The theme parks tend to be busiest between Christmas and New Year's Day, around Easter, and during the early months of summer, from mid-June through July, according to theme park officials. The weeks in which Thanksgiving and Christmas fall are especially crowded.

According to hotel occupancy rates and theme park officials, you'll find the sparsest crowds from mid-January through early February; the second week of September, from Labor Day through Thanksgiving Day; and during the first three weeks of December.

At Church Street Station's New Year's Eve Street Party in downtown Orlando, you can greet the New Year from 5 p.m. to 2 a.m. Tickets generally cost $40 to $50, and include entertainment by live bands, champagne at midnight, party favors and noisemakers; call (407) 422-2434, extension 405.

The fourth weekend of March brings the Harry P. Leu Gardens Annual Plant Sale. The 50-acre botanical garden opens all weekend for free, with dozens of vendors selling the latest plants and outdoor accessories. The gardens are at 1920 North Forest Avenue; (407) 246-2620.

The Orlando-University of Central Florida Shakespeare Festival begins in mid-September, at the Orange County Historical Museum Theatre in Loch Haven Park, at Princeton and Mills Avenues in Orlando. Tickets: $7 to $20; (407) 893-4600.

what to see

The Orlando Science Center, 777 East Princeton Street, (888) 672-4386, is a hands-on learning center with an array of exhibits for all ages. There are IMAX films in the CineDome and the Crosby Observatory, available for night sky viewing on weekends. Open daily.

At Discovery Cove, off Exits 27A and 28 of I-4, guests touch bottlenose dolphins, and trainers allow some patrons to play water games with the animals. The park requires reservations, and employs one staff member for every five guests. Admission is $179 for ages 6 and older who want to swim with dolphins; children 3 to 5 and those skipping a dolphin swim pay $89. Admission includes a meal outside at the Laguna Grill, use of snorkeling and beach gear (towels, chairs, hammocks), and a seven-day pass to nearby SeaWorld, home of Shamu; (877) 434-7268.

Otherwise, ticket prices are one area where Orlando's theme parks don't show much variety. Prices for a one-day, one-park ticket for ages 10 and up at Disney World's theme parks are $46; $37 for children ages 3 to 9. The Magic Kingdom and Disney-MGM Studios are off Exit 25B; Epcot and Animal Kingdom, Exit 26B. For all Disney parks information: (407) 824-4321.

Ticket prices are the same at SeaWorld, at Exits 27A and 28, (407) 351-3600; and at Universal, at Exits 30A and 29B, (407) 363-8000. Various multipark and multiday tickets are also available.

The theme-park attractions with the highest profile—certainly in the physical sense—are roller coasters, and Orlando boasts a crop of wild new ones. SeaWorld's Kraken rises 15 stories, then plunges its screaming passengers toward earth at 65 m.p.h. Riders on the Incredible Hulk are practically blown out of the starting gate from what looks like a giant missile launcher at Universal's Islands of Adventure park, which opened in May 1999.

The Rock 'n' Roller Coaster at Disney-MGM Studios treats its riders to an equally explosive start, accelerating from zero to 60 m.p.h. in 2.8 seconds, with the music of Aerosmith pumped through the seats.

A simulator game that pits guests of DisneyQuest, an indoor interactive playground, against the same motley gang from the Pirates of the Caribbean ride opened in June 2000 outside the park in Downtown Disney. Four players, wearing three-dimensional goggles, board a sailing ship under attack (its deck sickeningly weaves and rolls on springs controlled by computer) and defend themselves with cannons. Tickets cost $27 for adults, $21 for children age 3 to 9.

Universal's *Terminator 2,* a film at Universal Studios Theme Park, involves three-dimensional thrills and special effects, including fog and rain. It's the usual end-of-the-world scenario, starring Arnold Schwarzenegger, complete with guns booming and screeching pileups.

One of the most elegant new rides is the beautiful interactive carousel of Dr. Seuss animals—pull the reins and hair might fly up or a tongue stick out—at Islands of Adventure. The bright pink and blue carousel is based on the art of Dr. Seuss.

One park that has no problem with excessive crowds is Splendid China, a 76-acre park opened in 1993 by a Chinese company. It features nearly deserted gardens with more than 60 miniature models of historical Chinese sites. Sparse crowds usually greet its chief daily theatrical production, the "Mysterious Kingdom of the Orient"—a knockout performance of colorful costumes, traditional Chinese song and dance, acrobatics and martial arts. Follow Route 192 west from I-4 to Exit 25B in Kissimmee. Admission costs, which include the show and a terrible meal, are $19.95 for adults and $9.95 for children age 5 to 12. Call (407) 396-7111 or (800) 244-6226.

where to stay

BUDGET: A simple hotel tucked away off Interstate 4, the Comfort Inn Maingate South is an easy 15-minute ride from most of the theme parks. It is off I-4 Exit 23, eight miles west of Walt Disney World at 5510 U.S. Highway 27 North. Its 150 rooms cost $40 to $100, more on holidays; outdoor pool; (800) 255-4386, fax (863) 424-1723.

MODERATE: It's always easier to park your car and stay on the grounds of a theme park, but hotels and food usually cost more. A moderately priced choice is Disney's All-Star Resorts, at Exit 26B off I-4, with a mammoth complex of 5,760 basic rooms with outdoor pools, bakery, food court and free bus service to Disney attractions. Rooms are $74 to $104 a night; (407) 934-7639.

Minutes east of the theme parks is the Hampton Inn-Orlando Convention Center hotel, 8900 Universal Boulevard. The staff is helpful and friendly; there is a heated outdoor pool; the free Continental breakfast includes cereals, bagels, yogurt, fruit and waffles; and the 170 spotless rooms, with maple furniture and decorated in bright, tropical colors, are $69 to $109, depending on the season; (407) 354-4447, fax (407) 354-3031.

LUXURY: Elegant, sand-colored Italian marble and huge bouquets of native orchids give the lobby of the Peabody Orlando, 9801 International Drive, a distinctive Florida feel, and it's fun to watch the mascot ducks cavort in the fountain. Its 891 modern rooms are decorated in yellow and moss green; doubles are $330; it has an outdoor pool and kids' pool with waterfall; (407) 352-4000, fax (407) 351-0073.

The Grand Floridian Resort and Spa, Disney's sprawling Victorian-style hotel, boasts 900 quaint rooms, decorated with printed wall coverings, marble-top sinks, ceiling fans and Victorian woodwork. Big gingerbread porches with climbing roses overlook a lagoon on theme park grounds with a man-made beach and two outdoor pools. Off Exit 25B. Doubles are $304 to $400; (407) 824-3000, fax (407) 824-3186.

where to eat

At Universal's CityWalk, a 30-acre dining and entertainment complex, Jimmy Buffett's Margaritaville is completely casual. Try conch fritters dipped in honey-mustard sauce, followed by Caribbean grilled chicken salad, topped with almonds and habanero-mango ranch dressing, and key lime pie for dessert. Dinner for two with margaritas: about $50; (407) 224-2155.

Nearby, also at CityWalk, you'll find Emeril's, the Orlando branch of a series of restaurants owned by Emeril Lagasse. Reservations are recommended. Specialties include an appetizer of Maine lobster cheesecake; roasted rack of lamb with a Creole mustard sauce, and fresh Florida orange cake with strawberry compote. Dinner for two with wine: $125; (407) 224-2424.

Of all the theme parks, SeaWorld serves some of the best food, and its casual Bimini Bay restaurant, with waiters and waitresses wearing Hawaiian shirts, is typical. The menu features salads, pasta and seafood; try the fresh Florida grouper sandwich or marinated steak on a roll with sautéed onions and peppers. Lunch for two with beer costs about $40 (you must have a park pass); (407) 351-3600.

Two sessions of a gospel brunch occur every Sunday morning at the House of Blues Music Hall, at Downtown Disney, featuring nationally known and local gospel performers, and an all-you-can-eat Southern buffet. The meal and show cost $28; ages 3 to 9, $15. It's a good idea to buy tickets at least a week in advance at (407) 934-2583, fax (407) 934-2216.

A good family-style restaurant near Walt Disney World is Pebbles, 12551 State Road 535; (407) 827-1111. It serves a nice mix of dishes adults enjoy, like the excellent black bean soup ($3.25) or Mediterranean salad ($7.50), and child-friendly items like the cheeseburger ($6.95) and white chocolate mousse ($3.95).

vital statistics

POPULATION (1998 estimate): City 181,175; Metro area 1,504,569

HOTEL (not including Disney World): Room for one with tax $131.00

DINNER FOR ONE: With tax and tip but not drinks $23.55

TAXI (rates may vary by company): Upon entry $2.00; Each additional mile $1.75; From the airport $27.00

CAR RENTAL FOR A DAY: Midsize car with unlimited free mileage $50.00

FOR MORE INFORMATION: Telephone: (407) 363-5800; Web: www.go2orlando.com

Sources: Runzheimer International, U.S. Census Bureau, local businesses

Paris

From art to business to fashion, it's France in a nutshell

CORINNE LaBALME AND JOHN TAGLIABUE

Corinne LaBalme is senior editor of *La Belle France,* a newsletter.
John Tagliabue is a reporter in *The Times'*s Paris bureau.

No one can put Paris in a nutshell, for the City of Light is all things to all tourists. The movable feast includes foie gras at Taillevent, couscous in Menilmontant, a crusty baguette sandwich and a glass of red wine on the Boulevard Saint-Germain. Paris is a $6,600-a-night penthouse suite at the Meurice, a cramped student garret in the Latin Quarter—and lots more in between.

On the other hand, it is possible to say that Paris puts France in a nutshell. It is ground zero for art, entertainment, government, business, publishing, fashion, cuisine—you name it. Roll New York, Washington D.C., Los Angeles, and Boston into one capital city, and it approximates the towering importance of Paris to the French.

This explains why Paris is polished to perfection. The 1999–2000 season saw renovation and restoration of Notre Dame, the Place de la Concorde fountains, Pompidou Center, Théâtre du Châtelet, the Ópera, and Saint-Sulpice. Future projects include the beautification of the seldom-visited canals in eastern Paris.

For the traveler, Paris is supremely user-friendly. Streets are well-marked, restaurants display menus and prices outside the front door, and the public transport is exceptionally efficient (when not on strike). Hotels are better value than in most European capitals, and it's still hard to find a truly bad meal.

best of times

While April in Paris is often chilly, the clouds usually burn off by late May in time for the French Open tennis tournament. Bands blast on June 21 for the Fête de la Musique, although weekend concerts let Parisians party in the parks all summer long. On July 14, Bastille Day festivities start with a military parade down the Champs-Élysées, and end with fireworks and neighborhood dances. Bike fans gather on the Champs later in July for the dramatic finale of the Tour de France.

After the summer hiatus, the cultural season heats up in September. The Fête de la Seine, a recent addition, spotlights the Paris waterfront with exhibits, concerts and fireworks. Fashionistas storm the town for ready-to-wear shows in October and March and for haute couture showings in January and July.

Christmas and Easter, celebrated en famille, means that the city can look a bit deserted as the Parisian fauna heads home to the provinces, although there is more street decoration every year.

what to see

A stroll through the Latin Quarter, on the Left Bank, should not omit a stop at the Musée National du Moyen Âge, 6, place Paul-Painlevé, which has a new Garden of the Middle Ages. Set among brick paths and ringed by latticework fencing, the garden was inspired by the luxuriant detail of the museum's famed 15th-century tapestry "The Lady and the Unicorn." The small but richly planted garden, under soaring sycamores and chestnuts, features kitchen herbs, medicinal herbs and even plants that formed the basis of love potions. It also has a children's play area under trees. Open daily except Tuesday from 9:15 a.m. to 5:45 p.m. Admission: $3.95; call (33-1) 53.73.78.16.

If you're traveling with children, you might block out time for a visit to the big La Villette park, which includes the Cité des Sciences et de l'Industrie, 30, avenue Corentin-Cariou, in the 19th Arrondissement. The main museum building features hands-on exhibits, including a Cité des Enfants for ages 3 to 5 and another for ages 5 to 12, with games, robots and water mills. Outside, you can clamber into a full-size submarine, the Argonaute. A combined ticket of $7.25 includes admission to the Cité des Enfants, the Argonaute and museum exhibitions. Call (33-1) 44.84.44.84.

Take the No. 13 Métro to the suburb of St.-Denis and the venerable 12th-century Basilica of St.-Denis. The church, light and delicate despite its size, is generally considered the cradle of the Gothic style. Badly damaged during the French Revolution, it was restored in the 19th century. It is the burial ground of French kings, although the tombs were eventually emptied. It's located at 1, rue de la Légion d'Honneur. Entry is free. A visit to the tombs (closed when Mass is celebrated) costs $4.25; free for those under 18. Call (33-1) 48.09.83.54.

Avoid the endless lines at the Eiffel Tower by taking the elevator and a flight of stairs to the 11th-floor outdoor Panorama at the top of the Samaritaine Department Store—Store No. 2, 19, rue de la Monnaie. At an altitude of 243 feet, the 360-degree view opposite the Pont Neuf puts the Invalides Dome and Notre Dame gargoyles almost at eye level. Open Monday to Saturday 9:30 a.m. to 7 p.m., Thursday until 10 p.m. (depending on weather). Free.

Shopping is an essential part of Paris. Delicately carved Laguiole pocketknives from the Aveyron region can be found by the Place des Vosges at Le Laguiole du Marais, 6, rue du Pas de la Mule, (33-1) 48.87.46.88. The shop offers a wide selection of these hand-tooled collectors' items with curved bone, boxwood or mahogany handles: $25 to $195. Open daily.

In the 18th century, when wine bottles were sealed with wax, corkscrews were fitted with tiny brushes. Along with other enological gifts and gadgets, L'Esprit et le Vin, 81, avenue des Ternes, (33-1) 45.74.80.99, has special-edition whiskered and pewter corkscrews: $25 to $140. Closed Sunday.

where to stay

BUDGET: The Hôtel du Vieux Saule, 6, rue de Picardie, is in the Third Arrondissement on the edge of the Marais, about 10 minutes from the Métro stop Filles du Calvaire. It has 31 simply furnished rooms on a narrow side street just off one of the city's delightful old cast-iron covered markets. Doubles: $78 to $104; (33-1) 42.72.01.14, fax (33-1) 40.27.88.21.

The Hôtel des Grandes Hommes, at 17, place du Panthéon, across from the neo-Classical splendor of the Panthéon and near the Sorbonne, has 32 simply decorated rooms, many with timbered ceilings. Sixth-floor rooms have narrow balconies with views out to the glimmering white dome of Sacré-Coeur on the heights of Montmartre. Doubles: $112 to $158; (33-1) 46.34.19.60, fax (33-1) 43.26.67.32.

MODERATE: The Île St.-Louis is about as Parisian as you can get, and one of its delights is the Hôtel du Jeu de Paume, at 54, rue St.-Louis en l'Isle, set on a tiny courtyard reached through a timbered passageway. Its 32 rooms were created in buildings that began as covered tennis courts in the 17th century. Simple contemporary furnishings adorn the rooms. Doubles: $168 to $218; (33-1) 43.26.14.18, fax (33-1) 40.46.02.76.

On a small side street just off the Luxembourg Gardens is the Hôtel Le Ste.-Beuve, at 9, rue Ste.-Beuve, with 22 rooms done in soft pastel shades in a vaguely English style. Doubles: $100 to $224; (33-1) 45.48.20.07, fax (33-1) 45.48.67.52.

LUXURY: The Pavillon de la Reine, at 28, place des Vosges in the Marais, is a hidden jewel whose ivy-clad facade faces a tiny court-yard just off the arcaded square that is one of the architectural mas-terpieces of 17th-century Paris. It has 55 sumptuous rooms, many with beamed ceilings and equally grand bathrooms. Doubles: $290 to $350; (33-1) 40.29.19.19, fax (33-1) 40.29.19.20.

In June 2000, the elegant Hôtel Meurice, at 228, rue de Rivoli, the center-of-Paris landmark that once attracted the likes of King George VI and Salvador Dali, reopened after two years of renova-tion. Its 160 splendid rooms are hardly outshone by the late-19th-century charm of the Art Nouveau dome over the tea salon and the rococo interior of the main restaurant, Le Meurice. Doubles: $500 to $595; (33-1) 44.58.10.10, fax (33-1) 44.58.10.15.

where to eat

Hélène Darroze, 4, rue d'Assas, named for its noted chef, is a new favorite in town. Its casual downstairs room offers lighter dishes, while the more formal rooms upstairs, with eggplant-shaded velour on the walls and stark wooden floors, offer more elaborate fare. A meal upstairs might include foie gras of duck, followed by roast rabbit leg with poultry wings stuffed with herbs, then figs braised in honey and Port for dessert. Dinner downstairs, with wine, about $40 a person; upstairs, is about $110. Call (33-1) 42.22.00.11.

In the shadow of the Pompidou Center, Benoît, 20, rue St.-Martin, (33-1) 42.72.25.76, is a classic Paris bistro, with brass fit-tings and lace curtains. Dinner, with wine, is about $72.

In autumn, nicely done game can be enjoyed at Au Petit Marguery, 9, boulevard de Port-Royal, where a typical meal might begin with a pheasant terrine, followed by boned hare braised in a wine sauce with foie gras and truffles. For dessert, try a soufflé au

Grand Marnier. Dinner with wine is about $45; (33-1) 43.31.58.59.

Tucked away on a side street in the unpretentious 11th Arrondissement is Le Repaire de Cartouche, 99, rue Amelot, with dark wood paneling and jaunty murals of 17th-century life. Here dinner might consist of pork liver pâté with fig jam, followed by roast grouse packed in a cabbage leaf, and a fig tart. Dinner, with wine: $40; (33-1) 47.00.25.86.

Opened in March 2000, Bon, at 25, rue de la Pompe in the 16th Arrondissement, features three rooms—including a cozier area with low tables and couches, and a romantic boudoirlike room. Meals tend to be lighter—with organic, low-calorie and vegetarian menus. A more traditional dinner might consist of a salad of scallops, tuna steak with sautéed mushrooms, and one of a selection of desserts from Ladurée, the celebrated pastry shop. About $46, with wine. Call (33-1) 40.72.70.00.

If you're traveling with young children, try lunch at Hippopotamus, a chain of 20 Parisian restaurants, with packages of crayons and paper table covers for coloring, and TV's throughout the restaurant. A child's menu of salad, hamburger with fries, ice cream and soft drink or juice costs $6.25.

With its Naugahyde banquettes, pitted linoleum floors and crackled plaster, La Tartine, 24, rue de Rivoli, (33-1) 42.72.76.85, is a refreshing eyesore in the heavily gentrified Marais. At this low-key neighborhood wine bar, a garlic sausage sandwich, glass of Beaujolais and unlimited French ambience is $4.

vital statistics

POPULATION (1999): City 2,125,246; Île de France 10,952,011

HOTEL: Room for one with tax $296.00

DINNER FOR ONE: With tax and tip but not drinks $26.55

TAXI: Upon entry $1.73; Each additional kilometer 50 cents; From de Gaulle airport $33.20

CAR RENTAL FOR A DAY: Midsize car with unlimited free mileage $85.00

FOR MORE INFORMATION: Telephone: (33-1) 49.52.53.54; Web: www.paris.org

Sources: Runzheimer International, French Government Tourist Office, local businesses

Philadelphia
Layer upon layer of urban history

LAURA MANSNERUS

Laura Mansnerus, a reporter on the metropolitan staff
of *The Times*, is a former resident of Philadelphia.

In a nation more suburban by the day, Philadelphia is a city for
those who like cities. Here, every urban era lives on: the cobbled
streets of the 18th-century port, the gracious architecture of the
Colonial and Victorian rich, the stolid factories and narrow row
houses that received the hopeful from Ellis Island, the Deco and
postmodern skyscrapers.

With a gentility not found in New York and a street life not
found in Washington, Philadelphia has recently discovered itself
and dressed itself up skillfully. But it is not a city that lends itself to
marketing or manufactured entertainment. The pleasures, small
and profuse, are best taken in by the most urban means of transportation, walking.

Philadelphia owes much of its distinctiveness to its pre-automotive
scale; it is, some say, an HO-gauge city. In Center City, a two-mile
stretch between rivers, many shops and restaurants share narrow
streets with row houses.

Center City is also the locus of Philadelphians' reclamation,
with such an infusion of restaurants and hotels over the last few

years that locals are often startled by the new sheen that appears one day on dowdy spaces they've passed for years. The transformation is most visible in Old City, a formerly down-at-the-heels 19th-century commercial district where coffeehouses, galleries and clubs now keep the neighborhood alive night and day.

Still, this is a city largely allergic to newness; almost always, old facades are respected and old habits undisturbed. Philadelphia's anchors—from Independence Hall to the cavernous Reading Terminal Market to the gingerbread boathouses behind the art museum—have kept their looks. It all pretty reliably charms Americans from newer places—meaning, of course, almost anyplace.

best of times

After darkest winter comes the Philadelphia Flower Show, the nation's original flower show, the biggest and most extravagant. For eight days in early March, the Pennsylvania Convention Center is a vast landscape of gardens, all variations on a single theme, and hundreds of juried displays. For information: (215) 988-8899.

The Book and the Cook festival and fair brings dozens of cookbook authors to give demonstrations, sign books and cook at local restaurants, while by day the Convention Center fills with vendors and food people. Restaurant reservations should be made early for this weeklong event in late winter. Call the Visitors Center of the Convention and Visitors Bureau: (215) 636-1666.

At the nation's premier track and field meet, the Penn Relays, athletes from high schoolers to Olympic contestants compete at the University of Pennsylvania on the last Thursday, Friday and Saturday in April. Ticket information: (215) 898-6151.

The Philadelphia Folk Festival is a three-day outing (camping is encouraged) in the country on the weekend before Labor Day. The events at Old Pool Farm in Schwenksville, Pennsylvania, about 45 minutes from the city, include children's activities and folk and square dancing in addition to dozens of concert performances. Information: (800) 556-3655.

Then, for two weeks in September, the Philadelphia Fringe Festival does its best to bend traditions with hundreds of artists presenting drama, dance, art installations, poetry and music. Most of the venues, which may include parking lots, diners and warehouses, are in Old City. Information: (215) 413-9006.

what to see

In a city that never runs out of material, the Foundation for Architecture leads walking tours of about two hours—Saturday and Sunday at 2 p.m., and in summer on Tuesday, Wednesday and Thursday evenings at 6. Recent offerings included "20th Century Unlimited," around Center Square, and "Littlest Streets," along the old, once-bohemian residential alleys of Washington Square West. Adults $7, students $6; (215) 569-3187.

A different thread of history is on view at the hulking Eastern State Penitentiary, 22nd Street and Fairmount Avenue. Eastern State, one of the nation's first penitentiaries, opened in 1829 and was home to Al Capone and Willie Sutton. The gothic stone monster was only recently rescued from decades of decay and opened for tours of Capone's specially furnished cell and other exhibits on Wednesdays through Sundays. The fee is $7, $5 for students and ages 55 and up, and $3 for visitors under 17. Information: (215) 236-3300.

On the streets or in the galleries, plastic cups of wine in hand, people gather in Old City, just northeast of the Liberty Bell, on First Fridays. About 40 art galleries, on Second and Third Streets, open from 5 till 9 p.m. Call (215) 625-9200 or (800) 555-5191.

Walkers naturally seek out Society Hill, the core of Philadelphia's original civic life and of its downtown revival 30 years ago. It's a genteel quarter, red brick from the sidewalks up, encompassing Independence National Historic Park and dotted with courtyards and churchyards, with many Georgian and Federal buildings. But at its southern edge, South Street booms at night with bars and quirky shops.

Runners can always put on shorts and head up the Benjamin Franklin Parkway from Center City to the Philadelphia Museum of Art. A jogging and bike path continues another four miles along the Schuylkill, where the sights—bridges, scullers, masses of willows—are pretty much as Thomas Eakins painted them more than 100 years ago.

The Atwater Kent Museum, 15 South Seventh Street, is Philadelphia's history museum; admission is $3 for adults, $2 for ages 55 and older and $1.50 for children 3 to 12. Information: (215) 922-3031.

The African American Museum in Philadelphia is at 701 Arch Street, (215) 574-0380. Admission is $6 for adults, $4 for students, those aged 55 and older and the handicapped. It offers many evening and weekend activities, such as music and films.

where to stay

A hotel-building binge for the Republican National Convention resulted in a tourists' market for most weeks of the summer and fall. To find out about hotel packages, including tickets to cultural events, call (888) 467-4452.

BUDGET: The Hawthorn Suites, 1100 Vine Street, (215) 829-8300, fax (215) 829-8104, is crisp and new, if a bit spare. Each of the 294 suites, at $149 to $159 (sometimes less on weekends), has a refrigerator, microwave and wet bar, making life easier for families. At the northern edge of Center City, the hotel towers over the convention center and Chinatown.

MODERATE: The Sheraton Society Hill, Second and Walnut Streets, has a quiet, established niche in the historic district. Like its surroundings, the low-rise redbrick hotel is Colonial (except for the swimming pool) and sedate. The 365 traditional rooms and suites range from $155 to $270 for a double. Reservations:(215) 238-6000, fax (215) 238-6652.

A block from the convention center, Loews, 1200 Market Street, (215) 627-1200, fax (215) 231-7305, is an Art Deco creation in an old bank building (check out the vault doors). The 583 rooms are pure 1930's luxe. A standard double is $175 to $240.

Just off Rittenhouse Square, the Sofitel has opened at 120 South 17th Street, on a pleasingly unreconstructed block of tiny shops. The hotel, by contrast, is all modern and smooth, its 306 rooms furnished in gleaming woods and geometric prints. Doubles: $189; (215) 569-8300, fax (215) 569-1492.

LUXURY: The Park Hyatt Philadelphia at the Bellevue, Broad and Walnut Streets, is rich in detail and history, a match for the Academy of Music on the next corner of the theater district. With just 172 rooms, including suites, it has a ballroom, a conservatory, a rooftop rose garden and such amenities as a day spa. Doubles start at $275; (215) 893-1234, fax (215) 732-8518.

Rittenhouse Bed and Breakfast, 1715 Rittenhouse Square, (215) 545-1755, fax (215) 545-1750, is as elegant as the neighboring square, formal from its facade to its nightly shoeshine service. Some of the 10 individually decorated rooms, all with baths, have fireplaces and whirlpools. Rates are $220 to $340 and include full breakfast.

where to eat

An anchor of Center City's restaurant row, Susanna Foo, 1512 Walnut Street, (215) 545-2666, has done Asian fusion elegantly for years. Under silk lanterns, diners can make their way from Chinese soups and delicate dumplings to emphatically French desserts (apricot tart with almond ice cream, for one). Dinner for two with wine: about $125.

Fishmarket, 122 South 18th Street, (215) 569-9080, offers seafood in a town house with just enough painted wood to feel like a crab house. Take a stool at the glistening raw bar at happy hour and enjoy oysters for $1 each. Dinner for two, with a bottle of wine: about $120. Closed Sunday.

Le Bar Lyonnais, 1523 Walnut Street, (215) 567-1000, is the downstairs wing of Le Bec-Fin, the French restaurant that has been on national best-of lists for years. The bar offers many lighter Bec-Fin standards like the galette de crabe and vichyssoise au caviar at considerably lower prices. The atmosphere is rich, dark and close—it seats about 30. No reservations. Dinner for two with drinks: about $100. Closed Sunday.

On the other side of Rittenhouse Square, Audrey Claire, (215) 731-1222, opens its wide windows at the corner of 20th and Spruce Streets to a neighborhood of brownstones and small shops. The fare is Mediterranean—Audrey Claire is known for its grilled flatbreads—and simple. No reservations on Friday and Saturday. Bring your own wine. Dinner for two, about $60. Closed Monday.

Effie's, at 1127 Pine Street on Antique Row, (215) 592-8333, is a tiny Greek restaurant in a row house with a tiny, inviting garden. Effie's has fresh fish every day, usually served whole, brushed with lemon and olive oil and grilled. Bring your own wine. Dinner for two: under $40.

For those who cannot leave town without a cheesesteak, the pure South Philadelphia version is available at Pat's King of Steaks, (215) 468-1546, or Geno's, (215) 389-0659, competing cholesterol palaces at the intersection of Passyunk, South Ninth and Wharton Streets.

And for South Philly pizza, try Marra's, 1734 East Passyunk Avenue, (215) 463-9249, now in its third generation. Wear a tank top and bring $5 to $10 a person (that includes the beer).

vital statistics

POPULATION (1998 estimate): City 1,436,287; Metro area 4,946,562

HOTEL: Room for one with tax $187.50

DINNER FOR ONE: With tax and tip but not drinks $25.50

TAXI: Upon entry $1.80; Each additional mile $1.80; From the airport $22.00

CAR RENTAL FOR A DAY: Midsize car with unlimited free mileage $58.00

FOR MORE INFORMATION: Telephone: (215) 636-3300; Web: www.pcvb.org

Sources: Runzheimer International, U.S. Census Bureau, local businesses

Phoenix

Look closely, and you'll see the seams in a quilt of five cities

SUZANNE WINCKLER

Suzanne Winckler, who lives in Mesa, Arizona,
writes about natural history.

The Valley of the Sun is a sprawling amalgam of a dozen or so communities that budded in barren desert and then spread, thanks to ever more steady supplies of water pumped from underground or siphoned from other places. What looks like a seamless urbanscape from the air is in fact a handful of cities bumping up against each other.

Five of them—Phoenix, Scottsdale, Tempe, Glendale and Mesa—took root in the 1870's. More than 100 years later, each remains distinct, and their differences make the valley ripe for exploration. Mesa and Glendale are family towns, while Scottsdale is tony, and Tempe, home to Arizona State University, is laid back. Phoenix runs the gamut from urban chic to quiet bungalow neighborhoods.

The unifying chord through these communities is an obsession with water. Today, more than 1,200 miles of canals shunt it through the valley from reservoirs on the Salt and Verde Rivers, as well as from the Colorado. With all this water, the 2.8 million citizens of the valley have created an emerald-green city of grass and swaying palms, where most public spaces—museums, shopping centers, hotels—have some sort of babbling sculpture, fountain or sluice.

best of times

Phoenix is at its best from the autumnal to the vernal equinox—that is, from roughly Sept. 20 to March 20. This is the time when summer-cloistered Phoenicians come out of their air-conditioned houses and cars and inhabit their city, which in the sweltering months takes on the aspect of a ghost town. Their numbers are augmented by escapees from the higher latitudes, and from September to March, residents and visitors alike act like they are on vacation. You know the High Season, as it is called, has arrived when the predominant luggage on the carousels at Sky Harbor Airport are golf bags.

In these balmy, blissful months, major events and entertainment fall into several well-defined categories—horses, golf, weird desert plants and baseball—all of which are set against a backdrop of Southwestern culture steeped in Hispanic and Native American traditions.

If you prefer to sightsee from the saddle, check Cowboy Adventures or the Ranch Directory at www.arizonaguide.com for listings of trail rides and dude ranches in the Phoenix area. Or if you would rather watch other people ride horses, WestWorld Equestrian Center, 16601 North Pima Road, in Scottsdale, has a steady lineup of exhibitions and competitions and most events are free. Information: (480) 312-6802.

The Sonoran Desert is famous for its bizarre plants, including the saguaro, the cactus equivalent of Gumby. The Desert Botanical Garden, 1201 North Galvin Parkway, provides a wonderful introduction to desert flora, especially during Las Noches de las Luminarias, an annual holiday tradition in Phoenix. Information: (480) 754-8188.

In January, the Tournament Players Club of Scottsdale, 17020 North Hayden, hosts the Phoenix Open, billed as the world's best-attended golf tournament. Information: (602) 870-4431 or www.phoenixopen.com.

The finale of the High Season is Cactus League Baseball in March. Seven major-league teams (Angels, Cubs, Brewers, Athletics, Padres, Mariners and Giants) converge in metro Phoenix for spring training. They play ball in intimate, open-air stadiums full of deliriously happy sun- and beer-flushed fans. It feels like the olden days of baseball, and a spike in workplace absenteeism at this time seems to be an accepted part of the local economy. Information on spring training is available at www.arizonaguide/cities/mesa.

what to see

The Phoenix Art Museum is at 1625 North Central Avenue. The museum is open daily except Monday. General admission is $7 for adults, $5 for ages 65 and up and students, $2 for ages 6 to 18; free on Thursdays. Information: (602) 257-1222 or www.phxart.org.

The Heard Museum, 2301 North Central Avenue, houses the American Indian collections of Dwight and Maie Bartlett Heard, a couple who settled in the Valley in 1895. The museum's Spanish Colonial–style building is on what was their estate, in the historic Los Olivos neighborhood, north of downtown Phoenix. The museum is open daily. Admission is $7 for adults, $6 for ages 65 and up, $3 for ages 4 to 12; (602) 252-8848.

With the moderate temperatures from November through April, the best way to get a lay of the land is to park your car and start walking. More than 100 miles of hiking trails weave through metropolitan Phoenix, and AZ Trails, at www.azcentral.com/travel/hiking, has listings that include distances, difficulty and directions. Among the choices is the Summit Trail on Squaw Peak, (602) 262-7901, a fairly strenuous 2.4-mile round trip that provides a panoramic view of the city. The Waterfall Canyon Trail in the White Tank Mountains, (623) 935-2505, west of the city, is an easy two-mile trip that goes past Indian petroglyphs carved into boulders on the way to an 80-foot waterfall; much of this trail is accessible by wheelchair.

The 1983 *Guide to Architecture of Metro Phoenix,* though a tad outdated, is the best introduction to the valley's urban history. It costs $3.20 from the Central Arizona Chapter of the American Institute of Architects, 802 North Fifth Avenue; (602) 257-1925. The chapter is just north of downtown near several classic 1920's and 30's neighborhoods, including Encanto-Palmcroft, Willo and Coronado. These areas are living museums of such styles as Mission Revival, California Bungalow, Craftsman Bungalow, Art Moderne and International Style.

The palm-tree-lined campus of Arizona State University in Tempe offers a sleek modern setting for people-watching. The most avant-garde of the buildings is the A.S.U. Art Museum, Mill Avenue and 10th Street, an Egyptian-looking vault of shimmering pink cement designed by Antoine Predock. Regardless of what is on display, it's a joy to walk through the subterranean walkway adorned with sculpture and the three levels of large white, echoey galleries; (480) 965-2787.

where to stay

BUDGET: The Tempe Days Inn, 1221 East Apache Boulevard, (480) 968-7793, fax (480) 966-4450, has 102 rooms and is close to the Arizona State campus. Doubles run from $59 in the summer, to $99 in winter.

The Econolodge Scottsdale, 6935 East Fifth Avenue, (480) 994-9461, fax (480) 947-1695, is in the heart of Old Town, an area of shops, restaurants and galleries. It has 92 rooms, with doubles ranging from a summer low of $49 to $94 in February.

MODERATE: The 107-room Best Western Executive Park Downtown, 1100 North Central Avenue, (602) 252-2100, fax (602) 340-1989, is quiet, comfortable and convenient to museums and other central-city attractions. There is a restaurant, lounge, pool, sauna and exercise area, and in-room modems. Doubles average $110.

LUXURY: The Arizona Biltmore Resort and Spa, 24th Street and Missouri Avenue, (800) 950-0086, fax (602) 381-7600, is clois- tered within the 1,000-acre Arizona Biltmore Estates at the end of a long and winding road. Designed by Albert Chase McArthur, with assistance from Frank Lloyd Wright, it is a grand, rambling ghost-gray palace with a stark, cool lobby and spare Mission-style furniture. Of the 730 rooms, 120 are in a new wing that opened in 1999, less than two years after the resort built a spa and fitness area. There are eight swimming pools (including the original Catalina pool, with its gorgeous multicolored tiles), seven tennis courts, a croquet lawn and a chessboard with three-foot-tall pieces. Doubles start at $315, and winter rates will run from $330 for a double to $1,695 for a two-bedroom villa suite.

In Carefree, 12 miles north of Scottsdale, the Boulders, 34631 North Tom Darlington Drive, (800) 553-1717, fax (480) 488-4118, is a 1,300-acre retreat surrounded by two golf courses and the desert. Guests stay in their own little casitas, each with a deck and fireplace supplied with aromatic shaggy-bark juniper. There are five restaurants and three swimming pools. Rates: $185 in summer to $565 from mid-January through April.

where to eat

Cafe Terra Cotta, 6166 North Scottsdale Road, in the Borgata Scottsdale shopping center, offers such neo-Southwestern dishes as pork tenderloin adobado, corn risotto and pepper filet cooked rare when the customer says rare. The wine list focuses on zinfandels, but numerous other wines and beers are available. Dinner for two with wine costs about $80. Open daily for lunch and dinner; reservations recommended for evening weekends (480) 948-8100.

Marquesa, at the Fairmont Scottsdale Princess Resort, 7575 East Princess Drive, lies at the elegant extreme of dining in the Valley of the Sun. With indoor and patio seating, it specializes in generous portions of Catalan and Mediterranean food served by attentive waiters. Signature dishes include gazpacho, garlic soup and seafood paella. Dinner for two with cocktails and wine costs about $250. Open Tuesday through Saturday for dinner and Sunday for brunch. Reservations recommended; (480) 585-4848.

The Chuck Box, 202 East University Drive in Tempe, is the place for really big hamburgers, fries, onion rings and beer in mason jars. It prides itself on simple décor, with Arizona ranch and cowboy photos on the walls. A meal for two with beer costs about $15; (480) 968-4712.

Mrs. White's Golden Rule Cafe, 808 East Jefferson Street, is a downtown landmark, serving Southern-style plate lunches, including smothered chicken. Two can eat for less than $12. Open 11 a.m. to 5 p.m. Monday through Friday; (602) 262-9256.

A fine and friendly example of the city's many family-owned Mexican restaurants is Los Picos, 1542 West University Drive in Mesa, which focuses on seafood dishes from Mexico's Pacific Coast, like Sinaloa-style coctel de camaron with shrimp, salsa, cucumber and avocado. Dinner for two with appetizer and beer costs about $30. Breakfast, lunch and dinner daily; (480) 833-4711.

vital statistics

POPULATION (1998 estimate): City: 1,198,064; Metro area: 2,931,004

HOTEL: Room for one with tax: $187.00 (January to May); $91.00 (May to September); $153.00 (September to January)

DINNER FOR ONE: With tax and tip but not drinks $24.35

TAXI (rates may vary by company): Upon entry, including first mile $3.00; Each additional mile $1.50; From the airport $10.00

CAR RENTAL FOR A DAY: Midsize car with unlimited free mileage $68.50

FOR MORE INFORMATION: Telephone: (877) 225-5749; Web: www.accessarizona.com/partners/phoenixcvb

Sources: Runzheimer International, U.S. Census Bureau, local businesses

Pittsburgh

Mr. Rogers's neighborhood,
and Andy Warhol's, too.

BILL DEDMAN

Bill Dedman writes for *The Times* from Chicago.

It may be no surprise that Pittsburgh has direct flights to London, Paris and Frankfurt, but consider this: many of the tourists here have come from Europe to the capital of culture in the Alleghenies.

Surely Europeans aren't coming to take a tour of Mr. Rogers's neighborhood at the nation's first public television station, or to tramp two hours into the countryside to see Frank Lloyd Wright's masterpiece at Fallingwater. So what, then?

It must be Andy Warhol.

The son of an immigrant laborer from Czechoslovakia who came to work in Andrew Carnegie's steel mills, the pop artist is remembered at the seven-story Andy Warhol Museum, where Mick Jagger was once spotted kicking around the helium-filled Silver Clouds.

The city that produced Andrew Warhola and Fred Rogers has other surprises, just as the modern skyline is thrust at the visitor emerging from the Fort Pitt Tunnel on the drive in from the modern airport, with its 100 shops and a fitness center for passengers.

A city built on rivers and bituminous coal, Pittsburgh has survived the boom and bust years. The air is clear. Upscale shops are open downtown. Even a bit of a cafe society is emerging.

If Pittsburgh had always been like this, Mr. Warhol might never have left, and Mr. Rogers might not have stayed.

best of times

The city's weather is relatively moderate: winters are not too severe, long or snowy, summers not too hot and humid. But there is one outstanding characteristic: clouds. Almost 200 days a year on average are marked by overcast skies.

Spring and summer in Pittsburgh mean outdoor festivals. Four of the biggest celebrate children, heritage, art and jazz. The season starts with performing arts and plenty of child's play at the Pennsylvania International Children's Festival, in West Park, usually in late May. Visiting troupes from around the world perform acrobatics and stage puppet theater. Call (412) 321-5520.

The food, music and dance of a score of nationalities are on display at the Pittsburgh Folk Festival, at the end of May, (412) 278-1267, in Station Square, a renovated rail terminal beside the lovely Smithfield Street Bridge. Performers include Ukrainians, Bulgarians and the Coal Country Cloggers.

For most of June, the enormous Three Rivers Arts Festival takes over the Golden Triangle, where the rivers meet, with visual and performing arts, crafts, poetry and children's events. And it's free. Call (412) 281-8723.

what to see

Victorian refinement and industrial Pittsburgh merge at the Frick Art and Historical Center, 7227 Reynolds Street, (412) 371-0600, which combines a turn-of-the-century residence, a museum with pre-20th-century European and Asian paintings, and a car and carriage museum with more than 30 old masters of the Rolls-Royce variety. The mansion, known as Clayton, 20 minutes east of downtown in Point Breeze, belonged to the coal baron Henry Clay Frick, Carnegie's partner and rival. Open Tuesday through Saturday 10 a.m. to 5 p.m., and Sunday noon to 6 p.m. Admission is free to the museum, cars and greenhouse; mansion $8.

The best views of the city are had from Mount Washington, a 400-foot ride up one of the city's two funiculars, or inclined railways. Below is the city's birthplace, where the mud-bedded Monongahela ambles into the impatient, limestone-cutting Allegheny to form the wide Ohio, the gateway to the Gulf of Mexico. Remnants of the British Fort Pitt (1758) have been rebuilt with a museum.

To the right, east of downtown, is the Oakland neighborhood, the city's cultural center. One can easily spend a day exploring the pale sandstone Carnegie Museum of Art, the Carnegie Museum of Natural History, the University of Pittsburgh and its towering Cathedral of Learning, Carnegie Mellon University and the floral displays in the crystal palace of the Phipps Conservatory. The Carnegie Museums, 4400 Forbes Avenue, (412) 622-3131, are open Tuesday through Saturday, 10 a.m. to 5 p.m., and Sunday 1 to 5 p.m. Closed holidays. Admission is $6.

Straight ahead are the glass towers of downtown's Golden Triangle. Just beyond, beside the Allegheny, is the Strip, a district of produce stalls and fish markets now bustling with coffee shops and hot spots, including a floating boardwalk and nightclub. The John Heinz Pittsburgh Regional History Center, 1212 Smallman Street, (412) 454-6000, gives a tour of Western Pennsylvania history, from 1750 to the present. Open daily 10 a.m. to 5 p.m.; admission is $6.

For a street-level view of Pittsburgh at its finest, walk through Daniel Burnham's Beaux-Arts Penn Station (1898), at Liberty Avenue and Grant Street, or what some say is the finest building in the country, the Allegheny County Courthouse (1888), at Forbes Avenue and Grant Street, a Romanesque castle with its open interior courtyard and tower designed by Henry Hobson Richardson.

Mr. Warhol gets far more than 15 minutes at the Andy Warhol Museum, 117 Sandusky Street, (412) 237-8300, housed in a former warehouse that was renovated and converted into a museum in 1994. Here hot-pink Chairman Maos share wall space with Brillo and Marilyn. More revealing of Warhol may be his time capsules, file boxes in which he saved everything that crossed his desk (or his mind) until his death in 1987. Admission is $6. Open Sunday and Wednesday 11 a.m. to 6 p.m., Thursday through Saturday to 8.

"How can I keep a woodpecker from tapping on my house?" "A huge hawk is circling my house. Will it capture my dog?" Answers to these questions can be found at the National Aviary, (412) 323-7235. More than 200 species of bird are on display at this bird zoo on the city's North Side: red-crowned cranes, African pygmy falcons, eastern towhees. The glass-enclosed aviary, next to the Children's Museum, is a good place for a fair-weather walk. Admission is $5 for adults, $3.50 for children. Open 9 a.m. to 5 p.m. daily. And the answers? Provide another place for the woodpecker to display his percussive prowess, and no, your dog is probably too heavy for the hawk.

Wright's Fallingwater, on State Route 381 between Mill Run and Ohiopyle, (724) 329-8501, remains open while it awaits repair of a seven-inch settling of its cantilevered concrete floor. Steel cables are planned to keep the 60-year-old house from falling into Bear Run. Tours are $8 weekdays, $12 weekends. Open 10 a.m. to 4 p.m.; closed Monday.

where to stay

BUDGET: Mainstay Suites Pittsburgh Airport, 1000 Park Lane Drive, an extended stay hotel, is 10 minutes from the Pittsburgh International Airport in a quiet, hilly section. All 100 rooms have a sofa bed or recliner, iron and ironing board, and satellite television. Suites have kitchens and dining areas. Rates start at $70, including Continental breakfast on weekdays; (412) 490-7343, fax (412) 788-6097.

MODERATE: The Priory, 614 Pressley Street, makes an inviting stopover on the North Side. Port and sherry are served under the stamped-metal ceiling in the 111-year-old sitting room. Wines are served in fair weather in the shaded courtyard. The 24 guest rooms and suites, which are not large, have butterscotch walls, antique and reproduction beds, vintage lamps and armoires, and fireplace mantels. The Priory is just across the Allegheny River from downtown, near the Warhol Museum and the National Aviary. Standard rooms are $114; (412) 231-3338, fax (412) 231-4838.

In Oakland, the Wyndham Garden Hotel University Place, 3454 Forbes Avenue, opened in 1998, with a grand entrance of etched granite and marble and 198 guest rooms and suites. Includes a restaurant and lounge, shuttle service, an exercise room and room service. Standard rooms are $114 weekdays, $109 weekends; (412) 683-2040, fax (412) 683-3934.

The 465-room Pittsburgh Greentree Marriott, 101 Marriott Drive, (412) 922- 8400, three miles southwest of downtown, has a business center, a prime rib beef buffet, pizza parlor, comedy club, putting green and basketball courts. Rooms are $129 weekdays, $69 to $79 weekends.

LUXURY: The downtown Westin William Penn Hotel, 530 William Penn Place, built in 1916 by Frick as a showpiece for the city's steel and glass industries, completed a renovation in 1998. Guests sip afternoon tea under the 25-foot plaster and gilded ceilings in the lobby's Palm Court. Weekday rates start at $185, weekend specials are $99 to $129; (412) 281-7100, fax (412) 553-5252.

where to eat

"J'eet jet?" is still the standard way for a Pittsburgher to ask if you're ready for a meal, but the meal itself is no longer limited to chipped ham and an Iron City beer.

The most popular spot in town may be the barrel-vaulted ceiling and stained glass at the Grand Concourse Restaurant, in the Station Square entertainment center, (412) 261-1717. It opened in 1978 in an old railroad waiting room, with curved booths and lampposts. Fresh seafood is flown in daily. The jumbo lump crab cakes, with rice and vegetable, are $21.

Word of mouth leads to the Neapolitan home cooking at the new La Cucina Flegrea, 2114 Murray Avenue in Squirrel Hill, (412) 521-2082. In a narrow room, little more than an eat-in kitchen, the chef, Anna Fevola, serves sautéed cod, roasted vegetables and fresh pasta. Ravioli filled with eggplant is $15.25. B.Y.O.B.

The Penn Brewery, Troy Hill Road, (412) 237-9400, in the historic Eberhardt and Ober Brewery building, is in the North Side district known as Deutsch Town. The restaurant opened in 1989, with a full German menu, its own Penn Pilsner and, on weekends, live oompah music. Schweinebraten with sauerkraut and potatoes is $13.50.

Just to prove that Steeltown isn't dead, the lines are long at lunchtime for the sandwiches at Primanti Brothers, 46 18th Street in the Strip District, (412) 263-2142. Either a sandwich shop or a religious institution, Primanti serves fried bologna and cheese sandwiches, with fries and slaw wrapped inside thick crusty bread to save time ($3.95). You haven't tasted Pittsburgh until you've had one.

vital statistics

POPULATION (1998 estimate): City 340,520; Metro area 2,346,153

HOTEL: Room for one with tax $129.00

DINNER FOR ONE: With tax and tip but not drinks $31.35

TAXI: Upon entry $1.80; Each additional mile $1.40; From the airport $30.00

CAR RENTAL FOR A DAY: Midsize car with unlimited free mileage $65.00

FOR MORE INFORMATION: Telephone: (800) 359-0758; Web: www.visitpittsburgh.com

Sources: Runzheimer International, U.S. Census Bureau, local businesses

Prague

The wealth of architectural styles is unmatched in Europe

Prague

JEREMY BRANSTEN
Jeremy Bransten is a senior editor at
Radio Free Europe/Radio Liberty in Prague.

Prague's singular beauty has prompted many would-be poets or guidebook authors to outdo one another with metaphors. But perhaps the simplest and truest thing that can be said is this: wherever you've come from in Europe or North America, you're in for a visual feast. Few other cities on the Continent match Prague's architectural riches—a symphony of Gothic spires, Renaissance palaces, hidden gardens, Baroque churches and Art Nouveau facades.

Add to this a multitude of cultural offerings, including some of Europe's finest classical music venues, as well as the best beer in the world, and Prague becomes a feast that satisfies all the senses.

best of times

By the beginning of May, beer gardens once more sprout in the city's parks and courtyards. The orchards on Petrin Hill are covered in blossoms, and rowboats reappear on the Vltava. Every year, the defining cultural event of the season is the Prague Spring classical music festival. By tradition, a performance of My Country (Ma vlast) by the 19th-century Czech composer Bedrich Smetana, opens the festival on May 12 in the aptly named Smetana Concert Hall of the Art Nouveau Municipal House (Obecni Dum), Namesti Republiky 5, Prague 1; (420-2) 22 00 23 36.

Following concerts take place every night at venues around town. Tickets sell out fast, but can be bought in advance through the festival Web site: www.festival.cz. Festival ticket prices range from $13 to $90.

Summer is marked by an influx of tourists and a reduction in cultural offerings. Most Prague residents flee to their country cottages. One event of note, though two hours' drive outside the Czech capital, is the annual Karlovy Vary International Film Festival. The spa town plays host to domestic and international celebrities as dozens of new films are screened during the first week in July. Contact the Karlovy Vary Film festival office at (420-2) 2423 5412 or (420-2) 2423 8225.

Fall is inaugurated with the arrival of burcak—sweet, half-fermented new wine that is served in pubs and at street stands around town. It may taste like lemonade, but it packs a punch.

The weather usually deteriorates in the approach to winter, bringing gray days and cold rain. Time to take in some concerts and savor the smoky snugness of Czech pubs. The week before Christmas, Prague's streets teem with shoppers and buckets of live carp, which are brought up from the ponds of southern Bohemia.

what to see

In summer, it's nearly impossible to cross the pedestrian-only Charles Bridge. To avoid the multitudes, try to rise early to quietly savor the Old Town's twisting alleys, gardens and churches.

The tower of the Old Town Hall on Old Town Square is known for its 15th-century astronomical clock. The building also makes a fine vantage point for a panoramic view of Prague's red-tiled roofs and the Castle across the river. Open Tuesday to Sunday 9 a.m. to 4:30 p.m. and Monday 11 a.m. to 4:30 p.m. Admission, 85 cents; (420-2) 24 48 26 29.

Prague's old Jewish quarter, Josefov, bounded by Kaprova and Parizska Streets just northwest of the Old Town Square, is named after Joseph II, whose 1781 Patent of Tolerance permitted Jews to live in other parts of the city. But Jewish life continued to center on the area. The Holocaust claimed the lives of 78,000 of the 120,000 Jews in what is now the Czech Republic. Today, fewer than 1,500 Jews are active members of Prague's Jewish community.

The Old-New Synagogue, Cervena 2, dates back to the 13th century and is one of Europe's oldest. Inside is the wooden seat once occupied by Rabbi Loew, who, according to legend, created the fearsome Golem monster. His grave can be found among the jumbled headstones of the Old Jewish Cemetery about 100 yards down the street. The resplendent interior of the Spanish Synagogue, Vezenska 1, with its stained-glass windows and vaulted ceilings covered in gold leaf, is newly restored.

Tickets to the Jewish Quarter's synagogues and museums plus the cemetery cost about $13.75, and can be bought at any of the sites. Entry to the Old-New Synagogue alone costs $5.75. All the sites are open Sunday to Friday 9 a.m. to 4 p.m.; (420-2) 24 81 00 99.

Havelska Street, with its outdoor produce market, is a convenient spot to pick up a snack. For something more substantial, follow the street until it reaches Coal Market Square (Uhelny Trh on the street sign), where you'll find U Dvou Kocek (At the Two Cats), one of Prague's historic beer halls, founded in 1678. A half-liter of foaming Pilsner Urquell costs about 60 cents. Open daily 11 a.m. to 11 p.m; (420-2) 267 729.

Crossing the Charles Bridge over the Vltava River, the splendor of the Little Quarter rewards unhurried exploration. Its cobblestone streets lined with Baroque palaces climb toward Prague Castle.

The castle—a city within a city—is reached by following Nerudova Street. A ticket (about $3.50 for adults, $1.75 for students) covers admission to all the main sites, including St. Vitus's Cathedral, the Old Royal Palace and the 10th-century Basilica of St. George, the oldest structure in the citadel. The main sites are open daily 9 a.m. to 4 p.m., till 5 p.m. starting in April and through summer; (420-2) 2437 3368.

Besides a wealth of centuries-old architecture, Prague is also home to some modern treasures. The Trade Fair Palace (Veletrzni Palac), a seven-story 1928 Functionalist masterpiece, houses the Gallery of Modern Art, which boasts an impressive collection of paintings and sculptures from turn-of-the-century Cubism to post-Communist art in galleries that surround a soaring white atrium. The palace, at Dukelskych Hrdinu 47, in the Holesovice district, is open Tuesday to Sunday 10 a.m. to 6 p.m. Admission is free, $2.25 for special exhibitions; (420-2) 24 30 11 11.

where to stay

BUDGET: Sloping ceilings and exposed beams adorn some of the 12 rooms and 2 suites in King George's House (Dum U krale Jiriho), Liliova 10. The hotel is in a restored 14th-century building in the center of the Old Town, a five-minute walk from the Charles Bridge. Doubles are $85, suites $95; (420-2) 22 22 09 25, fax (420-2) 22 22 17 07.

Hotel Anna, Budecska 17, has 23 functional rooms in a converted turn-of-the-century apartment building in the residential Vinohrady neighborhood, near everything but just outside the tourist zone. Doubles are $85; (420-2) 22 51 31 11, fax (420-2) 22 51 51 58.

MODERATE: The Maximilian Hotel is on a quiet square in the heart of the Old Town at Hastalska 14 and combines the charm of a turn-of-the-century exterior with modern amenities. All rooms have satellite TV, a fax machine and a minibar. A big breakfast buffet is included in the price. The rate for a double is $210; (420-2) 218 06 111, fax (420-2) 218 06 110.

The small mansion that now is Pension Dientzenhofer, Nosticova 2, was the home of the 18th-century architect Kilian Ignac Dientzenhofer. He and his father designed many of the Baroque palaces of the Little Quarter. The seven rooms here, all of them wheelchair accessible, face a quiet garden. Doubles are $100; (420-2) 53 16 72, fax (420-2) 57 32 08 88.

LUXURY: Since the 1920's, the Hotel Palace Praha, Panska 12, has catered to the famous, from Josephine Baker to the Rolling Stones. This Art Nouveau landmark has 114 rooms and 10 suites, with the more opulent quarters featuring antiques and crystal chandeliers. Doubles: from $260; (420-2) 24 09 31 11, fax (420-2) 24 22 12 40.

The designers of the Radisson SAS Hotel Praha, Stepanska 4, have re-created the Art Deco touches in the lobby and the 211 guest rooms that gave this Prague classic its character when it was known as the Alcron. Doubles range from about $200 to $300; (420-2) 22 82 0000, fax (420-2) 22 82 01 20.

where to eat

Palffy Palac, Valdstejnska 14, is in a Baroque palace and illuminated by candlelight. This most atmospheric of restaurants, seating about 50, specializes in game. Try the haunch of deer in cranberry sauce and the homemade sorbets. Dinner for two with wine is about $70. Reservations recommended; (420-2) 57 32 05 70.

Ostroff, Strelecky Ostrov 336, is an oasis on its own small island in the Vltava. The restaurant is divided into three parts: a terrace offering one of the best views in town, a stylish bar and an Italian restaurant. Pumpkin and slivered almond soup can be followed by linguine with lobster, or rack of lamb with tarragon sauce. Dinner for two is around $70; a three-course prix fixe lunch is $12. Reservations are recommended; (420-2) 24 91 92 35.

Bellevue, Smetanovo Nabrezi 18, offers a Sunday jazz brunch with a castle view, at $20 a person, from 11 a.m. to 3:30 p.m. The buffet includes champagne, three kinds of salmon, oysters and a variety of hot dishes. Reservations are recommended; (420-2) 22 22 14 38.

The owners and staff at Kogo, a trendy but cozy spot at Havelska 27, are from Sarajevo, and the cuisine is a mixture of Balkan and Mediterranean, at reasonable prices. Risotto with frutti di mare, or the veal escalope in port wine sauce are both good main courses. The salads and desserts, including baklava, are excellent. Lunch or dinner for two costs about $22; (420-2) 24 21 45 43.

One of the best pizza joints in town, Pizzeria Rugantino, Dusni 4, is also child- and pet-friendly. The cost of a pizza averages about $3.50; (420-2) 231 81 72.

vital statistics

POPULATION (1997): City 1,200,455

HOTEL: Room for one with tax $207.00

DINNER FOR ONE: With tax and tip but not drinks $24.30

TAXI: Upon entry 46 cents; Most rides in town $4.50; From the airport $10.75

CAR RENTAL FOR A DAY: Midsize manual shift car with unlimited free mileage $125.00

FOR MORE INFORMATION: Telephone: (42-2) 24 21 22 09; Web: www.globopolis.com/prague

Sources: Runzheimer International, local businesses

Rio de Janeiro
Moving to the samba beat

Rio de Janeiro,
Brazil

LARRY ROHTER

Larry Rohter is the chief of the Rio de Janeiro bureau of *The Times*.

Rio de Janeiro is one of the world's most celebrated tourist spots, and nobody knows that better than the 6.5 million people who live here, who like to call their hometown "a Cidade Maravilhosa," or "the marvelous city." Beaches, mountains, an enviable climate, friendly people, nonstop nightlife and championship-caliber soccer: all do their part to bring millions of visitors calling year after year.

One of the most appealing characteristics of Cariocas, as natives of Rio are called in Portuguese, is their zest and joy for life. Get on a bus or the city's clean and efficient subway, and someone is likely to be tapping out a samba beat. Stop for a caipirinha or a cold beer at one of the multitude of casual neighborhood bars, known as botequins, and you will be welcomed like a long-lost relative if you are brave enough to venture even a few words in Portuguese. Rio is all about inclusion, not exclusion.

Compared to a decade—or even five years—ago, the city is also a much safer and better-policed place these days, at least in the areas tourists are likely to frequent. Still, it makes sense to be as cautious here as in New York City or any other big urban area.

That means that if you plan to go to the beach, for instance, you should not take a camera, your passport, jewelry or a large sum of money with you. In other words, don't do something just because you are in Rio that you wouldn't also do at home.

best of times

The high season, of course, is the Southern Hemisphere summer, from November through March, when the schools shut down, holidays come in clusters, and the city's languid rhythms relax even further. By the time Carnival, the annual bacchanal famous for its driving music, scanty costumes and nonstop partying, rolls around just before Ash Wednesday, Rio is almost purring with contentment.

The truth is, though, that almost any time of year is a good time to stop over in Rio. If the weather seems a bit too cold for lounging on Ipanema or Copacabana beaches and watching the locals, well, then, the restaurants and clubs are still filled until well past midnight. Clients are so exuberant that one popular beachfront spot posts a sign cautioning that "it is forbidden to beat out rhythms on tables or to sing aloud while eating."

New Year's Eve (Reveillon) is another day for celebration in Rio. And for two consecutive weekends in January, Rock in Rio brings some of the top rock-music performers to the city.

what to see

Rio de Janeiro occupies one of the most magnificent natural settings of any city in the world, and the view from the Christ the Redeemer statue atop Corcovado Mountain is every bit as spectacular as countless movies have portrayed it. Look one way, and all of Guanabara Bay lies before you; look another, and a series of mountain peaks dominates the scene. It is possible to drive or take a taxi to the top, but the easiest way is to take the cable car that leaves from 513 Rua Cosme Velho every half hour from 8:30 a.m. until 5:30 p.m. It costs $9.75; telephone (55-21) 558-1329.

The best place to observe Cariocas being themselves is seaside. Copacabana and Ipanema are the most famous beaches, and when the surf turns rough, there is still fun to be had in people watching: couples flirting, volleyball and soccer on the sand, strollers and skateboarders, vendors selling ice cream and coconuts. One of the best shows in town, and it's free.

Created by Emperor João VI in the early 19th century, the Jardim Botânico, or Botanical Garden, displays some 6,000 species of flower, plant and tree native to Brazil. But even for those not interested in tropical botany, a walk along the quiet paths of the gardens, with their splendid royal palms towering overhead, is both restful and romantic. At 920 Rua Jardim Botanico and open daily 8 a.m. to 5 p.m. Admission is $2.17; (55-21) 294-6012.

Americans who think soccer is boring often change their minds after attending a game at Maracanà Stadium, at Rua Profesor Eurico Rabelo. With a capacity of 120,000 spectators, Maracanà is home base for perhaps the most passionate fans in the world: they sing, dance, yell and chant their way through flamboyantly played matches, especially on weekends. Hotel concierges can arrange excursions, with tickets from $2.70 to $27.

Brazil's endangered Indians, who have been embraced in recent years as symbols of ecological awareness, are the subject at the Indian Museum, 55 Rua das Palmeiras in Botafogo, (55-21) 286-8899, open Tuesday to Friday 10 a.m. to 5 p.m., Saturday and Sunday 1 to 5 p.m.; and the International Museum of Naive Art, 561 Rua Cosme Velho in Cosme Velho, (55-21) 205-8612, open Tuesday to Friday 10 a.m. to 6 p.m., Saturday and Sunday noon to 6 p.m. Admission is $2.70 adults, $1.35 students and seniors.

When Brazil's top musical artists want to put themselves on display, they play at Canecão, 215 Avenida Venceslau Bras in Botafogo, (55-21) 543-1241. Shows start at 9 p.m. on weeknights and at 10 p.m. on weekends, with ticket prices generally ranging from $11.50 to $28.50. Consult concierges or Rio's newspapers for performers.

For jazz, try Mistura Fina, at 3207 Avenida Borges de Medeiros in the Lagoa district, (55-21) 286-4158. This is where leading American artists play when they come to town, so Brazilian musicians also like to test their chops here. Cover averages $11, with a $6.50 minimum.

where to stay

BUDGET: The 150-room Marina Palace, 630 Rua Delfim Moreira, is the only beachfront hotel in Leblon, the tree-lined neighborhood that is the quieter, calmer cousin to Ipanema. Each room offers a view of either the beach or Corcovado mountain, and some have both. With doubles from $107, it is definitely a bargain; (55-21) 259-5212, fax (55-21) 294-1644.

The 156 rooms at the Everest Rio Hotel, (55-21) 523-2282, fax (55-21) 521-3198, can be a bit small. But the location, at 1117 Rua Prudente de Morais just a block from the beach in the center of Ipanema, and the price (doubles from $152) more than compensate.

MODERATE: The Rio Palace Hotel, 4240 Avenida Atlântica in Copacabana, has been restored to the status it enjoyed a decade ago as one of the city's premier hotels. The 388 rooms are spacious, many with verandas, and the hotel also houses a highly regarded French restaurant, Le Pré-Catelan. A double room with a spectacular view of the full length of Copacabana starts at $342; telephone (55-21) 525-1232, fax (55-21) 522-0570.

The Sheraton Rio Hotel and Towers is both the largest and the most spectacularly situated of the city's main hotels. All 561 of its rooms overlook the crashing surf of Vidigal Beach, far from the hustle and bustle of Copacabana and Ipanema, and there are plenty of sports facilities, including tennis courts and a health club. After Easter, when prices fall, a standard double is $180; (55-21) 274-1122, fax (55-21) 239-5643.

LUXURY: The 75-year-old dowager of Rio's hotels, the Copacabana Palace, emerged from a complete face-lift more sparkling than ever. Old-fashioned elegance is the byword here, with plenty of marble and Art Nouveau architecture; the location, in the heart of Copacabana on the beach at 1702 Avenida Atlântica, is convenient. Double rates in the 226 rooms begin at $410; (55-21) 548-7070, fax (55-21) 235-7330.

The Caesar Park Hotel, 460 Avenida Vieira Souto in Ipanema, is more modern in design and offers easy access to the city's most famous beach. Double rates in the 221 rooms and suites start at $302; (55-21) 525-2525, fax (55-21) 521-6000.

where to eat

Rio gourmets tend to overrate their city's French restaurants and disparage the food of Brazil's mother country, Portugal. But the chefs at Antiquarius, 19 Rua Aristides Espinola, Leblon, work wonders with the humble codfish and other mainstays of Portuguese cuisine, such as the soup called caldo verde. Diners Club and MasterCard are the only credit cards accepted. Dinner for two with a modest South American wine will cost about $115; (55-21) 294-1049.

The city also boasts many excellent Italian restaurants; one of the most celebrated and bustling is Quadrifoglio, 19 Rua J. J. Seabra in Jardim Botânico. The various risottos on the menu come highly recommended, as does the lamb with rosemary. Dinner for two with wine is about $90; (55-21) 294-1433.

The idea of the rodizio, the all-you-can-eat grill where the waiters bring the meat to the table, is starting to catch on in New York and other American cities. Rio boasts some of the best of the lot. O Porcão is at 218 Rua Barão da Torre in Ipanema, (55-21) 522-

0999, and Marius is in Copacabana just up the street from the Rio Palace Hotel at 96 Rua Francisco Otaviano, (55-21) 521-0500. Dinner for two at either of these carnivore's delights runs about $65 to $81.

For seafood, A Cabaca Grande is a traditional favorite of Rio residents. The main location, near the docks downtown at 12 Rua do Ouvidor, (55-21) 509-2301, has been in business for nearly a century, specializing in a kind of Brazilian bouillabaisse known as sopa leão veloso. That branch is open only for lunch, but dinner is served in Ipanema at 422 Rua Barão da Torre, (55-21) 287-7177. Try any of the various moquecas, or seafood stews, and you won't go wrong. Dinner for two: about $60.

Also popular in Rio are restaurants that offer elaborate buffets whose price is calculated by weight. For lunch, Estação, 570 Rua Visconde de Pirajá in Ipanema, (55-21) 294-4233, features five separate establishments, on two floors, with everything from sushi to pasta. For dinner, Fellini, at 104 Rua General Urquiza in Leblon, (55-21) 274-2966, is a good bet. At both locations, meals cost about $5 a pound.

vital statistics

POPULATION (1996): City 5,551,538; State 13,406,308

HOTEL: Room for one with tax $227.50

DINNER FOR ONE: With tax and tip but not drinks $20.95

TAXI: Upon entry $1.37; Each additional kilometer 44 cents; From the airport $11.00 (to downtown); $16.50 (to Ipanema)

CAR RENTAL FOR A DAY: Midsize car with unlimited free mileage $77.00

FOR MORE INFORMATION: Telephone: (55-21) 217-7575; Web: www.rio.rj.gov.br/riotur

Sources: Runzheimer International, Brazilian Embassy, local businesses

Rome

The Jubilee Year leaves
a sparkling city behind

CELESTINE BOHLEN AND ELISABETTA POVOLEDO

Celestine Bohlen is a former chief of *The Times*'s Rome bureau,
where Elisabetta Povoledo is a researcher.

For cities, important events can serve as the catalyst for major improvements. Such is the case with Rome, where the 2000 Roman Catholic Jubilee, or Holy Year—a tradition that dates to 1300 and now takes place about every 25 years—was used as an excuse to get some of the city's notorious traffic under control, its museums brought up to scratch and its piazze and palazzi spruced up.

Rome has not looked so clean in years, but since the traffic has not been entirely tamed, the gleaming travertine marble and resplendent creamy colors of many facades are doomed to slowly sink back into exhaust-gray anonymity.

Hopefully, improvements to the city's museums will last longer. Priceless paintings by Raphael, Caravaggio and Titian now look more comfortably at home after the Borghese Gallery and the National Gallery of Ancient Art in Palazzo Barberini were brought to a matching splendor. The world's oldest collection of public art—the Capitoline museums—no longer looks its age and has opened a vast gallery overlooking the forum.

While the Jubilee has very specific Christian connotations,

Rome's pre-Christian past was not ignored, with the complete reorganization of the national Etruscan museum in Villa Giulia as well as the National Roman Museum, now divided among three new or improved sites. And for those who wonder what happened to the city between the Roman era and the Renaissance, the new Crypta Balbi museum uncovers the history of this period.

Finally, though the weight of thousands of years of artistic patrimony hangs over Rome, spaces dedicated to modern art have multiplied. Not only was the National Gallery of Modern Art entirely rearranged, but the city also opened its own contemporary art museum in a former brewery.

best of times

Rome's temperate climate—ranging between 52 and 90 degrees—makes visiting pleasant year round, so there is always a steady flow of tourists. Their numbers, however, tend to swell during important Christian holidays, like Holy Week and Christmas.

Still, spring (as well as autumn) is one of the best times to visit Rome, when the Spanish Steps are taken over by thousands of newly blooming azaleas, and it is still cool enough for the city to host three important sporting events: the Rome Marathon, the International Horse Show at the Piazza di Siena and the Italian International Tennis Tournament. (But it can rain in Rome in the spring, and when it does, it pours.)

The hot summer nights are made bearable by dozens of outdoor events, and many of Rome's archaeological sites, piazze and parks become open-air venues for cinema and for music, theater and dance.

And though the likelihood of having a white Christmas is practically nonexistent, still the air is crisp and long winter nights are brightened by Christmas lights. The Baroque Piazza Navona becomes a lively and noisy outdoor market bursting with toys, candies and Christmas decorations, and many of the city's churches vie with each other in an unofficial competition for who has the most elaborate Nativity crèche.

what to see

After a tour of the palatial ruins and gardens of the Palatine, a quick walk across the Circus Maximus and a steep climb up its southern embankment, you are already halfway up the Aventine—close enough to follow signs to Santa Sabina, Sant'Alessio and Sant'Anselmo, the three churches that crown the hill.

Of these, Santa Sabina is the gem: a perfect example of a fifth-century basilica, full of light and space. The carved panels on the door to the left of the main entrance beneath the covered portico are also from the fifth century, including one of the oldest known representations of the Crucifixion.

Across the courtyard from Santa Sabina is a walled garden filled with gnarled orange trees and with a lookout offering a panorama of the city and its cupolas. For a cozier view, walk farther down the Via Santa Sabina to the Sovereign Order of Malta garden gate, and peek through the keyhole for a dead-centered glimpse of the cupola of St. Peter's, built by Michelangelo.

An out-of-the-way museum in the same area is the so-called Art Center ACEA, or Centrale Montemartini, at 106 Viale Ostiense with an extraordinary collection of 450 ancient sculptures taken from the basements of the Capitoline Museums, displayed in what was Rome's first electric power generating station. The contrast of white marble and the giant black machines of the Industrial Age is novel and striking. Admission: $5.35; (39-06) 5748042.

Ostia Antica—with its acres of half-ruined houses, shops and theaters that, after Pompeii, give the best sense of ancient Roman life—is only a 25-minute subway ride away. From the Piramide station, take a train to the Ostia Antica stop. The station is a short walk from the archaeological site. Open Tuesday to Sunday 9 a.m. to 5 p.m., until 7 p.m. in summer. Tickets: $3.55; (39-06) 5635-8099.

where to stay

To avoid crowds, it makes sense to stay in one of the several small hotels on the Aventine, which are moderately priced, quiet and have a certain character

BUDGET: The Aventino, at 10 Via DI San Domenico, is managed by the Sant'Anselmo group. It is comfortable, and has its own garden. A double costs $111; (39-06) 574-5231, fax (39-06) 578-3604.

MODERATE: The Hotel Sant'Anselmo, at 2 Piazza Sant'Anselmo on a tiny square directly behind the church of the same name, is an old villa with 24 rooms set off a central staircase. There are antiques in the hallways and stenciled flowers on the walls. A double is about $142, breakfast included. Some rooms can accommodate four, at $178; (39-06) 5745-174, fax (39-06) 578-3604.

Slightly more expensive is the Domus Aventina, not far away at 11B Via di Santa Prisca. It was renovated three years ago, and now offers very modern rooms that are comfortable (if a bit uniform), many with little balconies overlooking a courtyard that belongs to the adjacent church. Doubles: $175, breakfast included; (39-06) 574-6189, fax (39-06) 5730-0044.

LUXURY: The Hotel Forum, 25 Via Tor Dei Conti, is perched on the edge of the Imperial Forum, with a roof-garden restaurant justifiably famous for its view. Many of the rooms also have views onto the ruins. Doubles start at $258 without breakfast; (39-06) 679-2446, fax (39-06) 678-6479.

One of Rome's very best hotels is the Eden, 49 Via Ludovisi, where the rooms are luxurious, the bathrooms even more so and the roof terrace fabulous. Doubles: from $514 with breakfast; (39-06) 478-121, fax (39-06) 482-1584.

where to eat

At night, parts of Rome's historic center still seem sunk in the Middle Ages, and the visitor can get lost in dark (but not dangerous) alleys that end abruptly in dimly lighted piazzas.

One of these is Piazza delle Coppelle, in the neighborhood near the Pantheon and Piazza Navona. Riccioli Cafe, on the piazza at No. 10/a, (39-06) 6821-0313, has a hip interior—lots of steel and primary colors. The menu favors light fish dishes. You can order fresh Belon oysters, or ventresca di tonno (red tuna belly) or marinated fish or salad made with curried shrimp, yogurt and cucumber. The chocolate cake or the millefeiulle with cream and figs are fine meal toppers. The wine list is extensive and meals start at $90 with wine.

Rome's restaurant scene is generally pretty stable, with names and menus staying the same for generations. One of the oldest and best is Checchino dal 1887 in 30 Via di Monte Testaccio, (39-06) 574-6318, run by the same family for five generations. It serves typical Roman "cucina povera," or poor cuisine, which makes use of just about every part of the animal carcass that can be eaten. It is a carnivore's dream and a vegetarian's nightmare: head of veal, veal's foot, tripe, oxtail, entrails, stomach lining—yum. There are also many varieties of cheese and a wine list of about 600 labels. Meal for two starting at $90.

But new places do crop up, like the innovative Ristorante Gusto, on 9 Piazza Augusto Imperatore, (39) 06 3226273, right in front of Augustus' mausoleum. In stark contrast with many traditional Roman trattorie, Gusto is large and very modern looking and includes a wine shop, wine bar and pizzeria. The food is original and includes eggplant and chickpea strudel with goat cheese and sesame sauce, spelt soup with cured goose meat and artichokes or various kinds of couscous. Dinner for two comes to about $90.   `

Another new entry on the Roman restaurant scene is Ditirambo, in Piazza della Cancelleria 74, (39-06) 687-1626, close to the boisterous Campo de Fiori, one of the preferred hangouts of young people—Italian and non. A cozy place with wooden beams and tables, where the pastas are homemade and the ingredients super fresh. Dinner for two—a first course of malfatti (a pasta made of almond flour and ricotta) with zucchini flowers, a main course of mixed boiled meats with green sauce, a tasty salad of spinach, pears, walnuts and cheese, and elegant desserts—comes to about $62 with a bottle of good Italian white wine.

At the tiny Tartaruga, at 53 Via del Monte della Farina, behind San Andrea della Valle on Corso Vittorio Emanuele II, the Limana family offers a menu that changes daily, with choices like the traditional Roman soup of fish and broccoli, fresh pastas and simple meat or fish dishes. Lunch for two with a bottle of wine is about $36, dinner from $67; (39-06) 686-9473.

For another kind of experience, try the wine bar at Trimani, 37B Via Cernaia, where in a modern, stylish atmosphere, you can have a drink, inquire about English-language wine-tasting courses, or choose from a large menu that offers everything from polenta to quiche to steak as well as a large assortment of cured meats and cheeses. Dinner for two, with a bottle of wine from the large and varied list, is $45 to $60; (39-06) 446-8351.

vital statistics

POPULATION (1999): City 2,654,000

HOTEL: Room for one with tax $234.00

DINNER FOR ONE: With tax and tip but not drinks $42.50

TAXI: Upon entry $2.00; Each additional kilometer 58 cents; From the airport $33.75

CAR RENTAL FOR A DAY: Midsize car with unlimited free mileage $92.00

FOR MORE INFORMATION: Telephone: (39-06) 4889-9253; Web: www.italiantourism.com

Sources: Runzheimer International, local businesses

Salt Lake City

Where Mormons once sought isolation, preparations for a world-class party

Mormon Temple, Salt Lake City

MATTHEW BROWN

Matthew Brown is a journalist in Salt Lake City.

Mormon pioneers came to this once desolate, high-desert valley to get away from the rest of the world. But 153 years later, the roughly one million people living at the base of the Wasatch Mountains are preparing to welcome the world for the 2002 Winter Olympics.

In Salt Lake City, work crews are erecting hotels and expanding the Salt Palace Convention Center. Interstate 15, widened to 12 lanes, will stretch the length of the valley, joining a new light-rail train to help handle the expected crowds of athletes, spectators and workers.

Athletes are already training at the Utah Olympic Park, about 30 miles east of the city. Visitors can tour the park ($5 a car) and even try out some of the bobsled runs and ski jumps.

But skiing, hiking and other outdoor sports aren't the only attractions in the area. The city and Park City, 30 miles east of Salt Lake City, are host to arts and film festivals, an international piano competition and other celebrations throughout the year.

best of times

Races at Park City Mountain Resort kick off the World Cup ski racing season every November. Spectators can stand and watch the world's top skiers for free or pay for lunch and a bleacher seat. For information, call (435) 649-9090.

More than 100 independent films are shown in January at the annual Sundance Film Festival, founded by Robert Redford. Most are shown in Park City, but screenings are also held in Salt Lake City, Ogden and Provo. Tickets go on sale in October and screenings often sell out. Call (801) 328-3456.

Each June the city is host to the Gina Bachauer International Piano Competition and festival. Depending on the year, pianists from around the world compete in various age groups. Performances are free except in Abravanel Hall. Tickets to the festival's workshops and lectures can be purchased individually or as a package. Call (888) 521-9200.

Also in June is the Utah Arts Festival, which runs for four days at the Utah State Fairpark, 155 North 1000 West. More than 100 artists from around the country sell their works, and entertainment includes jazz, folk, pop, along with modern dance, ballet and poetry readings.

In a celebration that surpasses Independence Day, the city nearly shuts down on July 24 to celebrate the Mormon pioneers' arrival to the valley in 1847. Salt Lake residents hold services, parades, running races, festivals and fireworks.

On first weekend in August, up to 100,000 people crowd onto Park City's historic Main Street for the GM Park City Art Festival. The two-day event features the work of 200 visual artists from around the country, ethnic food and three stages where local and regional musicians perform; call (435) 649-8882.

what to see

Visitors and lifelong residents alike marvel at the majestic mountains that ring the Salt Lake Valley. The peaks offer hiking for all levels. For an easy walk, head to City Creek Canyon just north of downtown. From Second Avenue and Canyon Road, walk north through a residential area and Memory Grove Park, then follow the road to a gatehouse, where a five-mile paved road begins. Walkers and cyclists have it to themselves on odd-numbered dates, and walkers share the road with cars ($2.50 a vehicle) on other days. The canyon is open 8:30 a.m. to 10 p.m. Call (801) 483-6880 to reserve picnic sites, which cost $2.50 to $30.

They say the sunsets are beautiful from Buffalo Point on Antelope Island. But the best time to visit the largest island in the Great Salt Lake in warmer months may be in the morning, when the pesky gnats and mosquitoes are not swarming. Antelope Island State Park, 30 miles northwest of Salt Lake City off Interstate 15, is home to 500 buffaloes that roam freely, along with mule deer, big horn sheep, antelope and coyotes. More than 30 miles of hiking trails offer spectacular views of the lake. Take your own water. In summer, the beach at Bridger Bay is the best place to experience the sensation of floating on the salt water. Park fees are $7 a vehicle or $4 per cyclist or pedestrian. The 30 campsites cost $10 a night. Information: (801) 773-2941; campsite reservations: (800) 322-3770.

At Olympic Park in Park City, tours of the bobsled run and ski jumps are given daily 11 a.m., and 12:30 and 2 p.m. The 60- to-90-minute tours cost $6 for adults, $4 for seniors and children age 5 to 11. For park information, call (435) 658-4200.

At Temple Square, visitors can learn about Mormonism, get a close-up view of the six-spired Salt Lake Temple and walk inside the domed Tabernacle.

Another popular place is across the street in the church's Family History Library, 35 North West Temple, (801) 240-2331. The library has the largest archive of its kind in the world and is a gold mine for genealogists of any faith or belief. It has computer terminals with easy-to-use software. Terminals are also at the Family Search Center in the Joseph Smith Memorial Building, 15 East South Temple. Use of the library and center is free. The library is open Tuesday through Saturday, 7:30 a.m. to 10 p.m. and Monday 7:30 a.m. to 5 p.m. Center hours are 9 a.m. to 9 p.m., Monday through Saturday.

where to stay

BUDGET: Downtown Hampton Inn, 425 South 300 West, is close to some of the city's best restaurants and microbreweries. The 158-room hotel has an indoor pool, hot tub and exercise room. A double is $79, with Continental breakfast; (801) 741-1110, fax (801) 741-1171.

MODERATE: Hotel Monaco, 15 West 200 South, with 1930's French décor, is a lively addition to the downtown hotel scene. The daily manager's social at 5 p.m. offers guests a free neck and shoulder massage with a glass of wine. The hotel is a refurbished 15-story bank building with 225 rooms, a restaurant and a bar. The

10-foot ceilings and extra-long beds make it a favorite for visiting professional basketball teams. A double room is $149; (801) 595-0000, fax (801) 532-8500.

For a more conservative setting there is The Inn at Temple Square, 71 West South Temple. The 90 rooms, most of which have views of either the Mormon Temple or Abravanel Hall, have the look and feel of a country inn. The inn and its restaurant do not serve alcohol. A double with a king-size four-poster bed is $130 on weekdays and $99 on weekends. Rates include a hot breakfast; (800) 843-4668, fax (801) 536-7272.

Little America Hotel and Towers, 500 South Main Street, offers a broad selection of accommodations—from the Governor's suite for $800 a night to motel-style rooms for $59 on weekends. There are 850 rooms in the tower and other buildings, and two restaurants and two pools. A double in the spacious tower suites is $164, while smaller garden rooms go for $129. Rates drop about $35 or more on weekends; (800) 453-9450, fax (801) 596-5911.

LUXURY: The most luxurious lodging in the area is at Deer Valley Resort in Park City. Among the hotels and condominiums is the Goldener Hirsch Inn, Post Office Box 859, Park City, Utah 84060, a European-style hotel with 20 rooms and a restaurant. All rooms have king-size beds, down comforters and large baths, and 17 have private balconies and fireplaces. Prices range from $210 to $900 in winter and $100 to $235 in the summer. The hotel is closed for about one month each during the spring and fall. Call (800) 252-3373; fax (435) 649-7901.

where to eat

Under state liquor laws, the New Yorker Club, 60 West Market Street, (801) 363-0166, is considered a private club, but nonmembers can buy a two-week membership for $10, which is valid for six people. It offers elegant rooms with Italian marble floors and soft lighting. Appetizers include ahi tuna roll with a rich wasabi butter sauce; a popular entree is roast rack of lamb with rosemary cream and fresh vegetables. Try the raspberry almond tart for dessert. A meal for two with wine is about $150. Like all but one of these restaurants, it is closed Sunday.

The food, rather than the décor, is the attraction of Chez Betty, in the Copperbottom Inn, 1637 Shortline Road, Park City. While the interior has the feel of a hotel coffee shop, the eclectic menu includes unique dishes such as Mediterranean eggplant salad ($9.50) and a delicious sautéed scallopine of turkey breast with rock shrimp and artichokes ($23). For dessert, there's a flavorful trio of gingerbread, spice and carrot cakes with a lemon-lavender jus ($7). Dinner for two with wine is about $110. Open Thursday to Tuesday. Call (435) 649-8181.

The basement location in a dingy strip mall belies the excellent Tuscan food at Michelangelo Ristorante, 2156 South Highland Drive, (801) 466-0961. Ravioli stuffed with porcini mushrooms and Parmesan cheese are served in a rich sauce of truffle oil and butter. The tiramisu is excellent. Dinner for two with wine: $75.

If it's a hot day, head up Emigration Canyon to Ruth's Diner, 2100 Emigration Canyon Road, (801) 582-5807. You can sit in the original dining car or on the patio next to the creek and try anything from burgers and salads to spicy coconut curried shrimp. Ruth's bananas is a parfait of sliced bananas, vanilla ice cream and warm rum sauce. Dinner for two with wine: $50. No reservations, and the wait can be long for Sunday brunch.

For a step back to the time of car hops, burgers and malts, head to Hires Big H, 425 South 700 East. The place is swarming with teenagers and families craving the Big H burger on a soft flour-dusted bun ($2.65), greasy fries ($1.65) and thick malts ($2.29). You can order from your car or eat inside.

vital statistics

POPULATION (1998 estimate): City 174,348; Metro area 1,267,745

HOTEL : Room for one with tax $149.00

DINNER FOR ONE: With tax and tip but not drinks $24.40

TAXI: Upon entry $1.60; Each additional mile $1.60; From the airport $20.00

CAR RENTAL FOR A DAY: Midsize car with unlimited free mileage $63.00

FOR MORE INFORMATION: Telephone: (801) 521-2822; Web: www.visitsaltlake.com

Sources: Runzheimer International, U.S. Census Bureau, local businesses

San Diego

Sun, sea, vine-covered hills:
a great place to nestle

JAMES STERNGOLD

James Sterngold is a correspondent in
The Times's Los Angeles bureau.

"**N**estled" is one of the first words that comes to mind when thinking of this sun-dappled pearl on the Southern California coast.

The city, large though quite manageable, is nestled along an arc of fabulous beaches on the Mexican border. Wonderful getaways like the La Jolla area are nestled into quiet coves of charm and affluence. And, though little known, the eastern reaches of this surprisingly varied county have everything from highly regarded vineyards to breezy apple orchards, all (you guessed it) nestled into auburn-hued hills and mountains.

Perhaps the other word that leaps to mind is "cozy." San Diego has grown into a high-tech center, and still houses some major military bases, but it has little of the boisterous energy of Los Angeles, 100 miles to the north. It is a retreat of sorts.

Not far from downtown is Coronado, a sandy island resort where ordering iced tea can make up a day's exercise. Also near the heart of the city is the 1,200-acre Balboa Park, the home to everything from art museums to the renowned San Diego Zoo, (619)

234-3153. And then head a couple of hours' drive east to the mountain village of Julian and visitors can feel like they stepped into the middle of a giant bakery. The town is famous for its apples and, of course, apple pies, sold from a number of cheerful bakeries lining the streets. This is, in short, a city to be taken in wearing, for the most part, flip-flops and a baseball cap pushed comfortably back on your head.

best of times

One of the great virtues of San Diego's weather is its consistency. High temperatures in winter are in the mid-60's, with about a 10- to 15-degree rise by the time summer arrives (expect wide variations, though, as you head eastward). There's very little rain May through October. The most notable weather component is the coastal fog during fall and winter.

Wildflower season in Anza-Borrego Desert State Park, in the eastern part of San Diego County, usually begins in late February and lasts two to six weeks; call (760) 767-4205.

It should come as no surprise that Fiesta Cinco de Mayo, in early May, is one of the city's most popular annual events. It consists of two days of vibrant celebrations of Mexican-American culture in Old Town San Diego State Park. There's music, dance and Mexican food. Call (619) 296-3161.

A parade, flyovers by Navy aircraft and a concert in Spreckels Park are part of Coronado's annual Independence Day celebrations. But it's all just a warm-up for fireworks that night over Glorietta Bay; (619) 437-8788.

The Mother Goose Parade, in nearby El Cajon in late November, brings together floats, clowns and mounted riders along Main Street. Call (619) 444-8712.

And San Diego Harbor sparkles with the Parade of Lights, a nighttime flotilla of illuminated ships and boats in mid-December. The fleet cruises from Shelter Island to Seaport Village.

what to see

A visit to San Diego can take in more than fabulous ocean vistas and busy theme parks, although they remain part of the attraction. Indeed, one place where these come together is La Jolla, on a beautiful stretch of coast where sea lions and the wealthy come to play. It is just a few miles from SeaWorld San Diego, 500 SeaWorld Drive, (619) 226-3901, and the San Diego Wild Animal Park, (619) 234-6541, which is about 35 miles northeast of downtown in

Escondido, just off I-15. La Jolla has everything from chic boutiques to the La Jolla Playhouse, 2910 La Jolla Village Drive, (858)
550-1010, one of the finer regional theaters in the country. And
don't forget the Hotel Parisi, where the first listing on the auto-
matic dial on the room telephones is the staff psychologist. Hey,
it's Southern California.

Drive an hour or two to the eastern reaches of giant San Diego
County, and a different world emerges, one of auburn-hued hills
and horse ranches. At the northeast end of the region is the town of
Temecula, which has blossomed over the past couple of decades
into a productive wine region with 14 active wineries. One of the
largest is Callaway, just up a pomegranate-lined driveway at 32720
Rancho California Road. There are tours hourly on weekends,
from 11 a.m. to 4 p.m., as well as tastings; (800) 472-2377.

Visitors can enjoy a much homier experience nearby at the
Cilurzo Vineyard and Winery, 41220 Calle Contento, (909) 676-
5250. All the tanks and equipment are right there to see at this small
operation, which produces some nice merlots, cabernet sauvignons,
petite sirahs and viogniers. Tastings are 10 a.m. to 5 p.m.

Rides in hot-air balloons are popular in this hilly area, which
can get roasting hot during the day, but is often cooled by breezes
from the ocean that sweep through a pass. Hour-long rides are
offered by Temecula Valley Balloons, (888) 695-9693, $125 a per-
son if one or two, $110 a person if three and $100 if four or five,
and A Grape Escape, (800) 965-2122, $130 a person. The Temecula
area is accessible via the Rancho California exit on Interstate 15,
about 100 miles south of Los Angeles. Call (909) 699-3626.

Southeast of Temecula, in the Cuyamaca Mountains, is Julian, a
historic village where some gold prospectors struck it rich in 1869.
It is about 60 miles northeast of downtown San Diego on Highway
78. The source of its fame has changed now, and that is never more
evident than in the fall, when a stroll along Main Street is like visiting a giant apple pie bakery, featuring the sweet products of the
many nearby orchards. Information: (760) 765-1857.

Julian consists of about 100 yards of shops on Main Street and
acres of orchards and rolling hills. In the town, the Julian Pioneer
Museum, 2811 Washington Street, (760) 765-0227, fills an attic-
like setting with Gold Rush artifacts; closed Mondays through
November; open weekends only through March. The Eagle and
High Peak Mine, at the far end of C Street, (760) 765-0036, is open
daily for tours of one of the original gold mines in the area. The
Farmers Mountain Vale Ranch, (760) 765-0188, has a picnic area
and farm animals, and visitors can watch cider pressing.

where to stay

BUDGET: There are a number of moderately priced hotels close to the traditional attractions like SeaWorld and the zoo. One convenient hotel is the Holiday Inn Mission Bay, which is a short hop from SeaWorld at 3737 Sports Arena Boulevard, San Diego, (800) 511-6909; fax (619) 224-9248. A double runs from $89 to $149.

In Temecula, one of the more pleasant places to stay is the Loma Vista Bed and Breakfast, 33350 La Serena Way; (909) 676-7047, fax (909) 676-0077. Set on a hill and up a narrow lane overlooking the Callaway vineyards, it has six rooms decorated in Spanish Mission style. Prices run from $105 to $155 Monday through Thursday, $10 higher on Friday, Saturday and Sunday nights.

MODERATE: In Julian and the vicinity, there are several dozen inns and B & B's. A fine place in town is the Orchard Hill Country Inn, 2502 Washington Street; (800) 716-7242, fax (760) 765-0290. The 22 rooms, done in a casual country style, run from $185 to $285, with full breakfast.

About a mile out of town on a heavily wooded site is the Wikiup B & B, (800) 694-5487, fax (760) 765-1512, at 1645 Whispering Pine Drive. The four rooms—each with fireplace and three with a Jacuzzi, two with Victorian décor—run from $155 to $175.

LUXURY: In La Jolla, the Hotel Parisi, 1111 Prospect Street, (858) 454-1511, fax (858) 454-1531, quiet and with understated elegance, occupies a prime spot on one of the main thoroughfares in this affluent community. The 20 suites, done in a contemporary Mediterranean style, cost $275 to $435, with breakfast.

where to eat

In Temecula, at the pleasant, midpriced Vineyard Terrace restaurant at Callaway, 32720 Rancho California Road, (909) 308-6661, lunch entrees cost $8 to $14; dinner entrees, such as beef tenderloin, $12 to $18. There is an extensive wine list. Lunch is served Thursday through Sunday, dinner Friday and Saturday.

For a little local color in Julian, you can go to the Miner's Diner, opposite the Town Hall, at 2134 Main Street, (760) 765-3753, for sandwiches, milk shakes and the like—as well as the old-fashioned soda fountain setting.

A standby in La Jolla is Harry's Coffee Shop, 7545 Girard Avenue, (858) 454-7381, run by Harry Rudolph for 40 years. Breakfast is served all day and the fare is solid coffee shop, with meals about $10.

One of San Diego's livelier areas is the Mission Hills–Hillcrest area, which has a large gay population and a vibrant, hip nightlife. The food at Parallel 33, 741 West Washington Street, (619) 260-0033, a new restaurant, combines influences from North Africa, Asia, India and California. Entrees run from $17 to $24.

A casual blues-themed restaurant in the same general neighborhood, the Gulf Coast Grill, 4130 Park Boulevard, (619) 295-2244, combines cuisine of two gulfs, California and Mexico, and Cajun. A huge fish near the entrance lets you know the specialty. Entrees, such as Mississippi mustard catfish, run from $9 to $19.

vital statistics

POPULATION (1998 estimate): City 1,220,666; Metro area 2,780,592

HOTEL: Room for one with tax $176.00

DINNER FOR ONE: With tax and tip but not drinks $29.90

TAXI: Upon entry $1.60; Each additional mile $1.90; From the airport $10.00

CAR RENTAL FOR A DAY: Midsize car with unlimited free mileage $52.00

FOR MORE INFORMATION: Telephone: (619) 236-1212; Web: www.sandiego.org

Sources: Runzheimer International, U.S. Census Bureau, local businesses

San Francisco

Through earthquakes and fire, its charms are irrepressible

Transamerica Pyramid &
Columbus Tower, San Francisco

EVELYN NIEVES AND CHRISTOPHER HALL

Evelyn Nieves is chief of *The Times*'s San Francisco bureau.
Christopher Hall contributes to *The Times* from San Francisco.

The seal of San Francisco depicts a sailing ship and a miner—references to the California Gold Rush—but the phoenix shown above them in its bed of fire is a more apt symbol for the city. Almost since 1776, when Spain established a presence here, San Francisco has periodically been reborn after fires, earthquakes and economic calamity.

Most dramatic were the booms that followed the discovery of gold in 1849 and the devastating 1906 earthquake and fire, but there have been modern rebirths as well. In the tumultuous 1960's, San Francisco emerged as a center of counterculture—a continuing influence on city politics. A revitalized waterfront followed the razing of an elevated freeway damaged in the 1989 quake. And the city, after years of watching helplessly as traditional businesses fled for greener pastures, now rides the crest of the high-tech wave.

These periodic rebirths have had an effect on those who live here, be it with flowers in their hair or a briefcase in their hand. San Franciscans cling to the past—witness the city's unabashed love affair with its gaily colored Victorian houses—even as they embrace new trends. This compact city of small neighborhoods, where it's often easier to find a cappuccino or a Chinese pork bun than a hardware store, invites you to enjoy life while you can. Inhale the toasty-sweet aroma from an Italian bakery, catch kaleidoscopic views of city and bay from a cable car, or savor the bounty of Northern California at one of the city's countless eateries.

Better yet, take a boat ride on the bay and notice how San Francisco seems to float in place. A trick, perhaps, of light on water, or maybe all that rebirthing has taught the city how to stay light on its feet.

best of times

Mark Twain may never have said that the coldest winter he ever spent was a summer in San Francisco, as some people claim he did, but the fact is that fog can put a damper on temperatures during the summer. San Francisco has an essentially Mediterranean climate, however, and temperatures are rarely extreme. Late spring and early fall are generally sunny and sometimes warm, and while winter and early spring are the seasons for rain, the city rarely looks finer than when the sun reappears after a February or March storm.

In January or February, the city's Chinese New Year Celebration, (415) 982-3071, culminates in a parade featuring a 200-foot-long dragon. In March, thousands of green thumbs flock to the San Francisco Flower and Garden Show; (800) 829-9751.

Carnaval, (415) 826-1401, a huge Latino street festival, arrives in May, while in June the city's gay pride parade, (415) 864-3733, fills Market Street for hours.

The San Francisco Blues Festival, (415) 979-5588, the oldest blues festival in America, is held in September, followed in October and November by the San Francisco Jazz Festival; (415) 788-7353.

what to see

The timeless attractions—the 43 hills that can make driving up and down neighborhood streets feel like riding in the first seat of a roller coaster; the hyperkinetic sidewalks of the Haight; the serene gardens of Golden Gate Park; the fog rolling like a great ghost through the streets, morning and night—are still free.

For people-watching, try the Haight-Ashbury, where there are plenty of outdoor cafes, a mix of old- and neo-bohemians, and gift and vintage clothing shops. One of the biggest, the Wasteland, at

1660 Haight Street, will be happy to look at your old flower-power jeans.

City Lights bookstore, the famous Beat hangout founded in 1953 by San Francisco's poet laureate, Lawrence Ferlinghetti, is still one of the most interesting bookstores around, with a poetry room upstairs. It's at 261 Columbus Avenue, off Jack Kerouac Alley in North Beach; (415) 362-8193.

North Beach, the popular stomping grounds for tourists, is much more enjoyable to walk around than to drive. (Parking is nearly impossible, anyway.) Rest your feet on one of the benches at Washington Square, where the old-timers from the old country mingle with the tai chi practitioners.

You might try the espresso at Mario's Bohemian Cigar Store Cafe, at 566 Columbus Avenue, (415) 362-0536, one of the last of the Old World hangouts, or the cannoli at Stella Pastry, 446 Columbus Avenue, (415) 986-2914.

One of San Francisco's biggest sources of pride, Golden Gate Park, boasts gardens, lakes, trails, playgrounds, sports facilities and several museums, not to mention musicians, skateboarders and in-line skaters who love to show off. The Strybing Arboretum and Botanical Gardens is filled with rare plants and trees from around the world. For free walking tours, call (415) 263-0991.

Maintenance crews go through hundreds of gallons of orange paint each week on touch-ups to the Golden Gate Bridge. It's all to keep this star looking its best. For the best way to cross the bridge, start at Fort Point Lookout, (415) 556-1693, on Marine Drive at the San Francisco end. The lookout has a gift center, a statue of Joseph B. Strauss, the bridge's designer, and a sample of the three-foot-thick suspension cable. A path from the lookout leads to the toll plaza and then about two miles across to Marin County.

The San Francisco Museum of Modern Art, at 151 Third Street, (415) 357-4000, is open daily except Wednesday from 11 a.m. to 6 p.m. (9 p.m. Thursday). Admission: $9 adults, children under 12 free. Half-price Thursday from 6 to 9 p.m., and free the first Tuesday of every month.

Pacific Bell Park, replacing the much-maligned Candlestick Park, made its debut in 2000. The stadium, billed as a "state-of-the-art old-fashioned ballpark," is in China Basin, seven blocks from the Moscone Center. Tickets for games: $8.50 to $42.

The Exploratorium, a family-friendly science museum in the Palace of Fine Arts, 3601 Lyon Street, (415) 563-7337, is open Tuesday to Sunday, 10 a.m. to 5 p.m., Wednesdays until 9 p.m.; closed Mondays except for most holidays. Admission: $9.

where to stay

BUDGET: The Dakota, 606 Post Street at Taylor, (415) 931-7475, fax (415) 931-7486, is a 41-room hotel dating from 1914, two blocks from Union Square. Most rooms come with refrigerators, microwaves and cable TV. Rates from $79 to $119; discounts for weeklong stays.

MODERATE: The Nob Hill Inn, 1000 Pine Street, is a sweet-looking little place filled with Victorian antiques, where tea is served at 4 p.m. (no charge). The 21 rooms are $109 to $259, with Continental breakfast. Telephone (415) 673-6080, fax (415) 673-6098.

The White Swan Inn, 845 Bush Street, a cross between a hotel and a bed-and-breakfast, has 26 well-appointed rooms, a breakfast room and a small garden. Doubles from $165; (415) 775-1755, fax (415) 775-5717.

LUXURY: Anchored by an Old Navy store that looks about ready to eat downtown Market Street, The Palomar, at 12 Fourth Street, occupies the top five floors of a converted nine-story 1907 landmark structure (the first concrete-and-steel-reinforced office building to rise above the rubble of the 1906 earthquake). The 1930's French-inspired interior is both hip and elegant, with rooms in Art Deco style with velvet-covered furnishings. And the hotel boasts one of the hottest tickets in town in its eclectic restaurant, Fifth Floor, which is usually booked six weeks in advance on weekends. Rooms start at $255, suites start at $425; (877) 294-9711, fax (415) 348-0302.

The Westin St. Francis, 335 Powell Street, is one of the city's most popular and luxurious hotels. Built just before the 1906 earthquake, it was completely rebuilt just after it, expanding to take the entire west side of Union Square. Crown moldings, chandeliers, antiques and muted yellows and blues lend an air of grandeur, while rooms are equipped with two phones (one cordless) and data ports (some have fax machines). Standard rooms start at $219, suites at $450; (415) 397-7000, fax (415) 774-0124.

The Hyatt Regency, 5 Embarcadero Center, across from the Embarcadero shopping plaza, has the 20-story lobby that gave Mel Brooks vertigo in *High Anxiety* and 805 rooms with contemporary furnishings (some are being renovated) starting at about $300; (800) 233-1234, fax (415) 291-6538.

where to eat

A two-to-three-week wait for dinner reservations says much about the Continental-influenced Vietnamese cuisine at the Slanted Door,

584 Valencia Street, (415) 861-8032, in the Mission District. The restaurant has an airy, contemporary feel, with high ceilings and a more formal space upstairs. The menu changes, but regular favorites include spicy organic green beans with shiitake mushrooms, garlic and chili sauce, and grapefruit and jicama salad with candied pecans. Dinner with wine for two: $40 to $50. Closed Mondays.

Watergate, 1152 Valencia Street, (415) 648-6000, has a stately ambience, with walls paneled in beige wood. The French-Asian menu includes a warm lobster martini appetizer (served in a martini glass) with cilantro and mashed potatoes; entrees include grilled rib eye with watercress salad and bordelaise sauce. Dinner and wine for two: $100.

Eos, 901 Cole Street, (415) 566-3063, favored for its East-West fusion cuisine, serves grilled spicy butterfish with grilled prawns and Thai spiced broth, and pan-seared drunken boneless quail with garlic chive and chevre dumplings and sautéed pea sprouts, among its adventurous dishes. Dinner for two with wine: $90.

Most of the old-fashioned spaghetti joints that occupied North Beach have yielded to the pasta-and-greens menus in favor nowadays. But Michelangelo Cafe, 597 Columbus Avenue, where there is always a wait to get in, still offers a traditional menu in a family-style atmosphere. Dinner for two with wine: about $45.

Kate's Kitchen, in the Haight district at 471 Haight Street, offers inexpensive, hearty meals in a cozy storefront. Specialties include scallion-cheese biscuits and lemon-cornmeal pancakes. Breakfast or lunch for two: about $20.

vital statistics

POPULATION (1998 estimate): City 745,774; Metro area 4,001,831

HOTEL: Room for one with tax $223.00

DINNER FOR ONE: With tax and tip but not drinks $32.05

TAXI: Upon entry $2.50; Each additional mile $2.40; From the airport $35.00

CAR RENTAL FOR A DAY: Midsize car with unlimited free mileage $56.50

FOR MORE INFORMATION: Telephone: (415) 391-2000; Web: www.sfvisitor.org

Sources: Runzheimer International, U.S. Census Bureau, local businesses

San Juan

A renaissance has the old city looking its best in years

San Juan,
Puerto Rico

JOHN MARINO AND MARTIN DELFIN

John Marino is the city editor of *The San Juan Star*.
Martin Delfin is a reporter for *The Star*.

There's a clear light in San Juan throughout the year. It takes on the blues of the coastline along San Juan's beaches, which stretch from Condado all the way out to undeveloped Piñones, and turns iridescent in Old San Juan, as it bounces from the sandstone facades of historic fortresses and chapels, and splashes across the pastel sides of old city homes.

Strolling around Old San Juan, whose narrow streets sculpted from ship's ballast climb from the San Juan Bay to a headland overlooking the Atlantic, it's possible to forget what year it is. Art Deco apartment buildings and storefronts from the 1930's are crowded into the mile-square peninsula amid 100-year-old Spanish-colonial mansions, towering 16th-century fortresses and historic churches. Yet most residences are two stories or less, painted in bright pastels, one reason Old San Juan lingers in the memory as an intimate place.

Old San Juan has been undergoing something of a renaissance lately, eliminating the once-common sight of ruined Spanish mansions spread across the zone; they're now being painstakingly restored to the Institute of Puerto Rican Culture's specifications to retain the sector's historic integrity. Retailers, hotel operators and restaurateurs have also been busy in Old San Juan. The boom has resulted in new lodging options (with more on the way) and new shops. The biggest impact has been in the number of new restaurants on the scene. The new pack includes Dragonfly, specializing in Latin-Asian cuisine, and Tantra, the island's first Indian restaurant.

best of times

With the exactness of a finger snap, San Juan's skies turn in mid-December, as the rainy season disappears into the dry, bright afternoons of winter. But even during wet months (around May and then again in November), the sun usually breaks through for a good portion of the day, and many spring, autumn and summer days can be just as delightful as the Caribbean winter. The only time it's not advisable to come is during late August and September, the peak of the hurricane season. High season, when most visitors come to San Juan, runs from around December 15 through April 15.

Old San Juan is lively throughout Las Navidades, Puerto Rico's Christmas season. It runs from late November to mid-January, when Las Fiestas de la Calle San Sebastián (the San Sebastían Street Festival) takes place in Old San Juan. By day, it's an impressive outdoor art show and crafts exhibit. By night, it's a street party.

The Heineken Jazz Fest, in late May, features Latin and United States performers. The festival, from Thursday through Sunday, takes place at Sixto Escobar Stadium, Munoz Rivera Avenue, Puerta de Tierra. Tickets cost $47.50 for the whole festival or $18 a day.

The feast day of Saint John the Baptist, the city's patron saint, is celebrated June 23 with La Noche de San Juan. Tradition mandates that people walk backwards into the ocean at midnight. Today, people go in droves to the beaches of San Juan, which are filled with music as people bring picnic foods and drinks. It's the one night of the year that city beaches are safe.

The Puerto Rico Symphonic Orchestra's season runs from January through May, at San Juan's fine arts center (Bellas Artes), in the heart of the city in Santurce. Tickets: $25 to $30. The center also is host to the Casals Festival each June, a two-week classical music event. There's something going on almost every night at Bellas Artes, formally known as the Luis A. Ferré Performing Arts Center, on the corner of Ponce de León and De Diego Avenues; (787) 725-7334 or (787) 725-7338.

Gallery Nights begin each year on the first Tuesday of February. More than 20 museums and art galleries in Old San Juan are open between 6 and 9 p.m. Several restaurants and nightspots also host openings, and the old city stays festive well into the evening. Information: (787) 723-7080. Gallery nights take place the first Tuesday of each month, from February through May, and from September through December.

what to see

The San Juan National Historic Site encompasses two Spanish fortresses used to defend the island from attack. The sprawling San Felipe del Morro, built between 1539 and 1783, is set dramatically on a promontory, and one can wander freely through five levels of the vast structure, looking out over ocean views. Its younger twin fortress, San Cristóbal, built in 1634 with a network of tunnels and trenches, is nearby. Both can be reached from Norzagaray Street in Old San Juan and are open daily 9 a.m. to 5 p.m. Admission: $2 for each fort; $1 ages 13 to 17. Information: (787) 729-6960.

Islanders can claim the oldest governor's residence in continuous use in the Western Hemisphere: Santa Catalina, better known as La Fortaleza. The imposing pale blue and white building flanked by two watchtowers dates back to the mid-1500's. Free tours include the lush gardens, which retain the Spanish colonial atmosphere. Tours are between 9 a.m. and 3:30 p.m., Monday to Friday by reservation at (787) 721-7000, extension 2211, 2323 or 2358.

The Puerto Rico Art Musuem, in a renovated Spanish colonial building, opened in July 2000. Besides temporary exhibitions, the museum also has botanical gardens, a theater and lots of activities for the kids. The museum is at 299 Avenida De Diego; (787) 977-627. Admission is $5 for adults, $3 for students, and $2.50 for senior citizens or the handicapped. Open Tuesday through Sunday 10 a.m. to 5 p.m., and Wednesday 10 a.m. to 8 p.m.

And for kids, the Museo del Niño has playrooms where children can hammer away in a makeshift carpentry section or climb in a small replica of a town center; 150 Cristo Street, (787) 722-3791. Open Wednesday through Sunday; $2.50.

where to stay

Rates are for peak season.

BUDGET: To stay within reach of Condado without being in the middle of all its touristy bustle, you could try the Hotel Excelsior, 801 Ponce de León Avenue, Santurce, (787) 721-7400, fax (787) 723-0068. The 140 simply furnished rooms are equipped with kitchenettes or microwaves; there is a pool and a restaurant. Doubles are $143 and up, plus tax.

The Hotel Iberia, 1464 Wilson Street, (787) 723-0200, fax (787) 724-2892, is a small, friendly inn near east Condado and within walking distance of shops and the beach. The 30 rooms are small and sparsely decorated but clean. Doubles from $88, plus tax.

MODERATE: The San Juan Marriott Resort and Stellaris Casino, 1309 Ashford Avenue, (787) 722-7000, fax (787) 722-6800, is one of the most popular resorts in Condado. A large pool with a tropical garden serves as a foyer to an Atlantic Ocean beach. At night in the immense lobby, an orchestra playing Spanish tunes competes with the clanging from the casino. The 525 rooms have a tropical flavor. Singles and doubles: from $285 for a city view to $305 for an ocean view, plus tax.

The open-air lobby of the 644-room Caribe Hilton Hotel, Los Rosales Street, San Geronimo Grounds, (787) 721-0303, fax (787) 725-8849, with its lush tropical plants and waterfalls, exudes a warm Caribbean feel. Double rooms in this recently remodeled hotel run from $295, which includes Continental breakfast but not tax.

LUXURY: When Sanjuaneros want to celebrate, they go to El San Juan Wyndham Resort Hotel and Casino, 6063 Isla Verde Avenue, (787) 791-1000, fax (787) 791-0390. The 389 elegant rooms, done in pastels with plush furnishings, range from $395 to $775 plus tax. There are seven restaurants, a casino, a disco and several lobby bars.

The palatial Ritz-Carlton San Juan Hotel, Spa and Casino, 6961 Avenue of the Governors, (787) 253-1700, fax (787) 253-1111, is 10 minutes from the airport. The hotel boasts shops, a spa and several restaurants. The 414 rooms, decorated in a Caribbean contemporary design with bright colors and large marble bathrooms, overlook the ocean (the hotel has a beach) or the Isla Verde strip with its shops and restaurants. Rates begin at $389, plus tax.

where to eat

Trois Cent Onze, 311 Fortaleza Street, is one of the newest restaurants in Old San Juan, serving French cuisine in Art Deco surroundings. Starters include lobster and salmon ravioli with fresh dill and shellfish, or lobster velouté with Cognac and fresh dill. Steamed fish in pesto and sole meunière are among the entrees. The chocolate mousse perfumed with rum is delicious. Dinner for two with wine is about $120; (787) 725-7959.

Another new entry is Luigi's, 104 Diez de Andino, where the Genovese owner and chef, Luigi Sanguineti, prepares the antipasto, gnocchi with pesto and eggplant lasagna. The small restaurant has a formal and romantic ambience. Dinner for two, including wine: $55; (787) 977-0134.

Authentic Mexican dishes can be found at Cielito Lindo, 1108 Magdalena in Condado. In addition to the combination plates—which include a tostada, guacamole taco, refrijoles and chalupa—Tampique steak and enchiladas are popular. Dinner for two, with beer or drinks: $45; (787) 723-5597.

To get away from the glitter of hotels and casinos and see a typical San Juan neighborhood, take a cab to La Casita Blanca, 351 Tapia Street, in Villa Palmeras, for Puerto Rican home cooking. An appetizer like cod fritters might be followed by rabbit or shrimp fricassee, grilled red snapper or the typical chicken asopao, a soupy rice stew. A liqueur on the house is served after the meal. Dinner for two: $30; (787) 726-5501.

No matter what time of day, Bebos Cafe, 1600 Loiza, in Santurce, always seems full. This is a place for good, cheap food. Roasted chicken and ribs, pork chops, chicken soup and club sandwiches are always on the menu. You may have to wait to get a table. Dinner for two, with beer: $15; (787) 268-5087.

vital statistics

POPULATION (1999 estimate): City 439,604; Puerto Rico 3,889,507

HOTEL: Room for one with tax $373.00 (December to May); $252.00 (April to November)

DINNER FOR ONE: With tax and tip but not drinks $24.80

TAXI: Upon entry $3.00; Each additional mile $1.60; From the airport to Coronado $12.00; to Old San Juan $16.00

CAR RENTAL FOR A DAY: Midsize car with unlimited free mileage $42.40

FOR MORE INFORMATION: Telephone: (787) 721-2400; Web: www.prtourism.com

Sources: Runzheimer International, U.S. Census Bureau, local businesses

Santiago
The return of democracy
brings a new vitality

Santiago, Chile

CALVIN SIMS
Calvin Sims is a former chief of the
Buenos Aires bureau of *The Times*.

Once considered the most militaristic country in Latin America, Chile has worked hard to overcome that stigma, emerging in the last decade as a model for economic and social change in the region. Its armed forces are no longer a threat, its restructured economy is among the fastest growing in the world and its reputation for innovation is firmly established.

Nowhere are these changes more evident than in Chile's capital, Santiago, a modern metropolis of five million people, set amid the august snowcapped Andes and fertile valley farmland.

In 1990, after losing a plebiscite, the military junta that had ruled Chile since 1973 relinquished power to an elected government. Free of repression, the city's intellectual and cultural communities are thriving again. And thanks to a steady flow of foreign investment, Santiago has all the trappings of a world-class city: skyscrapers, fancy and ethnic restaurants, trendy shopping malls, art galleries, rowdy demonstrations and pollution. While most buildings in Santiago are fairly new, the center of the old city, between the Mapocho River and O'Higgins Avenue, contains many historic colonial mansions, churches and government buildings.

During the day, most parts of the city of interest to tourists are safe to visit, and police officers are visible on major street corners and intersections. But visitors should exercise caution at night, when many petty thieves strike.

best of times

The ideal time to visit Santiago is during the Southern Hemisphere's spring, from late September to November, when pollution levels are low, temperatures mild and nature in full bloom.

A wide variety of cultural programs are offered in Santiago throughout the year. The majestic neo-Classical Municipal Theater, at San Antonio and Agustinas, (56-2) 369-0282, stages opera, ballet and symphony performances from March through December.

The University of Chile Theater, 043 Providencia Avenue at Plaza Baquedano, (56-2) 634-5295, hosts seasonal programs featuring the National Symphony Orchestra, the Chilean National Ballet, and Symphony Chorus. Call theater box offices for a listing of performances and prices.

what to see

Santiago's most historic buildings are on Constitution Plaza, downtown, where one can view the impressive changing of the guard in front of the Presidential Palace. The palace, which is known as the Casa de la Moneda because it was originally a mint, was built in 1786 in the Spanish colonial style, with high ceilings and large wooden doors and windows. It was partly ruined in the 1973 military coup, but the building has been restored, and tours can be arranged through Oscar Pizarro, (56-2) 690-4069.

Parque por la Paz, or Peace Park, 8200 José Arrieta Avenue, stands as a memorial to the 3,000 political prisoners who died or disappeared during General Pinochet's 17-year regime. The park, which is open on Saturday and Sunday from 11 a.m. to 5 p.m., was the site of a notorious military detention center—Villa Grimaldi—where torture, murder and other atrocities took place. The city government razed the villa two years ago to create an open green space with trees and benches. A monument under construction inside the park will contain the names of the 224 victims who perished at the villa.

For a panoramic view of Santiago, go to the top of San Cristóbal

Hill, (56-2) 777-6666, an 1,800-acre park with a zoo, botanical garden, public swimming pools, picnic area and a 120-foot statue of the Virgin Mary at its peak. The round-trip fare up the hill is $3 by cable car and $2 by funicular, (56-2) 737-6669, at the end of Avenida Pedro de Valdivia Norte.

A tour of the house where the Nobel poet Pablo Neruda lived with his last wife, Matilde Urrutia, is a magical experience. Known as La Chascona, (56-2) 777-8741 or 737-8712, the house, built in 1953 at 0192 Fernando Márquez de la Plata, was designed by Neruda to give the feeling of sailing in a boat. Tours in English, which are conducted from 10 a.m. to 1 p.m. and 3 to 6 p.m., Tuesday to Sunday, cost $6.

From 5 p.m. to midnight on weekends, the illuminated park behind the National Fine Arts Museum, Parque Forestal, becomes an open-air theater where young actors perform short plays, clowns and mimes display their wit, and amateur poets and writers read their works. The museum itself, (56-2) 633-3577, is open Monday to Friday 10 a.m. to 7 p.m. Admission: $1, Sundays free.

Nearly 30 years after it was conceived, the Salvador Allende Museum of Solidarity, at 360 Herrera downtown, (56-2) 681-4954, finally opened in late 1999 to much fanfare. In the historic Yungay district, the museum is named for the former Chilean president who died in the 1973 military coup. The museum contains a rare collection of works by artists from Latin America and Europe, who donated their sculpture and paintings to show support for Allende's newly elected government (1970-1973). Works by Chillida, Matta, Miró, Guayasamin and Tapis are among those displayed. The museum is open Monday through Sunday, 10 a.m. to 7 p.m. Guided tours are available Monday through Thursday but must be arranged by telephone.

Another fine arts museum is the Ralli Museum, 4110 Alonso de Soto Mayor, (56-2) 208-1798, open 10:30 a.m. to 4 p.m. every day except Monday and Thursday.

At the Chilean Museum of Pre-Columbian Art, 361 Bandera, (56-2) 695-3851, the permanent collection has works from Mexico to the southern tip of the continent. Hours: Tuesday to Saturday, 10 a.m. to 6 p.m., Sunday to 4 p.m. There are informative and free guided tours in English every hour. Entrance fee is $4; free Sundays.

The Lastarria neighborhood is filled with art galleries and cafes, which occupy pretty neo-Classical buildings. The heart of the neighborhood is Plaza Mulato Gil.

where to stay

Unless otherwise noted, rates include breakfast.

BUDGET: Hotel Turismo Monte Carlo, 209 Victoria Subercaseaux, (56-2) 633- 9905, fax (56-2) 633-5577, is a friendly place with a small lobby and reception area. Its 65 rooms are nondescript but comfortable. A double costs $50.

The Residencial Londres, 54 Londres, telephone and fax (56-2) 638-2215, has 28 simple rooms with high ceilings, wood floors, bed, table and chair. The sitting room has deep sofas and chairs. A double with private bath costs $29. Breakfast of coffee and a roll is $1.50 extra.

MODERATE: Los Españoles Hotel, 2539 Los Españoles, (56-2) 232-1824, fax (56-2) 233-1048, has 52 tidy rooms adorned in soft grays and pinks with simple furniture and lithographs of gardens and other nature scenes. A double room costs $100.

The 33 cozy rooms of the Montebianco Hotel, 2911 Isidora Goyenechea Avenue, (56-2) 233-0427, fax (56-2) 233-0420, have hand-woven Chilean rugs and modern furniture. Doubles: $107.

LUXURY: The Santiago Park Plaza Hotel, 207 Ricardo Lyon, (56-2) 233-6363, fax (56-2) 233-6668, is an elegant Old World hotel with 104 rooms, decorated with a European flair. The paneled lobby has velvet sofas, antique chairs, Persian rugs and elaborate flower arrangements. Doubles: $230.

At its existing property along the Mapocho River, Sheraton Hotels opened the San Cristóbal Towers, 1742 Santa María Avenue; (56-2) 233-5000, fax (56-2) 234-1729. The 139 luxury rooms are outfitted with mahogany antiques and large baths. The vast marble-floored lobby overlooks an outdoor pool and verdant grounds. A double room costs $400 a day.

where to eat

With the increase in foreign investment and tourism in Chile has come a new diversity of top-flight and ethnic restaurants.

Aquí Está Coco, at 236 La Concepción, (56-2) 235-8649 or 251-9143, serves superb seafood amid décor that features navigation memorabilia. House specialties include grilled crab cakes, sea bass stuffed with crab, and white chocolate pudding with orange sauce. Dinner for two with wine is about $90. Reservations are recommended.

La Cascade, 2930 Isidora Goyenechea, (56-2) 231-1887 or (56-2)

232-2798, is an upscale French restaurant with large windows and burgundy décor. Dinner of cocktail, goat cheese salad, duck à l'orange, homemade ice cream with berries and wine is about $100 for two.

The popular Café Santa Fe, 10690 Las Condes Avenue, (56-2) 215-1091, pulses with Mexican music. Frozen margaritas, fajitas of shrimp, beef or chicken, and raspberry yogurt cake are favorites on the Tex-Mex menu. Dinner for two is $60.

Frequented by local artists and designers, El Huerto, 54 Orrego Luco, (56-2) 233-2690, offers creative vegetarian cuisine, including fruits and juices, salads, bean soups, homemade cheesecake and pachamama—a regional dish of quinoa, black beans, corn soufflé and boiled vegetables. Dinner for two, with wine: about $40 for two.

In an old adobe-brick house in the bohemian neighborhood of Bellavista, El Caramaño, 257 Purisima, (56-2) 737-7043, serves up typical Chilean dishes like pescado escabechado (fish cooked in vinegar with onions and carrots), osso buco al vino blanco (beef in a white wine sauce with vegetables) and suspiro (meaning "sigh"), a sweet dessert of papaya stuffed with cream. About $40 for two, with wine.

vital statistics

POPULATION (2000 estimate): City 4,600,000

HOTEL: Room for one with tax $289.50

DINNER FOR ONE: With tax and tip but not drinks $17.10

TAXI: Upon entry 26 cents; Each additional kilometer 52 cents; From the airport $20.00

CAR RENTAL FOR A DAY: Midsize car with unlimited free mileage $63.00

FOR MORE INFORMATION: Telephone: (56-2) 632-7785; Web: www.visitchile.org

Sources: Runzheimer International, Santiago Information Center, local businesses

São Paulo
The embodiment of Brazil's racial democracy

São Paulo

LARRY ROHTER

Larry Rohter is chief of the Rio de Janeiro bureau of *The Times*.

Superlatives come quickly to mind when talking about São Paulo. With 18 million people in its metropolitan area, this is the largest city in Brazil, the largest in South America, indeed the largest in the Southern Hemisphere. It boasts of having the largest population of Japanese descent of any city outside Japan, the largest of Lebanese descent of any city outside the Middle East, the largest of Italian descent of any city outside Italy, and more wealth than any city in what used to be called the third world.

Paulistanos, as residents of the city are known, have always taken pride in the cosmopolitan environment they have constructed around them during the past century, with a melting-pot population that personifies the Brazilian ideal of racial democracy.

Those who come to São Paulo expecting to find a laid-back seaside tropical resort in the style of Rio de Janeiro or Salvador are in for a shock. São Paulo is a very different kind of Brazil: aggressive, sprawling and resourceful, with a different climate.

Instead, São Paulo's charms are distinctly urban: restaurants, museums, concerts, nightclubs, parks and window shopping along Avenida Paulista, the main commercial boulevard. So are the problems the city confronts, including poverty, crime and police brutality. But even a confirmed Tropicalist like the pop singer Caetano Veloso was forced to confess that, as he wrote in a homage to the busiest intersection in Brazil's busiest city, "something happens in my heart every time I turn the corner of Ipiranga and São Joao."

best of times

The Southern Hemisphere summer (December to March) is marked by temperatures in the 80's and afternoon rains, but because São Paulo is on a plateau, weather is generally milder than in Rio. Winter (June through September) sees cool temperatures during the day, sometimes falling to near freezing at night.

Any calender in Brazil rotates around Carnival, which occupies the week before Ash Wednesday (Feb. 28 in 2001). But São Paulo celebrates at many other times, too, with activities from music to sports.

The São Paulo State Symphony Orchestra, for instance, has made an effort to become a world-class ensemble since moving into a new home in 1999. The season begins in March, with concerts Thursday and Saturday and guest appearances by leading soloists and visiting orchestras sprinkled throughout the year. Call (55-11) 3351-8189 for schedules and prices.

The Free Jazz Festival in October features leading performers from the United States, Europe and Brazil on three different stages on three consecutive nights; (55-11) 3034-6514. October is also the month for the Mostra Internacional de Cinema, a major film festival.

The São Paulo Biennial is the largest artistic event in Latin America, with thousands of contemporary works by hundreds of artists from all over the world occupying two miles of corridors at Ibirapuera Park. The next exhibition is scheduled for April and May 2002; call (55-11) 5574-5922 for information.

Soccer is more than a sport, it is a national passion, and the São Paulo state championship features some of the country's finest players. The season runs from January through May, with games Saturday and Sunday. Try to see a game at giant Morumbi Stadium with one of the four main clubs: Corinthians, Palmeiras, Santos and São Paulo.

what to see

Ibirapuera Park is to São Paulo what Central Park is to New York: an island of green and calm amid traffic and skyscrapers. It has numerous museums and pavilions, many of them designed by the renowned Brazilian architect Oscar Niemeyer, and open spaces that include lakes and playgrounds, which draw large crowds of families on weekends. The planetarium, $2.85, displays the constellations of the Southern Hemisphere. The park is open daily, 6 a.m. to 8 p.m.; (55-11) 574-5177.

The Instituto Butantan, Avenida Vital Brasil 1500 in the Butanta area, is perhaps the city's most popular tourist attraction. One of the world's leading reptile research centers, it has a collection of more than 60,000 animals, and its small museum features live spiders and scorpions as well as poisonous snakes with exotic names like jararaca and mussurana. Open Tuesday through Sunday, 9 a.m. to 4:30 p.m. Admission is 85 cents for adults; 55 cents for children; (55-11) 813-7222.

The Memorial to the Immigrant, at Rua Visconde de Parnaíba 1316 in Bras, is Brazil's Ellis Island. Nearly three million people from 60 different countries, including the United States, came through this processing center during the 91 years it operated before closing in 1978. Their contributions to Brazil are honored in thorough, fascinating exhibits. Open Tuesday through Sunday, 10 a.m. to 5 p.m. Admission is $1.15 for adults, half price for children; (55-11) 6693-0917.

Installed in one of the city's uglier buildings is its best museum, known as the MASP, or Museu de Arte de São Paulo, Avenida Paulista 1578. The collection here is said to be the largest and most impressive in Latin America, with European masters as well as leading Brazilian artists such as Portinari, Anita Malfatti and Tarsila do Amaral. On Sunday an antiques and arts-and-crafts fair is held outside the museum. Open Tuesday through Sunday, 11 a.m. to 6 p.m.; admission $5.75; (55-11) 251-5644.

Also on Sundays, the "Discover São Paulo" program offers three bus tours departing from the Praça da República downtown. The Green route shows visitors parks and gardens, the Cultural itinerary visits the principal museums, and the Historic tour stops at old homes and monuments. Tickets—$2.85 adults, $1.15 for children—are sold at tourist offices or through (55-11) 6971-5000.

where to stay

By Brazilian standards, São Paulo hotels can be absurdly overpriced. But on weekends, when business travelers leave, rates at major hotels can drop by 30 percent.

BUDGET: São Paulo is awash in what are known as "flats," apartment hotels aimed primarily at the long-term business visitor but also available to the tourist. One especially good option is the Parthenon chain. Rooms at some, such as the Parthenon St.

Germain on Rua Padre João Manuel 202 in Cerqueira Cesar, start at $60, with breakfast. The top price at this chain is $100. Call (800) 111790 for reservations; fax (55-11) 883-2476.

The Best Western Pôrto do Sol, Rua Tutóia 77 in Cerqueira Cesar, is halfway between Avenida Paulista and Ibirapuera Park and convenient to many good restaurants. Its 198 rooms, while simple, are clean and attractive. A double starts at $100, with an ample breakfast buffet of tropical fruits and juices; (55-11) 3059-5000, fax (55-11) 3059-5193.

MODERATE: Few of São Paulo's hotels are more reliable or convenient than the Crowne Plaza, just off Avenida Paulista at Rua Frei Caneca 1360 in Cerqueira Cesar. Remodeled not long ago, it has 220 rooms and large beds and bathtubs in which to sink at the end of a long day. A standard double starts at $198 a night. Telephone (55-11) 253-2244 or (800) 227-6963; fax (55-11) 251-3121.

In the 1970's, the Grand Hotel Ca D'Oro, Rua Augusta 129 in Consolação, was the most elegant place to stay in São Paulo. The neighborhood has fallen on hard times, but the 265 rooms, most still decorated in the same style as they were back then, are large. The Italian restaurant is one of the best in town. Doubles are $150, breakfast included; (55-11) 236- 4300, fax (55-11) 236-4311.

LUXURY: Big, swaggering and always crowded, the Maksoud Plaza Hotel, Alamêda Campinas 150 in Bela Vista, has become something of a landmark since it opened 20 years ago. But the imposing atrium and 415 rooms are starting to show their age, and there is a certain air of snobbery that can be disconcerting. Doubles: from $350; (55-11) 253-4411, fax (55-11) 253-4544.

On the other side of Avenida Paulista, at Alamêda Santos 1123, sits the Inter-Continental São Paulo. The 193 rooms are larger than those at several other luxury hotels, the atmosphere is one of cool efficiency, and there are many good places to eat within walking distance. Doubles are normally $400. Telephone (55-11) 3179-2600 or (800) 327-0200; fax (55-11) 3179-2669.

where to eat

Year after year, Baby-Beef Rubaiyat is the runaway winner in every survey of São Paulo's best churrascarias, restaurants specializing in grilled meat. The cuts may seem unfamiliar to the American palate, but the meat here is extraordinarily tender and lean, perhaps because the restaurant has its own ranch. Of the two branches, the more convenient is at Alamêda Santos 86 in Paraiso. Dinner for two with beer: about $65; (55-11) 289-6366.

In theory, Antiquarius, Alamêda Lorena 1884 in Cerqueira Cesar, specializes solely in Portuguese cuisine. But a signature dish is a singular mixture of Lusitanian and Brazilian ingredients: a startlingly delicate codfish moqueca, or stew, laced with coconut milk. The atmosphere is charmingly rustic. Dinner for two with a bottle of sparkling Portuguese vinho verde: about $125; (55-11) 282-3015.

The menu at Amadeus, Rua Haddock Lobo 807 in Cerqueira Cesar, is devoted to seafood, freshly caught. Traditional Brazilian sauces, which make liberal use of coconut milk, palm oil, onions, tomato and peppers, are the main feature, but a terrific shrimp curry is also on the menu. Dinner for two with a bottle of Brazilian wine is about $110; (55-11) 3061-2859.

In a city blessed with dozens of excellent Italian restaurants and cantinas, Massimo, at Alamêda Santos 1826 in Cerqueira Cesar, stands at the head of the class. The osso buco almost melts off the bone, and the cheeses, eggplant, peppers and olives in the antipasto are extraordinarily fresh. Dinner for two is about $125 (no credit cards); (55-11) 284-3011.

For cheap, appetizing eating, Paulistanos often turn to restaurants offering food by the kilogram, most of which charge $4.50 to $5.50 a pound. There is a large concentration of these self-service buffet-style cafeterias in Rua Augusta. For a varied menu and mouthwatering desserts, try Parque Avenida Grill, Avenida Paulista 1776; (55-11) 283-0201.

vital statistics

POPULATION (2000 estimate): City 9,996,827; Metro area 18 million

HOTEL: Room for one with tax $228.00

DINNER FOR ONE: With tax and tip but not drinks $25.50

TAXI: Upon entry $1.78; Each additional kilometer 45 cents; From the airport $22.78

CAR RENTAL FOR A DAY: Midsize manual shift car with unlimited free mileage $114.00

FOR MORE INFORMATION: Telephone: (55-11) 289-7588; Web: www.saopaulobureau.com.br

Sources: Runzheimer International, Brazilian Embassy, local businesses

Seattle

The home of Microsoft is proudly anti-establishment

SAM HOWE VERHOVEK

Sam Howe Verhovek is a *Times* correspondent based in Seattle.

Seattle certainly made a name for itself in December 1999, as host to the World Trade Organization meeting. Civic boosters' idea of showing off their city as a world-class friend to free trade didn't exactly pan out—not amid all the demonstrations and the tear gas. But many residents think that the raucous protests against globalization were a badge of honor for Seattle.

The long-running tension here, between those who revel in the high-tech, high-wealth place Seattle has become and those who fret over its loss of quirky small-town charm, continues apace. One focus of lively debate is the Experience Music Project. Designed by Frank O. Gehry and located under the Space Needle, the museum is wildly curvy and colorful, an undulating aluminum and stainless-steel shell of gold, silver, red, blue and iridescent purple, built roughly in the shape of a smashed guitar. Some Seattleites consider it brilliant, a bit of Bilbao-on-Elliot-Bay; others, one of whom described it as looking like "open-heart surgery gone awry," call it a curse on the landscape. The museum is financed by Paul G. Allen, who co-founded Microsoft with a school chum by the name of Bill Gates.

Rising on lush hills, between Puget Sound and Lake Washington, Seattle is a city of wonderfully diverse, quirky neighborhoods. One good example is Fremont, just north of downtown, which bills itself as the "center of the universe." Its landmarks include a 53-foot-tall rocket, a large troll eating a Volkswagen Bug, and a statue of Lenin.

best of times

Dot-com frenzy and cultural activity of all kinds bloom throughout the year. As always, late spring, summer and early fall remain a time when the natural grandeur in and around Seattle is on particularly glorious—and somewhat drier—display.

And although late spring and summer are prime festival time, there is usually something going on, often at the renovated Seattle Center, bounded by Mercer and Broad Streets between First and Fifth. The Northwest Folklife Festival, at Seattle Center, (206) 684-7300, features over 5,000 participants, with arts and crafts, wandering performers and stage presentations, not to mention the food. It is held annually over the Memorial Day weekend.

Watch out for flying fish (that's how many vendors get them across the counter to customers) at the Pike Place Market Festival, a celebration of the city's famous fish and farm market, also Memorial Day weekend. Hours: 10 a.m. to 7 p.m.; First Avenue and Pike Street; (206) 587-0351.

The Seattle Film Festival, (206) 324-9996, showcases foreign and independent American films bypassed by the local cineplex. The festival usually occurs from around the middle of May to the middle of June. Women in Cinema, featuring films directed by women, usually occurs in the first week or two of November.

The Seattle International Children's Festival, usually mid-May, offers a wonderful lineup of performances from around the globe. The whole event is billed as "a festival for children and other adventurous people." Call (206) 684-7346.

The University of Washington is host to a Summer Arts Festival in July. Tickets start at $5. For information and tickets, call the university's Arts Ticket Office, (206) 543-4880.

One of the most popular festivals is Bumbershoot (British slang for an umbrella), attracting hipsters of all ages and usually held in early September, at the Seattle Center. It features, according to its sponsors, music ranging from Bach to hip-hop, outrageous sculpture, poetry slams, cutting-edge cinema, modern dance, literary readings, comedy, hands-on arts projects for kids and food from more than 50 area restaurants.

what to see

The Experience Music Project, which opened in June 2000, is undeniably fun on the inside, an interactive paean to modern American music in all its forms. Sound studios allow visitors to experiment with their own music, or to strum a guitar that lights the sequence of chords to play "Louie, Louie," a song whose lyrics sparked an F.B.I. file that is one of 80,000 artifacts collected for the museum. It's located in Seattle Center, (206) 367-5483.

Seattle boasts many bike trails offering glorious vistas of the city, Puget Sound and the Olympic and Cascade Mountains. At Blazing Saddles Bike Rentals, 1230 Western Avenue, (206) 341-9994, bikes (with helmet, locks and other accessories included) rent for $5 an hour and up.

If you don't feel so fleet of foot, join the other tourists and take Argosy Cruises' two-hour Lake Washington tour, which passes houseboats and the University of Washington on its way to the Gold Coast on the lake's east side. You'll see the techno-palace owned by Bill and Melinda Gates; a guide helpfully pointed out the trampoline room where, she said, Mr. Gates "can go and bounce all his troubles away." Argosy, (206) 623-4252, also has Puget Sound tours and dinner cruises. The Lake Washington tour is $24.

A cheaper but no less splendid way of seeing Seattle and the surrounding mountains is aboard one of the many state ferries that travel to nearby Bainbridge Island from Pier 52 downtown. Foot passengers pay $3.70 round trip; (206) 464-6400.

The Elliott Bay Book Company, one of the nation's best and largest independent bookstores, is a beloved institution, with a program of author readings and talks. Meet a friend for coffee or browse for hours amid the Western red cedar shelves, at 101 South Main Street; (206) 624-6600.

The Seattle Art Museum, in a soaring Robert Venturi building at 100 University Street, (206) 654-3100, has an extensive collection of Northwest Indian, African, Impressionist, Greek and other art. It is affiliated with the Seattle Asian Art Museum, 1400 East Prospect Street in Volunteer Park, which has a remarkable collection of art and artifacts from China, India, Korea and Japan. Both are open Tuesday through Sunday, 10 a.m. to 5 p.m., Thursday till 9. Suggested admission is $7 for the Seattle Art Museum, $3 for the Asian Art Museum.

where to stay

The visitors bureau's hotel line, (800) 535-7071, often features deals well below advertised prices.

BUDGET: The 24-room Ace Hotel, 2423 First Avenue; (206) 448-4721, fax (206) 374-0745, is not for everybody. But it is an epicenter of Seattle's hipster scene, surrounded by stores and galleries in the Belltown area near downtown. This former flophouse has been converted into a chic, sleek place with low beds and interesting steel fittings. Where one might normally look for the Gideon's Bible, expect to find stylized copies of the Kama Sutra. Standard rooms, with shared bath, start at $65; suites with private bath at $130.

The Seattle Inn, 225 Aurora Avenue North near downtown, (206) 728-7666, fax (206) 728-6108, has 159 standard rooms, an indoor pool, a whirlpool and parking. Double rates with Continental breakfast range from $59 to $115.

MODERATE: The Inn at the Market, 86 Pine Street, (206) 443-3600, fax (206) 448-0631, has 70 antiques-filled rooms, many with views of the Pike Place Market, Elliott Bay and the Olympic Mountains. Doubles from $170. If your room doesn't have a view, the rooftop balcony does.

"Sleep with the fishes" is the unusual offer made by the Hotel Monaco, 1101 Fourth Avenue, (206) 621-1770, fax (206) 621-7779, which promises to put a goldfish in a bowl in your room if you desire such company. The European-style boutique hotel has 189 rooms. Doubles from $195.

The Beatles slept there, and a 1964 picture of them fishing from the window of their suite proves it at the 236-room Hotel Edgewater, Pier 67, 2411 Alaskan Way; (206) 728-7000, fax (206) 441-4119. The rooms are Northwestern lodge style, many with stunning water and mountain views. Doubles from $169.

LUXURY: The Four Seasons Olympic, 411 University Street, (206) 621-1700, fax (206) 682-9633, restored several years ago to its pre-Depression Italianate Renaissance glory, has 450 spacious, classically decorated rooms, including 209 suites, and a chandeliered lobby and adjoining lounge. Rooms start at $305.

where to eat

The bounty of the Northwest's waters—clams, oysters, crabs, mussels, salmon, halibut—is astonishing. At Etta's Seafood, 2020 Western Avenue, (206) 443-6000, the menu often changes depending on what's freshest, but among the best of the regulars is Etta's spice-rubbed and pit-roasted Alaskan king salmon with cornbread pudding and shiitake relish, or the sea scallops with udon noodles in a lemongrass-miso broth. Dinner for two, with wine: $120.

Cafe Campagne, 1600 Post Alley, (206) 728-2233, is a delightful Parisian bistro half a block from the Pike Place Market, serving breakfast, lunch and dinner daily and a Sunday brunch. A good appetizer is the port and pistachio crepinettes, served with a roasted red beet and arugula salad. Specialties include pan-sautéed boneless trout with steamed potatoes and an almond, lemon and brown-butter pan sauce, and a daily rotisserie offering. Dinner for two, with wine: about $110.

With so many quirky neighborhoods, it follows that some of the most interesting restaurants are well away from downtown. In the Phinney Ridge area, Carmelita offers savory vegetarian fare in its colorful dining room and on a patio enclosed by an herb garden. The seasonal menu—strictly vegetarian and vegan—is creative enough for confirmed meat-eaters. Dinner for two with drinks from the extensive wine and microbrew list: $80. Open nightly except Monday; 7314 Greenwood Avenue North; (206) 706-7703.

At the Noodle Ranch, 2228 Second Avenue, (206) 728-0463, the pan-Asian menu, under the Vietnamese chef, Nga Bui, offers an array of moderately priced dishes: Mekong grill with tofu or meat in a Vietnamese-style marinade, house pad Thai, Singapore noodles, spicy Japanese eggplant in a ginger sauce, Laotian cucumber salad, Saigon-style lemongrass chicken, and on and on. An excellent lunch or dinner, daily except Sunday, can cost as little as $12 a person.

Chinook's, 1900 West Nickerson Street, (206) 283-4665, serving moderately priced seafood (about $40 for two with a microbrew) in the Fishermen's Terminal, has an extensive menu and lively atmosphere. It looks out on the Pacific's largest fishing fleet, which Seattle-based author Jonathan Raban describes as "this last bastion of old-fashioned work" and "outdoor faces" in a city that now derives wealth from indoor virtual reality. The busy fleet fascinates kids of all ages, and Chinook's menu includes alder-planked salmon, salmon burgers, a salmon pot pie, salmon cakes, teriyaki salmon—one gets the picture.

vital statistics

POPULATION (1998 estimate): City 536,978; Metro area 3,424,361

HOTEL: Room for one with tax $171.50

DINNER FOR ONE: With tax and tip but not drinks $32.85

TAXI: Upon entry $1.80; Each additional mile $1.80; From the airport $31.00

CAR RENTAL FOR A DAY: Midsize car with unlimited free mileage $57.00

FOR MORE INFORMATION: Telephone: (206) 461-5840; Web: www.seeseattle.org

Sources: Runzheimer International, U.S. Census Bureau, local businesses

Shanghai

A lot of its history has fallen to the wrecker's ball, but the past is there amid the new

CRAIG S. SMITH

Craig S. Smith is chief of the Shanghai bureau of *The Times*.

Until not very long ago, Shanghai was like a dilapidated museum of its 1930's heyday. Mothballed buildings stood relatively untouched, ghostly hulks of aborted expectations with all of their fixtures intact.

But China's 1990's economic boom brought the wrecking ball into old Shanghai, crumbling architectural charm like so much chalk. Still, the city's old self intrigues most visitors, and it is possible to trace Shanghai's old features, both grand and gaudy, amid the new. Tucked away on Ruijin Road, for example, is the mansion in which Chiang Kai-shek married Soong Mayling; and at 182 Ninghai Xi Road, a tool company occupies the former home of Big Ears Du, leader of Shanghai's notorious opium-running, brothel-keeping Green Gang of the 1920's and 30's.

And many of the office towers rising from the rubble have architectural merit of their own. Skidmore, Owings & Merrill's 88-story Jin Mao Building, a gleaming silver tower, is a spectacular sight—even if it was designed with too few window-washing gondolas. The architects didn't factor in Shanghai's superpolluted air.

best of times

Like most places in the temperate zones, late April through May and late September through October are the most pleasant months to visit, when streets come alive and the city's increasing number of outdoor restaurants are the most crowded. For two weeks in late April and early May, several Buddhist temples organize fairs during which they are decorated and handicrafts are sold from stalls. The fairs typically include performances of traditional opera, acrobatics and folk dances. Among the liveliest locales are Longhua Temple, in the southwest part of the city, and Temple of the City God in the southeast part of the city.

October brings the Mid-Autumn Festival, during which Shanghainese give one another dense pastries called moon cakes to commemorate the Harvest Moon, the full moon occurring closest to the autumnal equinox, when the sun is over the equator. Families gather for a big meal on the night of the full moon.

The most celebrated time of year is the Lunar New Year, also known as Spring Festival, which usually falls in early February. Shanghainese willing to brave the crowds gather at temples for traditional bell-ringing ceremonies. And despite a ban on fireworks, the town erupts into a war zone of firecrackers and skyrockets for more than a week. The barrage begins at midnight New Year's Eve and hits another peak at midnight four days later when Shanghainese appeal for favors from the God of Fortune.

On the 15th day of the new year the city celebrates the Lantern Festival. Children parade with lanterns (mostly plastic and battery operated these days), and several public parks are decorated with fantastic silk lanterns in the shape of everything from dragons to palaces. The narrow streets around the old Yu Yuan Gardens are the most heavily decorated.

what to see

The old parts of Shanghai are wonderful for walking; the rest of the city can be unpleasant and daunting given the traffic and pollution. The two subway lines cost less than a dollar to ride across town, but visitors shouldn't even think about using the crowded public buses unless they're in for an adventure (and speak Chinese). Taxis are plentiful and cheap (few trips will cost more than $5 or $6), but look for the newer aquamarine-colored cabs owned by Da Zhong Taxi.

An entertaining option to cross the Huangpu River to Pudong, the newest part of the city, is the ferry. It costs about 10 cents and leaves from the Bund, the famous riverfront. Everyone visits the Bund, but many miss the view from the roof garden of the Peace Hotel, one of the city's most famous when it was the Cathay Hotel. If they are not in use, you can ask to visit the private apartments of the hotel's former owner, Victor Sassoon of the British trading family, one floor below the garden.

Also often overlooked is the lobby of the domed Pudong Development Bank, originally the Hong Kong and Shanghai Bank, on the Bund. The lobby ceiling is a magnificent mosaic depicting the world's great centers of commerce as of 1923, when the building was completed. Open daily 9 a.m. to 4:30 p.m.

Beyond the Bund, old Shanghai is best discovered by exploring neighborhoods on foot. The most revealing sections are the longs, or lanes, the oldest of which are lined with shikumen, an architectural style derived from Europe but quintessentially Shanghainese. Shikumen (the name means stone-framed door) were originally built to house the middle-class Chinese who poured into the French Concession area from the chaos of the late-19th-century Taiping Rebellion. By the 1920's most of Shanghai's Chinese population lived in these narrow brick row houses with stone-framed doors. A large shikumen district lies to the south of Huai Hai Dong Road and to the west of Xizang Nan Road, but the city plans to level it.

Farther east is Nanshi, the original walled city of Shanghai (the circular wall is long gone, replaced by a road). Visitors usually go to the maze of mostly rebuilt Qing dynasty buildings around the Temple of the City God and Yu Yuan Garden. Around the temple, narrow curio-shop-crammed passageways snake beneath traditional Chinese eaves and upturned roofs, while the adjacent carp ponds and meditation halls of Yu Yuan Garden provide relative serenity.

People with esoteric tastes can sample Kunju opera, dating from the Tang dynasty, at San Shan Hui Guan Theater, 1551 Zhong Shan Nan Road. Tickets, $6 to $24; (86-21) 6437-7756. The more traditional Beijing opera can be seen most weekends at Yifu Theater, 701 Fuzhou Road. Tickets, $6 to $24; (86-21) 6322-5075.

No visitor should leave without seeing the future—across the river in Pudong. Both the Buck Rogers–style television tower and the sleek Jin Mao Building have observation decks with wonderful views. The TV tower is open 8:15 a.m. to 9:15 p.m., daily. Tickets are $6 to $12, depending on how high one wants to go. The Jin Mao observation deck is open 8:30 a.m. to 9 p.m. daily; $6. Nearly the same view can be had free from the Grand Hyatt in the building.

where to stay

BUDGET: Xingguo Guest House, 72 Xingguo Road, (86-21) 6212-9998, fax (86-21) 6251-2145, is a colonial lodging in a state-owned wrapper. The centerpiece for this collection of 1930's manses in a parklike setting is Building No. 1, the Swire mansion. Built by the British trading family of the same name, the building was later used by Mao Zedong. The large ground-floor drawing room that Mao used as a bedroom has been split into two smaller rooms; guests can stay in either and still claim to have slept in the same room as the Great Helmsman. The 38 rooms, among 4 buildings, range from $55 to $95 a night, plus a 10 percent service charge.

MODERATE: For a taste of 1930's elegance—seasoned with a heavy dose of state-owned clumsiness—the Peace Hotel, 20 Nanjing Dong Road, (86-21) 6321-6888, fax (86-21) 6329-0300, offers easy access to Shanghai's old commercial district and a chance to watch energetic Shanghainese practice tai chi or ballroom dancing along the Bund at dawn. The 300 rooms cost about $100 to $115 a night, not including a 15 percent service charge.

LUXURY: The newly renovated Portman Ritz-Carlton, 1376 Nanjing Xi Road, (86-21) 6279-8888, fax (86-21) 6279-8999, has 564 rooms with every amenity imaginable, including a pool and health club. The hotel is part of a complex of restaurants, shops, offices and apartments. Doubles cost $250, plus a 15 percent service charge.

Shanghai's most spectacular hotel is the Grand Hyatt, 88 Shiji Da Dao, (86-21) 5049-1234, fax (86-21) 5049-8382, occupying the top 30 floors of the Jin Mao Building. The hotel is an architectural and engineering feat, from the 30-story circular atrium to the 57th-floor swimming pool. The 550 rooms are ultramodern, appointed with original art and equipped with Internet access via televisions that can be operated using wireless keyboards. Standard rooms cost $160 to $280, plus a 15 percent service charge.

where to eat

M on the Bund is probably Shanghai's best Western restaurant outside of the big hotels, and certainly the most romantic. On the seventh floor at 20 Guangdong Road, the restaurant has a large veranda with a spectacular view of the Bund and the traffic on the muddy Huangpu. Try the salt-baked lamb, or sample some Chinese caviar. The special dessert, pavlova, is an airy Australian confection of ice cream, fruit and meringue. Dinner for two with wine: $95; (86-21) 6350-9988.

Phoenix Restaurant, on the eighth floor of the Peace Hotel, also offers river views, though the gaudy Chinese interior is entertaining. It serves Sichuan and Cantonese cuisine, but prefers to be known for its Shanghai dishes, like river crabmeat with tofu. When you order a fish, the waitress brings it to you live in a red plastic bucket. Try the dou miao, if it's in season—this delicate green vegetable is not widely available in the United States. Dinner for two with wine: $85; (86-21) 6321-6888.

Near Yu Yuan Garden is Lu Bo Lang (or Green Ripple Hall), one of Shanghai's oldest and most famous restaurants. Arrive well before noon to enjoy the dian xin. This meal, similar to dim sum, consists of 11 varieties of dumplings and other small dishes— including the city's famous xiao long bao, little basket dumplings. If you avoid the overpriced turtle soup and drink the long jing green tea, lunch for two should cost just $12 or so.

Don't be afraid of street food fresh from the griddle or steamer. Sheng jian mantou, addictive pan-fried pork-filled dumplings sold all over the city, cost about 13 cents each, and cans of soda or bottled water are usually 20 or 30 cents.

vital statistics

POPULATION (1999 estimate): City 8 million; Metro area 15 million

HOTEL: Room for one with tax $215.00

DINNER FOR ONE: With tax and tip but not drinks $23.70

TAXI: Upon entry $1.25; Each additional kilometer 25 cents; From the airport $5.00

CAR RENTAL FOR A DAY: Midsize car with unlimited free mileage $65.00

FOR MORE INFORMATION: Telephone: (86-21) 6439-9806; Web: www.tourinfo.sh.cn

Sources: Runzheimer International, Chinese Embassy, local businesses

Singapore

The climate may inspire a laid-back attitude,
but this is a fast-paced metropolis

WAYNE ARNOLD

Wayne Arnold contributes to *The Times* from Singapore.

Don't come to Singapore expecting a laconic equatorial city. Despite blazing heat and humidity year round, Singapore is a digital-age metropolis determined to make its name as a world capital.

Like the pink bougainvilleas that sprout from every highway planter and the stately angsana trees lining the roads, nothing here is serendipitous, least of all the approach to tourism. As part of what the government calls Tourism 21, Singapore is trying to become a must-see destination, as well as a hub for travelers bound elsewhere in Southeast Asia.

Delightfully green, safe and efficient, Singapore is a welcome refuge from its more exotic, bewildering neighbors and an impressive tribute to urban planning and immigrant pluck. The city is undergoing a renaissance, from confident new architecture like Kenzo Tange's UE Square near Fort Canning Park, to meticulously restored historic districts, with avant-garde clubs, quaint cafes and hip restaurants.

The way to appreciate Singapore is to go behind its squeaky-clean facade to find its cultural and historical kaleidoscope. Singapore is a melting pot of Malays, Indians and an array of Chinese groups with their own languages, among them Hokkien, Teochew and Cantonese.

best of times

The ideal time to experience Singapore's Chinese heritage is during celebrations of the Lunar New Year, which usually falls in late January or early February. The crowded streets of Chinatown are lined with red lanterns, banners and stands selling traditional holiday delicacies. There are fireworks on the downtown waterfront; Chinese opera companies and lion dancers also perform.

Just before the Lunar New Year comes Thaipusam, a ritual self-mortification ceremony honoring Murga, the Hindu god of youth. Devotees from Singapore's Tamil community gather in Little India at the Sri Srinavasa Perumal Temple, where skewers are run through their cheeks and tongues. They then carry elaborate shrines to Chettiar Hindu Temple about two miles away to make offerings before being relieved of their painful burdens.

Singapore's international film festival is in April, showcasing a wide variety of films from Japan to Iran. June brings the festival perhaps closest to Singapore's soul, the Great Singapore Sale, when shopping malls are packed with bargain hunters. June is also the month for the Singapore Arts Festival, which features music and theater from around the world.

Sometime between late October through November, depending on the Hindu almanac, Little India lights up for Deepavali, the festival of lights celebrating the triumph of good over evil.

If you are in Singapore between mid-November and December 31, you'll be treated to a tropical yuletide spectacle on Orchard Road, where each mall endeavors to outdo all the others with the most lavish Christmas display. Leave your sweaters and mittens at home, though: Singapore is hot and muggy year round, with temperatures between 75 and 90 every day. Showers are brief but common.

what to see

Singapore is not dotted with historic temples and monuments as other Asian cities are. But it does have several interesting neighborhoods worth exploring on foot. Go early or late enough to avoid the oppressive midday heat.

A good place to start is the Merlion, a water-spouting statue of a mythical lionheaded fish. While unspectacular as fountains go, it offers picturesque views near where legend says Sir Thomas

Stamford Raffles landed in 1819 to establish Singapore as a British trading port and lend his name to a hotel, a school and a shopping mall, among other places. The Merlion park is open daily 7 a.m. to 10 p.m.

South of the river, away from the high-rise hotels, lies Raffles Place and the heart of the financial district. On Cecil Street, the Stock Exchange sits where there once was a thriving spice market. Just off Telok Ayer Street, Pekin Street has been turned into a pleasant pedestrian promenade leading to Far East Square with a row of newly restored two- and three-story shophouses, built by Chinese immigrants to house their families above their businesses.

Farther up Telok Ayer is the intricately decorated Thian Hock Keng temple, built in 1840 along what until roughly 1930 was shoreline to honor the queen of heaven and protector of sailors. West of Telok Ayer, on Amoy and Club Streets, are some of the best examples of restored shophouses. This gentrified area's older establishments, like the Dried Goods Guild, now rub elbows with a trendy assortment of bars, restaurants and dot-com companies.

Also worth wandering through is Little India, a cluster of shops around Serangoon Road, north of the Colonial district, selling saris, bindis for women's foreheads and booming bhangra CD's. On Sunday evenings, this boisterous area is inundated with laborers from India, Bangladesh and Sri Lanka. Visitors may join them at the Veerama Kaliamman Temple and pay their respects to Kali.

East of the Rochor Canal, the perfume shops and textile merchants around Arab Street remain picturesque, although business is waning, and Sultan Mosque endures as a serene refuge for the faithful. Stop along North Bridge Road for a murtabak pancake filled with egg and chicken or mutton. Meander down Kandahar Street to find the dilapidated 160-year-old palace of Singapore's former Malay sultanate, whose descendants were evicted in 1999.

Singapore's zoo is one of the few in Asia to keep animals in natural-looking surroundings rather than in cages. Once the sun sets, the zoo offers a Night Safari, with nocturnal animals up and about. The leopards are mesmerizing, but the hands-down highlight is the bat enclosure, which you can enter to test your composure against cat-size fruit bats inspecting your coiffure. Admission to the zoo, which is open 8:30 a.m. to 6 p.m., is $6. The Night Safari, 7:30 p.m. to midnight, costs $9.

Singapore's aquarium, Underwater World, is south of the city on Sentosa Island, which is a little bigger than Central Park and has man-made beaches, golf courses and other attractions. In addition to tidal pools with touchable sea life and a moving sidewalk that takes visitors through fish tanks, the aquarium has a new dolphin pool and a shark tank where scuba divers can take a 30-minute guided dive for $55. Open daily 9 a.m. to 9 p.m.; admission is $7.60.

Another pleasant diversion is the Jurong Bird Park, west of the city, with its underwater penguin gallery and walk-in tropical aviary. It is open 9 a.m. to 6 p.m. Monday to Friday, and 8 a.m. to 6 p.m. on weekends. Admission is $6.

where to stay

BUDGET: High ceilings, lazy fans and wooden banisters lend character to the 24-room Sun Sun Hotel, on Middle Road, near Bugis, (65) 338-4911. Doubles, with shared bath, are $23.50, $26.50 with air-conditioning.

Hotel Bencoolen, 47 Bencoolen Street, (65) 336-0822, fax (65) 336-2250, sparkles from a renovation two years ago and is a short walk from the art museum and the colonial district. The 74 rooms start at $49, including breakfast.

MODERATE: The tranquil 50-room Duxton Hotel sits among the shophouses at 83 Duxton Road, adjacent to Chinatown. Aside from its coziness, the Duxton, (65) 227-7678, fax (65) 227-1232, also has what is reckoned by some to be Singapore's best French restaurant, L'Aigle d'Or. Doubles cost $105.

LUXURY: Built in 1900, the 235-room Goodwood Park Hotel, 22 Scotts Road, (65) 737-7411, fax (65) 732-8558, started out as the Teutonia Club and is a short walk from the main shopping district. The décor hasn't changed in 25 years, and its pool, surrounded by turf and white-enamel chaise longues, is pure Graham Greene. Doubles from $250.

The Ritz-Carlton, Millenia Singapore, 7 Raffles Avenue, in Marina Square, (65) 337-8888, fax (65) 337-5190, provides superior service and three restaurants. But another attraction is the octagonal windows in each bathroom of the 608 rooms, providing bathing guests views of the downtown skyline. Doubles from $252.

The Raffles Hotel, 1 Beach Road, (65) 337-1886, fax (65) 339-7650, opened in 1887, was the birthplace of the Singapore Sling, memorialized in prose by Conrad and Maugham. A makeover in the 80's tidied the hotel but replaced the musky charm of its Writers Bar with something more Martha Stewartish. Its 104 suites start at $380.

where to eat

The best food in Singapore is also the cheapest. You can eat your fill of something tasty for less than $6 at almost any hawker center or food court. For a good selection of local delights, like Hainanese chicken rice or nasi padang, drop into Lau Pa Sat, an old train station at Robinson Road and Cross Street near the financial district that is now an open-air food court.

For crispy roti prata, a savory pancake served with a curry dip, head to the Casuarina Curry House, a small open-air restaurant on Casuarina Road in Ang Mo Kio. Lunch or dinner for two costs about $8.

For something more elaborate, travel out along the East Coast to the Long Beach Seafood Restaurants, 1018 East Coast Parkway at the Singapore Tennis Center, (65) 445-8833, and 1202 East Coast Parkway, (65) 448-3636. Long Beach claims to have invented black pepper crab, a giant Sri Lankan crustacean suffused with pepper sauce. Equally delicious is Long Beach's chili crab, with its meat-laden piquant sauce. Wear old clothes and roll up your sleeves. Dinner for two with a pitcher of beer is about $60.

Ivins, 396 Alexandra Road in Bukit Merah, (65) 276-3721, specializes in Singapore's unique Peranakan cuisine, an adaptation of Chinese recipes with Malay ingredients. Try the beef rendang, chicken curry or steamed fish. Dinner for two with beers can be had for under $25.

Komala Villas, 76 Serangoon Road (65) 294-3294, in Little India, serves delicious South Indian vegetarian thalis, and if you come close to finishing, a waiter is lurking not far away to ladle more onto your banana leaf. Dinner for two: $7.

vital statistics

POPULATION (1999 estimate): City 3,900,000

HOTEL: Room for one with tax $230.50

DINNER FOR ONE: With tax and tip but not drinks $24.00

TAXI: Upon entry $1.41; Each additional kilometer 25 cents; From the airport $10.30

CAR RENTAL FOR A DAY: Midsize manual shift car with unlimited free mileage $113.56

FOR MORE INFORMATION: Telephone: (212) 302-4861; Web: www.singapore-usa.com

Sources: Runzheimer International, Singapore Tourism Board, local businesses

Stockholm

Be prepared to do some island hopping

Nybroviken Quay, Stockholm

ERIC SJOGREN
Eric Sjogren is a Swedish journalist living in Brussels.

At the foot of the soaring tower of Stockholm's modern Town Hall lies the gilded effigy of a medieval knight, Birger Jarl. He was the man who founded Stockholm 750 years ago—in 1252, to be precise—and the anniversary in 2002 will be celebrated with pomp and circumstance. Birger Jarl's fortified town, on an island where the waters of Lake Malaren rush out to meet the Baltic Sea, successfully denied access to the prosperous hinterland to pirates from across the sea.

The Old Town remains the center of Stockholm, but the city has spread over 13 more islands. The Stockholmers are convinced that theirs is the most beautiful city in the world, but they miss no opportunity to exchange the comforts of urban civilization for the more basic pleasures of country living with nature on their doorstep. So virtually every weekend a veritable flotilla of thousands of leisure craft fans out toward the sea and the 24,000 or so islands and skerries of the Stockholm Archipelago.

The Swedes become more informal with every layer of clothing they peel off as the weather gets warmer, and all speak English, at least after a fashion. They bring their blond-haired tots everywhere, and you'll meet plenty of them on the ferries and sightseeing boats that crisscross inlets and bays.

best of times

The tourist season begins in May, when the water turns from a forbidding gray to an inviting blue and temperatures climb to the low 60's. From June through August the average high is around 70 degrees, falling back to 60 in September.

The Circus Princess arrives in May like a harbinger of spring. For three weeks, women artistes from all over the world perform their aerial stunts in a male-free environment, and a jury chooses that year's Circus Princess. The tent is pitched next to the Royal Tennis Hall. Details from www.bronett.com.

At the delicious Drottningholm Court Theatre, everything—stage, décor, dressing rooms—is authentic Gustavian style. It stages 17th- and 18th-century operas and ballets from late May to early September. The royal family lives next door in Drottningholm Palace. Visitors can wander in the large formal park. Each season comprises 30 to 40 performances.

The Christmas season starts early in Stockholm with the coronation of the Stockholm Lucia the first Sunday in Advent at the Skansen open-air museum. On St. Lucia's Day, December 13, virtually every home, office and even some hotels have their own celebration, highlighted by a procession of Lucias (preferably blond) in white clothing and wearing a crown of candles, singing a song of Neapolitan origin honoring a Sicilian saint in nominally Protestant Sweden (never underestimate the power of traditions). Glogg—a strong, mulled, sweet wine that tastes like it sounds—is served throughout the day.

what to see

The Vasa Museum's 17th-century man-of-war has become an icon of Stockholm. The Vasa, which sank on her maiden voyage but survived for 333 years on the bottom of Stockholm Harbor, is a veritable time capsule of life during the Thirty Years' War. Galarvarvet, Djurgarden, (46-8) 519-548-00. Open daily 9:30 a.m. to 7 p.m. in summer, 10 a.m. to 5 p.m. Aug. 31 to June 1. Admission: $6.50.

A bit farther out on Djurgarden, a 15-minute walk from the Vasa Museum, is Skansen, (46-8) 442-80-00, the world's first open-air museum when it opened 100 years ago. Generations of Swedes have tramped over this hilly enclave to admire the old farmsteads assembled from all over Sweden, and thousands of couples first met on Skansen's outdoor dance floor. The old small-town quarter is inhabited by artisans. Open 10 a.m. to 10 p.m. June through August, earlier close other months; $6.50.

The Stockholm Archipelago begins with Fjaderholmarna, a group of islands 25 minutes by boat from the city center. It has been turned into a huge aquarium. You can buy seafood in the Smoke House, or dine in style with a splendid view. There's also a pottery shop. The round-trip boat ride comes to $7; admission to the aquarium is $3.80.

The unsurpassed way of experiencing Stockholm is by boat. You can choose between general city tours and more specialized trips, and longer trips around Lake Malaren or in the archipelago. A four-day coastal cruise on a renovated postal steamer from the 1930's visits stately homes and humble villages in between fine meals. The price per day, including transfers, is $140. Call (46-8) 5871-4000.

The 17th- and 18th-century kings fenced in large tracts of land adjoining the city for their private pleasure. In 1995, this land became the Eco Park, notable for its many stands of centuries-old oak trees. It comprises Djurgarden Island to the east and Haga Park on the Brunnsviken bay, north of the city, and Fjaderholmarna and Skeppsholmen islands.

Long before Stockholm existed, the Vikings had a major center, Birka, on Bjorko Island in Lake Malaren, west of the city. More than 3,000 burial mounds circle the settlement, and many of them have yielded treasures on display at the Viking Museum on Bjorko, along with reconstructions of daily life 1,200 years ago. Admission and a guided walk are included in the price ($21.75) of a boat trip from Stockholm. Boats leave from Stadshusbron, next to City Hall; (46-8) 587-140-10.

The Moderna Museet reopened in 1998 next to its former site, now a museum of architecture. The design consists of pavilionlike, high-ceilinged cubes with pyramidal roofs crowned by lanterns. It fits well on Skeppsholmen, the old naval base turned museum island, connected to the mainland by a narrow bridge. The permanent collection of more than 30,000 paintings, prints and drawings features most of the great names of the 20th century. Admission is $6.50; (46-8) 5195-5200.

The five-story Kulturhuset (House of Culture) looks a bit like a reclining office tower, but inside are a theater, performance venues, exhibitions and restaurants. One floor is dedicated to activities for and by children. Kulturhuset is at 3 Sergels Torg; (46-8) 5083-1400.

where to stay

Most Stockholm hotels offer lower rates on weekends and from the end of June to early August.

BUDGET: Ornskold, 6 Nybrogatan, 11434 Stockholm, occupies the second floor of an apartment building near the Royal Dramatic Theater. The 27 rooms in Belle Epoque style, many with leather wing chairs, are much sought after by actors and artists. Doubles are $130; (46-8) 667-02-85, fax (46-8) 667-69-91.

Tre Sma Rum, 81 Hogbergsgatan, 11854 Stockholm, has seven rooms with limestone floors, modern furniture an extra fold-away bed. Doubles: $65; (46-8) 641-23-71, fax (46-8) 642-88-08.

MODERATE: Lady Hamilton, 5 Storkyrkobrinken, 11128 Stockholm, in the heart of the Old Town, was converted into a hotel by an antiques dealer. The 34 rooms are identified by flowers painted on the doors. After a morning sauna, you can cool off in a 14th-century well that is now a pool. Doubles: $170 to $290 through March, then $180 to $305; (46-8) 506-401-00, fax (46-8) 506-401-10.

Other hotels in the same small group, also in the Old Town, are the Lord Nelson, Vasterlanggatan 22, (46-8) 506-401-20, fax (46-8) 506-401-30; and the more expensive Victory, 5 Lilla Nygatan, (46-8) 506-400-00, fax (46-8) 506-400-10.

Clas Pa Hornet, 20 Surbrunnsgatan, (46-8) 165-130, is an old inn with 10 rooms, decorated in 18th-century Gustavian style (a sort of pared-down Louis XVI). The busy, cozy restaurant is a showcase for the best of Swedish down-home cooking. Rooms are $125 to $177.50.

The Scandic Hotel Hasselbacken, 20 Hazeliusbacken, 10055 Stockholm, is by the Skansen open-air museum on Djurgarden. The 111 rooms have parquet floors, many have French doors and most have sofa beds in addition to double beds. Doubles cost $130 to $235; (46-8) 517-343-00, fax (46-8) 517-343-11.

LUXURY: There's only one Grand Hotel, 8 Sodra Blasieholm-shamnen, 10327 Stockholm, and it isn't getting any cheaper. Some of the 307 rooms and suites face the water with a view of the Royal Palace. The rooms, which have high windows, are individually decorated in pastel colors, and the suites have parquet floors and

Oriental carpets. There is a fitness club. Doubles start at $360; (46-8) 679-35-60, fax (46-8) 611-86-86.

where to eat

Pontus in the Green House, 17 Osterlanggatan, celebrates the genius of the under-30 Pontus Frithiof in the dual role of manager and chef. In the spacious first-floor restaurant, the eight-course tasting menu changes every day but always includes one or more variations of saltwater crayfish, a bravura performance and a good value at $92.40 a person. An à la carte dinner for two with wine comes to about $217. In the ground-floor bar, you can have a quick lunch for less than $11, or choose from an Asian-influenced menu; (46-8) 238-500.

The restaurateur Erik Lallerstedt's Gondolen, 6 Stadsgarden, at the top of the Katarina Elevator, which carries riders 125 feet to the top of the hill much of the South Side is built on, offers a sweeping view of the Old Town and the surrounding waterways. The menu changes often, because it is long on seafood. An à la carte dinner for two with a glass of wine is about $160; a fixed-price three-course dinner costs $45 a person; (46-8) 641-70-90.

Bon Lloc, 111 Regeringsgatan, was awarded a Michelin star only eight months after opening. The Mediterranean-inspired cooking includes appetizers like tuna carpaccio and lobster risotto with roasted scallops, and entrees like grilled prime veal with spring vegetable salad and truffle butter. Dinner for two with wine is about $135, and a six-course tasting menu is $75 a person; (46-8) 660-60-60.

Self-service museum restaurants deliver quality food at reasonable prices. One of the best is the Atrium at the National Museum. When did you last visit a cafeteria where you could eat tortellini stuffed with ricotta and dried tomatoes with smoked salmon, basil, spinach and Parmesan strips for $12?

vital statistics

POPULATION (1999): City 760,000; Metro area 1,600,000

HOTEL: Room for one with tax $214.00

DINNER FOR ONE: With tax and tip but not drinks $22.70

TAXI: Upon entry $2.90; Each additional kilometer 70 cents; From the airport $36.60

CAR RENTAL FOR A DAY: Midsize car with unlimited free mileage $83.60

FOR MORE INFORMATION: Telephone: (46-8) 789-24-96; Web: www.stockholmtown.com

Sources: Runzheimer International, Stockholm Information Service, local businesses

Sydney

It invites comparisons, but stands on its own

Sydney Opera House, Australia

SUSAN GOUGH HENLY

Susan Gough Henly is a freelance photojournalist
who lives in Melbourne.

While some may compare Sydney to San Francisco or Rio de Janeiro, this is a city that needs no analogy. Sydney is brazenly self-assured, from its brilliant Opera House to its rows of ornate Paddington terrace houses, from its teeming fish markets to its urban surfing beaches.

Casual and hip, Sydney creates the feeling that the entire place is on one long vacation. The city has been enveloped in Olympics hoopla for years now. One of the benefits is that there are loads of new hotels and restaurants. However, there is more than a hint of Los Angeles in the designer-slick feel to this new development. To feel the real Sydney spirit, be sure to get to older city hangouts—the beach at Bondi or the Taronga Zoo, for instance.

The best orientation point is Circular Quay. From there it's either a short walk in one direction to the oldest quarter of the city at The Rocks or in the opposite direction to the Opera House and the Botanical Gardens. Circular Quay is also a hub for ferries, tour boats, buses and trains.

best of times

Sydney has a remarkably mild climate, so visitors can come pretty much any time of the year and be assured of a pleasant stay. However, if you want to take advantage of the city's 70 bay or harbor beaches, you would do best to visit between September and May.

The Sydney Festival kicks off the year in January with three weeks of international and Australian music, theater, dance and visual-arts exhibitions that take place around the city. The Sydney Symphony Orchestra and Opera Australia present free programs in The Domain park as part of the Festival.

Australia Day is celebrated on January 26 in Sydney Harbour with a tall-ships race, a colorful ferry race and a Flags Afloat regatta. Fireworks take place at Darling Harbour.

The Gay and Lesbian Mardi Gras festival runs for three weeks in February and March; the highlight is the parade on the first Saturday in March.

The Royal Easter Show provides a sense of Australian rural life without leaving the city. It takes place for two weeks around Easter each year at the Showgrounds, near the Olympics site on Homebush Bay.

June activities include the Sydney Film Festival and the Feast of Sydney, a food and wine festival in various locations around the city.

what to see

The best way to get to know Sydney is on its harbor. Many companies run sightseeing cruises, including Captain Cook Cruises, Wharf 6, Circular Quay, (61-2) 9206-1111, and Vagabond Cruises, East Circular Quay, (61-2) 9660-0388. Less expensive are the low, sleek River Cats or chunky green and yellow ferries; call (61-2) 9207-3170 for routes and schedules. (Within Sydney, call 131-500.) Starting at Circular Quay, the possibilities include Taronga Park Zoo ($13.75 round trip, including zoo admission) and hip Balmain for its Saturday market ($4.20 round trip).

Bridge Climb, a 4,921-foot ascent of the Sydney Harbour Bridge, offers a 360-degree view of one of the world's most spectacular harbors. Groups of 10 don gray climbing suits (to blend in and to avoid distracting motorists), communications equipment, and safety harnesses and are escorted up a series of ladders and steps for a three-hour climb. Tickets are $83 during the day, $96 during the evening; call (61-2) 9252-0077. No experience required. Departure is from 5 Cumberland Street; reservations are essential.

The Sydney Opera House is not only a venue for opera, but also has a concert hall, theater and several other smaller performance spaces. It offers a year-round performance schedule. Call (61-2) 9250-7777.

Tour the Olympic Games site via an Olympic Explorer bus, $6.55, which leaves from the Homebush Bay Information Centre, 1 Herb Elliott Avenue, and makes 10 stops; entry to the Aquatic Center is $6 extra. A combined River Cat trip and bus tour costs $9.80, $14.40 on weekends, when it includes the Aquatic Centre admission. It leaves from Wharf 5, Circular Quay; (61-2) 9207-3170.

For a beach swim, you can take a ferry close to many harbor beaches such as Balmoral Beach (service until April 4), Nielsen Park (ferry to Rose Bay or Watsons Bay, then bus), as well as Watsons Bay or Manly (which has both bay and ocean beaches). You'll need a car or bus to reach the most popular ocean beach, Bondi, where sun-mad teenagers, office workers, mothers and children, and tourists enjoy the rolling surf and sweep of white sand. You can take a train from Central Station to Bondi Junction, then a bus, or take the bus all the way.

Darling Harbour is another must for the Sydney Aquarium, (61-2) 9262-2300, with Great Barrier Reef exhibits and glass tunnels through shark and stingray tanks. Admission: $10.40. The serenely beautiful Chinese Garden, (61-2) 9281-6863, and myriad harbor-side restaurants and shops are connected by monorail; $1.95, or $3.90 for an all-day pass.

The Djamu Gallery of Aboriginal and Pacific Islander Art, a branch of the Australian Museum, is in the refurbished Customs House on Alfred Street across from Circular Quay, (61-2) 9320-6429. Djamu, which means "I am here" in the local Eora language, features indigenous art alongside objects from diverse Aboriginal communities. Open daily. Admission: $5.25.

The Museum of Sydney, corner of Bridge and Phillip Streets, (61-2) 9251-5988, contains an innovative interpretation of the settlement of Sydney through historic artifacts, images and stories. Admission: $3.90. Open daily.

where to stay

BUDGET: The Y on the Park Hotel, overlooking Hyde Park at 5-11 Wentworth Avenue, Sydney City, (61-2) 9264-2451, fax (61-2) 9285-6288, offers a range of 120 budget accommodations from a double room with bath for $52 to a spacious dormitory for four people from $16.30 a person.

The Periwinkle Manly Cove, 18-19 East Esplanade, Manly; (61-2) 9977-4668, fax (61-2) 9977-6308, is a guesthouse dating from 1895 with 18 bright and airy period rooms, six with views of Sydney Harbour. Doubles with shared bath: $72; with private bath and water view: $92.

MODERATE: The new Westin Sydney is on the site of the original Sydney General Post Office, No. 1 Martin Place, (61-2) 8223-1111, fax (61-2) 9279-0569. Partly built inside the sandstone shell of the Historic Register building, partly an ultramodern high-rise, the foyer and hotel restaurants, bars and cafes are in a four-story open atrium joining the two buildings and decorated with vibrant glass art. The 417 hotel rooms and suites are done in light woods and white linens. Doubles in the tower start at $176, in the heritage building at $216.

Ravesi's, corner of Campbell Parade and Hall Street, Bondi Beach, (61-2) 9365-4422, fax (61-2) 9365-1481, is a 16-room hotel perched above Bondi Beach, with cool, fresh furnishings and mostly large bathrooms. Doubles with shower and no view start at $65; a split-level one-bedroom suite is $127, a penthouse with stunning view, $180.

LUXURY: Most of the rooms at the 158-room Park Hyatt Sydney, 7 Hickson Road, The Rocks, (61-2) 9241-1234, fax (61-2) 9256-1555, have water views, some including the Opera House. The understated décor in beiges and creams features polished wood and black-and-white photos of Sydney. Doubles start at $425.

The elegant, low-rise Observatory Hotel, 89-113 Kent Street, Millers Point, (61-2) 9256-2222, fax (61-2) 9256-2233, feels exclusive and tucked away, set above The Rocks area on the southwestern side of the Harbour Bridge. It offers top-of-the-line service with traditional British décor in its 100 rooms. Personal trainers are on hand in the basement gym. Doubles start at $324.

where to eat

Located in a grand, light-filled room with massive pillars reminiscent of the bank it once was, Banc, 53 Martin Place, (61-2) 9233-5300, serves sublime French-inspired cuisine with a light touch and an exceptional wine list. For an appetizer, try the seared tuna with ratatouille vegetables with fennel oil and tomato vinaigrette and follow it with roast squab breasts with rösti potato, savoy cabbage and foie gras. For dessert, don't go past the lemon tart with blueberry compote. Dinner for two with wine: $137. Lunch, Monday to Friday; dinner, Monday to Saturday.

In an airy Victorian terrace in the inner suburb of Potts Point, Cicada, 29 Challis Avenue, is a popular bistro that combines the best of Australian produce with a Provençal aesthetic. Try the seared tuna minute steaks with cherry tomato, caper and olive salsa and, for dessert, caramel pot de crème with passionfruit. The excellent wine list contains some boutique wines at very good prices. Lunch, Wednesday to Friday; dinner Monday to Saturday. Dinner for two with wine: $73. Telephone: (61-2) 9358-1255.

Five generations of Sydneysiders have enjoyed the seafood at Doyle's on the Beach at Watsons Bay, (61-2) 9337-2007. Take the ferry from Circular Quay for lunch or dinner on the beach. Specialties include a hot or cold fisherman's platter (half lobster, crab, oysters, king prawns, mussels, smoked salmon, octopus and calamari) and a rare char-grilled bluefin tuna steak. Three-course dinner for two with wine: around $72. Lunch and dinner daily.

At Sailors Thai Canteen, 106 George Street, The Rocks, (61-2) 9251-2466, you can dine with the locals at the long stainless-steel communal table and be seduced by the aromas coming from the open kitchen. Everything is excellent, but it's hard to get past the pad Thai rice noodles stir-fried with dried prawns and bean sprouts. Be sure to check out the specials, too. Dinner for two, with wine: $36.

There is possibly no better place to start your day than at Bill's, 433 Liverpool Street, Darlinghurst, (61-2) 9360-9631. The sun streams in the corner terrace house onto a large blond communal table or smaller tables where people are enjoying luscious fruit salads, ricotta hotcakes with honeycomb butter, sweet corn fritters and creamy scrambled eggs. Breakfast for two is about $16; lunch for two, without wine, is about $23.

vital statistics

POPULATION (2000): City 3,980,000

HOTEL: Room for one with tax $200.00

DINNER FOR ONE: With tax and tip but not drinks $24.95

TAXI: Upon entry $1.25; Each additional kilometer 70 cents; From the airport $12.75

CAR RENTAL FOR A DAY: Midsize car with unlimited free mileage $28.30

FOR MORE INFORMATION: Telephone: (61-2) 9255-1788; Website: www.sydney.com.au

Sources: Runzheimer International, Australian Tourist Commission, local businesses

Tokyo

A city of 20 million, but look close and
see its personal, charming side

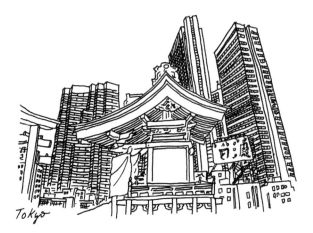

HOWARD W. FRENCH and STEPHANIE STROM

Howard W. French is chief of *The Times'*s Tokyo bureau.
Stephanie Strom is a correspondent in that bureau.

Tokyo, so imposing and impersonal from a distance, readily dis-
solves upon closer approach. Including Yokohama and other
nearby cities, this megalopolis is home to more than 20 million
people. But Tokyo is a huge collection of neighborhoods, each
built on a human, often charming, scale, perfect for exploration on
foot.

Some of the best starting points are near the Meiji Shrine.
Harajuku, abutting the shrine's south entrance, is overflowing with
boutiques that draw Japanese teenagers—a fact evident as soon as
you get off the JR Yamanote train at Harajuku Station. The pedestrian overpass leading to the shrine is the center of a Gothic fashion scene, with clusters of teenagers in outfits that look as if they
were inspired by the Addams family. Beyond this ghoulish gallery,
Harajuku is Tokyo at its Paris-like best. The Omotesando-dori, a
main avenue, is shaded by old trees and lined with cafes and
restaurants, and innumerable boutique-laden side streets radiate
from it.

The nearby Shibuya district is another walker's paradise. From

Harajuku, it is a leisurely 20 minutes or so by foot along Meiji-dori (the JR train makes the trip in a couple of minutes for $1.40). With its huge neon billboards, shimmering towers and crowds of pedestrians, Shibuya conjures up scenes from *Blade Runner*—no accident, since the movie's sets were inspired by this sort of postmodern Tokyo neighborhood.

A word about navigation: Tokyo streets often bear no names, and the city's address system is incomprehensible even to many longtime residents. Fortunately, the subway is among the world's best, and—for about $1.80—will bring you to virtually any neighborhood. English maps are available in every station, and English signs abound. When you reach the station nearest your destination, just show the address to a taxi driver (preferably in Japanese; few drivers speak English). Also know the Japanese name and address of your hotel—carrying one of its matchbooks should do the trick.

best of times

Almost like magic, sometime in late September, Tokyo is transformed from one of the world's muggiest, most miserable cities to a walker's paradise. The old joke holds that during the long summer months, Tokyo is a place where one can walk and swim at the same time. But with the passing of the season's typhoons, dry winds bring a crisp freshness.

For those with a choice, fall and spring are the only times to visit. Spring is famous for its cherry blossoms, but fall is no less celebrated for that other characteristic Japanese flower, the chrysanthemum, which blooms in October and was made famous by its use on Japan's imperial seal. And with temperatures in the 70's, Tokyo's denizens flock to major parks to view the blossoms.

The first of the season's major chrysanthemum exhibitions is at Yasukuni Shrine, 3-1-1 Kudan-kita in Chiyoda-yu, a major Shinto center just north of the Imperial Palace, usually from mid-October to early November. It's near the Kudanshita Station of the Tozai Subway. Information: (81-3) 3261-8326.

Kabuki performances at the main kabuki theater, the Kabukiza, 4-12-15 Ginza, Chuo-ku, (81-3) 5565-6000, are presented each month except July and August. The theater, a grand, Chinese-inspired building, is at the Higashi Ginza exit on the Hibiya Line. Tickets are $22.50 to $131. Headphones for English translations are available.

A personal favorite for viewing cherry blossoms (the season usually is in April) is Aoyama Bochi cemetery in the tony Aoyama district, southwest of downtown. Opened in 1874, it is the resting place of some of Japan's most illustrious figures. Another option is to float down the Sumida River, which is lined with cherry trees. The Tokyo Cruise Ship Company, (81-3) 3841-9178, operates a 45-minute o-hanami, or cherry-blossom viewing, cruise.

Two periods to avoid are the extended New Year's holiday, usually from about December 29 to January 7, and a week in late April through early May, with three national holidays. The city generally shuts down during these periods.

what to see

Sensoji, also known as the Asakusa Kannon Temple, is perhaps Tokyo's best-known temple complex and the emblem of Shitamachi, or the old city. It is equal parts bazaar and temple. The complex features a five-tiered pagoda and a beautiful Japanese garden called Dempoin, which is closed on Sunday and during religious events; have a hotel clerk call ahead to (81-3) 3842-0181 to check, and to let them know you are coming. The temple complex is a short walk from the Asakusa stop on the Ginza subway line or via the Tobu railway. Open daily.

Less well known is Taishakuten Daikyoji Temple in Shibamata, another pocket of the old city. Taishakuten is famous for its elaborately carved walls featuring episodes from Buddhist scripture. The $3.33 entrance fee includes the lovely Japanese garden in back of the temple. Open daily; (81-3) 3672-2661. To reach Shibamata, take the Keisei Railway to Takasago and change to the Kanamachi feeder train.

The Edo Tokyo Museum, 1-4-1 Yokoami, Sumida-ku, (81-3) 3626-9974, offers a peek at how Tokyo looked in the Edo Period from 1603 to 1868 using models of famous areas and structures. There are also models depicting the city during other eras. Closed Mondays. Admission: $5.

A thoroughly new part of town is Odaiba—an island built in Tokyo Bay in the 1980's. It has become a big draw in recent years, with amusement parks, futuristic gaming centers and spacious, ultramodern shopping malls, most of them open 11 a.m. to 10 p.m. Not all the merchandise is expensive, but don't expect bargains.

For children, there is the Tokyo Joypolis, a huge arcade run by Sega with life-size versions of its miniature games. Admission is $4.70 for adults, $2.80 for children; most games cost $4.70 to $6.60. It is open 10 a.m. to 11:30 p.m.; (81-3) 5500-1801. The island is reached by the Yurikamome monorail from Shimbashi Station.

Roppongi, a late-night amusement district, caters to Westerners.

The Lexington Disco, just off Gaien Higashi-dori, is probably Roppongi's most famous party place, but in this pulsing quarter, the choices are endless. Most clubs don't get rolling until after midnight, and many go till dawn. Cover charges range from $23 to $47. Take the Hibya Line to Roppongi Station; from there, you can't miss the neon signs.

where to stay

BUDGET: The Washington Hotel, 3-2-9 Nishi-Shinjuku, Shinjuku-ku, (81-3) 3343-3111, fax (81-3) 3342-2575, has 1,301 simple rooms in its main building and 337 in a new wing. It charges $140 for doubles, with breakfast.

Rooms with Western or traditional Japanese décor are available at the Atami-sou, 4-14-3 Ginza, Chuo-ku, Tokyo; (81-3) 3541-3621, fax (81-3) 3541-3263. In either case, the 74 rooms are small in this central Ginza business district hotel. Doubles with tatami-mats are $250; with Western furnishings, $185.

In a ryokan, or traditional Japanese inn, be prepared for sharing a bathroom, sleeping on the floor on a futon spread on a tatami mat and shoe-box-size rooms. Many are members of the Welcome Inn Reservation Center, (81-3) 3211-4201. Reservations are made by fax, (81-3) 3211-9009, using a form available from the Japan National Tourist Organization in New York, (212) 757-5640. Prices range from $33 to $66 a person a night.

MODERATE: The Ginza Tobu Hotel (Renaissance Hotel), (81-3) 3546-0111, fax (81-3) 3546-8990, is in central Tokyo, near the prestigious Ginza shopping district. Its 206 rooms are functional and of moderate size, but the hotel is spotlessly clean and has pleasant service. A double room with breakfast is $245.

Known for its good restaurants, the 375-room Odakyu Century Southern Tower Hotel, 2-2-1 Yoyogi, Shibuya-ku, Tokyo, (81-3) 5354-0111, fax (81-3) 5354-0100, is a 10-minute walk from Yoyogi Park, one of the prettiest in Tokyo, and is convenient to Shibuya, the bustling business and fashion center. This basic business hotel has good-size working areas and charges $205 for a double.

LUXURY: Tokyo's most famous hotel may be the 110-year-old Imperial, 1-1-1 Uchisaiwai-cho, Chiyoda-ku, (81-3) 3504-1111, fax (81-3) 3581-9146, with its cavernous Frank Lloyd Wright lobby, luxury boutiques, 1,059 rooms and proliferation of restaurants. Its location, across from Hibya Park near the Imperial Palace, is great for morning jogs or afternoon strolls. Doubles are $365 to $460.

Many business travelers pick the 858-room Hotel Okura, 2-10-4 Toranomon, Minato-ku, (81-3) 3582-0111, fax (81-3) 3582-3707. This big, old, impeccably maintained hotel near the United States Embassy features large rooms and plenty of restaurants and shops. Doubles are $375 or, with a tatami mat, $345.

where to eat

Goemon, 1-26 Honkomagome, (81-3) 3811-2015, serves traditional tofu cuisine in an old Japanese home. Fixed-menu lunches go for $25 and $33, and dinners for $52 to $70; beer or sake is $6.50. The restaurant is in the Bunkyo ward, a short walk from Hakusan Station, on the Mita Line.

Tsukiji, Tokyo's fish-market district, a short walk from the Tsukiji Station on the Hibya Line, naturally abounds in sushi shops and all have the traditional slatted doors and windows and long sushi bars. Sushi-ko, at 4-7-1 Tsukiji, Chuo-ku, (81-3) 3547-0505, is a great choice. Another area favorite is Sushi Iwa, 2-15-12 Tsukiji, Chuo-ku, (81-3) 3541-0655. Count on spending a minimum of $50 a person, without drinks, at either place for an indescribably fresh meal.

Among young Japanese, Ristorante Hiro, 5-5-25 Minami-aoyama, Minato-ku, (81-3) 3486-5561, is a top choice for Italian food. Dinner for two with drinks: $120. It's near the Omote-Sando Station.

For inexpensive Western-style food like burgers and sausages, try Tsubame Grill, 1-8-20 Ginza, Chuo-ku (Ginza-Ichome subway station), (81-3) 3561-3788. A dinner for two with drinks is about $55.

One affordable meal, closely associated with the cherry blossom season, is obento, a portable boxed meal. Mom-and-pop stands near transportation hubs display boxes of varying sizes and prices—just pick and point.

Yurakucho Station is home to a throng of tiny, inexpensive yakitori restaurants under the tracks. All that typically separates diners from the hustle-bustle outside is a plastic sheet, but the yakitori is piping hot and cheap. The cost is about $17 to $21 a person with a glass of beer.

vital statistics

POPULATION (2000): City 8,099,092; Metro area 20,018,050

HOTEL: Room for one with tax $276.00

DINNER FOR ONE: With tax and tip but not drinks $59.95

TAXI: Upon entry $6.18; Each additional 280 meters $4.57; From the airport $200.00

TRAINS: Bullet train to Osaka $135.90; Nozomi Super Express to Osaka $140.15; Bullet train to Kyoto $125.87; Nozomi Super Express to Kyoto $135.10; 7-day rail pass $269.45

FOR MORE INFORMATION: Telephone: (81-3) 5221-9084; Web: www.tcvb.or.jp

Sources: Runzheimer International, Japan National Tourist Organization, local businesses

Toronto
Proving that bigger is better, busier and brighter

ANTHONY DePALMA

Anthony DePalma is a former chief
of the Toronto bureau of *The Times.*

Toronto has never been a bigger attraction: In 1998, five surrounding suburbs were incorporated with the central core,
transforming Toronto overnight into the fifth-most-populous city
in North America, surpassed by only Mexico City, New York, Los
Angeles and Chicago. The new mega-city government is intent on
proving that (at least in this case) bigger is not only better but
busier, brighter and far more beguiling.

Toronto's charms as an international city that works are well
known. Through good planning and good luck, it is a city that
focuses far more of its energy on creating the future than on cor-
recting the mistakes of the past. It is, some say, New York without
attitude.

When the beacon atop the Canada Life Assurance Building on
University Avenue is capped by the green light that signifies clear
and sunny weather (red means overcast; flashing white, snow),
Toronto heads outdoors. The theater and entertainment district
around the CN Tower and the Skydome downtown stays thronged
until late at night, and even the disappointing waterfront on Lake

Ontario—cut off by an elevated highway—has something happening almost every day throughout the summer.

The 1,815-foot CN Tower (equivalent to 181 stories) provides a modern, unifying image for the city. But it is the many robust neighborhoods, each with its own ethnic flavor or historical ambience, that really show off what Toronto stands for. It has at least three Chinatowns, two Little Italys and a Greek neighborhood that stretches for miles. On a quick stroll, visitors can find window displays of fresh cannoli, smoked whole squid or boxes of exquisite Cuban cigars. But find one of Toronto's cigar bars and smoke the stogies there. Taking them across the border is prohibited.

best of times

Nature is kind to Toronto, providing an agreeable climate—by Canadian standards—most of the year. But the premium weeks in T.O., which is what some residents call Toronto, last only from late spring through early fall. During this time gray skies clear and sidewalks fill with people. Not surprisingly, the city puts the highlights of its year into this sweet season.

Around the third week of June, the Downtown Jazz Festival gets things going with 10 days of bebop, blues and Afro-Cuban jazz; (416) 928-2033. On the last Sunday of June, the marchers and floats of the city's Lesbian and Gay Pride Parade turn strait-laced Bloor Street into an uninhibited carnival; (416) 927-7433.

July 1 is Canada Day, and in Toronto that means the Symphony of Fire, a series of extravagant lakefront fireworks displays, (416) 442-3667, coordinated to classical music that is broadcast on a local radio station. Starting a few weekends before July 1 and continuing for a few weekends afterward, each show begins at 10:30 p.m. and lasts half an hour. You can reserve a seat at Ontario Place ($18) or, better yet, find a comfortable spot along the waterfront, turn on the radio, lean back and enjoy.

As the weather heats up, so does the excitement. Around the middle of July waterfront streets are closed for the Molson Indy, a grand prix for screaming Indianapolis 500-style cars; (416) 872-4639.

By the time August arrives, the city turns sultry, and that means the beginning of the Caribana Caribbean parade, the city's largest street party. For eight hours, the parade makes staid Toronto seem like a northern Rio de Janeiro; (416) 465-4884.

When summer ends, the city starts to head indoors. The largest groups left on the streets are usually movie enthusiasts who have come for the Toronto International Film Festival. Hundreds of films from dozens of countries are screened, and local restaurants vie to produce the greatest number of star sightings; (416) 968-3456.

what to see

It is tempting to think that Toronto is all future and no past. But a visit to the difficult-to-reach Historic Fort York, Garrison Road off Fleet Street west of downtown, (416) 392-6907, allows a look at the city's history. The fort dates from 1793 (although the buildings there now date from 1813–15) and is now surrounded by a maze of railroad tracks and superhighways. Guided tours are available in summer, and fabulous photo opportunities to combine the oldest buildings in Toronto with the futuristic CN Tower. Regular admission: $3.55. Open year round.

Another reminder of the past is the house of William Lyon Mackenzie, Toronto's first mayor. The small brick town house at 82 Bond Street, a block east of Eaton Center (the huge downtown mall), was his home from 1859 till his death in 1861. He became mayor in 1834, when the city had only 9,252 inhabitants, and later led an ill-fated rebellion against the Crown. Open Tuesday through Sunday; hours vary seasonally. Admission: $2.50. Information: (416) 392-6915.

Two of the city's leading museums are the Art Gallery of Ontario and Royal Ontario Museum. The former, at 317 Dundas Street West, is open Tuesday, Thursday and Friday, 11 a.m. to 6 p.m., Wednesday until 8:30 p.m., Saturday and Sunday 10 a.m. to 5:30 p.m.; (416) 979-6648. Its permanent collection includes Canadian, Inuit, European and American art. The Royal Ontario Museum, 100 Queen's Park, (416) 586-8000, is open Monday to Saturday 10 a.m. to 6 p.m., Friday until 9:30 p.m. and Sunday 11 a.m. to 6 p.m. Admission: $10.65. It is Canada's largest museum, with a mix of art, archaeological artifacts and science exhibits.

where to stay

BUDGET: Best Western Primrose Hotel, 111 Carlton Street, (416) 977-8000, fax (416) 977-6323, is slightly away from downtown. The 337 comfortable rooms have king, queen or two double beds. Doubles from $106.

MODERATE: Families are welcome at the Delta Chelsea Inn, 33 Gerrard Street West; (416) 595-1975, fax (416) 585-4302. Children under 18 stay free in their parents' room, and those under 6 eat free. There is a supervised playroom. For $3.55 per child for two and a half hours, parents get time alone. For peace of mind, they also receive a pager. Rooms are decorated in cheery pastels and florals. Doubles from $132.

If you want to be on the waterfront, the 968-room Westin Harbour Castle, One Harbour Square, (416) 869-1600, fax (416) 361-7448, is a moderately priced choice, especially with a summer package. There's an indoor pool, outdoor deck and a revolving restaurant on the 38th floor that is scheduled to reopen in 2001. Doubles start at $141.

LUXURY: For convenience and luxury, few hotels beat the Four Seasons, 21 Avenue Road, (416) 964-0411, fax (416) 963-6902, in the ritzy Yorkville neighborhood. Soothing cream tones and tasteful upholstery make the 380 rooms decadently comfortable. Doubles from $192.

The Sutton Place Hotel, 955 Bay Street, (416) 924-9221, fax (416) 324-5650, is one of Toronto's most luxurious European-style hotels. Its 292 rooms and suites are among the most spacious in the city. The furnishings are lush and the rooms bright and airy, especially those overlooking Yonge Street. Double rooms start at about $135.

where to eat

The area around College and Clinton Streets in West Toronto's Little Italy has been selected as one of the hippest places in North America by the *Utne Reader* magazine. One of the oldest restaurants in the neighborhood is the Cafe Diplomatico, 594 College Street, (416) 534-4637. This place is the essence of Toronto neighborliness: a sidewalk patio lined with petunias, a jukebox and plenty of opportunity for people watching. The menu at "the Dip" retains the hearty fare on which it was founded. Specials are the ubiquitous vodka rose sauce with choice of pasta, and extra-large panzarotti—a baked pizza dough with choice of stuffing. Dinner for two with a bottle of Chianti is $46. The cafe is open daily from 8 a.m. to 2 a.m. (until 3 on Friday and Saturday).

There are many good restaurants in Chinatown on Spadina Avenue, but make every effort to get into the Lee Garden, 331 Spadina Avenue, (416) 593-9524, even if it means sharing a table with strangers (they may not be strangers after you wait in line with them for 20 minutes). Plastic table coverings do not detract from the exquisitely prepared food: quail rolled in lettuce, deep fried and sweetly delicate soft-shelled crabs. A meal for two with beer and tea is about $45. Dinner daily.

Scaramouche, 1 Benvenuto Place, (416) 961-8011, remains a place to go for a special night. Its location on a small rise gives it a striking view. As meticulous with the menu as it is with reservations, Keith Froggett's restaurant delights in surprise. Arctic char poached in aromatic water, served with Ontario asparagus and fingerling potatoes, is $20. Dinner for two, with wine from the extensive list: $125. Dinner only, Monday through Saturday.

Rodney's Oyster House, 209 Adelaide Street East, (416) 363-8105, is less formal. It is easy to miss the entrance, but there is nothing subtle about Rodney's itself, where many other restaurants buy their seafood. The long bar is piled with more than a dozen types of oysters, purchased by the piece and taken raw. A quieter back room retains the free spirit of the place. Steamed clams and bowls of periwinkles are also available. Price: about $75 for two, with drinks. Open 11:30 a.m. to 1 a.m. Monday through Saturday.

For a taste of hearty Canadian fare, try the Acadian Room at the Royal York Hotel, 100 Front Street West; (416) 860-6949. Seafood chowder, Quebec duck with lavender wild honey, and delicious Canadian salmon are served in the kind of dark-wood, country-lodge setting that goes with the nation's image. Dinner for two, with an Ontario wine: about $100. Breakfast, lunch and dinner daily (no lunch Saturday).

For a bite on the run, try an enormous grilled hot dog from one of more than 1,000 street vendors in Toronto. On a hearty yellow bun, they usually take two hands to handle. Lunch for two, with soda (called pop in T.O.): about $4.

vital statistics

POPULATION (1999): City 2,100,000; Metro area 4,600,000

HOTEL: Room for one with tax $156.50

DINNER FOR ONE: With tax and tip but not drinks $20.20

TAXI: Upon entry $1.70; Each additional 1.2 kilometers 85 cents; From the airport $23.70

CAR RENTAL FOR A DAY: Midsize car with unlimited free mileage $27

FOR MORE INFORMATION: Telephone: (800) 499-2514; Web: www.torontotourism.com

Sources: Runzheimer International, Toronto Tourism, local businesses

Vancouver

A variety of cultural offerings and stunning
natural backdrop (but bring an umbrella)

Downtown Vancouver

MELISSA A. TRAINER
Melissa A. Trainer is a food and travel writer who lives in Seattle.

Sitting in the shadow of the undulating and snowcapped Coast Mountains, British Columbia's Vancouver has a temperate climate and boasts 187 parks within the city limits alone. Although the average annual rainfall of 45 inches may scare some sun lovers south, the city's eclectic cultural scene and naturally beautiful vistas more than compensate for the slow and steady rainfall. The favorable exchange rate for United States visitors also sweetens the appeal.

Because the city sits on the Burrard Peninsula and juts into the Strait of Georgia and the Burrard Inlet, there are endless opportunities for seaside exploration and relaxation. Cruise ship berths sit in the heart of downtown and welcome hundreds of visitors. The ships sail through the Inside Passage en route to Alaska, and each season, more than 300 sailings take place.

best of times

The summer months are the most popular time to visit, as the average temperature is about 63 degrees and the days are generally crystal clear and humidity free. Although these are also the busiest months in Vancouver, visitors are equally pleased during the entertainment season, which runs from October to May. Shortly after the cruise ships batten down their hatches, theaters and galleries open their doors and welcome some of the world's finest performers and artists.

Among the leading performance sites are the Vancouver Playhouse, 600 Hamilton Street, (604) 873-3311, and the Queen Elizabeth Theater, at Hamilton and Georgia Streets, (604) 683-0222. But a number of smaller theaters are worth investigating, including the Chan Center for the Performing Arts at the University of British Columbia, (604) 822-9197, Ticketmaster (604) 280-3311; it opened in 1997 and has been praised for the acoustics in the 1,400-seat Chan Shun concert hall.

Another plus to visiting at this time is that packages offer outstanding deals at the city's most luxurious hotels as well as at the appealing family-oriented properties. The packages vary, and theater tickets, restaurant meals and museum passes are usually included.

The du Maurier International Jazz Festival generally takes place at the end of June and beginning of July. Considered one of the best jazz festivals in North America, the 10-day event was started in 1985 and features more than 1,600 musicians from around the world. The free and ticketed concerts take place at more than 38 venues throughout the city, both indoor and outdoor. For information, call (888) 438-5200.

The Bard on the Beach Shakespeare Festival runs throughout the summer on an outdoor stage on the scenic False Creek Waterfront. Started in order to offer affordable Shakespearean productions, the festival entertains close to 60,000 people each season. For information or tickets, call (604) 739-0559.

Held annually during the beginning of October, Vancouver's International Film Festival takes place at seven venues throughout the city with over 300 films from more than 50 countries. Call (604) 685-0260.

Granville Island is the home of the Vancouver International Writers Festival at the end of October. More than 60 authors and poets from around the world usually turn out. Call (604) 681-6330.

what to see

Yaletown, on the waterfront just southeast of downtown, is one of the city's most vibrant neighborhoods. At the turn of the century, freight trains trundled through the area, and Yaletown retains much of its workhorse appearance. Many of the brick warehouses today serve as residential lofts, office space, funky boutiques and design studios. After rambling, you can recharge at a cafe or restaurant; the patio of the Yaletown Brewing Company, 1111 Mainland Street, is a fine perch for a boutique beer and people-watching.

Stanley Park, a thousand-acre oasis in the heart of the city, is ringed by a five-mile seawall that provides a popular path for walkers, runners and cyclists. Information: (604) 257-8526. Inside the park, the Vancouver Aquarium Marine Science Center is undergoing a major four-part renovation. The Pacific Canada Pavilion, completed in June 1999, is the first stage. The pavilion's viewing tank is stocked with creatures from the nearby Strait of Georgia. Killer-whale shows are held in the pool just outside the pavilion. The Vancouver Aquarium Marine Science Center, 845 Avison Way, (604) 659-3400, is open daily 10 a.m. to 5:30 p.m. Admission: adults $9.55, seniors and students $8, children 4 to 12 $6.30.

Behind the Marine Science Center is the Children's Farmyard and Miniature Railway; (604) 257-8531. For $4 a family of four can board the railway's steam engines and chug through the park's old-growth and second-growth coastal rain forest. At the farmyard, frisky goats take friendly nibbles at children's sleeves. The farmyard and the railway are open seven days a week.

Various drives offer different views of the province's majestic mountains and waterways. Northwest Marine Drive, beginning at the end of Fourth Avenue in the enclave of Kitsilano (where you can fortify yourself at any number of cafes and artsy bakeries), weaves through upscale neighborhoods and hugs the edge of Burrard Inlet and the Strait of Georgia. On the way it passes the enormous Pacific Spirit Regional Park, a lush chunk of land offering steep hikes down to the water, and goes through the University of British Columbia campus, where the Museum of Anthropology has an extensive collection of Northwest Coastal Indian artifacts. Marine Drive connects with Highway 99, which goes north to return downtown.

Heading south, the highway leads to Richmond, a city on the mighty Fraser River with fertile farmland and a large fishing fleet. Richmond is also the heart of Vancouver's rapidly expanding Asian community, centered at the intersection of Number Three Road and Cambie, where a cluster of shiny malls sells Asian imports. Tours of Aberdeen Center, one of the major Asian shopping malls, are given Wednesday at 11 a.m., with stops at a traditional teahouse, a Japanese bakery and a Chinese medicine shop; the tour costs $10 and includes a sushi lunch. Reservations: (604) 270-1234.

Southwest of Richmond, also off Highway 99, is the small fishing village of Steveston, one of the largest fishing ports on the West Coast, with boutiques and a lively wharf.

where to stay

Since January 1998, 10 hotels have opened throughout greater Vancouver, and others have been fully renovated.

BUDGET: Built in 1916, the St. Regis, 602 Dunsmuir Street, (800) 770-7929, was renovated in 1999. The chief attraction of this 72-room hotel is its proximity to all major attractions. Standard rooms are $70, the six suites $104; rates include Continental breakfast. There's a Starbucks on the lobby level.

The Jolly Taxpayer, 828 West Hastings Street, (604) 681-3550, fax (604) 682-2160, offers basic bed-and-breakfast accommodations in a renovated turn-of-the-century building. There are 31 rooms, each with TV, toilet and sink. Bathrooms with showers or tubs or both are down the hall. Doubles: $54, with Continental breakfast.

MODERATE: The Century Plaza Hotel and Spa, 1015 Burrard Street, (800) 663-1818, fax (604) 682-5790, is family owned. Each of the 236 suites (there are studios and one-bedroom units) has kitchen facilities. An indoor pool and eucalyptus steamrooms are on the level below the lobby, and the spa offers everything from maternity and reiki massages to lemon-ginger scrubs and rose-petal plunges. Rates are $103 for a studio, $144 for one bedroom.

Because it started life as an apartment building, the Coast Plaza Suite Hotel at Stanley Park, 1763 Comox Street, (604) 688-7711, fax (604) 688-5934, has rooms that are slightly larger than standard hotel rooms, although the décor is hotel plain-vanilla. Many of the 267 rooms boast sea breezes and views of English Bay. The hotel is in a quiet neighborhood. Rates: $124 to $198.

LUXURY: The new Westin Grand, in the shape of a grand piano, is in the entertainment district at 433 Robson Street; (888) 680-9393, fax (604) 647-2502. It has 207 suites, each equipped with a convenience kitchen and decorated in earth tones, and a large health club. Rates: $234.

The elegantly appointed Wedgewood, 845 Hornby Street, (604) 689-7777, fax (604) 608-5348, is a privately owned boutique hotel near the Vancouver Art Gallery. There are 89 rooms, decorated in European style, with tapestry fabrics, mahogany walls, and antique furniture from the owner's collection; many offer views of the nearby Law Court gardens. Rates: $134 to $240; suites start at $295.

where to eat

At Vij's Curry House, 1480 West 11th Avenue, (604) 736-6664, Vikram Vij, who owns the restaurant with his wife, Meeru, carefully blends all his own masalas and curry pastes. The menu changes frequently. Meat curries and a rockfish, scallop and langoustine curry with cumin rice are two standards. Dinner for two with wine: about $70. Open daily for dinner.

Hidden in a shopping mall, Lombardo's Pizzeria, 120-1641 Commercial Drive, (604) 251-2240, is worth tracking down. The crispy thin-crusted pizzas are baked in a brick oven with choice ingredients. A lunch for two of two 12-inch individual pizzas and beer is about $24. Pasta and salads are also available.

If a visit to the fishing community of Steveston leaves you hungry for seafood, stop at Dave's Fish and Chips, 3460 Moncton Street, Steveston; (604) 271-7555. The fish (halibut or cod) arrives crispy, hot and moist. Diners can eat inside at one of the oilcloth-dressed tables, or order takeout (slightly less expensive) and sit at one of the nearby picnic tables on the banks of the Fraser River. A large order of codfish and chips is $8.30, halibut and chips $10.30. Lunch for two with beer is about $20.

Piccolo Mondo, 850 Thurlow Street, (604) 688-1633, is an elegant restaurant serving simple Italian fare. The polenta gorgonzola soup and the seared sea bass with haricots verts were delicious, the staff condescending. Dinner for two with wine: about $90. Reservations required.

vital statistics

POPULATION (1999): City 554,062; Metro area 2,016,600

HOTEL: Room for one with tax $123.00

DINNER FOR ONE: With tax and tip but not drinks $17.50

TAXI: Upon entry $1.57; Each additional kilometer 83 cents; From the airport $15.57

CAR RENTAL FOR A DAY: Midsize car with unlimited free mileage $33.85 (summer); $25.38 (winter)

FOR MORE INFORMATION: Telephone: (604) 682-2222; Web: www.tourismvancouver.com

Sources: Runzheimer International, Statistics Canada, Tourism Vancouver, local businesses

Vienna

The newest museum says it all:
the House of Music

St. Charles Boromeo,
Vienna

PAUL HOFMANN

Paul Hofmann, a native of Vienna, is the author of *The Spell of the Vienna Woods: Inspiration and Influence from Beethoven to Kafka.*

A brand-new museum, the House of Music, epitomizes what the Austrian capital means above all to many visitors. Located in a formerly princely palace in the city center, once the home of the 19th-century founder of the celebrated Vienna Philharmonic Orchestra, the composer-conductor Otto Nicolai, the museum is devoted to musical geniuses who were born or lived in Vienna. It presents on seven floors an incomparable musical heritage with memorabilia from Haydn to Mozart, Beethoven to Schubert, Mahler to Schoenberg, while multimedia sections are devoted to the music of the present and the electronic future. The House of Music, (43-1) 51648, is at 30 Seilerstatte.

Besides claiming to be the world capital of music, Vienna is also an attractive and orderly place with great architecture, a wealth of art collections, magnificent public gardens (including the vast Prater with a 200-year-old amusement park and a century-old giant Ferris wheel) and a leisurely pace. The vaunted Viennese cuisine seduces with its schnitzels as well as its strudels, tortes and other rich desserts.

In fall and winter, many Viennese and their guests journey to the ancient vintners' villages, a 20- or 30-minute trolley ride from the center, to sample the young wine. Best known of those picturesque suburbs is Grinzing. The weather usually remains mild until November, and the fall foliage can rival New England's. The ancient Romans planted the first vines in this northern province of their empire, and grapes have been grown since then on the green slopes of the Vienna Woods, sylvan arms that reach into the old city. Drinking the barely fermented product of the autumn's grape harvest in one of the hundreds of rustic (or fake-rustic) taverns near the vineyards is an annual Viennese rite.

best of times

Vienna is at its loveliest in spring, when chestnut trees along the monumental Ringstrasse are in bloom, and in its mellow autumn. The ornate State Opera, the city's pride and one of the world's leading shrines to the lyric drama, offers 300 performances of some 40 productions from September through June. Tickets cost from $10 for a balcony seat to $180 in the dress circle; $15 will buy a satisfactory seat—except for galas. The ticket office, (43-1) 513-1513, is a block from the opera at 3 Hanuschgasse.

The annual Vienna Festival Weeks from early May to mid-June lavish a bounty of music, drama and dance on the city.

Summer months are enlivened by a jazz festival and an outdoor film marathon in the large square in front of the neo-Gothic City Hall. Vienna Modern, a parade of contemporary music, takes place every November.

what to see

A free folder describing more than 50 museums—from art galleries to collections specializing in circus clowns and burials—is available at the tourist information office on the Albertinaplatz, 9 a.m. to 7 p.m. daily; (43-1) 2111-4222. The Vienna Card ($16.15 at hotels and the tourist office) provides admission discounts, as well as free rides on the public transport system for 72 hours.

The world's largest Bruegel collection can be found at the Museum of Fine Arts, 1 Maria-Theresien-Platz, (43-1) 525-240, with such masterpieces as "The Hunters in the Snow" and "Peasant Dance" along with works by Dürer, Rubens, Velázquez, Titian and many others. Open 10 a.m. to 6 p.m. Tuesday to Sunday, Thursday until 9 p.m.; $7.70.

Paintings of more recent vintage—19th- and 20th-century

Austrian art—can be found in the Austrian Gallery in the upper part of the baroque Belvedere Palace, 27 Prinz Eugen-Strasse, (43-1) 7955-7134, with works by Klimt, Schiele and Kokoschka. Open 10 a.m. to 5 p.m. Tuesday to Sunday; $4.60.

The Museum of Applied Arts, 5 Stubenring, (43-1) 711-360, has a vast collection of Biedermeier, Art Nouveau and Art Deco objects, from bentwood chairs to tableware; the contemporary section includes works by American artists. Known as MAK, the acronym of its name in German, the museum, with its elegant coffeehouse, is open 10 a.m. to 6 p.m. Tuesday to Sunday (Thursday to 9 p.m.); $2.30.

In 1899 a local neurologist, Dr. Sigmund Freud, published *The Interpretation of Dreams.* Only 123 copies were sold in the first six weeks, but it marked the foundation of psychoanalysis. The Sigmund Freud Museum is at 19 Berggasse, where Freud lived for 47 years and received patients for six years. The doctor's hours are 9 a.m. to 4 p.m. (6 p.m. July to September). Admission is $4.60; (43-1) 319-1596.

The Fine Arts Academy, 3 Schillerplatz, (43-1) 588 16225, is open 10 a.m. to 5 p.m. Tuesday to Sunday; $5.40.

The Jewish Museum, 11 Dorotheergasse, is open 10 a.m. to 6 p.m. Sunday to Friday, Thursday until 9 p.m. The many artifacts on display regarding the 800 years of Jewish life in the Austrian capital focus on the Jewish contributions to Viennese culture. There are also exhibits on the Vienna of Theodor Herzl, Sigmund Freud and Gustav Mahler, and a re-creation of a Jewish-Viennese coffeehouse. Admission is $5.40. For information, call (43-1) 535-0431.

where to stay

BUDGET: Suzanne, 4 Walfischgasse, (43-1) 5132-5070, fax (43-1) 513-2500, is a friendly pension in a turn-of-the-century building near the State Opera, with 25 comfortable rooms; $68 to $100, with breakfast.

Near the monumental Ringstrasse, the Goldene Spinne, 1A Linke Bahngasse, (43-1) 7124-4860, fax (43-1) 713-1661, has 41 simply furnished rooms and a bar. Doubles with bath: $85 to $93 ($100 in November); buffet breakfast included.

MODERATE: Konig von Ungarn, 10 Schulerstrasse, (43-1) 515-840, fax (43-1) 515-848, a low-slung, yellow Baroque building, was once a guest house for prelates visiting the nearby Cathedral of St. Stephen, and has been a hotel since 1815. The interior courtyard, where the clerics' coaches were parked, is now a charming glass-roofed hall where breakfast and drinks are served. None of the 33 brightly furnished rooms are alike; but most include large, modern baths. Doubles: $154 to $181, including breakfast.

George Balanchine stayed at Schneider, 5 Getreidemarkt, (43-1) 588-380, fax (43-1) 5883-8212, and the many autographed photos in the lobby attest that the family-run house was and is a favorite of show business personalities. There are 35 rooms and 35 kitchenette suites. Doubles: $119 to $151, including buffet breakfast.

Another family-operated hotel, Zur Wiener Staatsoper, 11 Krugerstrasse, (43-1) 513-1274, fax (43-1) 513-1274-15, occupies a graceful late-19th-century building near the opera. The 22 rooms are mostly spacious, the bathrooms narrow, the atmosphere cozy. Doubles are $85 to $122, with buffet breakfast.

LUXURY: The Austrian Government puts up its state visitors at the 128-room Imperial, 16 Karntner Ring, (43-1) 501-230, fax (43-1) 50123-410, the opulent 125-year-old hotel. Cherry-wood paneling was recently added to top-floor rooms; lower rooms have crystal chandeliers and Belle Epoque furniture. It features superb service, a refined restaurant and a cafe. Doubles: $423 to $923, breakfast extra.

Palais Schwarzenberg, 9 Schwarzenberg Platz, (43-1) 7984-5150, fax (43-1) 798-4714, off the Ringstrasse, occupies a wing of the 18th-century palace still inhabited by members of the princely Schwarzenberg family. The 49 rooms, some large, some rather cramped, are furnished with antiques; many look out on a private park. There are six suites. Doubles: $262 to $446 without breakfast.

where to eat

Steirereck, 2 Rasumofskygasse, (43-1) 7133-1680, in an uninspiring neighborhood 10 minutes from the center, receives you with a wealth of fresh flowers and great cordiality. The cuisine successfully blends Viennese, rural Austrian and French cooking. The wine cellar contains 500 labels. Dinner for two with a medium-priced wine: $150 to $190. Open weekdays.

Gosser Bierklinik, 4 Steindlgasse, (43-1) 5356-8970, displays in one of several cozy dining rooms on two floors a cannonball that the Turks lobbed into the city when they unsuccessfully besieged Vienna in 1683. Backed by a brewery, the restaurant offers reliable Austrian wines in addition to schnitzel, sausages and other substantial fare in a convivial atmosphere. Open daily except Sunday. Dinner for two with beer or a glass of wine: about $50.

Cafe Landtmann, 4 Dr. Karl-Lueger-Ring, (43-1) 532-0621, with a large terrace, is where Freud used to play cards with friends. The 125-year-old coffeehouse is one of about 500 in Vienna—from the elegant, like the Landtmann, to the plain—where many Viennese seem to live. A cappuccino costs $3.50, apple strudel à la mode $4.75; a sample $8 lunch menu consists of beef broth with liver dumplings and stuffed zucchini. Open until midnight daily.

Hauermandl, 20 Cobenzlgasse, (43-1) 320-3027, in Grinzing (take the No. 38 streetcar), is informal with schmaltzy music. A chicken dinner for two with plenty of the local white wine is about $60. Open 5:30 p.m. to midnight, Monday to Saturday.

One of a chain of self-service dining spots, the Naschmarkt at 16 Schwarzenberg Platz, (43-1) 505-3115, is next door to McDonald's but far removed when it comes to menu choices: vegetable soup, halibut with herb sauce, potatoes and fruit costs $5.50. The restaurants are named after Vienna's biggest outdoor food emporium: Nosh Market.

vital statistics

POPULATION (1999): City 1,650,000

HOTEL: Room for one with tax $199.50

DINNER FOR ONE: With tax and tip but not drinks $27.45

TAXI: Upon entry $1.64; Each additional kilometer 82 cents; From the airport $30.00

CAR RENTAL FOR A DAY: Midsize car with unlimited free mileage $100.87

FOR MORE INFORMATION: Telephone: (43-1) 211-140; Web: info.wien.at

Sources: Runzheimer International, City of Vienna Press and Information Office, local businesses

Washington

A city of monuments, and diverse neighborhoods

The Capitol,
Washington, D.C.

CYNTHIA HACINLI

Cynthia Hacinli is co-author of *Romantic Days and Nights in Washington, D.C.*

Once you've done the monuments and the museums, there's still the real Washington to discover. The soul of this vibrant international city can be found in its neighborhoods: Georgetown with its chic boutiques and cafes, lively waterfront and lovely gardens, the most notable being Dumbarton Oaks and Tudor Place; Dupont Circle with its thriving gay culture, tall Victorian town houses and opulent embassies, art movie theaters and edgy restaurants; Adams-Morgan, the melting pot of Northwest D.C., where nightlife sizzles and West African, Latin, Caribbean and Middle Eastern restaurants and clubs sit side by side.

The city's generally mild weather means street and cafe life from May through October. Bikers revel in the long season as well, and a series of trails along the Potomac, looping around the Mall, and through Rock Creek Park, make for a novel approach to the Washington, Jefferson and Lincoln Memorials, the National Zoo, and the museums. The big news on the Mall is the National Gallery's long-awaited sculpture garden and fountain, which segues into an ice-skating rink during the winter. And on Sundays between 8 a.m. and 1 p.m., the fledgling Dupont Circle Farmers Market, 21st Street between P and Q Streets NW, where vendors hawk organic goat cheese and eggs and heirloom fruits and vegetables, is the place to be.

best of times

The cherry trees get all the press, and, granted, that sweep of pink cotton candy rimming the Tidal Basil is worth braving the crowds that descend for the Cherry Blossom Festival, held the first week of April on the Mall and environs; (202) 455-5663. The blossoming of the trees doesn't always coincide with the festival, so it's best to be loose about travel plans if you want to hit the peak.

Washington resonates on the Fourth of July. Independence Day festivities begin at noon with the annual parade along Constitution Avenue from 7th to 17th Streets. They continue with live music at the Sylvan Theater on the Ellipse in the afternoon and a National Symphony Orchestra performance on the Capitol's West Lawn at 8 p.m. Things end with a bang on the Washington Monument grounds with fireworks around 9:20 p.m.

Cultural doings pick up in the fall with new museum shows and theatrical offerings, and the beginning of the symphony, ballet and opera season.

In winter, the holidays kick off early with the lighting of the National Christmas Tree on the Mall, usually the first week of December. Merrymaking continues with free evening concerts on the Mall all month long. Even the White House gets into the spirit of things as volunteer elves deck the halls with yards of holiday finery, there for the viewing on special tours.

what to see

When the weather turns mild, pedaling the monuments is a favored pursuit. An easy route starts at the Lincoln Memorial, 23rd Street between Independence and Constitution Avenues, follows the Reflecting Pool east to the Washington Monument then bears right along the paved path closest to the southern edge of the Mall to the Tidal Basin and Jefferson Memorial. All monuments are open daily, free. Big Wheel Bikes, 1034 33rd Street NW, rents bicycles; (202) 337- 0254.

Claes Oldenburg's witty oversized eraser—the kind with a brush on one end—sets the mood at the National Gallery of Art sculpture garden on the Mall between Seventh and Ninth Streets.

The Phillips Collection, 1600 21st Street NW, was begun by

Duncan Phillips, who in 1921 opened his Dupont Circle home and art collection to the public and, in that instant, founded the nation's first modern-art museum. Admission: $7.50 (free on Wednesday). Closed Monday; (202) 387-2151.

The National Museum of African Art, 950 Independence Avenue SW, is open daily and is free; (202) 357-4600.

The ornate Elizabethan theater at the Folger Shakespeare Library, 201 East Capitol Street SE, will look familiar to anyone who has seen *Shakespeare in Love.* Exhibits at the Library Gallery are free, but closed Sunday; (202) 544-7077.

Ideal for a stroll are Georgetown's handsome streets. Amble along P Street to No. 3271, where Jacqueline and John F. Kennedy lived as newlyweds. A block or so over, off R Street, Dumbarton Oaks, 1703 32nd Street NW, is vibrant all year long (gardens open 2 to 5 p.m. daily, free); (202) 339-6410.

Though too far to walk from Georgetown—unless hiking is your thing—the Washington National Cathedral, Massachusetts and Wisconsin Avenues NW, offers respite for the weary. You can get lost in the cavernous interior; on the south grounds, through a door right out of a Grimm's fairy tale, is the Bishop's Garden, a lush oval of evergreens, boxwood and herbs. Cathedral tours lasting 30 to 60 minutes are given Monday through Saturday from 10 to 11:30 a.m. and 12:45 to 3:15 p.m. and Sunday from 12:30 to 2:45 p.m.; (202) 537-6200. Suggested donation: $3 for adults and $1 for children.

where to stay

BUDGET: Popular with finicky parents of students at the nearby George Washington University is the St. James Suites, 950 24th Street NW, on Washington Circle. The 195 suites, in shades of maroon or green, all have kitchens and living areas. Suites begin at $109, with Continental breakfast; (800) 852-8512, fax (202) 659-4492.

On a quiet street off Dupont Circle, the intimate all-suite Canterbury Hotel, 1733 N Street NW, has a sizable European clientele. The 99 green floral-themed junior suites in this modern hotel have queen- or king-size beds and kitchenettes. Rates are $140 to $235, including Continental breakfast and a pass to a nearby Y.M.C.A.; the AAA rate is $119; (800) 424-2950, fax (202) 785- 9581.

MODERATE: The Hotel George, 15 E Street NW, (800) 576-8331, fax (202) 347-4213, provides some of the city's hippest accommodations. This 139-room hotel on Capitol Hill has a 24-hour fitness center, spacious rooms and avant-garde art. Doubles start at $159 on weekends until mid-November, $129 in late November and $119 in December. Its Bistro Bis serves sophisticated French comfort food (vegetable tarts and escargot ragout).

What was once the infamous Watergate Hotel, 2650 Virginia Avenue NW, has received an overhaul of the 250 rooms and suites and a new name, Swissotel Washington. Rooms have mahogany and red chintz furniture, taupe bedspreads and marble baths. Doubles: $179 to $595; (202) 965-2300, fax (202) 337-7915.

LUXURY: A magnet for celebrities, the Four Seasons, 2800 Pennsylvania Avenue NW, has 260 rooms, a health club and spa, and an indoor pool. Standard doubles, in blue and yellow, are $315 on weekends, the newer, bigger rooms $410, including parking; (202) 342-0444, fax (202) 944-2076.

The Hay-Adams, 800 16th Street NW, is as close as you can stay to the White House. The 143 rooms and 32 suites have mahogany furniture and are done in shades of cream, blue and beige. Smallish doubles with a courtyard view begin at $310, while a larger room with a glimpse of a White House is $495; (202) 638-6600, (800) 323-7500, fax (202) 638-2716.

where to eat

Already one of the city's top Northern Italian restaurants, Galileo, 1110 21st Street NW, has added Laboratorio Galileo, a glass-walled kitchen and dining area, where a lucky few can watch the chef, Roberto Donna, work and indulge in a multicourse meal for $95 a person. The Lab menu varies, but past hits include leek custard with black truffle and prosciutto, and rockfish with pig ears and shallots. Reservations for the Lab at least six weeks ahead are suggested. The main dining room is easier to get into, and the banquettes along the left wall are particularly romantic. Dinner for two with wine is around $150; (202) 293-7191.

Goldoni has a new pale-hued home at 1120 20th Street NW, but the chef Fabrizio Aielli's modern Venetian cooking is as dazzling as ever: he dares to pair chocolate-scented pasta with rabbit ragout and eggplant with a sweet-sour glaze. The second level feels more private. Dinner for two with wine: $150; (202) 293-1511.

Mr. Aielli's newer showcase, Teatro Goldoni, 1909 K Street NW, dishes up pasta and Venetian seafood like lobster with black truffle sauce to a backdrop of harlequin glass and an open kitchen. Dinner for two with a glass of wine: about $110; (202) 955-9494.

In just a few months, Equinox, 818 Connecticut Avenue NW, at Pennsylvania, became a hit with the White House crowd. The chef, Todd Gray, conjures up lush pan-carmelized duck foie gras and barbecued salmon with corn and red peppers. Dinner for two with wine: around $100; (202) 331-8118.

Also new and justly popular is Johnny's Half Shell, 2002 P Street NW, which flies in French bread from New Orleans for its oyster and soft-shell crab po'boys. Corn pudding, seafood gumbo and Manhattan clam chowder are tops, too, and at lunch, the hot dog with onions and blue cheese ($5.95) steals the show. No reservations. Dinner for two with wine: about $85; (202) 296-2021.

The wood-oven pizzas at Pizzeria Paradiso, P Street between 20th and 21st Streets NW, are dead ringers for the crisp-crusted pies of Naples. Rounding out the menu are paninis, inventive salads, an extraordinary antipasto and homemade gelato. Dinner for two with wine: around $30; (202) 223-1245.

A mini-chain of serene tea shops known as Teaism are hip places for steaming pots of tea (there are more than a dozen green teas alone) and Asian-inspired meals. At breakfast, candied ginger scones are the choice. Lunch and dinner revolve around tea-smoked salmon, sandwiches, homemade soups and addictive chocolate crème brûlée. Dinner for two: around $25. Outlets at 2009 R Street NW, (202) 667-3827; 400 Eighth Street NW, and 800 Connecticut Avenue NW, (202) 835-2233, where dinner is not served.

vital statistics

POPULATION (1998 estimate): City 523,124; Metro area 4,673,902

HOTEL: Room for one with tax $204.00

DINNER FOR ONE: With tax and tip but not drinks $35.50

TAXI (rates are for one passenger): One zone $4.00; Two zones $5.50; From the airport $11.00

CAR RENTAL FOR A DAY: Midsize car with unlimited free mileage $70.00

FOR MORE INFORMATION: Telephone: (800) 422-8644; Web: www.washington.org

Sources: Runzheimer International, U.S. Census Bureau, local businesses

Zurich

It's not all Swiss bank accounts; it's rich culturally, too

PAUL HOFMANN

Paul Hofmann is a former *Times* correspondent in Europe.

Some 200 banks—including branches of major institutions in the United States, Japan and several European countries—are doing brisk business at this Swiss commercial and financial cross-roads-on-the-lake. Yet this rich "Little Big City," as Zurich calls itself, also boasts an enviable cultural life with an ambitious opera house, many concerts and interesting theater. Its Kunsthaus is a trove of modern art.

Zurich also dazzles with one of the world's major shopping boulevards. The Bahnhofstrasse, lined with linden trees, slices for almost a mile across the center from the busy Hauptbahnhof (central rail terminal) to the northern tip of the boomerang-shaped Zurich lake. Luxury stores and boutiques display high-priced watches and jewelry, famous-label fashions, furs, shoes, accessories and cosmetics.

Zurich, Switzerland's biggest city, is framed by rangy green hills east and west and is brightened by a profusion of flowers on balconies and in public gardens such as the Pestalazzi Park, at the center of the city, and the jogger-friendly landscaped promenade on the western lakeshore.

Many languages besides the near-impenetrable local patois are heard in this cosmopolitan city; nearly everyone knows English. The public transit network is admirable; Zurich Airport, in the town of Kloten, is well connected to the center of town ($3.25 by rail), making Zurich a Continental hub.

best of times

The supposedly staid Zurichers frolic with astounding abandon during their Fasnacht (Carnival). Small bands of amateur musicians drift from tavern to tavern, especially in the bohemian Niederdorf on the east bank of the Limmat River, to play with ear-splitting dissonance. On the Saturday after Ash Wednesday, the Children's Parade takes place in the afternoon; the following day, it's the Carnival Parade.

The memory of the medieval craftsmen's and merchants' guilds is revived on the third Monday in April by annual rites of spring with marches by costumed groups along the Bahnhofstrasse. That is followed at 6 p.m. by the burning of a man-size straw puppet (symbolizing winter) on a pyre near the opera.

The Opera House season runs from the end of September to the first week in July, with the most important productions in special performances during the Zurich Festival, an arts celebration in July. Admission to repertory operas is $20 to $250; the ticket office, (41-1) 268-6666, fax (41-1) 268-6555, is on the Theaterplatz.

Concerts and recitals are offered year round in the auditoriums of the prestigious Tonhalle, across the lake from the opera. Information and tickets: 7 Claridenstrasse; (41-1) 206-3434, fax (41-1) 206-3469.

what to see

The heart of the city, between Bahnhofstrasse and the Limmat River where it flows out of the lake, is dotted with half-timbered medieval houses. Several of these ancient buildings were the headquarters of medieval craft guilds and evoke an epoch of wealthy artisans and silk traders. Their interiors have been modernized to serve as restaurants, shops, offices and private homes.

The Church of St. Peter, dating from the eighth century, carries enormous clock faces 28 feet in diameter on its steeple. Nearby is the Romanesque-Gothic Fraumunster church. When he was 80, Marc Chagall designed the five stained-glass windows in the choir, depicting episodes from the Old and New Testaments. Open 9 a.m. to 12:30 p.m. and 2 to 6 p.m. daily.

Zurich's principal landmark, the twin-towered Grossmunster cathedral across the river, perpetuates the memory of the Protestant reformer Huldrych Zwingli, who preached there from 1518 to shortly before his death in 1531.

The pedestrian-only precinct, known as Niederdorf, stretching north from the cathedral along the east bank of the river, is lively until late at night with many taverns and clubs; during the day, bibliophiles comb its bookstores.

An outing by streetcar No. 6 from the rail station up the forested Zürichberg hill can be combined with a visit to the zoo. Its 2,000 residents include little Asian elephants, bred in captivity by the zoo, that are the darlings of Zurichers. Open 8 a.m. to 6 p.m. daily. Admission: $8 for adults, $4 ages 6 to 16.

The Kunsthaus contains significant works by French Impressionists, Munch, Klee, the Giacomettis, Chagall and Kokoschka, as well as a room with 18 important Picassos. The museum, at 1 Heimplatz, (41-1) 251-6765, is open 10 a.m. to 9 p.m. Tuesday to Thursday and until 5 p.m. Friday to Sunday. Admission: $9.60 for adults, students $4.80.

where to stay

BUDGET: The Poly, 63 Universitätstrasse, (41-1) 362-9440, fax (41-1) 361-6212, overlooks the city in the academic district. The 37 rooms are furnished in a simple, modern style, and service is friendly. Doubles with bath: $110 to $131, breakfast included.

The 14 rooms in the Hotel Limmatblick, 136 Limmatquai, (41-1) 254-6000, fax (41-1) 254-6010, are in a narrow six-story building looking out on the river. Doubles with breakfast: $97 to $124.

MODERATE: Zürcherhof, 21 Zähringerstrasse, (41-1) 269-4444, fax (41-1) 269-4445, in the Niederdorf section, has 35 rooms with comfortable, solid furnishings in a renovated four-story building. Doubles cost $134 to $179.

Most of the 73 rooms in the City-Hotel, 34 Löwenstrasse, (41-1) 217-1717, fax (41-1) 217-1818, are small and short on frills, but they are centrally located near the train station and feature recently renovated bathrooms. The staff is small in this clean, quiet hotel, which includes a generous buffet breakfast in the room rate. Doubles: $151 to $172.

LUXURY: Dolder Grand Hotel, 65 Kurhausstrasse, (41-1) 269-3000, fax (41-1) 269-3001, has 182 rooms of understated elegance, some in a 19th-century building with pagodalike half-timber towers, others in a modern annex. Both buildings are in a country-club setting on the forested Zürichberg hill. Double rooms, some looking down onto the city and lake, are $317 to $428, including breakfast.

Widder, 7 Rennweg, (41-1) 224-2526, fax (41-1) 224-2424, is one of the newest deluxe hotels in town, smack in the historic center. Eight ancient buildings were linked in a renovation that yielded 49 rooms with plenty of wood paneling, glass and chrome, tile floors and modern furniture under the original beams. All rooms have fax machines, and some suites have rooftop terraces. Doubles, including breakfast, are $324 to $434.

where to eat

Bouillabaisse, 87 Bahnhofstrasse, (41-1) 211-8317, with the adjoining Lobster and Oyster Bar and the Grill Room in the St. Gotthard Hotel near the rail terminal, is an upscale place that has fresh seafood flown in daily. Its fish soup couldn't be improved upon in Marseilles, and the other offerings are inspired by Provençal cuisine. The wine list is imposing. A three-course dinner for two with an average-priced wine: about $120.

Kaufleuten, 18 Pelikanstrasse; (41-1) 225-3333. Employees of the big banks nearby like this roomy place with its Art Deco portals for its interesting food and quick service. At lunchtime recently an excellent rabbit with roast potatoes was $19, with a glass of Swiss red wine at $5.20.

Zeughauskeller, 28A Bahnhofstrasse, (41-1) 211-2690, is centrally located in a niche just off the famous shopping street. This large brasserie in a 500-year-old former civic arsenal draws tourists (the lengthy menu comes in English and Japanese), but the place isn't outright touristy, and there are many local people, especially for lunch. Bratwurst and several other kinds of sausage, pork and that local classic, Geschnetzeltes (minced and creamed veal) with rösti (finely sliced and roasted potatoes), are the standbys. A three-course meal for two with beer may run to $80; sausage with a side order as a snack is $15 to $20.

Kronenhalle, 4 Rämistrasse, (41-1) 251-6669, has to be mentioned, although it is expensive and the food is uneven. Yet the bar and the dark-wainscoted dining rooms where James Joyce once drank his beloved Fendant wine and where today the glitterati hang out and bankers entertain important clients is a landmark. The restaurant was founded in 1842 in a Biedermeier building, and its lace curtains with a knit royal crown seem from that era. Original Picassos, Klees and Mirós hang on the walls. Stick to the St. Gall bratwurst as your entree, and you should enjoy your meal. Three-course dinner for two with wine: $150.

Mère Catherine, 3 Nägelihof, (41-1) 250-5940, has tables on two floors and seating in the tiny square outside near the Grossmunster. In this Provençal-style restaurant popular with younger diners, onion soup is $9.50, a cheese platter is $5.17, and the three-course menu costs $15. Dinner for two with the house wine is about $50.

For quick and casual meals, Sprüngli, 21 Bahnhofstrasse, (41-1) 224-4711, is an elegant cafe and confectionery. It also serves sandwiches and snacks like beef meatballs with tomato sauce and salad ($14.80) or a vegetarian platter ($13.40).

vital statistics

POPULATION (1999): City 360,000; Canton 1,300,000

HOTEL: Room for one with tax $210.00

DINNER FOR ONE: With tax and tip but not drinks $30.60

TAXI: Upon entry $3.37; Each additional kilometer $1.80; From the airport $28.00

CAR RENTAL FOR A DAY: Midsize car with unlimited free mileage $50.50

FOR MORE INFORMATION: Telephone: (41-1) 215-4000; Web: www.zuerich.ch

Sources: Runzheimer International, Swiss National Tourist Office, local businesses